Religion and American Politics

RELIGION
AND
AMERICAN POLITICS

From the Colonial Period
to the 1980s

Edited by
MARK A. NOLL

New York   Oxford
OXFORD UNIVERSITY PRESS
1990

Oxford University Press

Oxford   New York   Toronto
Delhi   Bombay   Calcutta   Madras   Karachi
Petaling Jaya   Singapore   Hong Kong   Tokyo
Nairobi   Dar es Salaam   Cape Town
Melbourne   Auckland
and associated companies in
Berlin   Ibadan

Library of Congress Cataloging-in-Publication Data
Religion and American politics: From the Colonial period to the 1980s
/ edited by Mark A. Noll.
p.   cm.   Includes index.
ISBN 0-19-505880-1   ISBN 0-19-505881-X (pbk.)
1. United States—Religion.   2. United States—Politics and government.
3. Church and state—United States—History.
4. Christianity and politics—History.
I. Noll, Mark A., 1946–
BR516.R34   1990   322′.1′0973—dc 19
88-37117   CIP

2 4 6 8 9 7 5 3 1
Printed in the United States of America
on acid-free paper

To
Robert W. Lynn

Acknowledgments

Abridged drafts of most of the essays below were first presented at a conference organized by the Institute for the Study of American Evangelicals (ISAE) at Wheaton College on March 17–19, 1988. The chapters by Richard Carwardine, Lyman Kellstedt and Mark Noll, and George Marsden were prepared especially for the book. Wheaton's sponsorship of the ISAE and funding provided by the Pew Charitable Trusts made possible both that stimulating gathering and what we hope will be a useful volume. The smooth running of the conference was the result of much hard work by the ISAE's professional staff, Dr. Joel Carpenter and Dr. Edith Blumhofer, along with an energetic crew of capable assistants, headed by Mrs. JoAnn Haley and including Teri Kondo, Mrs. Cassandra Niemczyk, Bill DiPuccio, Dave Rogers, and Marilyn Timm. The wisdom of Professors Patricia Bonomi, David Leege, Charles Long, James Mathisen, Richard Pointer, James Turner, and Grant Wacker also enlivened the proceedings, even as it aided the process of revision that resulted in the book's chapters.

It is a pleasure to thank Mr. Martin Trimble of the Pew Trusts for his part in making the conference possible.

The book's dedication is a token of appreciation for a long history of cheerful support given to the scholars who share in the activities of the ISAE.

Contents

Contributors

RUTH H. BLOCH, who teaches history at UCLA, is the author of *Visionary Republic: Millennial Themes in American Thought, 1756–1800* (Cambridge, 1985) and of essays on feminine ideals in the Revolutionary and early national periods.

RICHARD CARWARDINE has published *Transatlantic Revivalism: Popular Evangelicalism in Britain and America, 1790–1865* (Greenwood, 1978) as well as articles on antebellum American politics. He is a lecturer in history at the University of Sheffield and a fellow of the Royal Historical Society.

ROBERT T. HANDY is Henry Sloane Coffin Professor Emeritus of Church History at the Union Theological Seminary in New York. He is the author of many works in American religious history, including a history of Union Seminary (Columbia, 1987) and *A Christian America: Protestant Hopes and Historical Realities* (revised edition, Oxford, 1983).

NATHAN O. HATCH is the author of *The Sacred Cause of Liberty: Republican Thought and the Millennium in Revolutionary New England* (Yale, 1977) and *The Democratization of American Christianity* (Yale, 1989). He is professor of history and associate dean of the College of Arts and Letters at the University of Notre Dame.

JAMES HENNESEY, S.J., rector of the Jesuit Community and Professor of Religious Studies at Canisius College, is the author of *American Catholics* (Oxford, 1981) and *The First Council of the Vatican: The American Experience* (Herder and Herder, 1963).

DANIEL WALKER HOWE is a professor of history at UCLA and the author of *The Unitarian Conscience: Harvard Moral Philosophy, 1805–1861* (Harvard, 1970) and *The Political Culture of the American Whigs* (Chicago, 1980), as well as editor of *Victorian America* (Pennsylvania, 1976).

LYMAN A. KELLSTEDT teaches political science at Wheaton College in Illinois. He is the author of articles on religious variables in political behavior and on the recent political activity of Protestant evangelicals.

GEORGE M. MARSDEN, who is Professor of the History of Christianity in America at the Divinity School of Duke University, is the author of *Fundamentalism and American Culture* (Oxford, 1980) and *Reforming Fundamentalism: Fuller Seminary and the New Evangelicalism* (Eerdmans, 1987), and has edited *Evangelicalism in Modern America* (Eerdmans, 1984).

MARTIN E. MARTY has written widely on all phases of religion in America, including the general history *Pilgrims in Their Own Land: 500 Years of Religion in America* (Penguin, 1985) and the first volume of a projected four-volume history of religious life in modern America, *The Irony of It All, 1893–1919* (Chicago, 1986). He is Fairfax M. Cone Distinguished Service Professor of the History of Modern Christianity at the University of Chicago.

JOHN M. MURRIN, a professor of history at Princeton University, is the editor of *Saints and Revolutionaries: Essays on Early American History* (Norton, 1984) and the author of essays on nearly every phase of American life in the colonial and Revolutionary periods.

MARK A. NOLL, professor of history at Wheaton College, is the author of *Princeton and the Republic, 1768–1822* (Princeton, 1989) and *One Nation Under God? Christian Faith and Political Action in America* (Harper & Row, 1988).

GEORGE A. RAWLYK has published widely on Canadian-American relations, including *Nova Scotia's Massachusetts* (McGill-Queen's, 1973), and on evangelical religion in Canada, including *Ravished by the Spirit: Religious Revivals, Baptists, and Henry Alline* (McGill-Queen's, 1984). He is professor of history at Queen's University, Ontario, and sometime Winthrop Pickard Bell Professor of Maritime Studies, Mount Allison University, New Brunswick.

HARRY S. STOUT, professor of American religious history and religious studies at Yale University, is author of *The New England Soul: Preaching and Religious Culture in Colonial New England* (Oxford, 1986) and has edited *Jonathan Edwards and the American Experience* (Oxford, 1988).

ROBERT P. SWIERENGA is the editor of *The Dutch in America* (Rutgers, 1985) and *Beyond the Civil War Synthesis* (Greenwood, 1975). He has also served as editor of the periodical *Social Science History*. He is professor of history at Kent State University.

DAVID W. WILLS, professor of religion at Amherst College, has published *Black Apostles at Home and Abroad* (G. K. Hall, 1982) and other essays on the religious experience of American blacks.

JOHN F. WILSON is the Collord Professor of Religion and director of the Project on Church and State at Princeton University. He has published *Public Religion in American Culture* (Temple, 1981) and is the editor of the two-volume bibliographical guide *Church and State in America* (Greenwood, 1986, 1987).

ROBERT WUTHNOW, who teaches sociology at Princeton University, is the author of *The Restructuring of American Religion: Society and Faith Since World War II* (Princeton, 1988) and *Meaning and Moral Order: Explorations in Cultural Analysis* (California, 1987) and has edited *The New Christian Right* (Aldine, 1983).

BERTRAM WYATT-BROWN is the Milbauer Professor of History at the University of Florida. His books include *Southern Honor* (Oxford, 1982), *Yankee Saints and Southern Sinners* (Louisiana State, 1985), and *Lewis Tappan and the Evangelical War Against Slavery* (Case Western Reserve, 1969).

Religion and American Politics

Introduction

MARK A. NOLL

In America, as throughout the world, the intersection between religion and politics has always occurred at several levels. First thoughts on the subject often go instinctively to major crises of church and state—like the struggle between the Maccabees and the Romans in the second century BC, Constantine's battle to recognize Christianity in the early fourth century, the appeal in 1077 by the Holy Roman Emperor Henry IV to Pope Gregory VII in the snow at Canossa, the state-sponsored persecution of Protestants by Catholic regimes and Catholics by Protestant regimes in the sixteenth century, Roger Williams' protest against the early government of Massachusetts, and the resistance of the confessing German church to Hitler. Or we may think of more modern conflicts like those before the Supreme Court over prayer and Bible reading in the public schools. At this level the issue is the exercise of authority between the institutions of government and the structures of religion. But such matters, which so often produce spectacular conflicts, are far from the whole story.[1]

A second range of connections between religion and politics concerns more mundane political behavior. Especially in the Western democracies, political pundits and academic specialists have tried to fathom the relationship between religious beliefs, practices, and associations, on the one hand, and partisanship, voting, and political activity, on the other. At stake for such connections are highly practical matters: Can Democratic candidates really count on an Irish Catholic vote, or take for granted the support of their Jewish constituents? Will Episcopalians always vote for the Republican? For academics, the questions extend over time as they probe the often complicated conditions that create and dissolve affinities between religious and political groups.

At yet a third level, questions of religion and politics concern the fundamental ordering of society. Here the issue is not so much who controls whom, or who voted for whom, but the broader matter of how religious beliefs, practices, and communal values relate to the activities, expectations, and symbols of a society's public life. In one of the essays below, Harry Stout speaks of "rhetorical worlds" that bridge the domains of religion and politics—that is, of those deeply rooted assumptions that shape a community's perception of its role in both the eternal economy of God and the political economy of a nation. At this level the question concerns cultural balance of trade. Where do modes of thought derived from religious traditions, from scripture, from the charisma of religious leaders shape expectations for political life? Where do the tumults of negotiation, the struggle for community self-definition, or the battle for votes influence the way religious people conceptualize their lives? Where are the rhetorical worlds of religion and politics both shaped by still other circumstances—by patterns of economic organization, by expectations for family life, by prosperity, disease, or warfare? And why is it that the balance of trade between rhetorical worlds is always variegated, affecting different groups in different ways at different times?

This book is an effort to address all three levels of religion and politics for the history of the United States from the colonial period to the present. Its authors assume that in the United States there has always existed what a British scholar once described for his nation as "a complex inter-relationship between political attitudes, ecclesiastical allegiances and cultural traditions."[2] Their intent is to describe both the nature of that interrelationship and how it has developed over time.

A host of recent circumstances has dramatized the importance of the issue. In the United States, religion has been a highly visible factor in many of the most controversial political events of the last three decades— from the mobilization of the civil rights movement and the rise of the New Christian Right to the presence of ministers as presidential candidates, the public debate over "traditional values," and the Supreme Court's adjudication of moral conflicts and church-state conundrums. In addition, an intense theoretical discussion has been building behind the individual controversies. It concerns the proper place for religious convictions and their expression in a pluralistic democracy where virtually all theorists, commentators, and political activists affirm the nation's traditional separation between the institutions of government and religion.[3]

Increasingly, Americans have also come to realize that such matters, of both practice and theory, are not unique to themselves. In fact, the religious-political landscape is often even more tangled in other parts of the world. Warfare fueled by long-standing religious antagonisms bedevils Northern Ireland, Lebanon, and other parts of the Middle East. Muslim nationalists have turned the Persian Gulf upside down and created new political realities in Afghanistan. Demands for rights by religious minorities have fueled explosive international tensions in the Soviet Union, India, and elsewhere. Religious convictions—often drawn from similar theological sources—inspire the defenders of apartheid and its opponents in the Republic of South Africa. Religion enters deeply into the political structures of Latin America, with long-standing alliances between ecclesiastical hierarchies and ruling elites and more recent community organizations of common people inspired by religious convictions. Other nations besides our own entertain the notion that they enjoy God's special blessing and protection. Even communist governments have tacitly acknowledged the contemporary relevance of religious-political connections by encouraging, for whatever reasons, religious commemorations—as, for example, East Germany in 1983 for the 500th anniversary of the birth of Martin Luther, and the Soviet Union in 1988 for the millennial anniversary of the entrance of Christianity into Kievan Rus. As in the United States, the presence of such circumstances in recent decades has been accompanied by a growing academic interest in historical patterns of religious-political interaction. The resulting literature is diverse, but it shows Americans that, even if the terms of their discussion are singular, their more general concerns are mirrored in place after place and, mutatis mutandis, in circumstance after circumstance around the world.[4]

For their part, Americans in recent years have produced a cascade of books and articles on questions across the broad range of issues involving religion and politics.[5] While much of this publication is superficial or simply tendentious, much is also intellectually challenging. Among some of the better efforts are a number that have paused to reexamine the history of religion and politics in North America. Pioneering textbooks are now available for an introduction to the subject.[6] Several synthetic interpretations trace the whole of the picture.[7] And a number of narrower monographs have reflected on the first European settlements or the founding events of the United States in order to propose remedies for current crises.[8]

These books follow a path well marked by classic studies, the best of which remains Alexis de Tocqueville's *Democracy in America.* De Tocqueville's specific judgments may be limited by the American conditions he observed in the 1830s, but his skill at recording the intimate relations among political culture, political behavior, and church-state circumstances remains unsurpassed, as in this assessment of religion's influence on American public life:

> I have remarked that the members of the American clergy in general, without even excepting those who do not admit religious liberty, are all in favour of civil freedom; but they do not support any particular political system. They keep aloof from parties, and from public affairs. In the United States religion exercises but little influence upon the laws, and upon the details of public opinion; but it directs the manners of the community, and by regulating domestic life, it regulates the state.[9]

After de Tocqueville, other foreign visitors and a number of Americans materially advanced the discussion that lies behind the current upsurge of interest in the subject.[10]

What the recent spate of books has not yet included, however, is a general effort organized by specifically historical interest. Books that put history to use for the purpose of recommending a course of action in the present are of course legitimate.[11] But they also suffer the weaknesses of their strength. Mining the past for lessons relevant to an author's present concerns means that important aspects of the past remain unobserved. Historians are always fenced in by the assumptions and concerns of their own generation, and no history will ever be written "as it really happened." Yet there is a difference between using the past to chart a course for the present and attempting to recover the past in terms understandable by those who lived through it themselves. Put this way, what we have been missing is a book that, while not immune to modern interests, sets out to describe rather than prescribe, to offer informed historical judgment instead of passionate prophetic insight.

Religion and American Politics is such a book. It is also a book that draws self-consciously upon the recent flourishing of American religious history. This flourishing has come about for several reasons, including a greater willingness on the part of secular academics to acknowledge the importance of religion in the nation's past and a heightened desire by believing historians to set religious history into the context of social, economic, intellectual, and cultural developments. For these and other reasons, the result has been an explosion in the quantity and the quality of instructive writing on America's religious past.[12]

Religion and American Politics aims, first, to take stock of existing historical knowledge concerning the relation of religion and politics in the United States from the colonial settlements to the present. The scholars who have contributed to this book are accomplished authorities, well positioned to summarize the most important recent conclusions for their periods or specialized subjects, even as they share the results of their own research. Their notes, sometimes amounting to major bibliographies, suggest the wealth of pertinent literature on the subject.

The book hopes, second, to clarify the course of American development through comparisons with other societies. To that end one essay discusses British politics and religion in relation to parallel developments in the United States, another does the same for Canada, and several others refer in passing to conditions beyond these shores. The result is still more an advertisement than a definitive exposition of comparative developments. But even this start indicates the benefits to be gained by studying the history of the United States comparatively, especially with respect to its nearest cultural neighbors.[13]

A third purpose of the book is to expand consideration of religion and politics, to broaden the scope and deepen the analysis of the subject, especially for the United States. To accomplish this purpose the individual essays examine important groups, particularly blacks and Roman Catholics, that are often overlooked in telling the American story. In addition, the essays taken together show what can be done by studying the subject from a range of perspectives. In the pages that follow, historians write with attention to intellectual, cultural, and social developments, as well as to religious and political conditions. The methods of the social sciences also come into play, especially sociology, anthropology, and political science.

The result is a series of essays, arranged chronologically, and so treating many of the important chapters in the history of religion and politics in the United States. But it is also a group of essays diverse in their methodologies and themes, and so suggesting some of the richness of the topic.

With the diversity of perspective and richness of theme, however, a central argument does inform, sometimes implicitly, the book. The argument is that whenever researchers study the history of American politics comprehensively, religion rises as a vitally important matter. But, one must hasten to add, it rises in complex and sometimes ironical ways. On the most famous church-state question, as John Murrin and John Wilson show below, the country's Founding Fathers testified to the importance of religion in the new nation by neutralizing it in the Constitution. In addition, religion is usually only one among other important factors providing the deep structure for America's political life. Considerable nuance is therefore required to describe the place of religion within the network of other grounding circumstances.

It is also usually the case that several religious visions have been at work at any one time or with respect to any one episode in the nation's past. Several of the essays below testify, for example, to the relevance of denominational allegiance. Catholics have indeed often acted differently in politics than Protestants, but sometimes German Catholics have acted differently than Irish Catholics, and sometimes being Catholic has meant one thing in Boston and another in the upper Midwest. By the same token, Baptists in the South have been associated with several different political philosophies and several different sorts of political behavior, depending upon time, place, and circumstance. Other essays show that denominational allegiance has often not meant as much politically as have styles of worship, levels of education, or attitudes toward moral absolutes. Still others explore critical changes over time, the most important of which is the expansion of "American religion" from a branch of British Protestantism, through a broader Protestantism more indigenously American, which then yielded cultural space to Roman Catholics, followed by a pluralism of "Protestant–Catholic–Jew," and then an even more pluralistic stage filled with tension between advocates of a secular America and defenders of traditional Christianity. In a word, religion almost always turns out to be important for American political attitudes and behavior, but in often surprising ways explainable only by close attention to historical context.

Along with the conclusion that religion is important for American politics, several of the chapters show also that political activity growing out of religious motives has had ironical consequences. In terms set out classically by Reinhold Niebuhr, believers who have mobilized politically sometimes realize at the very moment of their triumph that they have brought about something other than, even opposite to, what they intended.[14] Thus, a radical dissenting Protestantism was one of the most important factors in the rise of a distinctly American democracy, but it was that same democracy which eventually made possible the displacement of Protestants as the nation's cultural arbiters. White supporters of the slave system used the Christian faith to pacify their slaves, but Christianity became a vehicle for blacks to organize themselves politically. Once again, it is not enough to see that religion has been important in American politics. That recognition is the start, rather than the end, of analysis.

Religion and American Politics begins with John Murrin's overview of the striking circumstances that led from American colonization by religious monopolists to the creation of constitutional freedom of religion in the early United States. Included in his study is a description of the "roads not taken" in American religion and politics, like the Puritan effort to restrict (not expand) religious freedom, the Quaker experiment of government by pacifists in colonial Pennsylvania, and the religious anarchy of early Rhode Island. Murrin also ponders the network of events that led from the writing of the Constitution, with its largely secular intentions shaped by its largely secular authors, to the flourishing of religion in the new nation, where very soon Americans were looking back with holy gratitude upon the work of those Founders.

Four chapters follow on the critical developments of the founding period. Ruth Bloch shows how important religious conceptions were, especially in New England, for the inspiration of the American Revolution, and also how religious sensibilities evolved as the ideological excitement of the war gave way to the urgent necessities of nation-building. Harry Stout looks at the way elite clergymen in New England found themselves unable to control, or even to understand, the course of politics from the Revolution (which they thought *they* had sponsored as a product of orthodox Christian convictions) to the realities of the democratic new nation (which they regarded as far gone along a road to godless dissipation and excess). John Wilson's more narrow focus on the place of religion at the Constitutional Convention and in the passage of the First Amendment is fraught with implications for the present. He argues that the needs of that political moment—specifically, the desire to create a national government from fragmented states jealous of their own prerogatives—dictated the constitutional provisions concerning religion. Along the way Wilson administers a much-needed lesson for the application of history to the present. Nathan Hatch, who returns from more narrowly political matters to broader cultural questions, takes democratization as his theme. His essay testifies to the incompleteness of any historical view that leaves out the achievements of lower-order, dissenting Protestants, who, drinking deep from the wellsprings of Revolutionary rhetoric, greatly advanced the democratization of American religion and, in so doing, the democratization of American society and politics.

Two essays then describe the place of religion in northern politics during the national era. Daniel Walker Howe and Robert Swierenga both make full use of a remarkable surge of "ethnoreligious" research, which demonstrates that religion was the single most important long-term factor in the political alignments of the period. Howe's chapter features an extended discussion of the evangelical contribution to antebellum intellectual and social life, a contribution that everywhere influenced more overt political behavior. Swierenga, a social-scientific historian at home with the techniques of statistical analysis, presents in accessible general terms the results of exacting quantifiable research into the complex, but regular, connections between voting, party affiliation, and religious allegiance that in large part characterized American politics from 1828 through the 1896 election between William McKinley and William Jennings Bryan.

Bertram Wyatt-Brown's essay, the last chapter covering the antebellum era, is different in subject—it is about the South—and in method—it considers not so much political behavior as the deep background of Southern culture that undergirded the political life of the region. His subject is the interplay between Southern honor and Protestant evangelicalism from the early settlements through the Civil War, and what that interplay reveals about the framework of Southern politics.

A section devoted to comparative themes follows these essays on the nineteenth century. David Wills finds it painful, at this late date, still to be insisting on the need to include blacks in the story of American politics and religion. His account shows why that necessity exists, but also how the integration of this critical minority into the larger picture might take place. Richard Carwardine examines British political history in the nineteenth century (with brief considerations of more recent matters) to test the notion of American exceptionalism. If Carwardine shows how much religious-political conditions in Great Britain resembled those in the United States, though it is thought they did not, George Rawlyk shows how much religious-political conditions in Canada have differed from those in the United States, though it is thought they are similar. Rawlyk's essay addresses several intriguing questions: How have American notions of a special divine status for the United States shaped Canadian suspicion of the southern neighbor? Why is a tradition of religiously inspired socialism so much more important in Canada than in the United States? His answers, along with the exposition of the other two chapters in this section, suggest that the whole story of religion and politics in America would be dramatically improved by bringing into play the comparative dimension, both minority to majority at home and culture to culture from abroad.

The chapters on developments in the last century begin with Robert Handy's analysis of the way that religious expectations comported with major political developments in the progressive era. His essay's account of American religion at the turn of the century serves also as a summary of ecclesiastical developments to that time and as a base from which to interpret the startling changes of the twentieth century. The next two chapters present the histories of different groups in that century. An essay by James Hennesey treats Roman Catholics in the period between 1900 (when the Catholic church had clearly emerged as a major force in America) and 1960 (when the election of John F. Kennedy as president marked a climactic Catholic breakthrough). At the same time, by ranging backwards in time through the preceding centuries and with fleeting, but telling, comments on more recent history, Hennesey shows how central the experience of Roman Catholics has become for recording and, even more, interpreting American politics. Martin Marty's chapter deals with Protestants in a twentieth century that has moved beyond an earlier evangelical culture. It also shows how "others," non-Protestants and non-Catholics, have become increasingly important for all questions involving religion and the political sphere. Marty's particular concerns are the nature of politics in America's rapidly pluralizing society and the revealing stages through which religious-political connections have passed in the current century.

Two chapters follow on conditions since World War II. Robert Wuthnow explores the "hidden chasm" stretching across the contemporary religious landscape, a chasm not between denominations but between more basic attitudes concerning the place of religion in both private and public life. Wuthnow describes the development of the new divide with respect not only to religious divisions, but also to fundamental recent changes in American society and political expectations. Lyman Kellstedt and Mark Noll then analyze social-scientific survey data from the post-war decades that chart both political behavior and religious affiliation. Their conclusion—that over the last half-century religious allegiance can still be correlated with voting patterns and partisan alignment—illustrates from the ground something of what Wuthnow has seen from the top of the trees.

The book's final essay, by George Marsden, ventures a broad overview of the whole course of religion and politics in America. If much can be gained from the particular conclusions of the book's earlier essays, much may also be learned from an effort to see the picture whole. Marsden holds that it is possible to view American history as a painful struggle to achieve a religious consensus on political matters, a struggle that may have witnessed both its culmination and its dissolution in the last quarter-century.

The chapters in this book do not pretend to be comprehensive, even for their limited themes. So vast is the general subject that many important issues, incidents, and groups receive only passing attention or no attention at all. Were this an encyclopedia instead of a single book, it would have to include extensive treatment of other groups like Jews, Native Americans, and the small sects that often become focal points for sensitive church-state problems.[15] Many telling episodes would also receive extended treatment, like the crisis of Mormon self-definition when Utah sought statehood, or the establishment of public schools as an extension of the Protestant "benevolent empire" before the Civil War, or the many-faceted role of religious groups in the history of America's wars. Still other topics that deserve more attention include religious lobbying for legislation at state capitols and in Washington, the religious convictions of leading politicians, and the symbolism of the country's mottoes ("In God We Trust," "One Nation Under God"), which in turn broaches the protean subject of civil religion. These are only some of the subjects pertinent to its theme that the book does not address directly.

As it is, however, *Religion and American Politics* still ranges widely over a vast subject. The chapters pay rigorous attention to the historical circumstances of America's different eras, and so illuminate both matters of grand historical consequence but little contemporary relevance and matters of enduring significance throughout American history. Taken together, they are an exercise testing the implications of de Tocqueville's cryptic observation that "religion in America takes no direct part in the government of society, but it must nevertheless be regarded as the foremost of the political institutions of that country."[16]

Notes

1. When, however, church-state concerns are viewed in broader cultural terms—as they are, for instance, in the essays contained in John F. Wilson, ed., *Church and State in America: A Bibliographical Guide*, 2 vols. (New York: Greenwood, 1986, 1987)—they lead naturally into the other levels of interaction between religion and politics.

2. Keith Robbins, "Religion and Identity in Modern British History," in Stuart Mews, ed., *Religion and National Identity* (Oxford: Basil Blackwell, 1982), 465.

3. Samples from a rapidly growing literature include Kent Greenawalt, *Religious Convictions and Political Choice* (New York: Oxford University Press, 1987); Robin Lovin, ed., *Religion and American Public Life* (Mahwah, NJ: Paulist, 1986); Richard P. McBrien, *Caesar's Coin: Religion and Politics in America* (New York: Macmillan, 1987); Richard John Neuhaus, *The Naked Public Square* (Grand Rapids: Eerdmans, 1984); Max L. Stackhouse, *Public Theology and Political Economy* (Grand Rapids: Eerdmans, 1987); and (with

special attention to British concerns) Kenneth Medhurst and George Moysen, *Church and Politics in a Secular Age* (Oxford: Clarendon, 1988); and Duncan B. Forrester, *Theology and Politics* (Oxford: Basil Blackwell, 1988).

4. The following recent symposia suggest the wide range of this literature: Charles Wei-hsun Fu and Gerhard E. Spiegler, eds., *Movements and Issues in World Religions—A Sourcebook and Analysis of Developments Since 1945: Religion, Ideology, and Politics* (New York: Greenwood, 1987); Daniel H. Levine, ed., *Religions and Political Conflict in Latin America* (Chapel Hill: University of North Carolina Press, 1986); Bruce Lincoln, ed., *Religion, Rebellion, Revolution* (New York: St. Martin's, 1985); Jim Obelkevich, Lyndal Roper, and Raphael Samuel, eds., *Disciplines of Faith: Studies in Religion, Politics and Patriarchy* (London: Routledge and Kegan Paul, 1987); Pedro Ramet, ed., *Eastern Christianity and Politics in the Twentieth Century* (Durham, NC: Duke University Press, 1988); and Richard L. Rubenstein, ed., *Spirit Matters: The Worldwide Impact of Religion on Contemporary Politics* (New York: Paragon, 1987). In addition, European publishers are producing many works relevant to the general subject, like the series *Politiques & Chrétiens* (Paris, Beauchesne) with books already published on Edmond Michelet, Aldo Moro, and Konrad Adenauer, and many more to come on other European and American political leaders. Conor Cruise O'Brien, *God Land: Reflections on Religion and Nationalism* (Cambridge, MA: Harvard University Press, 1988), is a short but thought-provoking essay on religious-political connections in several modern locations.

5. Literature on the New Christian Right, which now constitutes its own industry, is cited in chapters 15 and 16, below.

6. See, for example, these thoughtful volumes: Robert Booth Fowler, *Religion and Politics in America* (Metuchen, NJ: Scarecrow, 1985); David Chidester, *Patterns of Power: Religion and Politics in American Culture* (Englewood Cliffs, NJ: Prentice-Hall, 1988); and Robert D. Linder and Richard V. Pierard, *Civil Religion and the American Presidency* (Grand Rapids: Zondervan, 1988).

7. Among the most thoughtful of such books are Furio Colombo, *God in America: Religion and Politics in the United States*, trans. (from Italian) Kristin Jarratt (New York: Columbia University Press, 1984); A. James Reichley, *Religion in American Public Life* (Washington: The Brookings Institution, 1985); and Kenneth D. Wald, *Religion and Politics in the United States* (New York: St. Martin's, 1986).

8. See, for example, John P. Diggins, *The Lost Soul of American Politics: Virtue, Self-Interest, and the Foundations of Liberalism* (New York: Basic Books, 1984); Robert Bellah, Richard Madsen, William W. Sullivan, Ann Swidler, and Steven M. Tipton, *Habits of the Heart: Individualism and Commitment in American Life* (Berkeley: University of California Press, 1985); and Willism Lee Miller, *The First Liberty: Religion and the American Republic* (New York: Knopf, 1985).

9. Alexis de Tocqueville, *Democracy in America*, 7th ed., trans. Henry Reeve (New York: Edward Walker, 1847), 332.

10. Among the best books on the subject published before the 1976 presidential campaign, which thrust religion back into the public consciousness, are Robert Baird, *Religion in the United States of America* (Glasgow and New York, 1844); Philip Schaff, *America: A Sketch of Its Political, Social, and Religious Character*, trans. from German (New York: Charles Scribner, 1855); H. Richard Niebuhr, *The Kingdom of God in America* (New York: Harper and Bros., 1935); Anson Phelps Stokes, *Church and State in the United States* (New York: Harper, 1950); Winthrop S. Hudson, *The Great Tradition of the American Churches* (New York: Harper, 1953); Leo Pfeffer, *Church, State, and Freedom* (Boston: Beacon, 1953); John Courtney Murray, S.J., *We Hold These Truths: Catholic Reflections on the American Proposition* (New York: Sheed and Ward, 1960); Sidney E. Mead, *The Lively Experiment: The Shaping of Christianity in America* (New York: Harper & Row, 1963); and Cushing Strout, *The New Heavens and the New Earth: Political Religion in America* (New York: Harper & Row, 1974).

11. Several books written by contributors to this volume fall at least partially into that category, including Martin E. Marty, *A Nation of Behavers* (Chicago: University of Chicago Press, 1980); John F. Wilson, *Public Religion in American Culture* (Philadelphia: Temple University Press, 1981); Mark A. Noll, George M. Marsden, and Nathan O. Hatch, *The Search for Christian America* (Westchester, IL: Crossway, 1983); Robert T. Handy, *A Christian America: Protestant Hopes and Historical Realities*, 2nd ed. (New York: Oxford University Press, 1984); George A. Rawlyk, *Ravished by the Spirit: Religious Revivals, Baptists, and Henry Alline* (Toronto: McGill–Queens University Press, 1984); Martin E. Marty, *Religion and Republic: The American Circumstance* (Boston: Beacon, 1987); and Mark A. Noll, *One Nation Under God? Christian Faith and Political Action in America* (San Francisco: Harper & Row, 1988).

12. These developments are well charted in Henry F. May, "The Recovery of American Religious History," *American Historical Review* 70 (1964): 79–92, reprinted, with much other pertinent assessment, in May, *Ideas, Faiths and Feelings: Essays on American Intellectual and Religious History, 1952-1982* (New York: Oxford University Press, 1983); Martin E. Marty, "The Editors' Bookshelf: American Religious History," *Journal of Religion* 62 (1982): 99–109; and Marty, "The American Religious History Canon," *Social Research* 53 (1986): 513–528.

13. Besides the extensive citations from Richard Carwardine and George Rawlyk, below, the following titles are also useful for considering questions of religion and politics in Britain's recent history: Kenneth D. Wald, *Crosses on the Ballot: Patterns of British Voter Alignment Since 1885* (Princeton: Princeton University Press, 1983); George Moyser, ed., *Church and Politics Today: Essays on the Role of the Church of England in Contemporary Politics* (Edinburgh: T. & T. Clark, 1985); and many of the papers in *Religion and National Identity* (note 2, above).

14. Reinhold Niebuhr, *The Irony of American History* (New York: Scribner's 1952).

15. For useful summaries at different points in time of the political situation for Jews in America, see Jacob Agus, "Jerusalem in America," in Elwyn A. Smith, ed., *Religion and the Republic* (Philadelphia: Fortress, 1971); and Jonathan D. Sarna, "Christian America or Secular America? The Church-State Dilemma of American Jews," in Richard John Neuhaus, ed., *Jews in Unsecular America, The Encounter Series*, no. 6 (Grand Rapids: Eerdmans, 1987).

16. De Tocqueville, *Democracy in America*, 334.

BEFORE THE CIVIL WAR

1

Religion and Politics in America from the First Settlements to the Civil War

JOHN M. MURRIN

Religion in America, we like to believe, is not only freer than in Europe and the rest of the world, but has always been so—or nearly always. One of the most enduring American myths—I intend nothing pejorative by this term, which I use in the anthropological sense of a body of folklore or a series of stories that organizes the way a particular culture tries to understand the world—remains the belief that this country was peopled largely by settlers fleeing religious persecution and yearning for the opportunity to worship openly and without fear. It was never that simple. At one level even popular culture provides a corrective in the equally persistent stereotype of the Puritan as cold, hard, bigoted, unimaginative, humorless—terrified by human sexuality and the enemy of all fun. "The Puritans hated bearbaiting," Thomas Babington Macaulay once remarked, "not because it gave pain to the bear, but because it gave pleasure to the spectators."[1] American undergraduates still respond warmly to this quotation. Like their elders, they prefer to believe both clichés about religion in early America.

I

Of course, neither stereotype does justice to the religious complexity of early New England, much less colonial America as a whole. Most New England Puritans came to these shores not to establish religious liberty, but to practice their own form of orthodoxy. They experienced moments of tension and open conflict when they discovered that John Winthrop's orthodoxy was not Roger Williams's or Anne Hutchinson's. Perhaps Thomas Hooker's was not even John Cotton's. They spent much of the 1630s and 1640s trying to agree on what their orthodoxy was, a process that achieved institutional expression in the Cambridge Platform of 1648, bolstered on the civil side by the Body of Liberties of 1641 as it transformed itself into the law code of 1648. By 1648 most had made compromises that few had anticipated in 1630, but beyond any doubt they meant to narrow, not expand, the religious options available to people in seventeenth-century England.[2]

They succeeded. Outside of Rhode Island, religious belief and practice became far more uniform in early New England than in the mother country at the same time. Bishops, altars, vestments, choirs, the liturgical calendar, and *The Book of Common Prayer* all failed to survive this particular Atlantic crossing, but persecution did in a limited form. Puritans used the law courts to harass and punish the small number of Quakers and Baptists that remained among them. But even though they hanged four Quakers around 1660, few Puritans were comfortable with this behavior. They preferred to cope with dissent by shunning the dissenters. Advocates of severe repression always spoke in the name of a larger religious unity, but serious efforts to implement their program ended by dividing the community, not uniting it.[3]

Something analogous happened in seventeenth-century Virginia. The options available in England diminished sharply in the colony, but in this case dissent, not the establishment, failed to win a secure place in the new settlement. Governor Sir William Berkeley was delighted. "I thank God *there are no free schools* nor *printing*, and I hope we shall not have [either] these hundred years," he exulted; "for *learning* has brought disobedience, and heresy, and sects into the world; and *printing* has divulged them, and libels against the best government. God keep us from both."[4] Although Virginia never obtained its own bishop in the colonial era and clergymen were usually in short supply, the colony managed fairly well as a low-key, very Low Church Anglican establishment. It kept most dissenters far away even during the turbulent 1640s and 1650s, when the Church of England collapsed at home. During the last quarter of the seventeenth century and the first quarter of the eighteenth, the church made striking institutional gains in Virginia just when dissenting energies seemed to be flagging elsewhere. Few planters lamented these restrictions on their choices.[5]

Maryland, of course, began very differently. Although planned by the Calverts as a refuge for persecuted Roman Catholics, the proprietary family always encouraged a high degree of toleration and welcomed Presbyterian and Quaker dissenters to the province. But the hostility between Catholic and Protestant would not disappear. In the wake of the Glorious Revolution of 1688–89, Catholics were disfranchised and the Church of England became established by law. When a large majority of planters rapidly accepted the new order, dissent in all forms, Protestant or Catholic, became increasingly marginalized. The religious complexion of Maryland began to resemble that of Virginia ever more closely. Partly because they had experienced directly the bitter conflict that religious choice could foster, most Marylanders seemed relieved to be delivered from the anguish of this particular liberty. They, too, were content to enjoy fewer options than those who had remained in England.[6]

In 1740 about 63 percent of the people of British North America lived in the New England or Chesapeake colonies under a Congregational or Anglican establishment with few real religious choices.[7] Some dissent did exist, of course, but for the most part it was stagnant or declining. Baptists and Quakers had ceased to grow in New England before the end of the seventeenth century; in that region only Anglicans were still expanding at Congregational expense, and their numbers were still very small.[8] Dissent had been shrinking rapidly in Maryland since the 1690s and had never achieved significance in Virginia. In both regions the clergy worried more about popular indifference and laxity than about overt denominational challenges to the established order. More than a century after the first settlements, most of the people in British America lived within a narrower band of religious choices than fellow subjects enjoyed in England. A mere half-century before the drafting of the Bill of Rights, a well-informed observer could not easily have detected in most of the American colonies much of a popular base for the active separation of church and state as proclaimed in the First Amendment.

II

But the Chesapeake and New England were not the whole story. What was happening among the other third of the colonial population would help to shatter this older pattern and characterize all of nineteenth-century America.

Religion in the Middle Atlantic colonies marked the most striking departure from the European norm of an established church. In New Netherland, the Dutch Reformed Church was actively supported by government, and Peter Stuyvesant grimly persecuted Quakers and other dissenters. But the church lost its privileges after the English conquest of 1664, and the Church of England never came close to providing a substitute. No regular Anglican parish was established anywhere in the colony before the 1690s. The vast bulk of the English-speaking population consisted of dissenters, mostly New Englanders with little affection for formal Anglican ways. Few settlers from a non-English background would support an Anglican establishment. Even though the legislature did establish the church in the four southern counties of the province in the 1690s, the institution remained weak, incapable of attracting the loyalties of most colonists. Toleration vanquished establishment if only because even those who favored establishment were divided over which church to support. The established churches of England, Scotland, and the Netherlands all had committed adherents by the eighteenth century. None could win preeminence in either New York or neighboring New Jersey.[9]

In Pennsylvania and Delaware toleration became much more the preferred choice of the community as a whole. Lutheran, German Reformed, and Presbyterian clergymen lamented the "disorder" they detected all around them and sometimes all but despaired of bringing the proper worship of God to the American wilderness. But, beginning in the 1680s, the Quakers had set the tone for the Delaware Valley. At no point thereafter did an established church seem even a remotely viable option. Churches became voluntary societies that people joined only if they so desired and then supported through private contributions. They had to compete with one another for members and they received no special privileges from government.[10] Within its small corner of New England, Rhode Island had already moved in this direction beginning in the 1630s.[11] Somewhat less directly, North Carolina stumbled in the same direction within the colonial South. The Church of England was established there by law shortly after 1700, but most settlers seldom saw an Anglican clergyman. Dissent became the norm despite the law.[12]

III

Before 1740 the Chesapeake and New England colonies narrowed the religious choices that had been generally available in England. The

Middle Atlantic colonies along with Rhode Island and North Carolina expanded them. Were these trends utterly contradictory, or can we find any underlying uniformities between them?

Two points seem relevant here: the institutional possibilities that America created and the potential for sustained and effective governmental coercion. Colonial North America was not a place where everyone was "doomed" to be free. It was an institutional void. Because it lacked the fixed structures of European societies, people could try out in the wilderness a whole range of ideas and experiments impossible to attempt in Europe. Some had a liberating vision that we still find bracing. The Quakers of West New Jersey drafted and implemented a constitutional system that was as radical as anything yet tried by Europeans. Other novelties could be extremely repressive. The Americas, not Europe, witnessed the resurrection of chattel slavery on a gigantic scale.[13]

Puritans erected their godly commonwealth in New England because the English crown would not let them do so in England. To be sure, those who had remained behind overturned the monarchy and established their own Puritan regime, but it collapsed much more quickly than the one in America. Unlike Oliver Cromwell's Protectorate, the New England Way survived long enough to expose the tensions and contradictions inherent within the Puritan vision itself.[14] So did William Penn's Holy Experiment. Only in America did pacifists have three-fourths of a century to demonstrate whether they could or could not govern a complex society in a world often at war.[15] Even Lord Baltimore's Maryland, too often dismissed as a stodgy anachronism, embodied an equally bold vision. Where else did a Catholic elite try to rule a Protestant majority through toleration, disestablishment, and broad political participation? To the Calverts, the emphasis on feudal hierarchy probably seemed a necessary cement for an otherwise fragile structure. The manorial system had little impact after the first decade or two, but the rest of the experiment lasted more than half a century. After 1660 it was getting stronger, not weaker, until it was undermined by the Glorious Revolution in England.[16]

America may be, as Daniel Boorstin once argued, the burial ground for Europe's utopias. More important, it was the only place where these experiments could receive a serious trial. All were doomed to failure in Europe. In America they got the chance to prove what they could accomplish. Only in America did several of them survive long enough to expose their inherent contradictions and to fail, not primarily because of conflict with outsiders, but through their own momentum or social dynamic. This pattern has long been clear for the New England Way and the Holy Experiment, but the logic even applies to the Church of England in colonial Virginia.[17]

Well into the first quarter of the eighteenth century, the planters seemed quite content to remain a colonial outpost of the mother church. Then this aspiration began to collide with the underlying demographic realities of North America, which affected even public worship in profound ways. Few planters hoped to become clergymen or to have their sons ordained. William and Mary College, organized around the turn of the century, did little to change this situation. The Anglican church had to import clergy to survive. Just after 1700, the Society for the Propagation of the Gospel in Foreign Parts (SPG) made concerted efforts to send Oxford and Cambridge graduates into the colonies. In the Chesapeake the ratio of clergy to settlers reached its highest point in the 1710s. But the population of the colonies doubled every twenty-five years. Oxford and Cambridge were stagnant. Even by sustaining its efforts the SPG could not hope to keep pace with demand in North America. It too would have had to double its efforts every generation. Although it did draw increasingly upon more dynamic universities in Scotland and Ireland, it was already losing the struggle by the 1720s. Especially in the Piedmont, the Southside, and the Valley, many of the laity were slipping out of touch with the established church. The Great Awakening would soon give them a chance to improvise their own solutions to this religious dilemma.[18]

In other societies governmental coercion might succeed in imposing orthodoxy despite these difficulties, but in all of the colonies these instruments were weak. No governor commanded a permanent military force of any significant size. No reliable hierarchy of social and economic clientage or patronage helped to ensure that lesser people would accept the religious judgments of their social superiors. To an extraordinary degree, government relied instead on voluntary cooperation to be effective. The results could be quite authoritarian when the broader population accepted such goals, as New Haven's rigid Puritan regime well illustrates.[19] But when any sizable portion of the population rejected the values of those in office, government had little chance of securing broad compliance.[20] The Quaker magistrates of West Jersey could not surmount the open defiance of non-Quaker settlers by the 1690s.[21] When the justices of Albany County, New York, summoned individuals to court in the eighteenth century, a large majority never bothered to appear.[22] If any one feature of early America tells us how settlers who did not deliberately choose religious freedom got it anyway, the weakness of government is that factor.

IV

For most people during the first century of settlement and beyond, religious choice remained narrower, not greater, than what England allowed. After 1740 that pattern changed irreversibly. The reasons are not hard to find—the First and Second Great Awakenings with the Revolution sandwiched between them.

Together these events generated the most important denominational reshuffling in American history. Into the 1730s the prevailing denominations were Congregationalist in New England, Anglican in the South, and—somewhat less firmly—the Quakers and their sectarian German allies in the Delaware Valley. New York and New Jersey were already a mosaic of competing denominations that no one group could dominate, a pattern that also characterized Rhode Island and North Carolina. But Congregationalists, Anglicans, and Quakers remained far more influential than all other rivals. The First Great Awakening, a series of intense revivals concentrated in the 1730s and 1740s, made New England and Virginia far more pluralistic than they had ever been before. The Revolution disestablished the Church of England from Maryland through Georgia. The Second Great Awakening, which spread throughout the continent after 1800, captured the religious loyalties of most settlers in the South and West and also disestablished the Congregational Church in the New England states. By the 1820s religious pluralism, the lack of an establishment, and full toleration had become the traditional pattern. It prevailed everywhere but in Massachusetts, which finally came into line by 1833. By then even most clergymen considered the transformation a good thing. They believed that voluntaristic religion produced healthier varieties of Christian commitment than any form of state support could generate.[23]

In denominational terms, this shift meant that the three prevailing faiths prior to 1740 would lose influence and adherents to three newcomers by 1820. Baptists and Methodists vied for the largest membership in the United States, a contest that Methodists would win by a narrow margin before the Civil War. A distant third, but well ahead of all other rivals, were the Presbyterians. These three denominations shared one major feature—all had embraced evangelical piety in the eighteenth century. Anglicans and Quakers had rejected the Awakenings.[24] Congregationalists in New England were divided fiercely over the revivals. Old Lights generally prevailed in eastern Massachusetts and western Connecticut, the traditional heart of each colony; New Light strength was greatest on the periphery of each.[25] In the Middle Atlantic, the revivals also split the young Presbyterian church by 1741. Because Old Side antirevivalists outnumbered New Side awakeners at that point, the revivalists seceded from the Philadelphia Synod and organized their own synod in New York City by 1745, with the most dynamic leadership coming from the Tennent family in New Jersey and Jonathan Dickinson on Long Island. By the time this rift was healed in 1758, the New Side clergy had become far more numerous than their opponents simply because—first at the Log College in Neshaminy, Pennsylvania, and later at the College of New Jersey, finally located at Nassau Hall in Princeton in the 1750s—the New Side had acquired the means to train its own clergy. Old Side Presbyterians still relied on Ulster and Scotland as their source of ministers.[26]

Methodists and Baptists had even greater advantages in this respect. By not insisting on a college education and by emphasizing charismatic qualities over formal learning, they could train men quickly and were ideally situated to conquer the West. The three denominations that had dominated the colonies before 1740 never made much headway in the West. Anglican settlers who crossed the mountains almost never brought the Church of England with them, although many may have preferred Methodism to other evangelical faiths because it was an offshoot of Anglicanism. Similarly, New Englanders loyal to their ancestral faith rarely remained Congregationalists when they moved west. They were much more likely to become Presbyterians. Except for a few pockets in Indiana and elsewhere, Quakers made almost no headway in the West. From the 1750s through the War of 1812, the American frontier was an exceptionally violent place, as the Iroquois, Delaware, Shawnee, Creeks, Cherokee, and Seminoles organized the last heroic phase of their resistance to settler encroachment. Quaker pacifism did not thrive in this environment.[27]

V

The Revolution brought another momentous change to North America. By the late eighteenth century, the churches were no longer the only official spokesmen for public values. They had rivals. Today many Americans like to think of the Revolutionary generation as quiet and confident custodians of our fundamental values. They were less confused by their world than we are by ours. When we get into trouble, we can always turn to them to regain our moral bearings.[28]

This vision has a fatal weakness. The Revolutionary generation never shared a single set of fundamental values. Then, as now, people had to decide which of a half-dozen sets of competing fundamental values they wished to uphold. These choices became urgent, even agonizing, as the century roared to its passionate conclusion in the violence of the French Revolution, an upheaval that shook America almost as profoundly as Europe.

At least six discernible value systems competed for the allegiance of Americans: Calvinist orthodoxy, Anglican moralism, civic humanism, classical liberalism, Tom Paine radicalism, and Scottish moral sense and common sense philosophy. They did not exhaust the possibilities. For example, Roman Catholics and Jews affirmed very different constellations of values, but far into the nineteenth century both still remained well on the margins of American life.

The prevailing six differed dramatically. While some of their emphases could be reconciled with one another, many could not. Calvinist orthodoxy achieved its most systematic and eloquent statement in America in the writings of Jonathan Edwards and his students. It was no anachronism in the age of the Revolution. Edwardsians insisted on predestination, the inerrancy of Scripture, and the centrality of the conversion experience in the life of a Christian. To be converted, a person must first recognize his or her utter lack of merit in the eyes of God. Only then would God bestow saving grace on someone to whom He owed nothing whatever.[29] Anglican moralists, by contrast, rejected the necessity of a conversion experience and emphasized the need to lead an ethical life in this world. This tradition left few systematic expressions in eighteenth-century America, but it undoubtedly made a deep impact on gentleman planters and other elite groups.[30] Civic humanism went even farther in its concentration upon this-worldly activities. The fullest life, its apologists insisted, is that of the citizen who must always be willing to sacrifice self-interest for the common good.[31] Civic humanists gloried in their own rectitude and incorruptibility. Although many evangelical Calvinists could embrace the ethic of sacrifice that civic humanists demanded, few men who began as civic humanists could ever become evangelical Calvinists. They could not persuade themselves that their best deeds stank in the nostrils of the Lord. They could not achieve the humility essential to an orthodox conversion experience.[32]

Classical liberalism—the philosophy that society will be much better off if individuals are left free to pursue their self-interest with minimal governmental restraint—clashed with all three of the older value systems. In many ways it grew out of the natural rights philosophy of John Locke, a Socinian (or proto-Unitarian) in theology. Its principal European spokesmen after 1740—David Hume, Adam Smith, Jeremy Bentham, and, later, John Stuart Mill—were all atheists, although Smith never advertised his loss of faith. Liberalism seemed to transform the Christian sin of greed into a civic virtue. It seemed to mock the civic humanist commitment to disinterested patriotism.[33] Tom Paine's admirers posed equally dramatic challenges. Many were deists rather than unbelievers, but their challenge to Protestant orthodoxy drove many clergymen close to panic in the 1790s.[34] Radicals also challenged an assumption common among moderate and conservative civic humanists, that gentlemen of leisure made the best citizens and officeholders. To radicals, this claim was but a disguised assertion of aristocratic privilege. Only men who worked for a living deserved the confidence of other citizens.[35]

Scottish moral sense philosophy derived mostly from Francis Hutcheson of Glasgow and from the Edinburgh literati, a remarkably talented group that made important contributions to most fields of knowledge in the last half of the eighteenth century. The Scots tried to synthesize the best of existing knowledge. Moral sense philosophy tried to find a more compelling basis for human ethics than John Locke's highly cerebral reliance upon explicit understanding of natural law among people living in the state of nature. The Scots, whose curiosity drove them to read much of the descriptive literature about American Indians, had difficulty imagining the Iroquois, for example, rationally deducing the laws of nature in their long houses before embarking on moral behavior. Instead the Scots endowed every human with a moral sense, an ingrained and instantaneous response to external stimuli. Until corrupted by their cultures or by habit, people react positively to benevolent actions (for example, a mother nursing her infant) and negatively to malevolence (for instance, teenagers clubbing a grandmother). Common sense philosophy provided an antedote to the skepticism of David Hume by trying to establish, first, what people can take for granted and then by building larger philosophical systems upon this foundation. At first, many Calvinists regarded moral sense philosophy as a challenge to the doctrine of original sin, but by the end of the century Scottish learning had triumphed almost completely in American academic life. Scottish common sense philosophy is still taught today in fundamentalist schools. Its original enemies have become its warmest advocates.[36]

VI

Partly because disestablishment took government out of the business of proclaiming and defending fundamental values, the struggle among these systems was passionate but seldom violent. The state did not execute nonjuring clergymen—unlike the government of revolutionary France, which brought many priests to the guillotine. Although the officeholding class in the United States was probably no more orthodox than its counterparts in Britain and France, nearly all public officials deliberately minimized rather than emphasized how far they had strayed from ancestral beliefs. Thomas Jefferson and James Madison cooperated actively with Baptists and Presbyterians in Virginia politics to disestablish the Protestant Episcopal Church, but to the dismay of many Presbyterians they also refused to sanction tax support for any other denomination or combination of denominations.[37] Jefferson and Madison along with George Washington, John Adams, Benjamin Franklin, and nearly all of the Founding Fathers claimed to be Christians; but, by virtually any standard of doctrinal orthodoxy, hardly any of them was. They demanded the right to think for themselves on the most sensitive questions of faith, doctrine, and morals, but they did not try to impose their conclusions on others by force.

Yet these were precisely the men who led the way in drafting the nation's fundamental laws—its most admired constitutions, state and national, and its bills of rights at both levels. The first state constitutions usually invoked God somewhere in the text. "The People of this State, being by the Providence of God, free and independent," declared Connecticut in converting its royal charter into a constitution in 1776, "have the sole and exclusive Right of governing themselves as a free, sovereign, and independent State. . . ."[38] The preamble of the Massachusetts Constitution of 1780 explicitly recognized the providence of God while "imploring His direction" in framing a government derived from the people.[39] New Hampshire in 1784 based all "due subjection" to government upon "morality and piety, rightly grounded on evangelical principles."[40]

The explicit theism of these pronouncements made them exceptional at the time. Other constitutions were more perfunctory, or they used the language of the Enlightenment rather than Scripture or the ritual phrases of any of the Protestant churches. The preamble to the Pennsylvania Constitution, for instance, proclaimed that government exists to protect natural rights "and the other blessings which the Author of existence has bestowed upon man" and acknowledges "the goodness of the great Governour of the universe" for the people's opportunity "to form for themselves such just rules as they shall think best for governing their future society."[41] Even Massachusetts, while explicitly invoking providence, avoided the word "God." Instead the drafters acknowledged "with grateful hearts, the goodness of the Great Legislator of the Universe" in permitting the people of the commonwealth to assemble peaceably and create their own "original, explicit and solemn compact with each other."[42] The preamble to the Vermont Constitution of 1777 saluted natural rights "and the other blessings which the Author of existence has bestowed upon man."[43] Neither Pennsylvania nor Vermont joined Massachusetts in recognizing divine providence. Both assumed that the people had to make their political decisions for themselves. Even the Articles of Confederation, something less than a full organic document, explicitly invoked God, "the Great Governor of the world," who, however, assumed something more than a deistical role when He "incline[d] the hearts of the legislatures we represent in Congress, to approve of . . . the said articles of confederation and perpetual union."[44]

In some states the reference to God was casual and incidental, but it did reveal something about popular expectations. Virginia mentioned God only in the last clause of the Declaration of Rights, which guaranteed full religious freedom because "Religion, or the duty which we owe to our Creator, and the manner of discharging it, can be directed only by reason and conviction, not by force or violence."[45] The New Jersey Constitution closely followed this model. Georgia acknowledged a deity only in prescribing specific texts for several oaths. Maryland made no explicit mention of God's blessings, but in requiring all officeholders to be Christians, its constitution was in fact far more traditional than most others of the period. In a slightly weaker clause, North Carolina, after barring all clergymen from public office (as did several other states), required all officeholders to believe in God, an afterlife, the truth of the Protestant religion, and the divine authority of both the Old and New Testaments.[46]

In the light of this pattern, the failure of the Federal Constitution to mention God becomes all the more significant. The delegates to the Philadelphia Convention must have realized that they were doing something singular in this respect. They used the text of the Articles of Confederation quite often for specific clauses of the Constitution, but they omitted the passage that invoked God. They were used to seeing chaplains in their state legislatures and in the Continental Congress, but they invited none to participate in their deliberations. This choice was no mere oversight. When disagreements became particularly ferocious in late June 1787, Franklin moved to invite one or more clergymen to lead them in prayer at the beginning of each day. Hamilton objected on grounds of realpolitik. The delegates had sent for no chaplain until then; to do so at that moment could only inform the world how badly at odds they were. Edmund Randolph countered with the shrewd suggestion that they first invite a minister for the Fourth of July celebration and then continue the practice thereafter. The public would not realize that a transition had occurred. But the resolution won little support in either form—four votes, in all probability, with only Roger Sherman and Jonathan Dayton joining Franklin and Randolph. Yet even in a convention closed to the public, the majority was much too prudent to vote directly against God. Instead, Hamilton and Madison carried a motion to adjourn.[47]

The Federal Constitution was, in short, the eighteenth-century equivalent of a secular humanist text.[48] The delegates were not a very orthodox group of men in any doctrinal sense. The only born-again Christian among them was probably Richard Bassett of Delaware, a Methodist who generously supported the labors of Francis Asbury and other missionaries but who said nothing at the Convention.[49] Roger Sherman may have been another, but his advocacy of New Light causes in Connecticut seems more political than religious.[50] One cliché often applied to the Constitution is not correct in any literal sense—that at least the Founders, unlike the wildly optimistic French, believed in original sin and its implications for government and politics.

Quite possibly not a single delegate accepted Calvinist orthodoxy on original sin—that man is irretrievably corrupted and damned unless redeemed from outside. Washington, Franklin, Madison, Hamilton, James Wilson, and Gouverneur Morris gave no sign of such a belief at this phase of their lives. As a Methodist, even Bassett was probably an Arminian in theology, willing—like John Wesley—to give individuals some effective agency in their own salvation.

But if the delegates did not think that man is irrevocably corrupted, they did believe that he is highly corruptible and that a surrender to corruption had destroyed nearly every republic before their day. When combined with the vestige of aristocratic honor that most Founders shared, this fear came to mean something rather different, a conviction that *other people* are corrupt. The typical Founding Father repeatedly insisted that *his* motives were pure, disinterested, patriotic—a judgment often extended to one's close friends in public life as well. Jefferson had no higher praise for Madison, but he always suspected Hamilton of sinister designs.[51]

Although the dread of corruption had a genuine affinity for orthodox Christian values, it drew far more directly from civic humanist sources, the effort by the seventeenth and eighteenth centuries to understand why republics had failed in the past and how they could be constructed to endure. The Convention's answer to this problem, although not always civic humanist in content and emphasis, came very close in most particulars to what today's evangelicals mean by secular humanist.[52]

In their television sermons, Jerry Falwell and Jimmy Swaggart usually define three components as the essential ingredients of secular humanism. First is the willingness to elevate human reason above divine revelation whenever a conflict appears between them. Beyond any doubt nearly all of the Founders qualify on this score. Jefferson and Adams certainly fit that description.[53] Madison, although he probably contemplated entering the ministry as a young college graduate and affirmed some basic Calvinist tenets as late as 1778, seemed much more comfortable with nature's supreme being than with the God of revelation by the 1780s. He looked increasingly to history, not to the Bible, for political guidance.[54] James Wilson also believed that the Bible usefully reinforced moral precepts that we learn through our moral sense and reason, not the other way around.[55]

As a group, the Founders took Protestant private judgment a step beyond earlier eras and used it to evaluate the plausibility of Scripture itself. Most of them were extremely reluctant to use the word "God" or "Christ." They flatly rejected miracles, whether attested by Scripture or not. As Jefferson advised his nephew, one should read the Bible as one would any other book, accepting what is edifying and rejecting what is fantastic. He chose a sensitive issue on which to make his point. The Virgin Birth being impossible, Jesus of Nazareth must have been a bastard. "And the day will come," he assured John Adams several decades later, "when the mystical generation of Jesus by the supreme being as his father in the womb of a virgin will be classed with the fable of the generation of Minerva in the brain of Jupiter."[56]

A second criterion of secular humanism is the conviction that human solutions are adequate for human problems. Politicians need not invoke God or providence. At the Philadelphia Convention, a large majority explicitly refused to do so, as we have seen, and they proceeded to devise a constitution that, in the words of one nineteenth-century admirer, became "a machine that would go of itself." Built-in checks and balances pitted one human passion against another. The separation of powers kept Congress, the president, and the courts warily watching one another. The House and Senate likewise checked each other and within the broader federal system, so did the state and national governments as a whole. Madison hoped that he had created a political system that would routinely produce leaders who could identify and pursue the common good above narrow and selfish interests. In this respect he left little to chance— or providence. Instead, he put his confidence in the structure of the constitutional system as a whole.[57]

Ethical relativism has become the third component of secular humanism, at least as defined by televangelists. In the modern sense of a truly relative or situational ethics, the term does not apply to the Founders. But while they admired the moral precepts of Jesus of Nazareth, virtually all of them also believed that man can do better than what the Bible prescribes. Anticlerical in a rather gentle way, they were extremely reluctant to let any minister or church define their moral priorities for them. They believed that man was still making tremendous improvements in the moral character of public life, which, on the whole, they valued above traditional private morality. The churches, they noted quietly from time to time, had contributed much misery to the world through internal conflict and persecution. Rational man, they assumed, ought to do better. They aspired, in short, to something more perfect than the organized Christianity of their own day. They differed from ethical relativists of today in their expectation that reasonable men would someday find a loftier moral code that all could affirm and implement. When Jefferson predicted shortly before he died that most American youths would enter adulthood as Unitarians, he proved to be a terrible prophet. But what he really meant is that he expected them to embody a stronger morality than traditional churches had espoused.[58]

On all of these grounds the Founders meet the definition of secular humanism. If it is now ruining the republic, they started the process. At a minimum they expanded the content of American pluralism. Secular values became so prominent in the overall revolutionary achievement that, fully as much as the Puritan vision of an earlier age, they emerged as an essential part of the American experience. Of course, the two systems of thought overlapped at many points. Defenders of the Puritan tradition were already recasting its original emphasis on religious and civil liberty (which in 1630 had meant the political freedom to practice religious orthodoxy unrestrained from abroad) into a new hierarchy that valued civil over religious liberty. Secular apologists for the republic, if they had a taste for historical precedents, usually learned to admire Roger Williams and Anne Hutchinson, George Fox and William Penn. Yet, despite genuine similarities, the underlying motivations between seventeenth-century religious radicals and eighteenth-century revolutionaries were quite different. Williams and the Quakers favored a sharp separation of church and state because they were convinced that in any formal union, the state will always corrupt the church. Jefferson and Madison also favored rigid separation, but for the opposite reason. They believed that when any church is established by law, it will corrupt the polity.[59]

VII

The potential for conflict between secular leaders and the defenders of orthodoxy remained quite strong throughout the era of the Revolution and the early republic. At times clerical denunciations of the new godlessness became shrill and even hysterical, particularly in the assault upon the Bavarian Illuminati in 1798, a secret and conspiratorial group credited with the destruction of religion in France and who were now, supposedly, trying to repeat that triumph in America. When Jefferson ran for president in 1800, his religious convictions—or lack thereof—became a major campaign issue in New England.[60]

And yet the truly remarkable feature about the age as a whole is how contained this struggle was. About half of the clergy of France could not accept the Civil Constitution of the Clergy and became enemies of the revolutionary regime. In the United States nearly all of the clergy (including even a majority of Anglicans) supported the Revolution, the Constitution, and later the War of 1812. Some of them perfectly understood the secular vision of the Founding Fathers. "We formed our Constitution without any acknowledgment of God . . . ," reflected Timothy Dwight as the War of 1812 threatened to engulf the land in a new calamity. "The Convention, by which it was formed, never asked, even once, his direction, or his blessing upon their labours. Thus we commenced our national existence under the present system, without God."[61] But this tone was never the predominant one even among the clergy, most of whom greatly preferred the Constitution to the Articles of Confederation in 1788 and never saw reason to change their mind.[62]

How can we explain this conflict that never quite happened? Several reasons come to mind. One is the most obvious contrast between religion and revolution in France and America. France's radical republicans gloried in their assault upon orthodoxy, while the Founding Fathers all claimed to be "Christians." They used the word in a way that aroused the suspicions of numerous ministers, but in doing so they also signaled their unwillingness to fight, at least in public, about such issues. New England Federalists denounced Jefferson's godlessness in 1800. He never replied. Madison kept his religious opinions very much to himself as he drifted away from orthodoxy. Second, although the Constitution was in no explicit way a religious text, it was also not antireligious. It provided no overt threat to anybody's doctrinal convictions. Firm believers in original sin could find much to admire in it even if its drafters did not share their conviction. Finally, the secular humanists of 1787 eventually had to confront Madison's own logic about how things really worked in America. By 1798, as part of his own defense of the states' rights position of the Jeffersonian opposition, Madison insisted that the Philadelphia Convention never had power to implement and therefore define the meaning of the Constitution. That act took place through the process of ratification. Only the people in their separate state conventions had the power to put the Constitution into practice. Through the same process, only they could decide what it means.[63]

In the nineteenth century, the American public sacralized the Constitution. The extreme case is the Mormon church, which still teaches that the Convention was inspired by God, that the Constitution is thus the product of explicit divine intervention in history. Others did not go that far, but by the 1820s, mostly because of Jonathan Dayton's garbled recollections, they were quite happy to believe that Franklin's prayer motion at the Convention not only carried but was passed with at most a single dissent, and that it also marked the turning point in the debates. Soon after sending for a minister, according to Dayton's version, the large and small states agreed upon the Great Compromise, and the republic was saved. No effective answer to this claim was available until 1840, when Madison's notes were finally published. By then the public's eagerness to sanctify the secular had probably gone too far to reverse.[64]

VIII

Americans are indeed a peculiar people. The enormous range of religious choice available to the public since the late eighteenth century has generally favored evangelical Protestants over more traditional ones, but it has also energized Roman Catholics to a startling degree. While Catholicism faced a serious threat of decline nearly everywhere in nineteenth-century Europe, it built a larger and more faithful base of communicants in the United States than anywhere else in the world. American Catholics were also less inclined to heresy and more loyal to the pope than just about any other large body of Catholics in the world. Somehow the most traditional as well as the most evangelical of Christian churches were able to thrive in America. The land foreordained nobody's success, but it did provide amazing opportunities that groups and institutions could learn to use if they had sufficient energy and imagination.

The Revolution also liberated an important group of gentlemen from the constraints of orthodoxy long enough for them to draft the constitutions and bills of rights at both the state and federal levels. Major elements of the broader public have been trying to Christianize these texts ever since.

The real meaning of America and the American Revolution is not in one alternative rather than the other, but in their continuing and dramatic interaction. Neither the orthodox nor the skeptics have ever been able to destroy one another. Neither can ever do so without drastically redefining the whole of the American experience. At some periods, such as the New Deal era, this tension has been very much muted. At other times it has come close to defining the central issues of the age. Without the Northern evangelical assault upon slavery, there would have been no Civil War. Without the evangelical resurgence in the United States from the 1960s to the present, there probably would have been no Reagan Revolution—a lesser matter, to be sure, but hardly a trivial one.

The tension between secular humanist and orthodox or evangelical values has been an active part of American public life for two centuries. It shows no sign of abating.

Notes

1. Thomas Babington Macaulay, *The History of England from the Accession of James II* (London: Longmans, 1849–61), I, 161.

2. Puritans objected strenuously to the most recent contributors to religious diversity in the England of 1630, namely, the Arminians. See Nicholas Tyacke, *Anti-Calvinists: The Rise of English Arminianism. c. 1590–1640* (Oxford: Oxford University Press, 1987). On the growth and acceptance of religious pluralism in Restoration England, see the essays by Geoffrey F. Nuttall, Anne Whiteman, and Roger Thomas in Nuttall and Owen Chadwick, eds., *From Uniformity to Unity 1662–1962*, (London: SPCK, 1962).

3. Perry Miller, *Orthodoxy in Massachusetts, 1630–1650* (Cambridge, MA: Harvard University Press, 1933); David D. Hall, *The Faithful Shepherd: A History of the New England Ministry in the Seventeenth Century* (Chapel Hill: University of North Carolina Press, 1972); William G. McLoughlin, *New England Dissent, 1630–1833: The Baptists and the Separation of Church and State* (Cambridge, MA: Harvard University Press, 1971), I, 3–90; Jonathan Chu, *Neighbors, Friends, or Madmen: The Puritan Adjustment to Quakerism in Seventeenth-Century Massachusetts Bay* (Westport, CT: Greenwood, 1985).

4. William Waller Hening, ed., *The Statutes at Large: Being a Collection of All the Laws of Virginia from the First Session of the Legislature, in the Year 1619* (New York: Bartow, 1809–23), II, 517.

5. George M. Brydon's *Virginia's Mother Church and the Political Conditions Under Which It Grew* (Richmond: Virginia Historical Society; Philadelphia: Church Historical Society, 1947–52) remains the standard history.

6. Russell R. Menard, "Economy and Society in Early Colonial Maryland" (Ph.D. diss., University of Iowa, 1975); Michael Graham, "Lord Baltimore's

Pious Enterprise: Toleration and Community in Colonial Maryland" (Ph.D. diss., University of Michigan, 1983); Lois Green Carr, "Sources of Political Stability and Upheaval in Seventeenth-Century Maryland, 1634–1692," *Maryland Historical Magazine* 79 (1984): 44–70; John D. Krugler, "'With Promise of Liberty in Religion': The Catholic Lords Baltimore and Toleration in Seventeenth-Century Maryland, 1634–1692," ibid., 21–43; Lois Green Carr and David W. Jordan, *Maryland's Revolution of Government, 1689–1692* (Ithaca, NY: Cornell University Press, 1974).

7. Population estimates are calculated from U.S. Bureau of the Census, *Historical Statistics of the United States, Colonial Times to 1970* (Washington: U.S. Government Printing Office, 1975), II, 1168.

8. Susan M. Reed, *Church and State in Massachusetts, 1691–1740* (Urbana: University of Illinois Press, 1914), is still very useful although superseded for the Baptists by McLoughlin's *New England Dissent*. See also Bruce E. Steiner, *Samuel Seabury: A Study in the High Church Tradition* (Athens, OH: Ohio University Press, 1971), although the primary focus of this book is on Connecticut after the Great Awakening.

9. Frederick J. Zwierlein, *Religion in New Netherland, 1623–1664* (New York: Da Capo Press, 1971; orig. ed., 1910); George L. Smith, *Religion and Trade in New Netherland: Dutch Origins and American Development* (Ithaca, NY: Cornell University Press, 1973); Randall H. Balmer, "The Social Roots of Dutch Pietism in the Middle Colonies," *Church History* 53 (1984): 187–199.

10. Edwin B. Bronner, *William Penn's "Holy Experiment": The Founding of Pennsylvania, 1682–1701* (New York: Columbia University Press, 1962); Gary B. Nash, *Quakers and Politics: Pennsylvania, 1681–1726* (Princeton: Princeton University Press, 1968); John E. Pomfret, *The Province of West New Jersey, 1609–1702* (Princeton: Princeton University Press, 1956); Pomfret, *The Province of East New Jersey, 1609–1702* (Princeton: Princeton University Press, 1962); Jon Butler, *Power, Authority, and the Origins of American Denominational Order: The English Churches in the Delaware Valley, 1660–1730*, American Philosophical Society, *Transactions* 68 (Philadelphia, 1978); Martin E. Lodge, "The Crisis of the Churches in the Middle Colonies, 1720–1750," *Pennsylvania Magazine of History and Biography* 95 (1971): 195–220.

11. Sydney V. James, *Colonial Rhode Island: A History* (New York: Scribner's, 1975).

12. No adequate study of religion yet exists for colonial North Carolina, but in no year prior to 1750 were there more than three Anglican clergymen in the colony. Only for the three-year period 1768 through 1770 were there ten or more, the peak being sixteen. By contrast, the Baptists alone had thirty ministers in 1770, and other Dissenters, fourteen. Calculated from Frederick Lewis Weis, *The Colonial Clergy of Virginia, North Carolina, and South Carolina* (Boston: Society of the Descendants of the Colonial Clergy, 1955), 58–70.

13. For the extremes of West Jersey liberty and New World slavery, see *The West Jersey Concessions and Agreements of 1676/77: A Round Table of Histori-*

ans, New Jersey Historical Commission, Occasional Papers Number One (Trenton, 1979); Edmund S. Morgan, *American Slavery, American Freedom: The Ordeal of Colonial Virginia* (New York: W. W. Norton, 1975).

14. Perry Miller, *The New England Mind: From Colony to Province* (Cambridge, MA: Harvard University Press, 1953), is a brilliant exposition of this argument.

15. Among works not yet cited, see Alan Tully, *William Penn's Legacy: Politics and Social Structure in Provincial Pennsylvania, 1726-1755* (Baltimore: Johns Hopkins University Press, 1977); Ralph L. Ketcham, "Conscience, War, and Politics, 1755-1757," *William and Mary Quarterly*, 3rd ser., 20 (1963): 416-439.

16. See above, n. 6.

17. Daniel J. Boorstin, *The Americans: The Colonial Experience* (New York: Random House, 1958), 1.

18. Joan R. Gundersen, "The Anglican Ministry in Virginia, 1723-1776: A Study of Social Class" (Ph.D. diss., University of Notre Dame, 1972); Carol Van Voorst, "The Anglican Clergy in Maryland, 1692-1776" (Ph.D. diss., Princeton University, 1978). In the Chesapeake as a whole, the number of Anglican ministers did not reach twenty until 1680. It hovered around twenty-five for the next decade, rose dramatically to sixty or more by 1714, and then stagnated. Only in 1741 did it permanently exceed seventy. Calculated from Weis, *Colonial Clergy of Virginia, North Carolina, and South Carolina*, 1-57. For the Great Awakening in Virginia, see especially Rhys Isaac, *The Transformation of Virginia, 1740-1790* (Chapel Hill: University of North Carolina Press, 1982).

19. On New Haven, see the essays by Gail Sussman Marcus and John M. Murrin in David D. Hall, John M. Murrin, and Thad W. Tate, eds., *Saints & Revolutionaries: Essays on Early American History* (New York: W. W. Norton, 1984), 99-137, 152-206.

20. I develop this argument more systematically in "Colonial Government," in Jack P. Greene, ed., *Encyclopedia of American Political History: Studies of the Principal Movements and Ideas* (New York: Scribner's, 1984), I, 293-315.

21. This process can best be followed in Henry Clay Reed, ed., *The Burlington Court Book: A Record of Quaker Jurisprudence in West New Jersey, 1680-1709* (Washington: American Historical Association, 1944).

22. Douglas Greenberg, *Crime and Law Enforcement in the Colony of New York, 1691-1776* (Ithaca, NY: Cornell University Press, 1976), 87-88, 193.

23. William G. McLoughlin, "The Role of Religion in the Revolution: Liberty of Conscience and Cultural Cohesion in the New Nation," in Stephen G. Kurtz and James H. Hutson, eds., *Essays on the American Revolution* (Chapel Hill: University of North Carolina Press, 1973), 197-255; Sidney Mead, *The Lively Experiment: The Shaping of Christianity in America* (New York: Harper & Row, 1963).

24. Gerald L. Goodwin, "The Anglican Response to the Great Awakening," *Historical Magazine of the Protestant Episcopal Church* 35 (1966): 343-371;

Frederick B. Tolles, "Quietism versus Enthusiasm: The Philadelphia Quakers and the Great Awakening," in his *Quakers and the Atlantic Culture* (New York: Macmillan, 1960), 91–113.

25. C. C. Goen, *Revivalism and Separatism in New England, 1740–1800* (New Haven: Yale University Press, 1962); Conrad Wright, *The Beginnings of Unitarianism in America* (Boston: Beacon, 1953); Richard L. Bushman, *From Puritan to Yankee: Character and the Social Order in Connecticut, 1690–1765* (Cambridge, MA: Harvard University Press, 1967).

26. Leonard J. Trinterud, *The Forming of an American Tradition: A Re-Examination of Colonial Presbyterianism* (Philadelphia: Westminster, 1949); Howard Miller, *The Revolutionary College: American Presbyterian Higher Education, 1707–1837* (New York: New York University Press, 1976).

27. For a good survey of the denominational restructuring, see Sydney E. Ahlstrom, *A Religious History of the American People* (New Haven: Yale University Press, 1972), ch. 27, esp. pp. 436–437 on relative Methodist and Baptist strength. See also Gregory Evans Dowd, "Paths of Resistance: American Indian Religion and the Quest for Unity, 1745–1815" (Ph.D. diss., Princeton University, 1986).

28. For a fuller treatment of the issues in this section, see John M. Murrin, "Fundamental Values, the Founding Fathers, and the Constitution," paper read at the Capital Historical Society's March 1989 meeting, Washington, D.C.

29. Perry Miller, *Jonathan Edwards* (New York: William Morrow, 1949).

30. John Spurr, "'Latitudinarianism' and the Restoration Church," *Historical Journal* 31 (1988): 61–82; Norman Fiering, "The First American Enlightenment: Tillotson, Leverett, and Philosophical Anglicanism," *New England Quarterly* 54 (1981): 307–344.

31. Of an enormous literature, see especially J. G. A. Pocock, *The Machiavellian Moment: Florentine Political Thought and the Atlantic Republican Tradition* (Princeton: Princeton University Press, 1975).

32. For the impact of civic humanism on the evangelical clergy, see Bernard Bailyn, "Religion and Revolution: Three Biographical Studies," *Perspectives in American History* 4 (1970): 85–169; and Nathan O. Hatch, *The Sacred Cause of Liberty: Republican Thought and the Millennium in Revolutionary New England* (New Haven: Yale University Press, 1977). No explicit study exists emphasizing the difficulty of moving from committed patriot to reborn Christian, but it is probably no accident that republican convictions reached their peak in America at about the time that church adherence hit its lowest point, the two decades after independence. The Revolution intensified another trend already evident in American life. Young men aspired to be proud and independent. Young women were socialized to be humble and dependent. The abject humility of the conversion experience raised far fewer difficulties for women than for men. The gender balance among full church members in evangelical denominations, already skewed toward women before the Revolution, became much more extreme during the following generation. See Richard D. Shiels, "The Feminization of American

Congregationalism, 1730-1835," *American Quarterly* 33 (1981): 46-62; and, for the Middle Atlantic, Martha T. Blauvelt, "Society, Religion, and Revivalism: The Second Great Awakening in New Jersey, 1780-1830" (Ph.D. diss., Princeton University, 1974).

33. The fullest argument for the impact of classical liberalism on America is Joyce Appleby, *Capitalism and a New Social Order: The Republican Vision of the 1790s* (New York: New York University Press, 1984).

34. Gary B. Nash, "The American Clergy and the French Revolution," *William and Mary Quarterly*, 3rd ser., 22 (1965); 392-412; Michael Durey, "Thomas Paine's Apostles: Radical Emigrés and the Triumph of Jeffersonian Republicanism," *William and Mary Quarterly*, 3rd ser., 44 (1987); 661-688.

35. Gordon S. Wood, "Interests and Disinterestedness in the Making of the Constitution," in Richard Beeman, Stephen Botein, and Edward C. Carter II, eds., *Beyond Confederation: Origins of the Constitution and American National Identity* (Chapel Hill: University of North Carolina Press, 1987), 69-109.

36. The essays in Istvan Hont and Michael Ignatieff, eds., *Wealth and Virtue: The Shaping of Political Economy in the Scottish Enlightenment* (Cambridge: Cambridge University Press, 1983), provide an outstanding introduction to the main themes of the Scottish Enlightenment. For its impact on America, see David F. Norton, "Francis Hutcheson in America," *Studies on Voltaire and the Eighteenth Century* 151-155 (1976), 1547-1568; Garry Wills, *Inventing America: Jefferson's Declaration of Independence* (New York: Doubleday, 1978); Ronald Hamowy, "Jefferson and the Scottish Enlightenment: A Critique of Garry Wills' *Inventing America: Jefferson's Declaration of Independence*," *William and Mary Quarterly*, 3rd ser., 36 (1979): 503-523; Mark A. Noll, "Common Sense Traditions and American Evangelical Thought," *American Quarterly* 37 (1985): 215-238; and Noll, *Princeton and the Republic, 1768-1822: The Search for a Christian Enlightenment in the Era of Samuel Stanhope Smith* (Princeton: Princeton University Press, 1989).

37. Thomas E. Buckley, S.J., *Church and State in Revolutionary Virginia, 1776-1787* (Charlottesville: University Press of Virginia, 1977).

38. Benjamin Perley Poore, comp., *The Federal and State Constitutions, Colonial Charters, and Other Organic Laws of the United States* (Washington: Government Printing Office, 1877), I, 257.

39. Oscar Handlin and Mary F. Handlin, eds., *The Popular Sources of Political Authority: Documents on the Massachusetts Constitution of 1780* (Cambridge, MA: Harvard University Press, 1966), 441-442.

40. Poore, *Federal and State Constitutions*, II, 1280-1281.

41. Samuel Eliot Morison, ed., *Sources and Documents Illustrating the American Revolution, 1764-1788, and the Formation of the Federal Constitution*, 2nd ed. (Oxford: Clarendon, 1929), 162-163.

42. Handlin and Handlin, *Popular Sources of Political Authority*, 441-442.

43. Poore, *Federal and State Constitutions*, II, 1857.

44. Morison, *Sources and Documents*, 186.

45. Ibid., 151.

46. For New Jersey, see Julian P. Boyd, ed., *Fundamental Laws and Constitutions of New Jersey* (Princeton: Van Nostrand, 1964), 161; for Georgia, Maryland, and North Carolina, see Poore, *Federal and State Constitutions*, I, 383, 828; II, 1413.

47. Max Farrand, ed., *The Records of the Federal Convention of 1787*, rev. ed. (New Haven, 1937), I, 450–452; III, 467–473. I discuss this incident more fully in "Fundamental Values, the Founding Fathers, and the Constitution."

48. The phrase "secular humanist" was not used in the eighteenth century. It derives, in all probability, from the creation of secular humanist societies in New York City and elsewhere in the early twentieth century. In recent decades it has become primarily a code word among conservative evangelicals for intellectual forces—in schools and colleges, the media, and government—that they see destroying traditional American values. But even if the term had no currency in the eighteenth century, men of the Enlightenment had their own counterparts that meant nearly the same thing. The "party of humanity" is one example. This phrase usually signified a group of thinkers that derived its ethical values from reason and human experience, not revelation. See Peter Gay, *The Party of Humanity: Essays on the French Enlightenment* (New York: Knopf, 1963).

49. For evidence of Bassett's strong evangelical commitment both before and after the Philadelphia Convention, see Francis Asbury, *Journals and Letters*, ed. Elmer E. Clark (Nashville: Abingdon, 1958), I, 26n, 312–313, 337–338, 345, 449, 674 and passim.

50. Christopher Collier, *Roger Sherman's Connecticut: Yankee Politics and the American Revolution* (Middletown, CT: Wesleyan University Press, 1971), 36–37, 325.

51. Mark Noll, "James Madison: From Evangelical Princeton to the Constitutional Convention," *Pro Rege* (December 1987): 2–14; Thomas Jefferson, "The Anas," In Merrill D. Peterson, ed., *Thomas Jefferson: Writings* (New York: Library of America, 1984), 666, 671.

52. Gordon S. Wood, *The Creation of the American Republic, 1776–1787* (Chapel Hill: University of North Carolina Press, 1969); Ruth H. Bloch et al., "*The Creation of the American Republic, 1776–1787*: A Symposium of Views and Reviews," *William and Mary Quarterly*, 3rd ser., 44 (1987): 550–640.

53. John Adams seriously considered a career as a minister but gave it up because it threatened what he called his "liberty to think." Peter Shaw, *The Character of John Adams* (Chapel Hill: University of North Carolina Press, 1976), 9. The best study of Jefferson's religious beliefs is Eugene R. Sheridan, "Introduction," to Dickinson W. Adams and Ruth W. Lester, eds., *Jefferson's Extracts from the Gospels: "The Philosophy of Jesus" and "The Life and Morals of Jesus"* (Princeton: Princeton University Press, 1983), 3–42. The two compilations published in this volume represent Jefferson's effort to sort out those parts of Scripture that he could accept, versus the remainder that he rejected.

54. After graduating from the College of New Jersey in 1771, Madison spent

an extra year at Princeton studying Hebrew under President John Witherspoon, a commitment that suggests he was contemplating the ministry. See also Samuel Stanhope Smith to Madison, November 1777–August 1778, in William T. Hutchinson and William M. E. Rachal, eds., *The Papers of James Madison* (Chicago and Charlottesville: The University of Chicago Press and the University Press of Virginia, 1962–), I, 194–212. The Madison letter to which Smith is responding is no longer extant, but Smith's reply shows that Madison still accepted Calvinist orthodoxy on the central question of liberty and necessity. Cf. Ralph L. Ketcham, "James Madison and Religion—A New Hypothesis," *Journal of the Presbyterian Historical Society* 38 (1960): 65–90; and Ketcham, "James Madison and the Nature of Man," *Journal of the History of Ideas* 19 (1958): 62–76. Ketcham detects a stronger religious influence on the mature Madison than I do.

55. Robert Green McCloskey, ed., *The Works of James Wilson* (Cambridge, MA: Harvard University Press, 1967), I, 144.

56. Jefferson to Peter Carr, August 10, 1787, and to Adams, April 11, 1823, in Peterson, ed., *Thomas Jefferson: Writings*, 900–905, 1466–1469, quotation on 1469.

57. For Madison in particular, see especially *The Federalist*, Nos. 10 and 51. See also Michael Kammen, *A Machine That Would Go of Itself: The Constitution in American Culture* (New York: Knopf, 1987).

58. The drafters of the Pennsylvania Constitution of 1776 proclaimed, for example, that God "alone knows to what degree of earthly happiness mankind may attain by perfecting the arts of government." Morison, *Sources and Documents*, 163. For Madison's celebration of radical innovation during the Revolution, see the final paragraph of *The Federalist*, No. 14. See also Jefferson to Dr. Benjamin Waterhouse, June 26, 1822, in Peterson, ed., *Thomas Jefferson: Writings*, 1458–1459.

59. See Edmund S. Morgan, *Roger Williams: The Church and the State* (New York: Harcourt, 1967), for the very different seventeenth-century sensibilities on this question. For shifting priorities between civil and religious liberty, see Hatch, *Sacred Cause of Liberty*, ch. 1.

60. Vernon Stauffer, *New England and the Bavarian Illuminati* (New York: Columbia University Press, 1918); Constance B. Schulz, "Of Bigotry in Politics and Religion: Jefferson's Religion, the Federalist Press, and the Syllabus," *Virginia Magazine of History and Biography* 91 (1983): 73–91.

61. Timothy Dwight, *A Discourse in Two Parts, Delivered July 23, 1812, on the Public Fast, in the Chapel of Yale College*, 2nd ed. (Boston: Cummings and Hilliard, 1813), 24. My thanks to Harry S. Stout for bringing this passage to my attention. For Stout's own use of Dwight's comment, see below.

62. Although a slight majority of Congregationalist delegates in state ratifying conventions opposed the Constitution, most Congregational clergy favored it. See Jackson Turner Main, *The Antifederalists: Critics of the Constitution, 1781–1788* (Chapel Hill: University of North Carolina Press, 1961), 208; and Main, *Political Parties Before the Constitution* (Chapel Hill: University of North Caro-

lina Press, 1973), 377–379. Presbyterians probably reflected a similar pattern. See James H. Smylie, "Protestant Clergy, the First Amendment, and Beginnings of a Constitutional Debate, 1781–1791," in Elwyn A. Smith, ed., *The Religion of the Republic* (Philadelphia: Fortress, 1971), 116–153. See also William Gribben, *The Churches Militant: The War of 1812 and American Religion* (New Haven: Yale University Press, 1973).

63. For the French contrast, see Peter Gay, *The Enlightenment: An Interpretation: The Rise of Modern Paganism* (New York: Knopf, 1966). The tension between orthodoxy and the Enlightenment in North America resembled the tone already established in Scotland, where even David Hume refrained from overt attacks on the kirk. See, generally, Richard B. Sher, *Church and University in the Scottish Enlightenment* (Princeton: Princeton University Press, 1985). See also H. Jefferson Powell, "The Original Understanding of Original Intent," *Harvard Law Review* 98 (1984–85): 885–948.

64. Farrand, *Records of the Federal Convention*, III, 470–472.

2

Religion and Ideological Change in the American Revolution

RUTH H. BLOCH

This paper on the American Revolution is meant to address a basic historical question about religion and American politics, a question addressed in various ways by other papers in this volume as well. How did religious ideas contribute to the development of political ideology? Defining the topic this way necessarily brackets many other interesting questions about the role of religion in the American Revolution that fall more directly into the realms of social and political history—questions involving institutional structures and laws, the extent of clerical and lay activism, regional and denominational comparisons, and so on. To a certain extent, these subjects will inevitably bear upon my discussion, but the central issues I am exploring pertain to intellectual history: What elements of Revolutionary thought can be properly described as religious? How did they change over time? To what can we attribute these changes?

In a way, I am addressing an old historiographical problem. Beginning with the Revolutionary clergy itself, scholars have endlessly debated the importance of religion to the American Revolution. Some have stressed institutional factors, such as the weakness of the colonial religious establishments or the leadership role of the New England clergy, but most have argued over the interpretation of ideology. Was it best characterized as secular, Enlightened, or Protestant? Were the religious elements of Revolutionary thought primary or secondary, radical or conservative?

The main terms of this debate crystallized already in the Progressive generation. Historians such as Vernon Parrington and Carl Becker rejected the Protestant chauvinism of their nineteenth-century forebears and claimed the Revolution for Enlightenment rationalism. Lately, the debate has become more complex. The reigning interpretations of Revolutionary ideology no longer stress a monolithic Enlightenment but rather a less rationalistic "republicanism," one derived from a tradition of English political opposition to an expanding royal bureaucracy. This "republicanism," it is argued, incorporated both religious and Enlightenment ideas but subsumed them within its own hegemonic framework.[1] Some historians recently challenging this interpretation have stressed instead the emergence of another, still more fully secular ideology, that of free market liberalism.[2]

On yet a third side of this debate are those, including myself, who have argued for the centrality of religious ideas.[3] While on one level I intend this paper to remake this case in a new way, on another level I want to change the terms of the argument. Most historians now acknowledge the interpenetration of religious and secular themes in the ideology of the Revolution. So much scholarship of the last twenty years has documented the religious symbolism of the Revolutionary movement that the debate over the importance of religion is less over the existence and pervasiveness of this language than over its intellectual and social role.

Typically this debate revolves around conflicting assessments of the relative significance of religious compared to secular ideas. Did religion serve as a vehicle carrying secular political ideas to a Protestant populace?[4] Did American Protestantism itself decisively shape political ideology?[5] Or is the relationship between religious and secular thought best seen as a kind of momentary merger of otherwise distinct intellectual systems?[6] Beneath this dispute lurks yet another issue, which is the one I would like to stress. Virtually all such interpretations, whatever their differences, depict religion as essentially traditional. Thus the role of religion is typically either the dressing of new secular ideas in old, comfortable Protestant garb or, conversely, the ascetic critique of worldly modern fashions. When religion is depicted as a force of revolutionary change, its radical primitivism, not its conceptual creativity, usually receives emphasis.[7] Changing religious ideas appear more often as mirrors reflecting nonreligious intellectual developments than as dynamic components of the process of ideological change itself.[8]

This paper proposes to survey familiar historical territory from a somewhat different angle of vision. Without seeking to measure the relative importance of other influences upon Revolutionary ideology, I wish to highlight a few specifically *religious* contributions to its development between 1763 and 1789. This task requires that I begin by identifying, in very general terms, some basic religious orientations defining early American Protestantism. Drawing such generalizations is admittedly hazardous. Plenty of exceptions can be found—some of these themes are more pronounced in certain regions, social classes, and denominations than in others—yet there was also enough commonality among Revolutionary American Protestants to justify a synthetic interpretation. The popular support for the American Revolution came overwhelmingly from Congregationalists, Baptists, Presbyterians, and Southern lay Anglicans, almost all of whom can be loosely described as Calvinist. Here I am following David Hall, who has gone so far as to assert that "Calvinism was the common faith of people in America before the Revolution."[9] What Hall claims about colonial Americans is even more true of the Revolutionary movement. To be sure, the Revolution also enlisted the support of a number of religious rationalists, particularly among the urban elite and the Southern gentry, but, on a more popular level, the religious faith of American revolutionaries was in the main Calvinist. The non-Calvinist Quakers, Methodists, and Northern Anglicans drifted disproportionately towards neutrality and Loyalism, and typically Calvinist preoccupations underlay much of the development of Revolutionary ideology.

Calvinism in early America was, as Hall and others have recently emphasized, not a rigid system of doctrines so much as an open-ended and ambiguous effort to resolve a series of fundamental tensions posed by the Reformation: grace versus preparation, evangelicalism versus sacerdotalism, sect versus church. The common denominators of American Calvinism that most centrally pertained to the American Revolution were so basic that they can be boiled down to two: first, the experiential approach to salvation, with its uneasy connection to the necessity of righteous behavior in the world; and second, the definition of an elect community—ambiguously visible and invisible, churchlike and sectlike—with a secular history overseen by Providence.

These two basic themes weave in and out of the political ideology of the Revolution. Religious concerns about the conditions of salvation helped shape the understanding of the key Revolutionary values of liberty and virtue. The belief in Providence underlay the patriots' conviction that the secular history of the Revolution had a higher, transhistorical meaning. And the perennial effort to define the godly community contributed to the formulation of American nationalism. The historical roots of many of these ideological developments can be traced back to revolutionary Puritanism of the seventeenth century. Indeed, even the Lockean theory of the social contract as the basis of civil society was largely derived from Puritan ideas about the covenanted church. Far from having become secularized by the eighteenth century, the religious preoccupations that had always informed political ideology remained vitally important to Americans of the Revolutionary generation.

On the one hand, religion during the American Revolution responded flexibly to a shifting course of events, lending its authoritative vocabulary to legitimate an essentially secular process of change. On the other hand, however, ideological change occurred within a symbolic structure largely defined by the Calvinist experiential approach to salvation and providential understanding of the collective experience of God's people on earth. What happened in the Revolutionary period was that the conflict with Britain raised unusually fundamental questions about the justification of political authority and the moral and spiritual basis of collective life—questions so fundamental as to lay bare these religious underpinnings. The interpenetration of religious and political symbolism in patriot discourse signified neither a newfound politicization of nonpolitical religion nor a newfound sacralization of secular politics, but expressed the very depth and intensity of the crisis. This crisis not only exposed the underlying fusion of preexisting religious and political outlooks but gradually forced these outlooks to change. Neither static nor simply reactive, the religious symbolism of salvation and godly community was both general and problematic enough to allow room for creative reinterpretation over time. The following sketch of three major phases of ideological development during the Revolutionary era—roughly characterized by the periods 1763–1774, 1774–1778, and 1778–1789—illustrates the dynamic quality of this religious contribution to Revolutionary ideology.

1763–1774

These years of protest against the new British imperial policy have rightly been called a period of "resistance" rather than of "revolution."[10] This characterization points to the limited organization and goals of the early patriot movement as well as to the Americans' repeated declarations of loyalty to king and empire. Despite the momentary display of intercolonial unity during the Stamp Act crisis, American resistance in this period was organized locally, both in the provincial assemblies and in the city streets. The only place that consistently gave widespread popular support to the patriot cause was New England, particularly Boston. Just as the movement remained geographically decentralized, its strategy was for the most part confined to piecemeal responses to a number of different issues. These issues included not only the legendary taxation-without-representation but efforts to regulate colonial currency, the expansion of the royal bureaucracy, multiple officeholding by appointed officials, and the maintenance of a standing army. There were specifically religious issues as well—most importantly, the rumors in the early 1760s that the Church of England was planning to install an American bishop and, in 1774, the news that Roman Catholicism would be permitted by the British Crown to remain the official religion of conquered Quebec.[11]

Despite the early and persistent constitutional arguments against British claims that the Americans were "virtually represented" in Parliament, this great variety of issues lacked a specific constitutional focus. What united the protests and gave them an ideological coherence was instead a mythic perception of the violation of a sacred past. Bernard Bailyn and others have argued that the main terms of this myth were borrowed from the ideology of the English political opposition, a radical Whig version of history that featured a virtuous, liberty-loving citizenry under attack by an expanding, corrupt, and tyrannical executive power. Yet, as several other historians have demonstrated, it is clear that early patriot ideology had strong religious components as well.[12] Without seeking precisely to unravel the religious elements from the secular ones, one can identify several ways in which basic American Calvinist concerns about the definition of the godly community and the conditions of grace found immediate expression within early patriot discourse.

Inherited from the Puritans, the language of the covenant spoke directly to the question of an elect community and its protection by Providence. Although Perry Miller once argued that a moribund covenant theology was finally buried in the Great Awakening, only to be temporarily brought back to life in the Revolutionary period, Harry Stout has recently shown the enduring vitality of New England's belief in its special, covenanted relationship with God.[13] Just as the polemics of the radical Whigs idealized a mythic past of English liberty within a balanced constitutional order, New England sermons looked backwards towards the covenant of early colonial days. In both these ways, patriots were called to preserve the legacy of an earlier era.

In contrast to the more expansive, imperial framework of radical Whig ideology, the vocabulary of the covenant sharply differentiated America from Great Britain. At this early stage of the patriot movement, however, the concept of the godly community defined by the covenant was still highly provincial, remaining for the most part confined to New England alone.[14] New England patriot ministers spoke in defense of their regional history as a whole, moreover, without distinguishing between the social, religious, and political aspects of the past. They simply presumed the New England tradition to be both Christian and free, and their covenant terminology fused together church, state, and society into an undifferentiated godly community set apart from the British forces of sin and tyranny.[15]

Often combined with appeals to the covenant, and likewise involving the Calvinist effort to define the perimeters of God's people, was a Manichaean tendency to polarize the world between the forces of God and the forces of Antichrist. A dualistic understanding of history as a struggle between good and evil had as long a history in the colonies as covenant theology. By the 1760s both the conflicts of the Great Awakening and the anti-Catholic crusade of the French and Indian War had reinforced the inclination of American Calvinists to see themselves engaged in a cosmic battle with Satan. Whereas references to the covenant typically appeared in sermons by New England ministers, the Manichaean tendency to conceptualize the imperial conflict in terms of good and evil appeared first within lay political argument and popular patriot ritual as early as the mid-1760s.[16] The symbolic link forging the connection between Great Britain and Antichrist was typically the pollution of Roman Catholicism. In Boston and elsewhere, traditional anti-Catholic Pope Day celebrations became occasions for dramatizing the patriot cause. Orations, cartoons, and public hangings of effigies depicted the royal ministers as in league alternately with the pope and the devil.[17] Just as these symbols and rituals characterized the royal government as the agent of Antichrist, other purifying rituals of fasting and abstinence from imported British goods, along with appeals to the covenant, reinforced the connection between American resistance and the legions of God.[18]

In different if occasionally overlapping ways, both the covenant and the Manichaean symbolism of the early patriot movement sought to clarify the relationship between the colonial protests and God's providential plan for the world. Both types of religious symbolism aimed to delineate boundaries that defined the righteous community—either, in the case of the covenant, through identification with New England history or, in the case of Manichaeanism, through detestation of the British Antichrist. Alongside these efforts to specify the godly community, American patriots brought Calvinist preoccupations about salvation into their understanding of imperial politics. These concerns were expressed above all in the religious use of the central Revolutionary symbol of liberty.

In New England, especially, historians have found many examples of clergymen endorsing Whig ideas about the importance of constitutional liberty well before the outbreak of the Revolutionary conflict. Nathan Hatch stressed its assimilation into New England religious vocabulary during the French and Indian War, and more recently Harry Stout has offered a detailed account of how the Whig conception of liberty had been incorporated into New England covenant theology by the early eighteenth century.[19] The essentially religious status of the concept of liberty depends, however, only in part on such pre-Revolutionary endorsements of specifically Whig political ideas. As important was the more diffuse and fecund meaning of the word "liberty" within colonial religious vocabulary. For the term referred not only to the civil liberty of the English constitution but also to the religious liberty craved by religious dissenters and to the spiritual liberty of grace—"the liberty wherewith Christ made us free."[20] When New Englanders fought in the name of liberty against the French Catholics during the Seven Years' War, they had religious and spiritual as much as civil liberty in mind. When colonists in the religiously pluralistic middle colonies engaged in competitive denominational politics, they too demonstrated their commitment to a religious version of liberty.[21]

What was new in the 1760s was not the conflation of religious and political values but the shift of the British government from the side of liberty and Christianity to the side of tyranny and Antichrist. In the early Revolutionary movement, patriots repeatedly associated the Church of England and the royal ministers with papal tyranny. The ease with which so many Americans in the 1760s expanded their definition of Christian liberty to include civil as well as spiritual and religious liberty is comprehensible only when one realizes how these different definitions of liberty were already mixed together. To be sure, some American Protestants, most notably the Baptists, specifically resisted this equation, arguing against the devaluation of spiritual liberty by its association with profane political liberty.[22] They did so, however, well aware that they were seeking to sever the common linkage made within the patriot movement.

By the mid-1770s, then, religion was so deeply intertwined with Revolutionary political ideology that it seems virtually impossible to distinguish between them. The overlapping vocabulary of Whig ideology and American Protestantism wielded particular power, of course, in New England, where the fusion of the religious and secular had a long institutional history. Whatever other reasons can be offered to explain the primacy of New England in the early Revolutionary movement, the strength of this symbolic association between politics and religious experience must be taken into account. Nor was New England altogether unique. As suggested by the example of a 1765 Philadelphia Presbyterian crowd calling, "No King but King Jesus," or by the Virginian Richard Bland's 1771 description of High Church plans to found a colonial bishopric as "Papal Incroachments upon the Common Law," the overt blurring of religious and political categories was a feature of popular Revolutionary politics elsewhere in the early years of resistance as well.[23]

The fact that there were plenty of "secular" political treatises that never referred to the covenant, to Antichrist, or to the liberty of grace—and, conversely, plenty of "religious" discourses that altogether ignored politics—in no way undercuts this point. Surely there were Americans for whom liberty primarily meant the relative autonomy of the colonial legislatures, and others for whom it primarily meant the salvation provided by grace. The widespread resonance of such terms as "virtue," "corruption," or "liberty" in the early patriot movement depended, however, on their multivalent, civil and spiritual references. A connection between what we normally distinguish as religious or secular was embedded in the very meaning of Revolutionary language itself.

1774-1778

Religious and political terminology continued to fuse during the next period of open rebellion, warfare, and Revolutionary state-building. The basic religious orientation expressed in Revolutionary ideology from roughly 1775 to 1778 remained essentially the same. The underlying religious issues were still the spiritual quest for salvation and the purification of a godly community on earth. Liberty continued to have a sacred meaning in large part because of its intimate symbolic connection with grace. And revolutionaries persisted in defining their collective experience in providential and morally dichotomous terms: they were the nation under God, the Loyalists and the British were the representatives of Antichrist.

But, for all these fundamental continuities, both the context and the form of much of the specific religious symbolism in patriot ideology changed as America moved from resistance to revolution. The concrete catalysts for this change were several parliamentary measures of 1774—the so-called Coercive (or Intolerable) Acts leveled against intransigent

Massachusetts and the Quebec Act protecting Catholicism in French Canada. In response to these events, the colonists mobilized across geographical lines as never before, forming the Continental Congress, extralegal committees, provincial governments, and an army—steps that led within less than two years to national independence. These political developments took place alongside important shifts on the level of religious symbolism. It is possible to identify three particularly significant changes, all involving new efforts to formulate a sacred national identity. These efforts reveal a creative religious interaction with unfolding events. Encompassed within the broader symbolic framework of election and Providence, they suggest ways that American religion not only responded to the pressures of circumstances but, through a process of reinterpretation, structured the very meaning of revolutionary change.

One important symbolic change of the mid-1770s was the geographical extension of the definition of God's community. Earlier, the Manichaean, covenant, and providential language describing the virtues and obligations of God's people had been largely embedded within a provincial New England vocabulary. Now this symbolism expanded to cover the entire nation. In the wake of the Quebec Act, especially, the depiction of Great Britain as Antichrist became frequent throughout the colonies.[24] The New England clergy continued to appeal to its distinctive covenant theory, but, as Harry Stout has argued, even there patriot ministers began in 1775 to stretch the terms of the covenant to include the American colonies as a whole.[25] Covenant imagery appeared prominently elsewhere as well, permeating official proclamations by the Continental Congress, including its calls for fast and thanksgiving days.[26] Jefferson's Declaration of Independence emerged from the drafting committee of the Continental Congress with a reference to the controlling hand of Providence.[27] And other secular political leaders in the mid-1770s, ranging from the cool Anglican Alexander Hamilton to the semi-evangelical Patrick Henry, appealed in public to the unity and religious duty of Americans as a Protestant people under God.[28] This rapid redefinition of the righteous community cannot be explained simply as the product of New England influence or as the automatic response to a political situation. The underlying Protestant tendency to conceptualize secular experience in providential, collective terms—a tendency that extended beyond New England and the specific language of the covenant—shaped the emerging expression of American nationalism in the mid-1770s.

A second symbolic shift concerned the location of this righteous community in time. Earlier, New England patriots typically evoked the image of a hallowed past. Beginning in the mid-1770s, however, Congregational ministers instead increasingly stressed the prospects of a millennial future. These millennial hopes, like the image of a national community under God, extended well beyond New England alone, appearing both in sermons and in secular patriot writings in many regions of Revolutionary America.[29] In fact, a recent study of my own on the frequency of millennial statements in printed literature suggests that such ideas may well have been as common among Presbyterian and Baptist patriots in the middle and Southern regions as they were among New England Congregationalists.[30] Millennial symbolism was a standard feature of much American Protestantism of the late colonial period, weaving in and out of providential theories about the meaning of contemporary events. It was, however, only in the mid-1770s that this symbolism came to pervade Revolutionary ideology, enabling Americans to perceive the outbreak of war and assertion of national independence as steps towards the realization of God's Kingdom on Earth.

Both in its national scope and in its millennial optimism, then, the providential language of the mid-1770s differed sharply from that of the 1760s and early 1770s. The third important symbolic shift of this period gave a new sacred status to republican government. Earlier, the symbol of liberty had diffusely referred both to the experience of salvation and to the legitimate rights and traditions of the British political order. The term "virtue" likewise ambiguously evoked both Christian moral duties and the self-sacrificial patriotism of the public-spirited citizen. In the early years of the Revolutionary movement, however, this was the vocabulary of resistance to, not endorsement of, the state. As the colonists moved towards the establishment of an independent republican system, the symbols of liberty and virtue continued to be imbued with these manifold religious and political meanings, but they acquired a new, positive relationship to conceptions of government. The godly community of the virtuous citizenry became virtually indistinguishable from the republican state.

As Harry Stout has emphasized in his study of New England sermons, ministers now upheld the model of the Jewish republic, a development revealing not only the plasticity of biblical interpretation but the new-found fusion of the state with the godly community.[31] In the millennial literature of these years, the triumph of Christianity and republican government likewise merged together as the joint measure of progress towards the latter days.[32] This symbolic fusion of the state and the Christian community can also be discerned in the *rage militaire* during the beginning of the war, when enlistment in the army became the consummate expression of virtue.[33] Many Revolutionary state governments, including constitutionally radical Pennsylvania, sought to institutionalize this connection by passing test acts and other laws limiting inclusion in the republican polity to Revolutionary Protestants or, more broadly, Christians, alone. And, of course, in several New England states, the Congregational church remained legally established long after the Revolution.[34]

On the one hand, these legal provisions show us the obstacles that the modern principle of religious freedom had yet to overcome.[35] The identification of the secular state with the people of God was scarcely a new theme within the history of providential thought in America, particularly in New England, where the Puritan state had been patterned precisely on this Old Testament model. On the other hand, the forceful symbolic and institutional reassertion of this connection in the years surrounding independence—however retrograde this may seem from a modern perspective—gave powerful religious legitimacy to the new republican system of government.

Together with the national definition of the chosen community and the visionary hopes of a coming new day, this fusion of the religious and the political orders largely defined the ideological shift from resistance to revolution in the mid-1770s. The religious cast of these expressions of Revolutionary nationalism, optimism, and loyalty to republican government reveals the continuing allegiance of American Protestants to a concept of Providence and to the idea of a righteous community on earth. Similarly, the repeated Revolutionary appeals to liberty and virtue spoke to long-standing concerns about the experience and assurance of salvation. Never unproblematic, however, these basic religious orientations were frought with creative tensions that enabled religion to play a dynamic—not merely either a reactive or a determining—role in the shaping of Revolutionary ideology. Inevitably, fundamental religious questions remained unresolved. To what extent could Providence be relied on? How closely did the saintly community approximate the secular one? What was the path to salvation? Inasmuch as such questions continued to structure the religious understanding of the Revolution, the ideological answers changed over the course of the Revolution itself.

1778–1789

The third major phase in the development of Revolutionary ideology began during the dispirited years of the war after 1778. With a brief respite in the early 1780s, after the welcome news of Yorktown and during the settlement of peace, a mood of anxiety descended over the new nation that lasted at least until the ratification of the Constitution. The increased apprehensiveness during the so-called Critical Period has been often noted by historians, although they have debated whether or not this anxiety reflected serious political problems subsequently solved by the Constitution.[36] In any case, the crisis of this period was, as Gordon Wood has convincingly argued, moral as much as political.[37] American public spokesmen repeatedly lamented what they perceived to be a decline of virtue, a decline they saw as threatening the very basis of republican liberty.

Several developments underlay this perception. One, emphasized by Wood as most critical, was the outbreak of political conflicts on the state level over both currency policy and the framing of constitutions. A second was the increased consumerism stimulated by postwar access to imported foreign luxuries. These developments exacerbated latent social antagonisms and challenged the republican ideal of a united citizenry willing to sacrifice individual economic interests in the service of the greater public good. According to Wood, the Constitution, with its mechanisms for dividing and balancing power, represented an ideological solution to this moral crisis by divesting the government of the need to rely on popular virtue for the preservation of liberty.[38]

There is, however, another way of looking at the same process, one that emphasizes instead the religious reformulation of republican thought in the 1780s. Clergymen in this period, like secular spokesmen, frequently denounced symptoms of corruption as a threat to the republic, typically in the form of the jeremiad.[39] The millennial zeal of the 1770s abated, replaced by an upsurge of lurid, apocalyptical predictions of doom.[40] The solution advocated by these patriot ministers was neither rededication to public service, financial sacrifice, nor the cessation of factional disputes, but faith. As the Reverend Asa Burton of Vermont explained in his election sermon of 1786, "Political virtue may serve as a support for a while, but it is not a *lasting* principle." Rather, he insisted, the true basis of free states was a popular spirit of religious benevolence that arose from the fear of God.[41] If national happiness depended on virtue, the religious literature of the 1780s repeatedly proclaimed, virtue depended on piety.[42]

Whereas at the height of the Revolutionary excitement of the mid-1770s the religious and political orders were symbolically merged, this connection proved very short-lived. Within less than a decade religious leaders were urging American Protestants to reconceptualize their relationship to the state. On the one hand, it is possible to understand this

development as a logical response to the deflation of high hopes as the
new nation turned away from struggles with Great Britain and faced its
own inevitable imperfections. The logic of this disillusionment was, however, structured not merely by practical realities but by religious considerations as well. The strong identification of the righteous community
with the republican state that characterized the mid-1770s violated an
alternative sense of the righteous as an invisible church before God.
During the same years, as Virginians moved towards ecclesiastical disestablishment, Northern Protestants—including those in the established
churches of New England—were on a conceptual level disengaging from
the state as well. An emphasis on the legal and institutional differences
between Virginians and New Englanders obscures this common development. Although the principle of religious freedom came late and incom-
pletely to most American revolutionaries, the 1780s witnessed a growing
insistence on a religious space separate from republican government.

This increased detachment of religion from the state helped set the
stage for what Gordon Wood has called "the end of classical politics."[43]
The passage of the United States Constitution, with its mechanisms of
checks and balances, marks a shift away from a reliance on popular
virtue. No longer did the republic depend on extensive public involvement in the military or government. The more limited idea of public
virtue that remained in the minds of the proponents of the Constitution
hinged instead, as Daniel Howe has argued, on the superior reason of
statesmen.[44]

This shift in the definition of public virtue away from popular participation in republican government did not, however, produce an alternatively private or individualistic sense of morality. Despite these developments on the level of political thought, many Americans continued to
believe that the future of the republic depended on popular virtue. Far
from giving up on the superior righteousness and collective moral imperative of the American people, Protestant leaders in the 1790s rede-
fined the way this popular virtue would be generated and expressed.
Instead of being located directly within the institutional perimeters of
representative government, public virtue was increasingly defined as a
quality of nonpolitical organizational life. Of course, the ministerial
jeremiads of the 1780s most typically called the nation back to the
churches; but schools and families began to receive greater emphasis as
bulwarks of liberty and Christianity as well. In addition, the 1780s and
1790s saw the foundation of early voluntary reform associations designed
to correct various social ills, ranging from imprisonment for debt to
slavery, often also with a religious purpose in mind. What emerged by the

end of the Revolutionary period was a sense of a virtuous American society distinct from the institutions of government. A major source of this development was, I would like to suggest, the endemic tensions within the American Protestant tradition over the relationship of the godly community to the state. Already by the mid-1770s the definition of this community had extended to encompass the nation and, with it, republican government. In the 1780s, however, this unstable equation came apart, leaving a strong, religiously informed nationalism that was divested of much of its earlier association with the state.

I have sketched three intellectual stages through which Revolutionary American Protestants moved between 1763 and 1789, a movement characterized, first, by a rapidly expanding definition of liberty—one simultaneously embracing spiritual, ecclesiastical, and civil concerns—and, second, by an expanded definition of the righteous community—one encompassing not only the church and the province but the nation. If American Protestantism was not tied to the specific political policies or constitutional structure of the state, it did come to identify itself strongly with the American people and the broad republican values of liberty. This identification drew upon older quests for spiritual redemption, older commitments to religious community, and older struggles against tyrannical, "papist" government, but it was also critically shaped by the successive crises, hopes, and fears of the American Revolutionary process itself.

The expanded definitions of liberty and community did not mean that specific spiritual and religious commitments were displaced or subsumed by political ones. The religious involvement in institutionalized political life was, with the brief exception of the mid-1770s, qualified and contingent. Like the framers of the Constitution and unlike the classical republicans whose thought underlay much of the early Revolutionary movement, articulate American Protestants resisted the equation of virtue and political participation. As Nathan Hatch has shown, post-Revolutionary popular evangelical religious denominations would become more individualistic than their predecessors in their emphasis on personal salvation and scriptural interpretation.[45]

Unlike the Founders, however, and unlike subsequent generations of liberty theorists, they and other American Protestants continued to believe that virtue was indispensable to the public good. The rhetorical connection between piety, social happiness, and national destiny lived on, structuring major themes in American ideology. One of the major achievements of the Revolutionary era was the birth of a new dimension of American public life, neither church nor state, characterized by voluntary moral and social activism. Typically religiously inspired and nationalistic, these reform movements emerged as powerful and distinctive features of the American republican way of life. This development was, I would suggest, a direct consequence of the religious experience of the Revolution, an experience that drew upon the basic conceptual materials of the colonial past to forge new ways of thinking about the spiritual significance and moral imperatives of collective life.

Notes

1. The most comprehensive statement of this position is J. G. A. Pocock, *The Machiavellian Moment: Florentine Political Thought and the Atlantic Republican Tradition* (Princeton: Princeton University Press, 1975). Other key works are Bernard Bailyn, *The Ideological Origins of the American Revolution* (Cambridge, MA: Harvard University Press, 1967); and Gordon S. Wood, *The Creation of the American Republic, 1776–1787* (Chapel Hill: University of North Carolina Press, 1969).

2. See especially Joyce Appleby, *Capitalism and a New Social Order: The Republican Vision of the 1790s* (New York: New York University Press, 1984).

3. Ruth H. Bloch, *Visionary Republic: Millennial Themes in American Thought, 1756–1800* (New York: Cambridge University Press, 1985); Nathan O. Hatch, *The Sacred Cause of Liberty: Republican Thought and the Millennium in Revolutionary New England* (New Haven: Yale University Press, 1977); Alan Heimert, *Religion and the American Mind from the Great Awakening to the Revolution* (Cambridge, MA: Harvard University Press, 1966). Older literature includes Perry Miller, "From the Covenant to the Revival," in his *Nature's Nation* (Cambridge, MA: Harvard University Press, 1967); and Edmund S. Morgan, "The Puritan Ethic and the American Revolution," *William and Mary Quarterly*, 3rd ser., 24 (1967): 3–43.

4. This is the main dynamic traced in Hatch, *Sacred Cause*; and Harry S. Stout, *The New England Soul: Preaching and Religious Culture in Colonial New England* (New York: Oxford University Press, 1986).

5. For examples of this way of conceptualizing the issue, see Heimert, *Religion*; Bloch, *Visionary Republic*; and David S. Lovejoy, *Religious Enthusiasm in the New World: Heresy to Revolution* (Cambridge, MA: Harvard University Press, 1985).

6. James T. Kloppenberg, "The Virtues of Liberalism: Christianity, Republicanism, and Ethics in Early American Political Discourse," *Journal of American History* 74 (June 1987): 9–33.

7. For example, Rhys Isaac, *The Transformation of Virginia* (Chapel Hill: University of North Carolina Press, 1982); and Lovejoy, *Religious Enthusiasm*.

8. The assimilation of changing political ideas into older religious forms is the

process of intellectual change described, for example, in Hatch, *Sacred Cause*, and Stout, *New England Soul.*

9. Hall, "Religion and Society," in Jack P. Green and J. R. Pole, eds., *Colonial British America* (Baltimore: Johns Hopkins University Press, 1984), 323.

10. Pauline Maier, *From Resistance to Revolution* (New York: Knopf, 1972).

11. On the Bishop's Scare, see Carl Bridenbaugh, *Mitre and Sceptre: Transatlantic Faiths, Ideas, Personalities, and Politics* (New York: Oxford University Press, 1962); and Patricia Bonomi, *Under the Cope of Heaven: Religion, Society and Politics in Colonial America* (New York: Oxford University Press, 1987), 199–209. On the Quebec Act, see Bloch, *Visionary Republic*, 58–59; and Stout, *New England Soul*, 261.

12. See the works cited in notes 1–3, above.

13. Miller, "Covenant to Revival"; Stout, *New England Soul.*

14. The extent to which Calvinists in other regions during the early Revolutionary movement regarded America as their New Israel deserves more exploration. Only in New England, however, had such a perspective become so hegemonic as to provide an important basis of a regional patriot identity. I thank Patricia Bonomi for raising this issue with me.

15. The localism of the covenant language in this period is stressed by Stout, *New England Soul*, especially 284. His and other descriptions of the use of New England covenant language in the Revolution illustrates this undifferentiated sense of godly people. See also Miller, "Covenant to Revival"; and Sacvan Bercovitch, *The American Jeremiad* (Madison: University of Wisconsin Press, 1978).

16. Bloch, *Visionary Republic*, 56–57. See also William Pencak, *War, Politics and Revolution in Provincial Massachusetts* (Boston: Northeastern University Press, 1981), 226–227.

17. See, for example, John Hancock, *An Oration Delivered March 5, 1774* (Boston, 1774), 9–10; Paul Revere, "A Warm Place—Hell" (1768), in Elbridge H. Goss, *The Life of Colonel Paul Revere*, 5th ed. (Boston: Howard Spurr, 1902), 60. See also Peter Shaw, *American Patriots and the Rituals of Revolution* (Cambridge, MA: Harvard University Press, 1981), 15–18, 177–183, 197–199, and 204–226.

18. On the religious significance of the abstinence required by the nonimportation agreements, see Morgan, "The Puritan Ethic."

19. Hatch, *Sacred Cause*, 21–54; and Stout, *New England Soul*, 166–181.

20. Bloch, *Visionary Republic*, 44–45, 61–63, 81–82; Stout, *New England Soul*, 216, 259, 277, 297–299, 307; and Mark Noll, *Christians in the American Revolution* (Grand Rapids: Eerdmans, 1977), 56–57.

21. Bonomi, *Cope of Heaven*. On religious pluralism as a basis of American liberty, see also Sidney Mead, *The Lively Experiment* (New York: Harper & Row, 1963).

22. For example, Isaac Backus, "Appeal for Religious Liberty" (1773), in William G. McLoughlin, ed., *Isaac Backus on Church, State, and Calvinism*

(Cambridge, MA: Harvard University Press, 1968); Nathaniel Niles, *Two Discourses on Liberty* (Newburyport: Thomas and Tinges, 1774); and the eloquent anonymous example quoted in Stout, *New England Soul*, 273.

23. As quoted in Eric Foner, *Tom Paine and Revolutionary America* (New York: Oxford University Press, 1976), 115; Isaac, *Transformation*, 188.

24. Bloch, *Visionary Republic*, 58–60.

25. Stout, *New England Soul*, especially 296, 302.

26. For example, *Journals of Congress: Containing their Proceedings from September 5, 1774 to January 1, 1776*, 3 vols. (Philadelphia: Folwell's, 1800), I, 110, 172; II, 90; III, 370.

27. Carl Becker, *The Declaration of Independence* (New York: Knopf, 1922).

28. Hamilton, *Full Vindication of the Members of Congress*, in Harold C. Syrett and Jacob E. Cooke, eds., *The Papers of Alexander Hamilton* (New York: Columbia University Press, 1961), I, 69. On Patrick Henry, see Isaac, *Transformation*, 266–269; and Charles L. Cohen, "The 'Liberty or Death' Speech: A Note on Religion and Revolutionary Rhetoric," *William and Mary Quarterly*, 3rd ser., 38 (1981): 702–717.

29. Bloch, *Visionary Republic*, 75–87.

30. Bloch, "The Social and Political Base of Millennial Literature in Late Eighteenth-Century America," *American Quarterly* 40 (1988):378–396.

31. Stout, *New England Soul*, 393–396. The chief example is the election sermon by Samuel Langdon, *Government Corrupted by Vice and Recovered by Righteousness* (Watertown: Benjamin Edes, 1775), especially 11–12.

32. Bloch, *Visionary Republic*; and Hatch, *Sacred Cause*.

33. Charles Royster, *A Revolutionary People at War* (Chapel Hill: University of North Carolina Press, 1979), 25–53.

34. Francis N. Thorpe, ed., *The Federal and State Constitutions, Colonial Charters and other Organic Laws of . . . the United States of America*, 7 vols. (Washington, D.C.: Government Printing Office, 1909).

35. See the recent argument of Stephen Botein, "Religious Dimensions of the Early American State," in Richard Beeman, Stephen Botein, and Edwards C. Carter II, eds., *Beyond Confederation: Origins of the Constitution and American National Identity* (Chapel Hill: University of North Carolina Press, 1987).

36. The main lines of this debate can be followed in John Fiske, *The Critical Period* (Boston: Houghton Mifflin, 1888); Charles Beard, *An Economic Interpretation of the Constitution of the United States* (New York: Macmillan, 1913), and Merrill Jensen, *The New Nation* (New York: Knopf, 1950).

37. Wood, *Creation of the American Republic*.

38. Ibid.

39. Ibid.; Hatch, *Sacred Cause*; and Bloch, *Visionary Republic*.

40. Bloch, *Visionary Republic*.

41. Asa Burton, *A Sermon Preached at Windsor . . . On the Day of the Anniversary Election, October, 1785* (Windsor, VT: Hough and Spooner, 1786), 22.

42. Other salient examples include Charles Backus, *A Sermon Preached at Long Meadow, at the Publick Fast* (Springfield, MA: Weld and Thomas, 1788); Samuel Magaw, *A Sermon Delivered at St. Paul's Church* (Philadelphia: Young and M'Culloch, 1786); and Thomas Reese, *An Essay on the Influence of Religion, in Civil Society* (Charleston, SC: Markland and M'Iver, 1788).

43. Wood, *Creation of the American Republic*, 606.

44. Daniel Walker Howe, "The Political Psychology of *The Federalist*," *William and Mary Quarterly*, 3rd ser., 44 (1987): 485–509.

45. Nathan O. Hatch, "*Sola Scriptura* and *Novus Ordo Seclorum*," in Hatch and Mark A. Noll, eds., *The Bible in America: Essays in Cultural History* (New York: Oxford University Press, 1982); and Hatch, "The Christian Movement and the Demand for a Theology of the People," *Journal of American History* 67 (1980): 545–566.

3

Rhetoric and Reality in the Early Republic: The Case of the Federalist Clergy

HARRY S. STOUT

Timothy Dwight was no stranger to the inherited Puritan vocabulary of America as a new Israel. Speaking at a July 4 oration in 1789, Dwight invited his hearers to "look through the history of your country, [and] you will find scarcely less glorious and wonderful proofs of divine protection and deliverance . . . than that which was shown to the people of Israel in Egypt, in the wilderness, and in Canaan."

But in July 1812, amidst ongoing Federalist defeats at the national level and an unpopular war with England, a darker note sounded in Dwight's national assessment—one that he did not often repeat, but that surely loomed large in his and other Federalist clergymen's minds. Speaking at a public fast in Yale College Chapel, Dwight confessed that America's Constitution was non-Christian:

> We formed our Constitution without any acknowledgment of God; without any recognition of his mercies to us, as a people, of his government, or even of his existence. The [Constitutional] Convention, by which it was formed,

never asked, even once, his direction, or his blessing upon their labours. Thus we commenced our national existence under the present system, without God.[1]

That Dwight and most other Federalist clergy would speak of America both as a Christian nation and, less often but with equal intensity, as a godless republic, reveals in graphic fashion the tensions between Christian religion and republican government that lay at the heart of the new republic. These tensions reflected two conflicting "realities" or points of departure: the one political and constitutional, which explicitly separated church and state and left God out of the formulation; and the other rhetorical and religious, in which "America" inherited New England's colonial covenant and where God orchestrated a sacred union of church and state for his redemptive purposes. These tensions, not to say contradictions, never erupted in violent upheaval, but they did divide American society in profound ways that persist throughout American history.[2]

While the contradictions between America as a chosen nation and a godless republic are clear, the reasons for them are not. How could intelligent, honest ministers and statesmen proclaim such opposite sentiments without any sense of impropriety or deception? In what follows, I will suggest that if we are to understand the paradox of conflicting speech over the meaning of America, we must reach through and beyond the early republic to the rhetorical world of the Puritans and see how they bequeathed to their New England descendants an identity as a Christian people that was blind to contrary facts and that quite literally reshaped current realities to fit traditional rhetorical ends.

In speaking of the Puritans' "rhetorical world," I am taking a cue from Gordon Wood's magisterial reconstruction of the mental world of the Founding Fathers.[3] In that work Wood asks how the Founding Fathers, as intelligent and insightful as they were, could both create a democratic republic and, at the same time, remain blind to its radical egalitarian implications. Further, he asks, how could these same wise Fathers be so "scientific" about politics and yet be so taken with conspiratorial explanations of history that completely missed the larger economic and demographic forces that were transforming their society? His conclusion is that the Founders were neither pathological liars nor paranoids, but intelligent men who, like all peoples, were bounded by the symbols they possessed. Symbols, myths, and language open up and tame reality at the same time that they impose limits on the perceiver. In all symbol systems or rhetorical worlds some things come clearly into focus, while others remain hidden and inaccessible.

As used in this essay, the phrase "rhetorical worlds" refers to one particular type of "paradigm" or symbol system that operates in the world of public speech. Just as interpretive paradigms function to shape and mold "reality" in science, literature, or social theory, so also do they function to supply the operative rules and binding assumptions for communities of discourse. In this sense, rhetorical worlds are not a form of "propaganda" in which speakers consciously manipulate symbols to exploit baser ends. Quite the opposite, rhetorical worlds become shared realities that are as binding on the speaker as they are on the audience. They represent the master assumptions that speakers and their audiences cannot prove or disprove, but which both accept because, intellectually, they conform to the community's passionately held assumptions of self, society, and the cosmos and, socially, because they make the system work.

In the case of the Founding Fathers, Wood discovers a symbol system whose reality definitions were largely classical and aristocratic in origin. The rhetorical world of classical republicanism opened the founders' eyes to the meaning of liberty at the same time that its aristocratic context closed their eyes to the possibility of positive social change originating "from beneath," among the ordinary people. Like a gigantic presence from another world this classical rhetorical world towered over the mundane (and contrary) facts of the Revolution and shaped "reality" for those Founders who shared in its discourse. Try as they might, the Founders could not transcend their world and see the secular and democratic forces that were reshaping their society from the bottom up. Rhetorical worlds derive their power from the community's shared insistence that their formulations are not rhetorical inventions, but reality as it "really is." At the moment an individual or community peers around their rhetorical world, it ceases to exist and the once gigantic presence dissolves into a mist of dated "fiction" and "mere" rhetoric.

While the classical rhetorical world described by Wood was central in shaping the mental universe of the Founders, it was not monolithic. Recent studies have documented the presence of other, competing rhetorical worlds that held sway with different speakers and their audiences. Thus, for example, Alfred Young and Gary Nash have reconstructed a "popular ideology," or "small producer" ideology, of urban artisans and laborers and subsistence farmers that was organized around more egalitarian assumptions of popular sovereignty and a "moral economy."[4] Among elites themselves, Joyce Appleby has described a "liberal" ideology premised less on classical concepts of civic virtue and the sacrifice of self-interest than on the active promotion of the self-interested pursuit of happiness.[5] Unlike seventeenth-century New England, which featured one public speaker—the minister—and entire communities of captive listeners, the early republic encompassed a plurality of rhetorical worlds competing for popular audiences.

In turning to the New England Federalist clergy in the early republic, I would suggest that we are seeing yet another rhetorical world with a different set of actors and accompanying symbols. While the clergy shared a common classical education with the Founders that supplied some common assumptions, it did not shape their perception of reality at the most formative level. Rather, their reality was shaped by an inherited Puritan rhetorical world that overlapped the Founders' world at some points, but diverged dramatically in others. Most important, the inherited Puritan rhetorical world was incapable of seeing the constitutional realities of the First Amendment as "really real." Lying behind that Constitution, was another, more important reality of America as a Christian nation.

Before contrasting the rhetorical worlds of the Framers and the Federalist clergy more fully, it is important to recognize some convergences between their worlds that allowed for common action and a multilayered republican ideology. On a biographical level, many Federalist clergymen were good republicans, and many republican legislators were good Protestants. When faced with common threats from without or from beneath, they could close ranks in common opposition. Differences that would radically divide "secular humanists" and "evangelicals" in the late nineteenth century were, in 1787, still more potential than real.

One reason that neither the Founding Fathers nor the Federalist clergy could see the new forces around them was that both shared an elitist sense of history and society. Next to tyranny, the greatest threat these leaders perceived was anarchy, which they defined as any movement whose leadership bypassed them. If the Founders could not concede the legitimacy of democratic "parties" that were led by self-made commoners, neither could the Federalist clergy tolerate the self-trained Methodist itinerants and new "Christian" denominations that were threatening to dominate the nineteenth-century religious scene.[6]

Besides sharing a common elitism, the Founders and Federalist clergy shared a common, premodern sense of history that was essentially deductive and "personalistic."[7] As statesmen and clergymen surveyed the changes taking place in their society, they did not look for impersonal movements or environmental forces for explanation, but for faces and names. The central question for them was not *what* caused an event, but *who*? Who is responsible for the trials we endure or the blessings we enjoy? Such a view of history was neither modern nor commonsensical. One did not begin with the "facts," which would supposedly sort themselves into self-evident patterns, but with the archetypal causes to which the facts were able to adhere. Chief among these archetypal causes was the highly personal and individual confrontations between good and evil men. In this world there could be no sense of history such as the ironical one described by Reinhold Niebuhr as the dilemma of "moral man and immoral society."[8] Rather, there was a one-to-one correspondence between individual morality and social morality and, in both cases, a "moral tendency" or correlation between personal morality and national well-being.[9]

Yet if the classical and Puritan rhetorical worlds had much in common by virtue of a shared classical education and Protestant ethos, there were also profound differences that made inevitable the ongoing tensions between America as a secular republic and America as a Christian nation. In the early years of the republic these differences were largely inferential and philosophical—more matters of emphasis and priority than mutually exclusive categories. But in time, as the non-Protestant sector of American society grew ever larger, the possibility for division became greater.

Of all the differences separating the classical and Puritan rhetorical worlds none were more important than the alternative texts each looked to for explanation and inspiration. Where the Framers derived their sense of the American republic from classical and "Real Whig" political texts, the clergy oriented their speech and commentary around the vernacular Bible—read and internalized by most New England inhabitants for one and a half centuries. For most of the Framers the Bible stood to the side of political oratory as a more or less licit guest that could be brought in to legitimate truths that enlightened reason made clear.[10] Conversely, while the clergy did not ignore enlightened reason and the law of nature— particularly in election sermons and July 4 orations—those texts were subordinated to the eternal truths of sacred writ. The Bible supplied ministers with most of their metaphors and analogies, both religious and political. It also supplied a self-contained history of redemption that identified the ultimate force behind evil persons—the Antichrist—and that identified the ultimate end of history in the millennial creation of a new world freed from sin.

Beyond textual differences, the two rhetorical worlds differed substantially over the question of what constituted a truly moral, virtuous society. At its core, the Puritan vision of the good society was fixed by an idea—the idea of a "peculiar" national covenant between God and His sovereignly chosen people. New England was inhabited by such a chosen people and, by virtue of America's support for New England during the Revolution, the nation became engrafted onto New England's special destiny.[11]

In Puritan rhetoric the iron law of God's covenant explained all. This covenant, rather than the science of politics, determined the course of American history and represented the lens through which the nation-state was viewed. Obedience to God's covenant and His prophets was the sole criterion by which America would stand or fall. Where the classical rhetorical world subordinated religion to politics and privatized "conscience" for the public welfare, the Puritan rhetorical world subordinated forms of government to covenant-keeping and *imposed* conscience—"rightly informed"—on a public who desperately needed to observe the covenant whether they knew it or not.

Clearly, republican realities diverged dramatically from Puritan rhetoric on the level of textual authority and governing assumptions. But, equally clearly, the two did coexist in more or less peaceful harmony. And here we are again confronted with the problem of explanation. How could such rival rhetorics peacefully coexist? The answer is found far back in colonial New England's past, in the Glorious Revolution, when, in circumstances remarkably similar to 1787, the Puritan clergy learned to accept a new, non-Puritan authority without sacrificing their rhetorical identity as a "peculiar" people of the Word. When, in 1684, England acted to deprive Massachusetts Bay of its charter, the Puritan state, or "theocracy," came to an official end. Under the new royal charter, government was defined in new terms that made no reference to New England's covenant. The Act of Toleration meant that religion—at least in its Christian manifestations—had become a matter of private conscience beyond the power of the state to control.

Yet, in what surely stands as one of the clearest illustrations of the power of rhetoric to shape and mold contrary realities, New England preachers continued to speak of God's national covenant with the "nation" as if nothing had changed. Instead of attacking the new charter as godless and anti-Puritan, most ministers celebrated it enthusiastically, and then went on doing what they had always done.[12] Because the Act of Toleration granted Protestant movements the freedom to use words any way they pleased, ministers were freed to invoke terms like "liberty" in restricted ways that meant simply the liberty to preserve New England's inherited covenant. On the one hand preachers would praise England's policy of religious toleration, while on the other they continued to address New England audiences as a people still bound in an ancient yet ongoing covenant. Thus, in his 1692 election sermon, Cotton Mather followed up a celebration of the new royal government with the reminder that New England's destiny continued to hang on covenant-keeping: "If any one ask, unto what the Sudden and Matchless thriving of *New-England* may be ascribed? It is the Blessing of God upon the *Church-Order*, for the sake whereof . . . this Plantation was first Erected." The new charter did not change the terms of God's covenant with New England, and if the people forgot that, no nation or constitution on earth could protect them from the avenging hand of God: "If we don't go *Leaning* upon God, every step, we shall *go wrong*, and nothing will go *well* in our Hands."[13] As long as speakers and audiences continued to define New England as a peculiar covenanted people, the rhetoric would live on whatever the contrary realities.

The success of the clergy in bending the new realities to conform to the old covenant hinged on two considerations: intellectual and social. Intellectually, the clergy made their peace with the new regime by exploiting the multiple meanings and studied imprecision of terms like "liberty" and "nation."[14] From the first Puritan settlement these terms possessed distinct insider and outsider meanings. To outside audiences, whether they be Charles I, William and Mary, or the national Congress, "liberty" would be defined in its fullest meaning as the freedom of all religious groups to worship as they pleased and for speakers to compete for the loyalty of the citizenry. To insiders, however, "liberty" always assumed an instrumental, more restricted meaning as the liberty to create a covenantal society in which the inhabitants voluntarily established public support for their churches, ministers, schools, chaplains, and colleges. In like manner the word "nation" could mean the broad boundaries of the political state or, to insiders, the "holy nation" of convenanted believers for whose sake God would bless the larger political affiliation.

Socially, the preservation of Puritan rhetoric required a region sufficiently homogeneous for a clear majority of the inhabitants to endorse the rhetorical vision. Rhetorical worlds, after all, are *shared* worlds and require the willing incorporation of speaker and audience in a common script. From colonial origins to the first waves of nineteenth-century Irish immigrants, New England was uniquely such a region.[15] It remained, in Perry Miller's apt characterization, a "laboratory" whose population expanded almost exclusively through a vast natural increase of interconnected families. Thus, as long as the question of religious establishment and support was left to the will of the town majorities, and as long as speakers were free to define terms as they pleased, the Puritans could compete for and win the loyalty of the towns which, in turn, constituted the core of the "holy nation."

Clearly, much had changed in the century separating the royal charter of 1692 from the federal republic of 1787. Constitutional monarchy was replaced by democratic republic, religious tests for office were eliminated at the national level, and New England was no longer several colonies but states integrated in a larger union. Yet, in surveying Federalist preaching in the early republic, one is struck by how little the rhetorical strategy had changed as Federalist preachers unveiled the innermost meaning of America in a number of election, fast, or July 4 orations. Sermons preached and printed on "national" occasions were, in fact, remarkably provincial, such that "America" became New England writ large. The new constitutional realities that originated outside of New England and that ignored God did nothing to alter the rhetorical world of the Federalist clergy and their audiences. Constitutional realities were reinterpreted and subordinated to the sacred pretense of a covenant people. And by shouting the pretense loudly enough over competing voices, the rhetoric prevailed. Liberty remained sacred and instrumental. Because New Englanders utilized their liberty within "gospel bounds," the "nation"—now America—would enjoy the same covenant blessings that New England had enjoyed since first settlement.

In extending the idea of covenant to the nation, the Federalist clergy fastened on three interrelated corollaries that fixed "reality" for their listeners, even as the neoclassical rhetorical world of the Founders pointed in opposite directions. The first, and all-important, corollary to the clergy's Christianization of America was the proposition that America originated ultimately not through social compact but by divine fiat. Arguments from natural law and the consent of the governed were not sufficient explanations for the meaning of America. In the beginning God created New England. And from that sacred origin the larger nation evolved.

Almost without exception, Federalist clergy in the early republic devoted significant portions of their occasional oratory to a rehearsal of the "great errand" into America inaugurated by the Puritans and their covenant God. The real America—that is, sacred America—began, David Tappan explained in his 1792 Massachusetts election sermon, not in 1787 or 1776, but in 1620 when "our fathers were led out of the house of bondage in Britain, into the wilderness of America, and planted here, as in the land of promise, by the same divine Shepherd who led ancient Israel from deep oppression and misery, to the joys of freedom and plenty." Here, as elsewhere, speakers engrafted New England onto the sacred history of Israel, and then extended that history to America. Such a society, Josiah Bridge explained, was "by no means the result of chance," but of Providence.[16]

For the national convenant to endure, individual salvation was not required at all, but corporate morality was. In addressing the national covenant, occasional speakers spent far more time on the subject of "virtue" and "morality" than on personal salvation, while in their Sunday preaching—to insiders—they reminded their hearers that there could be no saving morality without personal faith.[17] Contained in the identification with Israel was far more than regional pride; it was sacred pretense. As far as the Founders were concerned, the New England migration was simply one among many competing colonial strains that collectively made up the American mosaic. But for New England speakers and their audiences, the Puritan strain was *the* strain of American history (and destiny), for it represented the covenant around which America must revolve if it was to retain God's blessings. So crucial was New England to American destiny that occasional speakers routinely identified the term "constitution" not with the federal Constitution, but with their state constitution, which, according to Samuel Deane, "approaches so near to perfection . . . that it can hardly be [revised]."[18]

The second organizing corollary to New England's identification of a Christian America was its millennial destiny.[19] The promise of millennium also appeared in Puritan rhetoric from first settlement, and completed their rhetorical world by moving from a sacred past instituted by divine fiat to a glorious future state ruled by Christ. As a people of Providence rather than compact, Americans could expect that the same God who orchestrated New England's beginnings would launch them into a glorious future as a redeemer nation.

Just as Federalist speakers identified America's past with biblical analogies or "types" from the Old Testament, so did they identify the republic's future with millennial texts. The most frequently cited text to fix America's future in the Revolutionary era was Isaiah 66:8: "Shall the earth be made to bring forth in one day? or shall a nation be born at once?" This prophecy, speakers argued, was fulfilled on July 4, 1776. That was the day God had in mind when he inspired Isaiah to record his prophecy. With independence, the text continued to resonate with sacred meanings for America. For example, in his 1793 election sermon Daniel Foster reminded the governor in attendance—John Hancock—that "it was under your presidency and direction, that ancient prophecy was literally accomplished, ' a nation born in a day'—America declared free, sovereign, and independent."[20]

If Americans were to inherit the millennial promise, they must keep the covenant. Along the way they could be sure there would be evil men and diabolical plots aimed at destroying the covenant. Alongside the promise of Christ was the threat of Antichrist, defined as anyone opposing the ongoing life of the covenant. The Federalist clergy, like the Founders, were attuned to plots and conspiracies in explaining history. But behind evil men, they discovered the even more diabolical presence of Satan. After the Revolution, Federalist clergy continued to discover the plot of Antichrist in the atheism of the French Revolution, and in international conspiracies such as the Bavarian Illuminati.[21] Within America itself the figure of Antichrist could be discerned amidst domestic unrest and violence and in the failure of America to follow the warnings of New England's prophets regarding war with England. Only by returning to the God of New England and His prophets could America remain in God's favor.

The third corollary to a Christian America was the proposition that religion must be *both* a matter of private conscience and public policy.[22] If the first two corollaries were largely subjective and interpretive, the third was practical and political. America's God was a jealous God who would have no other gods before Him. In the Puritan rhetorical world the greatest threat to republican government was not population expanse, war, or runaway inflation, but infidelity—bad faith. For most of the Founders, the greatest enemies to the republic were those who threatened disunity through party and factions. In the Puritan rhetorical world, however, the greatest enemies were atheists. Such people, Frederick Hotchkiss explained, were "unfit for human society." A nation "habitually irreligious," Samuel Taggart warned, cannot be long free: "Those who are endeavoring to eradicate the principles of religion and virtue, by discarding Christianity, however extensive the benevolence may be which they profess, are our worst enemies." The unforgivable sin of atheism, Timothy Dwight explained, was its "worship of Abstract terms" to the exclusion of a personal deity. Atheists depersonalized the cosmos and, in so doing, denied the possibilities of providential origins, ongoing covenant, and millennial hope—each of which depended on a transcendent presence in the life of the nation.[23]

The Framers could tolerate (if not endorse) the presence of deists and atheists in the national government as long as such citizens were bound to the dictates of reason and civic virtue. Not so the Federalist clergy—and most of their listeners—whose governing assumptions precluded the acceptability of an atheistic leadership. To insure that atheists and infidelity would not triumph in America, ministers never tired of pointing out that God required His people to elect a "Christian legislature" willing to acknowledge an overseeing deity and committed to supporting such Christian institutions as schools, colleges, churches, chaplains, and biblically derived laws. To insure such leaders—at least in New England—some form of religious test for office was necessary. Speaking in 1801 at the outset of a new century, Aaron Bancroft conceded that while personal conversion and the covenant of grace was "too sacred for human regulation" [i.e., private], that did not mean there should be no religious establishment. To the contrary, "it clearly falls within the province of a Christian legislature, to support institutions, which facilitate the instruction of people in the truths and duties of religion, which are the means to give efficacy to the precepts of the gospel, and are calculated to instill the spirit of morality and order into the minds of the community."[24]

Having established New England's covenant as the key to America's survival, Bancroft, like other speakers, would appropriate the traditional rhetoric of the jeremiad and apply it to the new nation. In words that echoed almost exactly the colonial threat of "almost" destruction, but not "quite yet," Bancroft openly wondered whether "the period that is now passed, in future [will] be remembered as the golden age of America? Have not too many fallen off from the principles of their ancestors?" If reform was not immediately forthcoming, Bancroft warned, "our nation will be rent by party. . . . By our vices we shall forfeit the blessings of our God . . . and we shall suffer the miseries of impiety and wickedness, of faction and anarchy, of tyranny and oppression." America's only hope was to turn back to the religion of New England's founders, to turn to the "protecting arm of Deity," rather than "become the sport of atheistical chance and accident."[25]

When national policy ran contrary to New England preference, as in the War of 1812, the Federalist clergy invariably invoked America's "true" constitution (the national covenant) as grounds for dissent and resistance. In nineteenth-century America, as in eighteenth-century New England, there were limits to the fusions of rhetorics. When these boundaries were crossed—in 1776 with George III or in 1812 with "Mr. Madison's War"—the clergy did not hesitate to denounce the outside "nation" and separate themselves from its constitutional pretenses. The blindness to contraries that marked ordinary discourse in times of peace broke down in 1812 into a prophetic New England "we" against a covenant-threatening "them who wanted war." For support the clergy turned to

America's "true" founders—the Puritan founders—who had articulated the "true" standards from which the nation had sadly "declined." Thus, in his July 4, 1812, oration Francis Blake dispensed with the customary paean to America and angrily wondered "how far we have wandered from the landmarks of our political fathers." Those landmarks, it soon became clear, were blazed almost exclusively in New England, and the "fathers" were the fathers of New England. John Fiske concurred in his 1812 address: "For the religious leaders of this land, especially of New-England we have reason to believe that war has been commenced on our part, without the approbation of heaven." Consequently, Fiske concluded, Americans must resist their nation's policy or risk a broken covenant.[26]

It is in such moments of tension and disjunction as 1812 that the full variance in republican and Puritan sentiments becomes clear. In fact, all of the corollaries attached to the Puritan notion of a Christian America contradicted the main outlines of the federal Constitution and the republic on which it rested. Yet they continued to define reality for many Americans. In times of dissent, the Federalist clergy condemned the "godlessness" of America's Constitution and invoked the Puritan founders and their own state constitutions as their true rhetorical standard. That standard enjoyed a longer New World history and, in their view, its genius defined America's true destiny.

What lessons can we take from the persistence of Puritan rhetoric in the early republic? For one, we are cautioned against completing intellectual revolutions in religious thought too quickly. Habits of speech, like habits of the heart, die hard, and loyal listeners rarely perceive the inner contradictions. The triumph of an individualist, egalitarian evangelicalism with its antihistoricism and commonsense realism was a more gradual transition than historians have generally allowed. In many ways the transition is still incomplete. Lying beneath the new evangelicalism of nineteenth-century America was an older rhetorical world, one that was corporate, coercive, providential, deductive, and elitist.

As religious historians need to qualify the triumph of an individual evangelicalism, so do constitutional and political historians need to examine the dominance of the secular enlightened naturalism that informed the Constitution. Alongside the celebration of religious liberty, separation of church and state, and the privatization of religious conscience lay a competing rhetorical world, with a longer New World history, that was every bit as real and compelling for its hearers as the language of the Constitution. Logically speaking, the two worlds could not peacefully coexist. But in fact they did, proving once again that America is a disproving ground of logic. It is in the inability of either rhetoric to triumph over the other that we find part of the explanation for the "unstable pluralism" that Michael Kammen sees lurking about the soul of an American "people of paradox."[27] Americans continue to peer through, but never around, their rhetorical worlds, thus leaving perpetually open the question of what is really real: the rhetoric or the reality?

Notes

1. Timothy Dwight, *The Duty of Americans* (New Haven: Green, 1798), 29–30; and *A Discourse in Two Parts*, 2nd ed. (Boston: Flagg and Gould, 1813), 24. Sentiments like Dwight's were not uncommon in 1812. In the year following Dwight's address, Chauncey Lee reflected on the republic's godless origins:

> Can we pause, and reflect for a moment, without the mingled emotions of wonder and regret; that that publick instrument, which guarantees our political rights of freedom and independence—our *Constitution* of national government, framed by such an august, learned and able body of men; formally adopted by the solemn resolution of each state; and justly admired and celebrated for its consummate political wisdom; has not the impress of *religion* upon it, not the smallest recognition of the government, or the being of GOD, or of the dependence and accountability of man. Be astonished, O earth!—Nothing, by which a foreigner might with certainty decide, whether we believe in the one true God, or in any God; whether we are a nation of Christians, or—But I forbear. The subject is too delicate, to say more; and it is too interesting to have said less. I leave it with this single reflection, whether, if God be not in the Lamp, we have not reason to tremble for the ark? (*The Government of God* [Hartford: Hudson and Goodwin, 1813], 43).

My analysis in this chapter is part of a larger study of preaching in the early republic. It is based on an examination of fifty printed occasional sermons delivered primarily by Congregational clergymen in the period 1787–1813.

2. For a recent explication of divergent tendencies in Protestant thought, see George M. Marsden, *Fundamentalism and American Culture* (New York: Oxford University Press, 1980).

3. See especially Gordon S. Wood, *The Creation of the American Republic, 1776–1787* (Chapel Hill: University of North Carolina Press, 1969); and Wood, "Rhetoric and Reality in the American Revolution," *William and Mary Quarterly*, 3rd ser., 23 (1966): 3–32.

4. See Gary B. Nash, *The Urban Crucible: Social Change, Political Consciousness, and the Origins of the American Revolution* (Cambridge, MA: Harvard University Press, 1979); and Alfred F. Young, Ed., *The American Revolution: Explorations in the History of American Radicalism* (Dekalb, IL: Northern

Illinois University Press, 1976). The term "moral economy" is taken from E. P. Thompsons's pioneering work on English popular ideology in *The Making of the English Working Class* (New York: Pantheon, 1964). For a recent survey of the extensive literature on social classes and class-linked political dissent, see Gary B. Nash, "Also There at the Creation: Going Beyond Gordon S. Wood, "*William and Mary Quarterly*, 3rd ser., 41 (1987): 602–611.

5. On the theme of liberalism, see especially Joyce Appleby, *Capitalism and a New Social Order: The Republican Vision of the 1790s* (New York: New York University Press, 1984): J. G. A. Pocock, *The Machiavellian Moment: Florentine Political Thought and the Atlantic Republican Tradition* (Princeton: Princeton University Press, 1975); and John P. Diggins, *The Lost Soul of American Politics: Virtue, Self-Interest, and the Foundations of Liberalism* (New York: Basic Books, 1984).

6. See especially Gordon S. Wood, "The Democratization of Mind in the American Revolution," in *Leadership in the American Revolution* (Washington, DC: Library of Congress, 1974), 63–89; Nathan O. Hatch, "The Christian Movement and the Demand for a Theology of the People," *Journal of American History* 67 (1980): 545–576; and Hatch, *The Democratization of American Christianity* (New Haven: Yale University Press, 1989).

7. For a description of the "personalistic and rationalistic mode of explanation" that dominated eighteenth-century elite discourse, see Gordon S. Wood, "Conspiracy and the Paranoid Style: Causality and Deceit in the Eighteenth Century," *William and Mary Quarterly*, 3rd ser., 39 (1982): 401–441.

8. Reinhold Niebuhr, *Moral Man and Immoral Society* (New York: Scribner's, 1932). See also Niebuhr's classic statement, *The Irony of American History* (New York: Scribner's, 1952).

9. This theme is developed extensively in J. Earl Thompson, "A Perilous Experiment: New England Clergymen and American Destiny, 1796-1826" (Ph.D. diss., Andover Seminary, 1965).

10. The best description of the "Real Whig" ideology is Bernard Bailyn, *The Ideological Origins of the American Revolution* (Cambridge, MA: Harvard University Press, 1967).

11. On the New England clergy's extension of covenant promise from New England to "America," see Sacvan Bercovitch, "How the Puritans Won the American Revolution," *Massachusetts Review* 17 (1976): 597-630.

12. I have developed this theme in *The New England Soul: Preaching and Religious Character in Colonial New England* (New York: Oxford University Press, 1986).

13. Cotton Mather, *Optanda, Good Men Described and Good Things Propounded* (Boston: Harris, 1692), 77, 83, 51-53. See also Samuel Willard's election sermon, *The Character of the Good Ruler* (Boston: Harris, 1694).

14. The theoretical work of J. G. A. Pocock is useful here in describing the unavoidable "multivalency" of language that grows from the different "social

worlds" in which terms and ideas are communicated. See especially Pocock, *Politics, Language and Time: Essays on Political Thought and History* (New York: Cambridge University Press, 1971) 3–41.

15. Gary B. Nash describes the unique cultural and ethnic homogeneity of colonial Boston in contrast to New York and Philadelphia in *The Urban Crucible*, 361. This homogeneity persisted until undermined in the 1830s by the first waves of Irish immigrants. See Oscar Handlin, *Boston's Immigrants, 1790-1865* (Cambridge, MA: Harvard University Press, 1941), 128–155.

16. David Tappan, *A Sermon Preached* (Boston: Adams, 1792), 23; and Josiah Bridge, *A Sermon Preached* (Boston: Adams and Nourse, 1789), 36. See also, for example, William Emerson, *An Oration* (Boston: Manning and Loring, 1802), 7–9.

17. These distinctions were traced in Chandler Robbins's Massachusetts election sermon, *A Sermon Preached* (Boston: Adams, 1791), 32; and Samuel Parker, *A Sermon Preached* (Boston: Adams, 1793), 21.

18. Samuel Deane, *A Sermon Preached* (Portland, ME: Wait, 1796), 21.

19. The best discussions of millennialism in the early republic are Nathan O. Hatch, *The Sacred Cause of Liberty: Republican Thought and the Millennium in Revolutionary New England* (New Haven: Yale University Press, 1977); and Ruth H. Bloch, *Visionary Republic: Millennial Themes in American Thought, 1756-1800* (New York: Cambridge University Press, 1985).

20. Daniel Foster, *A Sermon Preached* (Boston: Adams, 1790), 28. See also Festus Foster, *An Oration* (Brookfield: Merriam, 1812), 5; or Samuel Taggert, *An Oration* (Northampton: Butler, 1804) 3.

21. Vernon Stauffer, *New England and the Bavarian Illuminati* (New York: Columbia University Press, 1918).

22. See James Fulton Maclear, " 'The True American Union' of Church and State: The Reconstruction of the Theocratic Tradition," *Church History* 28 (1959): 41–59.

23. Frederick Hotchkiss, *On National Greatness* (New Haven: Green, 1793), 20; Taggert, *An Oration*, 25. See also John Allyn, *A Sermon Preached* (Boston: Young and Minns, 1805), 20–24, 32.

24. Aaron Bancroft, *A Sermon Preached* (Boston: Young and Minns, 1801), 21.

25. Ibid., 13, 17, 28.

26. Francis Blake, *An Oration* (Worcester: Sturtevant, 1812), 3; John Fiske, *A Sermon Delivered* (Brookfield: Merriam, 1812), 25. See also Foster, *An Oration*, 14–15; and Samuel Austin, *The Apology of Patriots* (Worcester: Sturtevant, 1812), 16.

27. Michael Kammen, *People of Paradox: An Inquiry Concerning the Origins of American Civilization* (New York: Oxford University Press, 1972), 57–58.

4

Religion, Government, and Power in the New American Nation

JOHN F. WILSON

While the historical discussion of "The Separation of Church and State" naturally centers in the "Founding Period," and while I want to focus on the codification given to religion and politics in that period, the subject is, in a sense, always current, and interest in it always derives from contemporary concerns. For this reason, consideration of "church and state" inevitably emphasizes the dialectical relationship between present and past. The present is reflected in concern with a past that gives it legitimacy, and the past is clarified in the present, which is perceived to flow from that past. Accordingly, I propose to develop the discussion in terms of this dialectical relationship, believing it will yield better history and, as a secondary matter, a more adequate understanding of both the possibilities and hazards of our own time.

Two paradigms govern current interpretation of how the Constitution regulates the relationship of religion to the federal regime whose bicentennial we have so recently celebrated. These are the separationist and the accommodationist. Both are modern positions, worked out within the last half-century or so, although each grounds its legitimacy on the same texts and supports itself by extensive historical argumentation. Not surprisingly, each reflects modern interests and is advanced in that light. Because contemporary discussion of the broader issue of religion and government in America tends to be polarized according to these paradigms, we need to know their limitations. As a constructive move I offer a third reading of this topic. While it certainly produces better history, it will not necessarily appeal to the chief interested parties or encourage them to modify their positions.

The separationist reading of the founding period of our nation was codified in the *Everson* case, which initiated modern interpretation of the First Amendment's establishment clause.[1] It is astonishing to moderns that the two religion clauses of the Bill of Rights went virtually unapplied—and thus unexplored—until well into this century. This is, of course, because they were an explicit limitation on the powers of Congress only. They were proposed—and adopted—largely at the behest of the Anti-Federalists, who were antagonistic to the proposed new national government. This opposition was not concerned with rights per se except in the case of states' rights, for it wanted to insure that the new federal regime would not be strong enough to usurp the powers of the several states. The religion clauses of the First Amendment therefore guaranteed Connecticut, Massachusetts, and New Hampshire, for example, that their statewide provisions for local tax support of settled congregations were secure against federal intervention and reassured the Baptists and Quakers in Rhode Island, for example, that their precious liberty of conscience would be similarly safe. Only as these clauses became limitations upon the states and local governments through application of the due process clause of the Fourteenth Amendment did these provisions become foundational for the separationist paradigm. As already noted, this determination did not take place until the middle of the twentieth century.

The *Everson* case ruled acceptable the reimbursement by the local school board of bus fares paid by parochial school students from Ewing, New Jersey. But Justice Black's opinion gave voice to a full-blown separationist interpretation of the establishment clause:

> The "establishment of religion" clause of the First Amendment means at least this: Neither a state nor the Federal Government can set up a church. Neither can pass laws which aid one religion, aid all religions, or prefer one religion over another. Neither can force nor influence a person to go to or to remain away from church against his will or force him to profess a belief or disbelief in any religion. No person can be punished for entertaining or professing religious beliefs or disbeliefs, for church attendance or non-attendance. No tax in any amount, large or small, can be levied to support

any religious activities or institutions, whatever they may be called, or whatever form they may adopt to teach or practice religion. Neither a state nor the Federal government can, openly or secretly, participate in the affairs of any religious organizations or groups and *vice versa*. In the words of Jefferson, the clause against establishment of religion by law was intended to erect "a wall of separation between church and State."[2]

The disjunction between this position and the outcome of the case led Justice Jackson to comment in his dissenting opinion: "The case which irresistibly comes to mind as the most fitting precedent is that of Julia, who, according to Byron's reports, 'whispering "I will ne'er consent"—consented.'"[3]

The Black opinion suggests the separationist logic. The First Amendment clauses were interpreted through the metaphor of the wall of separation Thomas Jefferson had used in conveying his political support to the Baptists of Danbury, Connecticut, for their struggle against their Federalist opponents. The image had exercised a powerful hold on the collective imagination before Justice Black appropriated it for the first full explication of the meaning of the establishment clause, but once he had done so, it became virtually an orthodoxy.[4]

In the world of symbols that concerns the legitimation of politics, this step made the struggle in Virginia on behalf of religious liberty—a struggle in which James Madison played a critical role (especially during Jefferson's absence in Europe)—normative for interpreting the First Amendment clauses.[5] Through Virginia's history, the latent meaning of the federal experience could be discovered. Of course, James Madison's role in drafting the Constitution proper, as well as initiating consideration of the amendments we know as the Bill of Rights, provides additional support for this interpretation.[6]

In general, the classic separationist position resolves the vexing question of how the two religion clauses relate to each other by positing a particular version of religious liberty. Religious liberty is understood as the absence of government constraint upon individuals in matters of religion. This is the fulcrum on which issues of church and state turn. Note that emphasis falls on religious liberty as entailing unfettered *individual* action, and then extrapolating that freedom to groups. It is the individual, devoid of participation in society or culture, who engages in the most basic religious action without reference either to others or to an existing tradition. Further, liberty is conceived negatively as absence of external constraint. This position incorporates an essentially radical Protestant view of faith focused through an Enlightenment emphasis upon the individual that effectively denies the importance of communal dimensions or social categories.

To this point we have explored the separationist paradigm. Now let us turn to the alternative position, usefully identified as accommodationist. Like separationists, accommodationists see religious liberty as a basic right—but they construe religion less in terms of individual action and give liberty a positive value as something more than the absence of restraint. Thus they are more concerned with the exercise of religion, and are aware of its communal aspects.

Here we do not have the benefit of such a legal *locus classicus* as the *Everson* decision. What we do have is an invitation by the current Chief Justice, William Rehnquist, to rethink the interpretation of the establishment clause on the basis of more adequate history: "Nothing in the Establishment Clause requires government to be strictly neutral between religion and irreligion, nor does that Clause prohibit Congress or the States from pursuing legitimate secular ends through non-discriminatory sectarian means."[7] At its basis, the accommodationist paradigm takes a more catholic position on the nature of religion.

Accordingly, the accommodationist position observes that in narrowly defining religion in terms of the individual, the separationist point of view may lead to a virtual caricature of religion, perhaps vaguely relevant only to the radical Protestant traditions of the modern United States. The accommodationist perspective emphasizes rather that the First Amendment was clearly not intended to be antireligious—indeed, as already suggested, it was drafted precisely to protect the various religious practices of the states, including preferential establishments in some of them. Accommodationists therefore reinterpret the First Amendment to make of religious liberty a positive right, the exercise of which is to be encouraged by government. By the same token they believe that the First Amendment excludes only the direct establishment of, or preferential treatment for, a particular religion. Indeed, government should facilitate the practice of religion by both individuals and collectivities as essential to the common good.

This position is very different from that of the separationists and leads to markedly different contemporary policies and practices. In addition, as the point of departure for historical interpretation, it focuses attention upon the residual religious quality of this founding period, which was hardly secularistic. The same congress that proposed the First Amendment was opened with prayer and named a chaplain. Indeed, most of the early presidents declared occasional days of thanksgiving—and even of humiliation. Provision was made for support of religion in opening

Western lands. And in time the resources of religious groups were utilized in making government policy for relations with Native Americans. In sum, accommodationists consider that the operative ideal of the early republic was a nonpreferentialist posture of support for religion on the part of government.[8] In turn, that seems to point toward a twentieth-century ideal of accommodation of government to religion in ways that secure the greater common civil good as well as serve the spiritual ends of numbers of citizens.

I trust I have made the case that too much interpretation of the First Amendment construes the founding period selectively so as to respond to a modern casting of issues. Instead, can we return to that founding period and understand it in a fuller and more adequate way than is permitted through the separationist and accommodationist viewpoints? Certainly we should make that attempt, only recognizing that selectivity inevitably affects interpretation. Our title, "Religion, Government, and Power," suggests a starting point for such a reconstruction.

The central issue in seeking to understand church and state in the new nation is recognizing that one—and only one—basic objective was held in common by the Founding Fathers, determining their work in and after the Constitutional Convention. Put bluntly, theirs was an acknowledged conspiracy to frame a government that was adequate to make the infant nation of recently liberated states viable. To that end the new government had to have sufficient power to give the authority of the nation credibility against the states that constituted it—and which claimed (implicitly, if not explicitly) to represent sovereign jurisdictions. Meeting in camera, delegates from the states framed a scheme of government that, while it would have to be ratified by those states, would then claim to have its own direct relationship to the citizens, who would owe allegiance to both. As the delegates in Philadelphia made their drafts, they found that compromise was the one strategy that worked. In sum, the Constitution represented something of a balancing act or, in a less flattering light, a shell game. The balancing act included calculation of what would work outside and beyond the convention as well as within it. Supporters of the new federal government, despite their differences (like Hamilton and Madison, for example), argued their cases energetically against those who opposed the new polity, the Anti-Federalists. For everything finally reduced to an essentially political issue: could a viable federal regime be first proposed, then ratified, and finally organized?

Unless we understand that highly political frame of reference, which reduced all other considerations to insignificance, and recognize how deeply and to the exclusion of various other objectives the Founders believed in the necessity of a more adequate government for the states as united, I do not think we can understand how the question of religion and regime appeared to them. For the delegates to the convention proper, this question of how to treat religion was not only a diversion from the central issue, it was also among the most divisive issues, if not potentially the most divisive issue, facing them. In many of the states represented at the convention there were traditions of preferential support for one or another religious "denomination." The settled churches of Massachusetts, Connecticut, and New Hampshire were an actual form of "establishment" in those states. Rather mixed patterns of preference for one or several religious bodies characterized some of the other states. Virginia, after a decade of avoiding the issue, had just disestablished the Church of England.[9]

Of greater relevance, however, were the religious tests for office, which were more widespread than the provisions requiring public support of church congregations. The formulations of these tests varied markedly, as did their observance. But the proposed federal government could not include religious tests for office if it were to survive after the convention or succeed in the subsequent ratification process, even though these tests were standard constitutional provisions in the constituent states. At root, while the Founding Fathers were not antireligious individually or collectively, their overriding and commonly held objective of achieving an adequate federal government could only be frustrated if the issue of religion's relationship to regime were allowed to introduce a dimension of continuing divisiveness into their work.

The outcome is well known to us. The Constitution proper as it emerged from the convention did include a provision regarding religion, but whose significance is often entirely overlooked—Article VI, Section 3: "No religious Test shall ever be required as a Qualification to any Office or public Trust under the United States." This seems to have been taken over from Charles Pinkney's early draft proposal and appears to have occasioned no dissent or even significant discussion in the convention. But it did set the federal government on a different course from most of the state governments. (Of course, one reason this section is overlooked is because the modern Supreme Court has used the First Amendment establishment clause to rule religious tests for office unconstitutional at other levels of government.)

Occasionally a counter-factual hypothesis will test the significance of an interpretation. Imagine, if you will, that the convention had proposed a generic religious test for office, or even taken a position in support of a favored church or churches at local option. As we reconstruct the possible alignments of religion and regime in the founding period under this hypothesis, only one conclusion is possible: no version of a proposal to favor one denomination could have contributed to the design and ratification of an adequate federal regime; and had such a scheme been proposed, it would have assured rejection of the document. Similarly, had a religious test for office been put forward, defeat of this desperately sought viable government would have been guaranteed.

I have as yet said nothing of liberty of conscience or religious freedom as a factor.[10] That is deliberate. The point is not that this construct was undervalued or lacked respect—though attitudes and practices varied from state to state. Rather, at the level of accommodation in the states between freedom for the practice of religion or liberty for conscience, effective toleration existed in relationship to widely varying patterns of support for denominations and religious test oaths. In sum, a proposed federal guarantee of religious liberty in opposition to state practices could not have mobilized support for ratification of this new federal venture, for that would have been to expand national authority and power decisively. Once again, the issue of religion had the vast potential to be positively divisive where support for the Constitution was concerned. Accordingly, for this tactical reason alone, it was excluded from the proposed mandate of the new government. To hypothesize again, I am confident that had the religious test oath—or support for one denomination or a particular set of them—been a potentially positive ground for enlisting support for this new government, then so desperate was the need as perceived by the Founders that the convention would have proposed such an oath and/or an appropriate pattern of public support for religion.

As it was being reviewed prior to ratification, numerous shortcomings were "discovered" in the proposed Constitution. As I have noted, the Anti-Federalist opposition, which was scarcely intellectually coherent, centered on the degree of centralization of power the document would legitimate. In response its proponents acceded to the notion of a series of amendments that would make explicit additional limitations on the power of the federal government. Ratification finally occurred with the presumption, at least in some states, that such amendments would follow, and in the first Congress James Madison took the lead in proposing them. Some further reference to religion had seemed called for beyond that in Article VI. Thus, the First Amendment religion clauses were designed to place explicit limitations upon Congress, assuring those skeptical of federal power that the existing state practices regarding religion—which varied widely—would be protected from federal intervention.

Modern interest in the religion clauses of the First Amendment has resulted in a great deal of scrutiny of both their legislative history and the process of ratification that followed. In capsule form, the story goes like this. Madison's initial proposal was comparatively expansive, doubtless reflecting his own convictions: "The civil rights of none shall be abridged on account of religious belief or worship, nor shall any national religion be established, nor shall the full and equal rights of conscience be in any manner, or on any pretext, infringed." [11] Having revised it several times and reduced it markedly in scope, the House finally forwarded to the Senate the following language: "Congress shall make no law establishing religion, or to prevent the free exercise thereof, or to infringe the rights of conscience." [12]

In turn the Senate proposed a different, but also reduced, version: "Congress shall make no law establishing articles of faith or a mode of worship, or prohibiting the free exercise of religion." [13]

The reduced language we know was finally worked out in a Committee of Conference between the houses: "Congress shall make no law respecting an establishment of religion, or prohibiting the free exercise thereof." [14] It then went through the process of ratification with numerous other provisions, only by accident of that process becoming part of the First Amendment. We have already noted that the clauses remained virtually unapplied and uninterpreted until the middle decades of this century, aside from their interpretation in the context of the federal prosecution of polygamy in the Territory of Utah in the late nineteenth century. [15]

Where does this leave us? I suggest that interpretation of the genesis of the religion clauses of the Constitution, including Article VI, Section 3, and the two provisions in the Bill of Rights, must start from recognition of the major objective of which they were a secondary expression. This was the overriding preoccupation of the Founders with designing and achieving an adequate national government. Their meaning derived from that context. They possessed no independent significance to which, in recent times, both separationist and accommodationist objectives might be related. At root the outcome the founding generation intended, and sought, was neither pro- nor anti-religion in the abstract. The Founding Fathers' overriding concern was to neutralize religion as a factor that might jeopardize the achievement of a federal government. Here Jefferson is less helpful than Madison, who suggested strategic or theoretical grounds, beyond the practical ones, for making the government of the United States independent of churches. He recognized that religion provided one basis for a factionalism that could destroy a regime. He did not seek to eliminate the causes of faction (religion being one), because in his view the polity stood the best chance of survival if factions (including those based on religion) counterbalanced each other.[16] We may also view the churches' separation from government as in certain formal respects similar to the deliberate separation of the executive, legislative, and judicial branches of government so as to use to advantage the checks and balances thus constructed among different centers of power. Religion, as one locus of power in the new United States, was to be respected as such and allowed an appropriate role; it was one among many social institutions and cultural activities out of which the new nation would be formed.

In proposing an adequate national government with a reasonable chance of being ratified, the Founding Fathers did not mention many issues that we might wish they had: provision for education; the status of the family; political parties—the list is long and the silences of the Founders witness to their overriding objective of achieving a limited national government. In consequence, it has fallen to subsequent generations to work out with respect to such issues how the principles that underlay the American polity would in fact apply. And although the Constitution was not in the end silent with regard to religion, I suggest we must approach religion in the same light. To interpret, and finally apply, the religion clauses, we must look for the strategic or theoretical considerations that led to the denial, from the first, of the federal government's competence in the area. What the Founding Fathers proposed in their minimalist attention to religion was not its wholesale segregation from government—the kind of resolution proposed in the French Revolution—for separationist logic opens the way for radical secularization as a social policy. Nor did they propose that the federal regime should take over (and thus make use of) churches—for an Erastianism of substance (if not form) is the outcome of accommodationist logic. Rather, they proposed that religious institutions should lie beyond the authority or competence of government. Religious activities were a part of the social and cultural life of the new nation which the distinctly limited federal government had no mandate to supervise or to depend upon. Such was appropriate for a religiously plural social order in which religion, left free of regulation, could easily be capable of destructive, as well as highly constructive, roles.[17]

In my own view, this was also a significant step in the resolution of a long-standing issue in Western cultures. This step was not so much a wholly new scheme, an abstract separation of religion and polity, as it was a new status for religions, primarily Christianity—and by implication Judaism as well—that had not been possible for the millennium and a half since the Constantinian revolution had made Christianity the favored religion of empire and religious uniformity under its sponsorship had been mobilized to guarantee social unity.

The framework I would suggest for understanding the genesis not only of the First Amendment religion clauses but also of the religious test clause of the Constitution, is that of the broadly political matrix within which the overriding objective was securing a more adequate federal government for the new nation. This government would necessarily compromise the sovereignty of the constituent states by drawing legitimacy from both them and their constituent citizens. This was a balancing act, requiring that limits be set to those powers the federal regime might exercise. To those skeptical of this polity because it might unduly infringe on the existing state governments, limitations were promised. And among the more prominent was forgoing the authority to require religion to support regime (as in religious test oaths), or to meddle either with existing preferential relationships between the states and particular religious bodies, or with liberty of conscience as it had come to be respected in the various sovereign states. But this balancing act certainly did not exclude government acquiescence in religious ministrations to the members of Congress, or to those in the military, nor did it rule out recognizing that the people as a collectivity—and as one source of federal authority—potentially stood in a relation to higher powers, for example, in exercises of fasting or thanksgiving.[18]

Interpreting the resolution of the church-state question in these contingent terms, seeing it as a product of the political necessities of the new nation rather than as a deduction from philosophical and theological doctrines, however formulated, makes it more comprehensible than accepting either the modern separationist or accommodationist paradigms. On the one hand, the separationist paradigm finds it difficult to interpret the ease with which practices like appointing congressional chaplains were adopted, or monies appropriated to make good on relations with the Indian tribes through the agencies of religious communities. Nor does it easily comprehend the recognition accorded to religion and morality in the new territories. On the other hand, the accommodationist paradigm does not readily make sense either of the variety of religious interests in the new nation or the strategic or theoretical grounds for making religion and government, both concerned with power, independent of each other. The denominations themselves had only just begun to organize and in any case had little centralized authority. And the young republic offered fertile ground for numerous new religious movements—to use our modern conception—that immediately took advantage of it and flourished in the next half-century. In sum, the accommodationist version of early American religious culture is too "Whiggish," reading more cultural coherence and more thoroughly developed religious institutions back into the late eighteenth and early nineteenth centuries than is warranted.

But the other side of this more contingent reading of the place of religion in the new nation and in the Constitution poses haunting questions. How durable were the formulations embodied in the Constitution? How does the Constitution so read with respect to its religion clauses address our era? Two hundred years later, a reading of the First Amendment origins such as we have given may be more acceptable history, but does it have any payoff in terms of understanding our contemporary United States and, for that matter, making possible constructive approaches to current issues that will be litigated under the Constitution?

To answer these questions we must first recognize that the United States has developed in remarkable ways over two centuries. Without attempting to, or wanting to seem to, preempt the discussion in subsequent chapters, let me simply indicate a few factors that make the context in which church-state issues are faced in 1989 rather markedly different from the context of 1789.

First, the authority and power of the federal government now decisively outweigh those of the states. Here the chief circumstance has been the conduct of war, whether international or civil, imperial or cold. It is beyond doubt that the power to conduct war claimed by the new national government—and all that claim entailed—has been basic to this shift in relationships between center and parts. Ours is now a continental society in a way that distances us from the founding era. This factor decisively affects reflection on our questions.

Second, the development of a continental, and now international, economy has had a great influence. Related both positively and negatively to the conduct of war, our dynamic economy has created a national culture which in the last half-century has reduced significant regional differences to tourist attractions. Ours is now in important respects a common culture. This factor also intersects with our questions.

Third, in spite of this commonality, we also have a variety of new cultural traditions entering the society and constituting vigorous, and not so vigorous, subcultures in tension with the common culture. Ours is a religiously plural nation beyond the powers of the Founders' imagination to conceive.

Fourth, religious institutions have progressively expanded their influence beyond the local level so that there has been a pronounced, if changing, religious complexion to the nation. Early in the nineteenth century a broad hegemony developed, first generally Protestant, then more inclusively Christian, followed by a "Judeo-Christian" axis in the mid-twentieth century. In sum, at least until recently, there has been at least the shadow of a common religion in American society. This factor, too, is not a neutral consideration in relation to our questions.

Fifth, religious innovations (both within the hegemonic tradition and as counterbalances to it) have developed in remarkable ways. In important respects, social deviance, frequently identified in ethnoreligious terms, has represented the rubric under which cultural pluralism has flourished. This factor also intersects with our questions.

By way of parenthesis, neither of the two prevailing paradigms—separationist or accommodationist—seems adequate to do justice to these basic features of our national development. The separationist ideal does not come to terms with the pervasive cultural aspects of religion, especially in relation to this powerful expansion of American society. Nor does the accommodationist paradigm enable us to comprehend either the pluralism of religion in today's culture or the divisive implications of links between government and particular religions. Thus, not only do both paradigms prove inadequate as a basis for interpreting the origin of the United States with respect to religion and regime, but they are also severely flawed as explanations of the place of religion in contemporary national experience. Does our historical reading offer a better approach to understanding the relationship of religion and government in an America that has developed in this fashion?

By recognizing that religion concerns power much as government does, and by understanding that making the two of them independent was a tactical but also a strategic commitment, we are positioned to see that the Founding Fathers' insistence on the independence of religion from the national government was tied to the theoretical foundations of our republic. Ironically, therefore, the thrust of this interpretation is to propose that Article VI, Section 3—the neglected clause of the Constitution—provides a better insight into the world of the Framers and their intent with respect to religion than the contested clauses that became the First Amendment of the Bill of Rights. Article VI, Section 3, meant that the new national government was accepting a limitation on its own sources of power and authority—religion should not be a category used in the conduct of government. In the eighteenth century, of course, this left the states free to do so. But for the federal side, such a limitation on the central government was a part of the complex of notions—including the division of powers, the strategy of checks and balances, belief in an informed citizenry, the reality of reserved powers, etc.—that provided the theoretical foundation for the new nation. In short, the issue of church and state was securely located within the framework of limited government, thus eliminating for the United States the synergistic relationship between religion and regime typical of other sovereign states and nations.

In this perspective, the role of the two clauses of the First Amendment was to reassure the states and their citizens that the implicit limitations upon the federal government would most explicitly leave each free of interference by the other. By virtue of incorporation those clauses now represent guarantees to the citizens against other levels of government— states and municipalities among them.[19] But the theory remains roughly the same though extended down to these other levels. Government shall be conducted without respect to religion. This does not mean society is necessarily rendered free of religious hegemony but that, should such exist, government policies must not be determined on that basis. The other side of this coin, however, is that policies may be determined on bases that accord with such a hegemony. Thus the religion clauses together form a most explicit constitutional basis, dating from the founding era, for support of at least one class of cultural activities independent of regime. We must think of them as among the best guarantees, along with the rest of the First Amendment, of cultural pluralism.

Ironically, when approached at this level, the insights behind the separationist and accommodationist readings of our history begin to come together. Each grasps a truth that is only part of a more adequate understanding of the American experiment. Put succinctly, separationist logic pertains to linkages between religious institutions and governments, accommodationist logic to the cultural reality of religion. In our political culture these join as complementary in the context of the undergirding federal theory of limited government. Neither has an independent grounding, however, apart from the contingent achievement of the founding generation, which must be rediscovered, renewed, and reapplied by each successive generation, even our own.

Notes

1. *Everson* v. *Board of Education of the Township of Ewing* (330 U.S. 1 [1947]).

2. *Everson* is excerpted in John T. Noonan, Jr., *The Believer and the Powers That Are* (New York: Macmillan, 1987), 370–374 (quotation on 373).

3. Quoted in John F. Wilson and Donald L. Drakeman, eds., *Church and State in American History*, 2d ed. (Boston: Beacon, 1987), 203.

4. *Reynolds* v. *United States* (98 U.S. 145 [1879]) makes reference to the metaphor; see Noonan, *Believer*, 197. See also Thomas Jefferson's letter to the Danbury Baptists in Wilson and Drakeman, *Church and State*, 78–79.

5. A good discussion of the events in Virginia is in Thomas J. Curry, *The First Freedoms: Church and State in America to the Passage of the First Amendment* (New York: Oxford University Press, 1986), ch. 6, "Religion and Government in Revolutionary America, Part I, The Southern States," 134–148.

6. For a recent general treatment of Madison, see Robert A. Rutland, *James Madison, the Founding Father* (New York: Macmillan, 1987). Chapters 2 and 3, pp. 23–71, delineate his roles in making and implementing, including amending, the Constitution.

7. Justice Rehnquist developed this position in his dissent in *Wallace* v. *Jaffree* (105 S. Ct. 2479 [1985]). See relevant excerpts in Wilson and Drakeman, *Church and State*, 243–245 (quotation on 245).

8. That this is closer to the original effect of the clauses than the implication of the "wall metaphor" is clear. What it does not do, however, is to locate the proscription of federal action about religion in its setting of a theory of limited government and, in particular, in relation to strategies for limiting the power of that federal government.

9. The most useful summary overview is Curry, *First Freedoms*, 105–133, in which he emphasizes the variety in understandings of the term.

10. Curry's discussion also summarizes this set of issues in the colonies-become-states; see ibid., 75, 78–104.

11. Wilson and Drakeman, *Church and State*, 75.

12. Ibid., 77.

13. Ibid., 77–78.

14. Ibid., 78.

15. See *Reynolds* v. *United States*, available (in part) in Noonan, *Believer*, particularly his chapter on Mormon marriage practices as occasioning litigation, 194–207.

16. See Madison in *The Federalist*, No. 10.

17. In a larger sense this essay is written in the context of the current discussion of the founding period so brilliantly delineated by Gordon S. Wood in "The Fundamentals and the Constitutions," *New York Review of Books* 25, 2 (February 18, 1988): 33–40. While taking seriously the return to texts (in this case of the Constitution) so assiduously cultivated by the disciples of Leo Strauss, Wood argues that the context must govern their interpretation. By implication, their application to another context properly entails understanding both contexts.

18. I have addressed some of these issues in my *Public Religion in American Culture* (Philadelphia: Temple University Press, 1979). See especially the discus-

Religion

The Court ruled that states may permit tax deductions for educational expenses even if parochial schools reap nearly all the benefit. The 5-to-4 decision in Mueller v. Allen was the first time the Court endorsed a form of tuition aid for parochial schools, but the majority's insistence that the benefit be at least nominally available to public school parents as well cast doubt on the Reagan Administration's plan for tuition tax credits for private school tuition.

The Court ruled in Marsh v. Chambers that the Constitution permits a legislature to pay a chaplain to open each day's session with a prayer.

In Larkin v. Grendel's Den, the Court declared unconstitutional a Massachusetts law giving churches a veto power over the issuing of nearby liquor licenses.

sion of Thanksgiving on pp. 56–63. See also ch. 4, "Ritualistic Behavior of American Public Life," pp. 67–93.

19. Indeed, *Torcaso* v. *Watkins* (367 U.S. 488 [1961]), which concerned religious oath-taking on the part of local officials, subsumed this issue under the establishment clause as interpreted in *Everson*, thus voiding the question of whether Article VI, Section 3, applies to other than federal officeholders.

5

The Democratization
of Christianity
and the Character
of American Politics

NATHAN O. HATCH

This essay will argue that at the very inception of the American republic the most dynamic popular movements were expressly religious. However powerful working-class organizations became in cities such as New York and Baltimore, their presence cannot compare with the phenomenal growth, and collective elán, of Methodists, Baptists, Christians, Millerites, and Mormons. It was lay preachers in the early republic who became the most effective agents in constructing new frames of reference for people living through a profoundly transitional age. Religious leaders from the rank and file were phenomenally successful in reaching out to marginal people, in promoting self-education and sheltering participants from the indoctrination of elite orthodoxies, in binding people together in supportive community, and in identifying the aspirations of common people with the will of God.

The vitality of these religious ideologies and mass movements has had a considerable long-term effect upon the character and limits of American politics. Churches, after all, came to serve as competing universes of discourse and action. And the political implications of mass movements that were democratic and religious at the same time are far more profound than merely predisposing members to vote Federalist or Republican, Democrat or Whig. As mass popular movements, churches came to be places in which fundamental political assumptions were forged: ideas about the meaning of America, the priority of the individual conscience, the values of localism, direct democracy, and individualism, and the necessity of dynamic communication, predicated on the identification of speaker or author with an audience.

This paper will suggest that to understand the democratization of American society, one must look at what happened to Protestant Christianity in the years 1780–1830. In an age when people expected almost everything from religion (and churches) and almost nothing from politics (and the state), the popular churches are essential to comprehending the enduring shape of American democracy. The first half of the paper will explore the character of these mass religious movements. I will then consider three dimensions of these movements which have long-term implications for American politics: the importance of churches as basic classrooms for molding perceptions about the meaning of America; the competing impulses of democratic dissent and desire for respectability within these movements; and the role of populist forms of Christianity in the forming of a liberal society that is individualistic, competitive, and market driven.

I

The American Revolution is the single most crucial event in American history. The generation overshadowed by it and its counterpart in France stands at the fault line that separates an older world, premised on standards of deference, patronage, and ordered succession, from a newer one to which we are attuned since it continues to shape our values. The American Revolution and the beliefs flowing from it created a cultural ferment over the meaning of freedom, a debate that brought to the fore crucial issues of authority, organization, and leadership.[1]

Above all, the Revolution dramatically expanded the circle of people who considered themselves capable of thinking for themselves about issues of freedom, equality, sovereignty, and representation; and it eroded traditional appeals to the authority of tradition, station, and education. Ordinary people moved towards these new horizons as they gained access to a powerful new vocabulary, a rhetoric of liberty that would not have occurred to people were it not for the Revolution. In time, the well-being of ordinary people edged closer to the center of what it means to be American, public opinion came to assume normative significance, and leaders could not survive who would not, to use Patrick Henry's phrase, "bow with utmost deference to the majesty of the people." The correct solution to any important problem, political, legal, or religious, would have to appear as the people's choice.[2]

The profoundly transitional age between 1776 and 1830 left the same kind of indelible imprint upon the structures of American Christianity as it did upon those of American political life. Only land, Robert Wiebe has noted, could compete with Christianity as the pulse of a new democratic society.[3] The age of the democratic revolutions unfolded with awesome moment for people in every social rank. Amidst such acute uncertainty, many humble Christians in America began to redeem a dual legacy. They yoked together strenuous demands for revivals, in the name of Whitefield, and calls for the expansion of popular sovereignty, in the name of the Revolution. It is the linking of these equally potent traditions that sent American Christianity cascading in so many creative directions in the early republic. Church authorities had few resources to restrain these movements fed by the passions of ordinary people. American Methodism, for example, under the tutelage of Francis Asbury, veered sharply from the course of British Methodism from the time of Wesley's death until the end of the Napoleonic Wars. The heavy, centralizing hand of Jabez Bunting kept England's potent evangelical tradition firmly grounded in traditional notions of authority and leadership. After 1800, the leaders of British Methodism were able to bar the eccentric American revivalist Lorenzo Dow from contaminating their meetings. In America, however, Dow took the camp meeting circuit by storm despite periodic censure from bishops and presiding elders. Given his effectiveness and popular support, they were unable to mount a direct challenge to his authority.

A diverse array of evangelical firebrands went about the task of movement-building in the generation after the Revolution. While they were intent on bringing evangelical conversion to the mass of ordinary Americans, rarely could they divorce that message from contagious new vocabularies and impulses that swept through American popular cultures in an era of democratic revolution: an appeal to class as the fundamental problem of society, a refusal to recognize the cultural authority of elites, a disdain for the supposed lessons of history and tradition, a call for reform using the rhetoric of the Revolution, a commitment to turn the press into a sword of democracy, and an ardent faith in the future of the American republic.

At the same time, Americans who espoused evangelical and egalitarian convictions, in whatever combination, were left free to experiment with abandon, unopposed by civil or religious authority. Within a few years of Jefferson's election in 1800, it became anachronistic to speak of dissent in America—as if there were still a commonly recognized center against which new or emerging groups had to define themselves. There was little to restrain a variety of new groups from vying to establish their identity as a counterestablishment. The fundamental history of this period, in fact, may be a story of things left out, as Roland Berthoff has recently suggested.[4] Churches and religious movements after 1800 operated in a climate in which ecclesiastical establishments had withered, in which the federal government had almost no internal functions—a "midget institution in a giant land"[5]—and in which a rampant migration of people continued to snap old networks of personal authority. American churches did not face the kind of external social and political pressures which in Great Britain often forced Christianity and liberty to march in opposite directions. Such isolation made it possible for religious "outsiders" to see their own destiny as part and parcel of the meaning of America itself. If the earth did belong to the living, as President Jefferson claimed, why should the successful newcomer defer to the claims of education, status, and longevity?[6]

The reality of a nonrestrictive environment permitted an unexpected and often explosive conjunction of evangelical fervor and popular sovereignty. It was this engine that greatly accelerated the process of Christianization with America popular culture, allowing indigenous expressions of faith to take hold among ordinary people, both white and black. This expansion of evangelical Christianity did not proceed primarily from the nimble response of religious elites meeting the challenge before them. Rather, Christianity was effectively reshaped by ordinary people who molded it in their own image and threw themselves into expanding its influence. Increasingly assertive common people wanted their leaders unpretentious, their doctrines self-evident and down-to-earth, their music lively and singable, their churches in local hands. It was this upsurge of democratic hope that characterized so many religious cultures in the early republic and brought Baptists, Methodists, Disciples, and a host of other insurgent groups to the fore. The rise of evangelical Christianity in the early republic is, in some measure, a story of the success of common people in shaping the culture after their own priorities rather than the priorities outlined by gentlemen, such as the Founding Fathers.[7] A style of religious leadership that the public had deemed "untutored" and "irregular" as late as the First Great Awakening became overwhelmingly successful, even normative, in the first decades of the new nation.

It is easy to miss the profoundly democratic character of the early republic's insurgent religious movements. The Methodists, after all, retained power in a structured hierarchy under the control of bishops; the Mormons reverted to rule by a single religious prophet and revelator; and groups such as the Disciples of Christ, despite professed democratic structures, came to be controlled by powerful individuals such as Alexander Campbell, who had little patience with dissent. As ecclesiastical structures, these movements often turned out to be less democratic than the congregational structure of the New England Standing Order.

The democratization of Christianity, then, has less to do with the specifics of polity and governance and more with the very incarnation of the church into popular culture. In at least three respects the popular religious movements of the early republic articulated a profoundly democratic spirit. First, they denied the age-old distinction that set the clergy apart as a separate order of men and they refused to defer to learned theologians and received orthodoxies. All were democratic or populist in the way their instinctively associated virtue with ordinary people rather than with elites,[8] exalted the vernacular in word and song as the hallowed channel for communicating with and about God, and freely turned over the reigns of power. These groups also shared with the Jeffersonian Republicans an overt rejection of the past as a repository of wisdom.[9] By redefining leadership itself, these movements were instrumental in shattering the centuries-old affinity between Christianity and the norms of high culture. They reconstructed the foundations of religion fully in keeping with the values and priorities of ordinary people.

Second, these movements empowered ordinary people by taking their deepest spiritual impulses at face value rather than subjecting them to the scrutiny of orthodox doctrine and the frowns of respectable clergymen. In the last two decades of the century, preachers from a wide range of new religious movements openly fanned the flames of religious ecstasy. Rejecting in 1775 the Yankee Calvinism of his youth, Henry Alline found that his soul was transported with divine love, "ravished with a divine ecstasy beyond any doubts or fears, or thoughts of being then deceived."[10] What had been defined as "enthusiasm" increasingly became advocated from the pulpit as an essential part of Christianity. Such a shift in emphasis, accompanied by rousing gospel singing rather than formal church music, reflected the success of common people in defining for themselves the nature of faith. In addition, an unprecedented wave of religious leaders in the last quarter of the century expressed their own openness to a variety of signs and wonders—in short, an admission of increased supernatural involvement in everyday life. Scores of preachers' journals, from Methodists and Baptists, from North and South, from white and black, indicated a ready acceptance to interpret dreams and visions as inspired by God, normal manifestations of divine guidance and instruction. "I know the word of God is our infallible guide, and by it we are to try all our dreams and feelings," conceded the Methodist stalwart Freeborn Garrettson." But, he added, "I also know, that both sleeping and waking, things of a divine nature have been revealed to me." Those volatile aspects of popular religion, long held in check by the church, came to be recognized and encouraged from the pulpit. It is no wonder that a dismayed writer in the *Connecticut Evangelical Magazine* countered in 1805: "No person is warranted from the word of God to publish to the world the discoveries of heaven or hell which he supposes he has had in a dream, or trance, or vision."[11]

The early republic was also a democratic moment in a third sense. Religious outsiders were flushed with confidence about their prospects and had little sense of their own limitations. They dreamed that a new age of religious and social harmony would spring up naturally out of their own efforts to overthrow coercive and authoritarian structures.[12] This upsurge of democratic hope, this passion for equality, led to a welter of diverse and competing forms, many of them structured in highly undemocratic ways. The Methodists under Francis Asbury, for instance, used authoritarian means to build a church that would not be a respecter of persons. This church faced the curious paradox of gaining phenomenal influence among laypersons with whom it would not share ecclesiastical authority. Similarly, the Mormons used a virtual religious dictatorship as the means to return power to illiterate men. Yet, despite these authoritarian structures, the fundamental impetus of these movements was to make Christianity a liberating force, giving people the right to think and act for themselves rather than being forced to rely upon the mediations of an educated elite. The most fascinating religious story of the early republic is the signal achievements of these and other populist religious leaders, outsiders who brought to bear the full force of democratic persuasions upon American culture.

The wave of popular religious movements that broke upon the United States in the half-century after independence did more to Christianize American society than anything before or since. Nothing makes that point clearer than the growth of Methodists and Baptists as mass movements among white and black Americans. Starting from scratch just prior to the Revolution, the Methodists in America grew at a rate that terrified other denominations, reaching a quarter of a million members by 1820 and doubling again by 1830. Baptist membership multiplied tenfold in the three decades after the Revolution, the number of churches increasing from 500 to over 2500. The black church in America was born amidst the crusading vigor of these movements and quickly assumed its own distinct character and broad appeal among people of color. By the middle of the ninteenth century, Methodist and Baptist churches had splintered into more different denominational forms than one cares to remember. Yet together these movements came to constitute nearly 70 percent of Protestant church members in the United States and two-thirds of its ministers.[13]

This essay grows out of research on five distinct traditions or mass movements that came to the fore early in the nineteenth century: the Christian movement, the Methodists, the Baptists, the black churches, and the Mormons. Each was led by young men of relentless energy who went about movement-building as self-conscious outsiders. They shared an ethic of unrelenting labor, a passion for expansion, a hostility to orthodox belief and style, a zeal for religious reconstruction, and a systematic plan to labor on behalf of their ideals. However diverse their theologies and church organizations, they were able to offer common people, especially the poor, compelling visions of individual self-respect and collective self-confidence.

II

In his highly suggestive book *The Revolution of the Saints*, Michael Walzer explores the character of the Puritan "saint," the stalwart figure of burning zeal who ignored age-old customs and traditional loyalties to reconstruct the social order of seventeenth-century England. Walzer suggests that the saint's personality itself was his most radical innovation. Hardened and disciplined by a compelling ideology, the saint could offer his own vision and pattern of life as an alternative to traditional social forms. What made the cadre of Puritan saints so formidable, and in Walzer's view so similar to the modern revolutionary, was their extraordinary capacity to mobilize people for a cause and to build organizations sustained by ideological bonds rather than ties of residence, family, and patronage.[14]

This chapter suggests that the social and intellectual ferment of the early republic gave rise to a generation of populist "saints." Their alienation from the established order matched their aptitude for mobilizing people. This set them apart from the generation of George Whitefield and Gilbert Tennant in the mid-eighteenth century, who labored to revive lukewarm establishments but left the creation of new institutional forms to the will of Providence and the discretion of those who pursued a New Light call. In the main, the creation of new congregations was an unintended and episodic consequence of the preaching of the earlier Great Awakening.

Dissent in America after the Revolution was characterized by a shift from seeking conversions to movement-building from the ground up. A battery of young leaders without elite pedigree constructed fresh religious ideologies around which new religious movements coalesced. W. R. Ward has noted that Francis Asbury was an entrepreneur in religion, a man who perceived a market to be exploited. The itinerant-based machine which he set in motion was less a church in any traditional sense than "a military mission of short term agents." [15] Similarly, the founder of the Churches of Christ, Barton W. Stone, eschewed normal pastoral duties and dedicated himself utterly to the pursuit of "causes" in religion. Elias Smith went so far as to define religious liberty as the right to build a movement by intinerating without constraint.[16] All of these leaders eventually defined success not by the sheer number of converts but by the number of those who identified themselves with a fledgling movement. This quest for organization lay at the heart of Methodism's success. One unfriendly critic observed that the movement produced such great results "because it took hold of the doctrines which lay in the minds of all men here, and wrought them with the steam, levers, and pulleys of a new engine." [17]

Above all, these upstarts were radically innovative in reaching and organizing people. Passionate about ferreting out converts in every hamlet and crossroads, they sought to bind them together in local and regional communities. They continued to refashion the sermon as a profoundly popular medium, inviting even the most unlearned and inexperienced to respond to a call to preach. These initiates were charged to proclaim the gospel anywhere and every day of the week—even to the limit of their physical endurance. The resulting creation, the colloquial sermon, employed daring pulpit storytelling, no-holds-barred appeals, overt humor, strident attack, graphic application, and intimate personal experience. These young builders of religious movements also became the most effective purveyors of mass literature in the early republic, confronting people in every section of the new nation with the combined force of the written and spoken word. In addition, this generation launched bold experiments with new forms of religious music, new techniques of protracted meetings, and new Christian ideologies that denied the mediations of religious elites and promised to exalt those of low estate.[18]

The result of these intensive efforts was nothing less than the creation of mass movements that were deeply religious and genuinely democratic at the same time. Lawrence Goodwyn has suggested that the building of significant mass democratic movements involves a sequential process of recruitment, education, and involvement that allows a "movement culture" to develop. This new plateau of social possibility, based on self-confident leadership and widespread methods of internal communication, permits people to conceive of acting in self-generated democratic ways, to develop new ways of looking at things less clouded by inherited assumptions, and to defend themselves in the face of adverse interpretations from the orthodox culture. Like the later Populist Movement about which Goodwyn writes, insurgent religious movements such as the Methodists, a variety of Baptists, the Christians and Disciples, the Millerites, and the Mormons dared to aspire grandly, to surmount rigid cultural inheritances, to work together in order to be free individually. If nothing else, these movements were collective expressions of self-respect, instilling hope, purpose, meaning, and identity in thousands upon thousands of persons whom the dominant culture had defined as marginal.[19]

All of these movements challenged common people to take religious destiny into their own hands, to think for themselves, to oppose centralized authority and the elevation of the clergy as a separate order of men. These religious communities could embrace the forlorn and the uprooted far more intensely than any political movement and offer them powerful bonds of acceptance and hope. As one new Methodist convert recalled, "I now found myself associated with those who loved each other with a pure heart fervently, instead of being surrounded by those with whom friendship was a cold commerce of interest."[20] These new movements could also impart to ordinary people, particularly those battered by poverty or infirmity, what Martin Luther King called "a sense of somebodiness"— the kind of consolation that another Methodist found so appealing in worship held in the crude environment of a log cabin: "an abiding confidence that he was a subject of that powerful kingdom whose Prince cared for his subjects."[21] These movements also allowed common people to trust their own powerful religious impulses. They were encouraged to express their faith with fervent emotion and bold testimony. In the most democratic gesture of all, some preachers even began to take their cues for evidence of divine power from expressions in the audience. During a camp meeting on an island in the Chesapeake Bay, Lorenzo Dow was interrupted by a woman who began clapping her hands with delight and shouting "Glory! Glory!" In a response that was the opposite of condescension, Dow proclaimed to the audience: "The Lord is here! *He is with that sister.*"[22]

In passing, it is instructive to suggest at least four reasons that historians have failed to explore the dynamics of popular religion in this era. First, during the last three decades the quickened interest in religion as a cultural force emerged within a broader historiographical tendency to downplay the social impact of the Revolution. Second, historians have interpreted the Second Great Awakening as an attempt by traditional religious elites to impose social order upon a disordered and secularized society—revivalism as an attempt to salvage Protestant solidarity. A third reason is that church historians from the more popular denominations have had reasons to sanitize their own histories. Modern church historians have chosen to focus on those dimensions of their own heritage that point to cultural enrichment, institutional cohesion, and intellectual respectability. William Warren Sweet, for instance, was committed to a vision of Methodists and Baptists as bearers of civilization to the uncouth and unretrained society of the frontier. Churches were instruments of order, education, and moral discipline.[23]

A fourth reason that popular religious movements remain unexplored is surprising given the deep commitment by a new generation of social historians to understand the lives of common people in the age of capitalist transformation. While considerable attention has been focused on the changing nature of markets, on the decline of independent artisans and farmers and the rise of the American working class, surprisingly little energy has gone into exploring the dynamics of insurgent religious movements.[24] This neglect stems both from the neo-Marxist preoccupation with the formation of social classes and the assumption that religion is generally a conservative force and a pernicious one.[25] What these studies fail to take into account is that, for better or worse, the most dynamic popular movements in the early republic were expressly religious.

III

The dissident movements of the early republic championed nothing more than the separation of church and state. Yet they were given to embrace the American republic with as much enthusiasm as had any of the orthodox traditions that still yearned for a Christian nation. These dissidents endowed the republic with the same divine authority as did defenders of the Standing Order such as Timothy Dwight and Noah

Webster, but for opposite reasons. The republic became a new city on a hill not because it kept faith with Puritan tradition, but because it sounded the death knell for corporate and hierarchic conceptions of the social order. In sum, a government so enlightened as to tell the churches to go their own way must have also had prophetic power to tell them which way to go.[26]

This is certainly not to suggest that political idioms uniformly colored the thinking of popular preachers in the early republic or that their message was not profoundly religious in purpose and scope. The early Methodist preachers, for instance, were preeminently soul savers and revivalists and saw political involvement as a distraction at best.[27] Their transatlantic connections, furthermore, kept before them the movement of Providence abroad as well as at home. Yet even Francis Asbury was given to affectionate reflections on the religious privileges offered in his adopted land. Repeatedly he made a sharp contrast between the state of Methodism in America and in Great Britain, noting the success of the daughter in outstripping the parent. A Methodist preacher without the slightest interest in politics or in the millennium still had to take note of the phenomenal growth on these shores of a movement that began as "the offscouring of all things."

Even the Mormons, who seemed to have rejected American values and who seemed to impose biblical models upon politics rather than vice versa, developed an eschatology that was explicitly American. Joseph Smith made the Garden of Eden a New World paradise, with America becoming the cradle of civilization. In due time, the *Book of Mormon* recounts, God prevailed upon Columbus "to venture across the sea to the Promised Land, to open it for a new race of free men."[28] A variety of Mormon authors suggest that it was the free institutions of America that prepared the way for the new prophet, Joseph Smith. The early Mormon missionaries to Great Britain made a literal appeal that converts should leave the Old World, bound in tyranny and awaiting destruction, and travel to the New. The contrast is explicit in this early song by John Taylor sharply pointing out the standard which British society does not meet:

> O! This is the land of the free!
> And this is the home of the brave;
> Where rulers and mobbers agree;
> 'Tis the home of the tyrant and slave.
>
> Here liberty's poles pierce the sky
> With her cap gaily hung on the vane;

The gods may its glories espy,
But poor mortals, it's out of your ken.

The eagle sours proudly aloft,
And covers the land with her wings;
But oppression and bloodshed abound,
She can't deign to look down on such things.

All men are born equal and free,
And their rights all nations maintain;
But with millions it would not agree,
They were cradled and brought up in chains.[29]

Not political in any conventional sense, the early Latter-day Saints envisioned a theology of America that was less explicit but far more concrete than any of their rivals. Despite extreme dissent from mainstream America, the Mormons never claimed that the entire stream of American identity, like that of the church, had become polluted. There was a special character to this land and its people that would allow the kingdom of heaven to be restored even if the current generation remained mired in corruption and oppression. This ambivalence allowed Joseph Smith to establish an independent kingdom at Nauvoo while at the same time announcing his candidacy for the presidency of the United States, calling Americans to "rally to the standard of Liberty" and "trample down the tyrant's rod and the oppressor's crown."[30]

Putting this another way, the alienation of insurgent groups in the early republic did not produce "sects" in a traditional European sense. A main reason was that all were convinced that the very meaning of America was bound up with the kind of new beginning which their own movement represented. The kingdom of God could yet be built in America if they were true to their own special calling. The pull was towards Providence as much as towards purity, to subdue the culture as much as withdraw from it. The call was to preach, write, convert; to call the nation back to self-evident first principles.

The Latter-day Saints, for instance, were as alienated from mainstream culture as were Roger Williams and the Quakers from the Massachusetts Bay Colony. Yet, in withdrawing from society, Joseph Smith and his followers did not retreat to modest aims and private ambitions. They were fired with a sense of providential mission of national, even international scope, a conviction that God's kingdom would yet rise in America, their own endeavors serving as decisive leaven. Much more like Puritan "saints" than Williams or the Quakers, they set their faces to accomplish great and mighty things. Sidney Rigdon's recollections about the charged atmosphere in a log house in 1830 magnificently captures the compelling sense of mission that transformed simple farmers and artisans into thundering prophets intent on shaping the destiny of a nation:

> I met the whole church of Christ in a little log house about 20 feet square . . . and we began to talk about the kingdom of God as if we had the world at our command; we talked with great confidence, and talked big things, although we were not many people, we had big feelings . . . we began to talk like men in authority and power—we looked upon men of the earth as grasshoppers; if we did not see this people, we saw by vision, the church of God, a thousand times larger . . . we talked about the people coming as doves to the windows, that all nations should flock unto it . . . and of whole nations being born in one day; we talked such big things that men could not bear them.[31]

A similar hunger for achievement and sense of providential mission propelled other saints to take up different causes, Methodist, Baptist, Universalist, or Christian. One simply cannot underestimate the force of this democratized "errand into the wilderness" in assessing the Christianization of popular culture and the relative weakness of other ideologies of dissent. In all of its diversity, this thundering legion stormed the hinterland of the nation empowered by an incomparable ideology of action: that popular innovation was the handiwork of God and the essential meaning of America.

IV

It is also important to emphasize that popular denominations were socially uniform and thus politically predictable. By the second decade of the century a struggle occurred within Baptists and Methodists between those who wanted respectability, centralization, and education and those who valued the tradition of democratic dissent—localism, antielitism, and religious experience fed by the passions of ordinary people. The fault line often ran between cosmopolitans and localists, between urban and rural interests. The example of Nathan Bangs superbly captures the tension in popular denominations between democratic dissent and professional respectability.

Although he declined election as bishop of the Methodist Church in 1832, Nathan Bangs left an indelible imprint upon the church in the generation after Francis Asbury. Bangs's early career was typical of those called to service in Asbury's missionary band. A largely self-educated young man who spent his youth in Connecticut and his teenage years in rural New York, Bangs moved to Canada at the age of twenty-one and taught school in a Dutch community near Niagara. Troubled by the perplexities of Calvinism, Bangs came under the influence of a Methodist itinerant, James Coleman, experienced a riveting conversion and sanctification, and, conforming to severest Methodist custom, removed the ruffles from his shirts and cut his long hair, which he had worn fashionably in a cue. In 1801, a year after he joined the church and three months after he was approved as an exhorter, he was licensed to preach and given a circuit. Riding circuits from Niagara to Quebec for the next decade, Bangs became the principal force in establishing Methodism in the lower St. Lawrence Valley.[32]

In 1810, the New York Conference presented a charge to Nathan Bangs that would profoundly alter the emphasis of his ministry: he was named "preacher in charge" of the five preachers, five preaching places, and 2,000 members that comprised the single circuit of New York City.[33] Bangs remained a dominant influence in Methodist affairs until the time of the Civil War—when Methodists could boast sixty churches and 17,000 members in the city. Yet despite the Methodist rule of biennial change of appointment, Bangs never managed to leave New York. His career and influence represent the tremendous allure of respectability that faced insurgent religious movements in Jacksonian America as their own constituencies grew in wealth and social standing and it became more difficult to define leaders' pastoral identity as defiant and alienated prophets. Bangs envisioned Methodism as a popular establishment, faithful to the movement's original fire but tempered with virtues of middle-class propriety and urbane congeniality. If Asbury's career represented the triumph of Methodism as a populist movement, with control weighted to the cultural periphery rather than to the center, then Bangs's pointed to the centripetal tug of respectable culture. In America, dissenting paths have often doubled back to lead in the direction of learning, decorum, professionalism, and social standing.

From the time Nathan Bangs arrived in New York City he set his face to dampen the popular spontaneity that had infused Methodist worship. "I witnessed," he said "a spirit of pride, presumption, and bigotry, impatience of scriptural restraint and moderation, clapping of the hands, screaming, and even jumping, which marred and disgraced the work of God."[34] Bangs called together the Methodists of New York in the John Street Church and exhorted them to be more orderly in their social meetings. Later Bangs also went on record as opposed to the spiritual songs of the camp meeting, "ditties" that in his words, "possessed little of the spirit of poetry and therefore added nothing to true intellectual taste."[35] With a view of his responsibilities not unlike that of his British counterpart, Jabez Bunting, Bangs depicted his role in the church as that of an overseer of a garden beset with the dangerous snake of disorder. Bangs's charge was to strike harder and harder with the whip of the Discipline.[36] One of the consequences of bringing more order and decorum to the John Street Church was that a large faction led by Samuel and William Stillwell, men who opposed centralized control, broke away to set up their own church. The immediate occasion for the split was a plan, backed by Bangs, to rebuild the church in a grand and expensive style, a controversial move at best given a church whose Discipline instructed that church buildings "be built plain and decent . . . not more expensive than is absolutely necessary."[37] The expensive style of the building, which even contained a carpeted altar, exacerbated a smoldering tension between what Bangs called "down-town" and "up-town" members. The simpler folk from uptown, led by the Stillwells, rallied against the new building and the heavy-handed tactics of its clerical supporters as "departure from the primitive simplicity of Methodism."[38]

Nathan Bangs also threw his remarkable energy and political savvy into building powerful central agencies for the expanding Methodist church. After serving for two years as the presiding elder for the New York Conference, he was elected the agent of the Methodist Book Concern in 1820, a position which would keep him permanently in New York and provide a strategic base from which to promote Methodist publications, missions, Sunday schools, and educational institutions. Under his direction the Book Concern grew from a struggling agency embarrassed by debt and without premises of its own to a publishing house which was the largest in the world by 1860.[39] Bangs reinvigorated the monthly *Methodist Magazine* and launched, in 1826, the *Christian Advocate and Journal*, a weekly newspaper that became an official organ of the church in 1828 and rapidly developed the largest circulation of any paper in the country—an estimated 25,000 subscriptions.[40] He was the father of the Missionary Society of the Methodist Episcopal Church and for twenty years its guiding hand. He was also tireless in his efforts for the church's Sunday School Union and was the first to use the powerful agency of the denominational press to push for required ministerial education.[41]

As Methodism's first major polemicist, theological editor, and historian, Nathan Bangs pushed relentlessly for raising the intellectual standards of the church. He was determined to "redeem its character from the foul blot cast upon it, not without some reason, that it had been indifferent to the cause of literature and science."[42] Bangs deplored Asbury's conclusion that the failure of early Methodist schools was a providential sign that Methodists should not attempt to found colleges. Frankly embarrassed and apologetic for the "little progress we have hitherto made in general literature," Bangs set about to make the church "'not be a whit behind the very chiefest' of the Churches in Christendom in the literary and theological eminence of her ministers." In 1830 Bangs transformed the monthly *Methodist Magazine* into the more serious and literary *Methodist Quarterly Review*, a journal to "draw forth the most matured efforts of our best writers . . . and lead others to the cultivation of a similar taste."[43] In his tenure as doorkeeper of Methodist thinking, Bangs used his considerable resources to accelerate a process by which many Methodists, particularly those in urban settings, shed their populist distinctives and stepped into ranks of "influential" Christians. By 1844 even the bishops of the church were forced to confess that the church was well on the way to selling its original birthright: "in some of the Conferences little or nothing remains of the itinerant system."[44]

While there was nothing uniform about this quest for respectability, it is a process powerfully at work among second-generation leadership of insurgent movements such as the Methodists, the Baptists, and the Disciples. The uneducated Methodist itinerant Hope Hull (1785–1818), for instance, settled permanently in Athens, Georgia, the place selected as the home for the University of Georgia, so that his sons could have the value of a liberal education. One of his sons became a lawyer and eventually Speaker of the Georgia House of Representatives and the other two were professors at Franklin College.[45] With similar intent, Methodists also came to domesticate the camp meeting, deemphasizing its emotional exercises and restricting its spontaneous exuberance.[46] By the middle of the century Methodists would remove their proscriptions on pew rentals, a move Peter Cartwright lamented as "a Yankee triumph."[47] Most important, in the three decades before the Civil War the Methodists founded over thirty colleges in nineteen different states; the Baptists, over twenty colleges in sixteen states.[48] By the 1840s, Methodist leadership had shifted firmly into the Whig political camp.[49]

In the long run, basic fault lines of class, education, and social status within a single denomination may have been more significant then sectional tensions, even between Northern and Southern churches. Despite the regional schisms in their churches, the difference between the Methodist Nathan Bangs or the Baptist Whig Francis Wayland and the "gentlemen theologians" of the South were simply not all that great, as Wayland noted ruefully about the 1845 division in the Baptist church. He argued that the Southern Baptist Convention was led by men representing the very best of enlightened Southern life, "governors, judges, congressmen, and other functionaries of the highest dignity."[50] What deserves much greater study are those churches and religious leaders that flourished on the fringes of Southern society, those upland whites who defiantly retained their own councils. Exploring their religious convictions, Bertram Wyatt-Brown has suggested, will reveal the "confused internal cleavage between the folkways of the poor and their social betters, a conflict that belies the notion of a monolithic southern cultural unity in opposition to a northern counterpart."[51]

Similar tensions in the North associated with social status played a key role in the political upheaval within the Methodist church during the 1820s, turmoil that led to the formation of the Methodist Protestant Church. In Massachusetts, for example, a local preacher was expelled for clashing with a congregation over the construction of a new chapel. Claiming to speak for the "plain, meek, humble, and old-fashioned Methodist" as opposed to the new "gay, assuming, proud, new-fashioned" ones, he thundered against new forms of ostentation that Methodists came to allow.[52] Furthermore, leaders of that movement, such as Nicholas Snethen, employed the rhetoric of democracy with telling effect to stigmatize the hierarchy of Methodism. Similarly, an intense commitment to local autonomy kept Baptists in states like Kentucky, Tennessee, and Missouri absolutely opposed to state, much less national, organization. When infrequent conventions were held, "sovereign and independent" churches would send messengers rather than delegates to insure that the convention could not claim "a single attribute of power or authority over any church or association."[53] In the American religious economy, moves toward dignity, solemnity, and gentility were sure to bring a swift and strident challenge. New sets of insurgents had ready access to the visions of apostolic simplicity that had inspired their parents and grandparents in the faith. Democratic dissent has been important over the last two centuries not because it has retained control of the major Protestant denominations, but, rather, because it has served as a residual dynamism unsettling church traditions, breaking out into new and distinctive religious movements, and providing a receptive audience for populist politicians capable of infusing events with moral significance.

V

An additional benefit of piecing together the story of these democratic religious movements is new insight into crucial questions about how America became a liberal society, individualistic, competitive, and market driven. In an age when most ordinary Americans expected almost nothing from government institutions and almost everything from religious ones, popular religious ideologies were perhaps the most important bellwethers of shifting worldviews. The passion for equality that came to the fore in these years decisively rejected the past as a repository of wisdom. Far from looking backward and clinging to an older moral economy, insurgent religious leaders espoused convictions that were essentially modern and individualistic. These persuasions defied elite privilege and vested interests, and anticipated the dawn of a millennial age of equality and justice. Yet, to achieve these visions of the common good, they espoused means inseparable from the individual pursuit of one's own spiritual and temporal well-being. They assumed that the leveling of aristocracy, root and branch, in all areas of human endeavor would naturally draw people together in harmony and equality. In this way, religious movements fervent about preserving the supernatural in everyday life had the ironic effect of accelerating the breakup of traditional society and the advent of a social order given over to competition, self-expression, and free enterprise. In this moment of fervent democratic aspiration, insurgent religious leaders had no way to foresee that their own assault upon mediating structures could lead to a society in which grasping entrepreneurs could erect new forms of tyranny in religious, political, or economic institutions. The individualization of conscience, which they so greatly prized, moved them to see the very hand of providence in a social order of free and independent persons with interests to promote.[54] Nothing better shows this process than the tumultuous career of John Leland, a career illustrating dramatically the ties in the early republic between popular religion, democratic politics, and liberal individualism.

In 1814 Leland was one of the most popular and controversial Baptists in America. He was most famous as a protagonist of religious freedom. As a leader among Virginia Baptists in the 1780s, Leland had been influential in petitioning the legislature on behalf of Jefferson's bill for religious freedom and for the bill to end the incorporation of the Protestant Episcopal Church. There is strong evidence that James Madison personally sought his support for the federal constitution, which Leland had first opposed. At the same time, Leland also marshalled Baptist opposition to slavery in Virginia. After returning to New England in 1791, he became the outstanding proponent of religious freedom as preacher, lecturer, and publicist and served two terms in the Massachusetts legislature representing the town of Cheshire.[55]

On a national level Leland was best known for the 1,235-pound "Mammoth Cheese" he had presented to President Thomas Jefferson. In New

York and Baltimore crowds flocked to see this phenomenal creation, molded in a cider press supposedly from the milk of 900 cows and bearing the motto "Rebellion to tyrants is obedience to God." Leland made the presentation to Mr. Jefferson at the White House on New Year's Day 1802 as a token of esteem from the staunchly republican citizens of Cheshire. Two days later, at the president's invitation, he preached before both houses of Congress on the text "And behold a greater than Solomon is here." One congressman who heard that sermon, Manasseh Cutler, a Massachusetts Federalist and Congregationalist clergyman, had few kind words to say about Leland's politics or his religion, dismissing "the cheesemonger" as a "poor ignorant, illiterate, clownish creature." "Such a farrago, bawled with stunning voice, horrid tone, frightful grimaces, and extravagant gestures, I believe, was never heard by any decent auditory before. . . . Such an outrage upon religion, the Sabbath, and common decency, was extremely painful to every sober, thinking person present." [56]

Leland's political notoriety has often masked the fact that fundamentally he was a preacher and itinerant evangelist. In 1824 he confessed that he had preached 8,000 times, had baptized over 1,300 persons, had known almost 1,000 Baptist preachers, and had traveled an equivalent of three times round the world. [57] Given Leland's stature and connections, it is not at all surprising that he attended the Baptists' first Triennial Convention in Philadelphia and preached at William Staughton's church the night before the first session. That sermon sounded a sharp alarm for Baptists who were hungry for respectability. Even before any decision had been made about forming a missions organization, Leland warned against the danger of "Israel" insisting on having a king so that they could be like other nations: "like the people now-a-days; they form societies, and they must have a president and two or three vice-presidents, to be like their neighbors around them." [58] After Baptists joined the Protestant quest for voluntary association, Leland stepped up his attacks upon missionary agencies and the clerical elites that stood behind them. For the next decade and a half, he went on the offensive against the organizational schemes and clerical professionalism at the core of American Protestant denominations. Leland ridiculed the mercenary foundation of foreign and domestic missions, [59] the oppression of "a hierarchical clergy—despotic judiciary—[and] an aristocratic host of lawyers," [60] the mechanical operations of theological seminaries, the tyranny of formal structures, [61] and the burden of creedalism—"this Virgin Mary between the souls of men and the Scriptures." In a letter to John Taylor, the stalwart foe of mission activity in Kentucky, Leland confessed in 1830 that his calling had been "to watch and check *clerical hierarchy*, which assumes as many shades as a chameleon."[62]

John Leland had every reason to take up the path of order and decorum that appealed to other Baptist leaders. Yet he seemed to come out of Revolutionary times with a different set of impulses stirring within. Rather than looking for ways to instill energy in government and to promote vigorous central policies, Leland sought at every step to restrain the accumulation of power. "I would as soon give my vote to a wolf to be a shepherd," he said in an oration celebrating American independence in 1802, "as to a man, who is always contending for the energy of government, to be a ruler."[63] John Leland's dissent flowed out of a passion for religious liberty that exalted the individual conscience over creedal systems, local control over powerful ecclesiastical structures, and popular sensibility over the instincts of the educated and powerful. As prolific publicist, popular hymn-writer, amusing and satirical preacher, Leland strongly advocated freedom in every sphere of life. Self-reliant to an eccentric degree, Leland is fascinating and important in his own right. He also stands as an important bridge between the Revolutionary era and the quest for localism and independence that confounded Baptist history through the Jacksonian period. The importance of this story, played out on the fringes of denominational life, is not fully appreciated given its lack of coherence and the orientation of early denominational historians to celebrate the opposite, the growth of respectability and organizational coherence.[64]

Brought up as a fervent New Light, John Leland found resources to accept, even defend, his own "rusticity of manners."[65] Chief among these was a Jeffersonian view of conscience that championed intellectual self-reliance. In a pamphlet published in 1792 attacking the New England Standing Order, Leland explained how he came to trust his own reasoning rather than the conclusions of great men. Having once had "profound reverence" for leading civic figures, Leland discovered that in reality "not two of them agreed."

> What, said I, do *great* men differ? boys, women and little souls do; but can learned, wise patriots disagree so much in judgment? If so, they cannot all be right, but they may all be wrong, and therefore *Jack Nips for himself.*[66]

Leland hammered out his view of conscience as he battled the state-church tradition of Virginia during the 1780s and of New England thereafter. In over thirty pamphlets and regular contributions to Phinehas Allen's staunchly Jeffersonian *Pittsfield Sun*, Leland spelled out a vision of personal autonomy that colored his personal life, his theological views, and his conception of society.

As early as 1790 Leland began to sound his clarion call that conscience should be "free from human control." His passion was to protect the "empire of conscience," the court of judgment in every human soul, from the inevitable encroachments of state-church traditions, oppressive creeds, ambitious and greedy clergymen—even from family tradition. "For a man to contend for religious liberty on the court-house green, and deny his wife, children and servants, the liberty of conscience at home, is a paradox not easily reconciled. . . . each one must give an account of himself to God."[67] Upon returning to New England in 1791, Leland assailed the Standing Order in a pamphlet entitled *The Rights of Conscience Inalienable . . . or, The High-flying Churchman, Stripped of his Legal Robe, Appears a Yaho* (New London, 1791). With language borrowed directly from Jefferson's *Notes on the State of Virginia*, he argued that truth can stand on its own without the props of legal or creedal defense. He reiterated the theme that "religion is a matter between God and individuals."[68] In addition to repeating his warning to parents that it was "iniquitous to bind the consciences" of children, Leland clarified his explicitly democratic view of conscience: that the so-called wise and learned were actually less capable of mediating truth than were common people. Leland dismissed the common objection that "the ignorant part of the community are not capacited to judge for themselves":

> Did many of the rulers believe in Christ when he was upon earth? Were not the learned clergy (the scribes) his most inveterate enemies? Do not great men differ as much as little men in judgment? Have not almost all lawless errors crept into the world through the means of wise men (so called)? Is not a simple man, who makes nature and reason his study, a competent judge of things? Is the Bible written (like Caligula's laws) so intricate and high, that none but the letter learned (according to the common phrase) can read it? Is not the vision written so plain that he that runs may read it?[69]

In an 1801 sermon, *A Blow at the Root*, published in five editions in four different states from Vermont to Georgia, Leland continued to project an image of the autonomous person besieged by the coercive forces of state, creed, tradition, and clerical hierarchy. The political triumph of Jefferson, the "*Man of the People*," convinced Leland that the "genius of America," which had been slumbering, had finally "arisen, like a lion, from the swelling of Jordon, and roared like thunder in the states, 'we will be free; we will rule ourselves; our officers shall be honorable servants, but not mean masters.'"[70]

Leland's legacy is an exaggerated opposition to official Christianity. He articulated a twofold persuasion that operated powerfully in the hinterland of Baptist church life: an aversion to central control and a quest for self-reliance. One reason that it is so difficult to write Baptist history in the early republic is that centrifugal forces were so powerfully at work, giving free reign to regional distinctives and take-charge entrepreneurs. Whatever success cosmopolitan leaders like Richard Furman or Francis Wayland had in building central institutions, their way was dogged at very step: by serious defections to the antiformalist appeals of Alexander Campbell and, later, William Miller,[71] by the rise of significant Antimission Baptist associations in regions as diverse as New York, Pennsylvania, Illinois, Kentucky, and North Carolina; and by the appearance of charismatic dissenters such as J. R. Graves and his Landmark Baptists.[72] Equally important was the entrenched opposition to central authority among those who remained within the regular Baptist fold. The Triennial Convention, after all, had never represented Baptist churches themselves, but only individuals and societies willing to pay appropriate dues to the organization. After 1826 it was virtually dismembered when its champions from different regions locked horns over issues of authority and control.[73]

John Leland is also important because of the way he turned a quest for self-reliance into a godly crusade. Like Elias Smith, James O'Kelly, Lorenzo Dow, Barton Stone, and William Miller, he fervently believed that individuals had to make a studied effort to prune away natural authorities: church, state, college, seminary, even family. Leland's message carried the combined ideological leverage of evangelical urgency and Jeffersonian promise. Choosing simple language and avoiding doctrinal refinements, he proclaimed a divine economy that was atomistic and competitive rather than wholistic and hierarchical. The triumph of liberal individualism, in this form at least, was not something imposed upon the people of America from above. They gladly championed the promise of personal autonomy as a message they could understand and a cause to which they could subscribe—in God's name no less.

Notes

1. Two recent books are superb on these themes: Robert H. Wiebe, *The Opening of American Society* (New York: Knopf, 1984), particularly ch. 8, "Revolution in Choices"; and Sean Wilentz, *Chants Democratic: New York City and the Rise of the American Working Class, 1788–1850* (New York: Oxford University Press, 1984). See also James A. Henretta, *The Evolution of American Society, 1700–1815* (Lexington, MA: Heath, 1973); Robert A. Gross, *The Minute Men and Their World* (New York: Hill and Wang, 1976); Edward Countryman, *A*

People in Revolution: The American Revolution and Political Society in New York, 1760–1790 (Baltimore: Johns Hopkins University Press, 1981); and Joyce Appleby, *Capitalism and a New Social Order: The Republican Vision of the 1790s* (New York: New York University Press, 1984). My own book, *The Democratization of American Christianity* (New Haven: Yale University Press, 1989), expands on the themes of this chapter in a more general consideration of religion in the early republic.

2. Henry Mayer, *A Son of Thunder: Patrick Henry and the American Republic* (New York: Watts, 1986), 444–445. On the rise of public opinion as an authority, see Gordon S. Wood, "The Democratization of Mind in the American Revolution," *Leadership in the American Revolution* (Washington, DC: Library of Congress, 1974), 63–89.

3. Wiebe, *Opening*, 142–144. Daniel A. Cohen has provided an insightful interpretation of the young hero of Charles Brockden Brown's novel, *Arthur Mervyn* (1799), as the story of a young man's struggle for survival and success in an age in which it was no longer clear how a young man was supposed to behave. Cohen sees Arthur Mervyn as caught between, on the one hand, the conflicting demands of traditional social patterns based on landed property, ascriptive rank, authoritative moral inculcation, household apprenticeship, and ordered general succession and, on the other, a disordered and relentlessly competitive social world—that is, between morality as submission to authority or morality as autonomous enlightened reason. "Arthur Mervyn and His Elders," *William and Mary Quarterly* 3rd ser., 43 (1986): 362–380.

4. Rowland Berthoff suggests about the early nineteenth century that it is difficult to write "a coherent account of so disjunctive a history." "The assumption persists that the history of America can be written without reflecting on what was missing from its unestablished religion, self-made elite, negligible government, discontinuous literary tradition, and loyalty to lofty but impersonal abstractions." See "Writing a History of Things Left Out," *Reviews in American History* 14 (1986): 1–16.

5. The phrase is from John Murrin in "The Great Inversion, or Court Versus Country: A Comparison of the Revolution Settlements in England (1688–1721) and America (1776–1816)," in J. G. A. Pocock, ed., *Three British Revolutions: 1641, 1688, 1776* (Princeton: Princeton University Press, 1980), 425.

6. R. Laurence Moore, *Religious Outsiders and the Making of Americans* (New York: Oxford University Press, 1986), 3–24.

7. Gordon S. Wood makes this argument in "Ideology and the Origins of Liberal America," *William and Mary Quarterly*, 3rd ser., 44 (1987): 637.

8. The canonical eighteenth-century distinction between vulgar and refined language denied the possibility of virtuous intelligence in vernacular expression. In the age of democratic revolution no change was more essential and far-reaching than the act of faith that attributed virtue to the vernacular expression of ordinary people. On this intellectual revolution, see Olivia Smith, *The Politics of Language, 1791–1819* (New York: Oxford University Press, 1984).

9. Appleby, *Capitalism and a New Social Order*, 79.

10. George A. Rawlyk, *Ravished by the Spirit: Religious Revivals, Baptists, and Henry Alline* (Toronto: McGill-Queens University Press, 1984), 14.

11. Doris Elizabeth Anderews, "Popular Religion and the Revolution in the Middle Atlantic Ports: The Rise of the Methodists, 1770-1800" (Ph.D. diss., Princeton University, 1986), 140. Richard Bushman, *Joseph Smith and the Beginnings of Mormonism* (Urbana, IL: University of Illinois Press, 1984), 59.

12. In a similar sense, Lawrence Goodwyn defines the populist movement of the late nineteenth century in democratic terms not because of its achievement but because of the intense democratic aspirations and hope that gave it birth. See *Democratic Promise: The Populist Movement in America* (New York: Oxford University Press, 1976).

13. Richard Carwardine, "Methodist Ministers and the Second Party System," in Russell E. Richey and Kenneth E. Rowe eds., *Rethinking Methodist History: A Bicentennial Historical Consultation* (Nashville: Abingdon, 1985), 134. David Benedict, *A General History of the Baptist Denomination*, 2 vols. (Boston: Lincoln and Edmonds, 1813), II, 552-553. Timothy L. Smith, *Revivalism and Social Reform: American Protestantism on the Eve of the Civil War* (Nashville: Abingdon, 1957), 22. C. C. Goss, *Statistical History of the First Century of American Methodism* (New York: Carlton and Porter, 1866), 106.

14. Michael Walzer, *The Revolution of the Saints: A Study in the Origins of Radical Politics* (Cambridge, MA: Harvard University Press, 1965), 1-21; and "Puritanism as a Revolutionary Ideology," *History and Theory* 3 (1964): 59-90.

15. W. R. Ward, "The Legacy of John Wesley: The Pastoral Office in Britain and America," in Anne Whiteman, J. C. Bromley, and P. G. M. Dickson, eds., *Statesmen, Scholars and Merchants: Essays in Eighteenth-Century History Presented to Dame Lucy Sutherland* (Oxford: Oxford University Press, 1973), 346-348.

16. Ralph E. Morrow, "The Great Revival, the West, and the Crisis of the Church," in John F. McDermott, ed., *The Frontier Re-Examined* (Urbana, IL: University of Illinois Press, 1967), 72.

17. Parsons Cooke, *A Century of Puritanism and a Century of Its Opposites* (Boston: Whipple, 1855), 258, quoted in Paul G. Faler, *Mechanics and Manufacturers in the Early Industrial Revolution: Lynn, Massachusetts, 1780-1860* (Albany: State University of New York Press, 1981), 47.

18. Richard Carwardine has argued that many of the "new measures" supposedly introduced by Charles Finney (the "anxious bench," women praying in public, colloquial preaching, protracted meetings) had been widely employed by the Methodists before Finney. See "The Second Great Awakening in the Urban Centers: An Examination of Methodism and the 'New Measures,'" *Journal of American History* 59 (1972): 327-340. For the innovative techniques of the Methodists, see Terry D. Bilhartz, *Urban Religion and the Second Great Awakening: Church and Society in Early National Baltimore* (Rutherford, NJ: Farleigh Dickinson University Press, 1986).

19. Lawrence Goodwyn, *The Populist Movement: A Short History of the Agrarian Revolt in America* (New York: Oxford University Press, 1978), vii–xxiv, 34–35, 293–296.

20. W. P. Strickland, ed., *Autobiography of Dan Young, a New England Preacher of Olden Time* (New York: Carlton and Porter, 1860), 34.

21. John M'Lean, ed., *Sketch of Rev. Philip Gatch* (Cincinnati: Swormstedt and Poe, 1854), 135.

22. The itinerant Methodist Joshua Thomas reported two such incidents with Dow. See Adam Wallace, *The Parson of the Islands: A Biography of the Rev. Joshua Thomas* (Philadelphia: Merrill, 1861), 76, 59.

23. Moore, *Religious Outsiders*, 3–21. Richard Carwardine has also made this point: "Yet later denominational and local church historians often under emphasized or deliberately ignored a side of evangelical life whose emotionalism, disorder, and impropriety were an embarrassment to them." *Transatlantic Revivalism: Popular Evangelicalism in Britain and America, 1790–1865* (Westport, CT: Greenwood, 1978), xiv.

24. For examples of the focus on cities and industrial workers, see Faler, *Mechanics and Manufacturers*; Charles G. Steffen, *The Mechanics of Baltimore: Workers and Politics in the Age of the Revolution, 1763–1812* (Urbana, IL: University of Illinois Press, 1984); and Wilentz, *Chants Democratic*. Wilentz is perceptive in treating the role of popular religion in New York City, particularly the role of Methodism, but religion remains only incidental to his work.

25. David Hempton notes this about the work of E. P. Thompson, in *Methodism and Politics in British Society, 1750–1850* (Stanford: Stanford University Press, 1984), 75–76.

26. Elias Smith devoted a sermon of 120 pages to the subject of how republican values should be applied to the church. See his *The Whole World Governed by a Jew; or the Government of the Second Adam, as King and Priest* (Exeter, NH: Roulet, 1805).

27. Carwardine, "Methodist Ministers and the Second Party System," 134–147.

28. W. H. Oliver, *Prophets and Millennialists* (Auckland: Oxford University Press, 1978), 235.

29. John Taylor, *Millennial Star* (London, November 15, 1847).

30. These phrases are from a camping song for Smith written by Parley Pratt. Quoted in Levette J. Davidson, "Mormon Songs," *Journal of American Folklore* 58 (1945): 277.

31. Rigdon's sermon was reported in a Mormon newspaper published by Joseph Smith's brother William. See *The Prophet*, June 8, 1844, p. 2, as quoted by Marvin S. Hill, "The Role of Christian Primitivism in the Origins and Development of the Mormon Kingdom, 1830–1844" (Ph.D. diss., University of Pennsylvania, 1968), 72–73.

32. Abel Stevens, *The Life of Nathan Bangs, D.D.* (New York: Carlton and Porter, 1863), 1–65.

33. Ibid., 182.

34. Ibid., 183.

35. Nathan Bangs, *A History of the Methodist Episcopal Church*, 4 vols. (New York: Methodist Book Concern, 1840–1853), II, 105.

36. Stevens, *Life of Nathan Bangs*, 184–185.

37. *The Doctrines and Discipline of the Methodist Episcopal Church* (New York: Methodist Book Concern, 1820), 165.

38. Samuel A. Seaman, *Annals of New York Methodism* (New York, 1892), 219, as quoted in Emory Stevens Bucke, ed., *The History of American Methodism*, 3 vols. (New York: Abingdon, 1964), I, 626.

39. Stevens, *Life of Nathan Bangs*, 239–252. By 1860, the Methodist Book Concern, with Eastern and Western branches and five depositories, employed four "Book Agents," twelve editors for its periodicals, 460 other workers, and between twenty and thirty cylinder and power presses. Its multiple periodicals had an aggregate circulation of over one million copies per month, and its quadrennial sales for the period ending in 1860 were over one million dollars (ibid., 248–249).

40. Bangs, *History of the Methodist Church*, IV, 434.

41. As early as 1820 Bangs proposed a seminary in New York, a move bitterly opposed by the same people who balked at building a new John Street Church. In 1824 Bangs was also unsuccessful in persuading the General Conference of the Methodist Church to establish a central college or university. Stevens, *Life of Nathan Bangs*, 232, 254.

42. Bangs, *History of the Methodist Church*, IV, 70.

43. Ibid., 289, 281–282.

44. *Journal of the General Conference of the Methodist Episcopal Church* (New York, 1844), 157.

45. William B. Sprague, *Annals of the American Pulpit*, Vol. VII, *The Methodists* (New York: Carters, 1865), 112–114.

46. For a description of this process in camp meetings around Baltimore ca. 1820, see Bilhartz, *Urban Religion and the Second Great Awakening*, 93–94.

47. *Autobiography of Peter Cartwright, the Backwoods Preacher*, ed. W. P. Strickland (New York: Methodist Book Concern, 1856), 481.

48. Donald G. Tewksbury, *The Founding of American Colleges and Universities Before the Civil War* (New York: Teachers College, Columbia University, 1932), 104–106, 115–117.

49. Carwardine, "Methodist Ministers and the Second Party System," 140.

50. Bertram Wyatt-Brown, "The Antimission Movement in the Jacksonian South: A Study in Regional Folk Culture," *Journal of Southern History* 36 (1970): 528.

51. Ibid., 503.

52. Alexander M'Lean, *An Appeal to the Public* (Belchertown, MA: Warren, 1828), 4, 6, 54–55, as quoted in Steven J. Novak, "The Perils of Respectability: Methodist Schisms of the 1820s," unpublished paper, American Historical Association, 1980.

53. Walter Brownlow Posey, *The Baptist Church in the Lower Mississippi Valley, 1776–1845* (Lexington, KY: University at Kentucky Press, 1957), 115–127.

54. The religious sources on which this chapter depends bear out the contention of Gordon S. Wood that a liberal social order was not simply foisted on the country by merchants and aristocrats, but percolated up from the convictions of the mass of ordinary Americans. See the lively discussion on these issues in the essays on Wood's book, *The Creation of the American Republic, 1776–1787*, in the *William and Mary Quarterly*, 3rd ser., 44 (1987): 549–640, particularly the essays by Gary B. Nash, John M. Murrin, and Gordon S. Wood. My own perspective has also been influenced by Appleby, *Capitalism and a New Social Order*.

55. The best assessments of Leland's activities are L. H. Butterfield, "Elder John Leland, Jeffersonian Itinerant," *Proceedings of the American Antiquarian Society* 62 (1953): 155–242; William G. McLoughlin, *New England Dissent, 1630–1833: The Baptists and the Separation of Church and State*, 2 vols. (Cambridge, MA: Harvard University Press, 1971), II, 915–938; and Edwin S. Gaustad, "The Backus-Leland Tradition," *Foundations: A Baptist Journal of History and Theology* 2 (1959): 131–152. On Leland's antislavery activity in Virginia, see James D. Essig, *The Bonds of Wickedness: American Evangelicals Against Slavery, 1770–1808* (Philadelphia: Temple University Press, 1982), 67–72.

56. W. P. Cutler and J. P. Cutler, *Life, Journals and Correspondence of Rev. Manasseh Cutler*, 2 vols. (Cincinnati: Clarke, 1888), II, 66–67. On the creation and presentation of the cheese, see Butterfield, "Elder John Leland," 214–229.

57. L. F. Greene, ed., *The Writings of John Leland* (New York: G. W. Wood, 1845), 513–515.

58. Ibid., 377.

59. On Leland's significant role in Antimission activities, see Byron Cecil Lambert, *The Rise of the Anti-Mission Baptists: Sources and Leaders, 1800–1840* (New York: Ayer, 1980), 116–152.

60. Leland, "A Little Sermon Sixteen Minutes Long," in *Writings of John Leland*, 410.

61. Leland's opposition to formal theological education was expressed in a widely circulated poem, "The Modern Priest."

62. Leland, *The Virginia Chronicle* (Fredericksburg; Prentis and Baxter, 1790), 34. "Extracts from a Letter to Rev. John Taylor of Kentucky, Dated Dec. 10, 1830," in *Writings of John Leland*, 601.

63. Leland, *An Oration Delivered at Cheshire, July 5, 1802, on the Celebration of Independence* (Hudson, NY: Allen, 1802), 12.

64. Three early historians of the Baptists in America all chronicle the rise of a movement from persecution to respectability. All make an implicit appeal that Baptists be accorded the same respect as were other churches. See Robert B. Semple, *A History of the Rise and Progress of the Baptists in Virginia* (Richmond: Lynch, 1810); David Benedict, *A General History of the Baptist Denomination* (Boston: Lincoln and Edwards, 1813); and Isaac Backus, *A History of*

New England with Particular Reference to the Denomination of Christians Called Baptists (Newton, MA: Backus Historical Society, 1871). The same approach is also evident in the writing of Methodist history, as, for example, Nathan Bangs's *History of the Methodist Episcopal Church.*

65. Leland, "Events in the Life of John Leland Written by Himself," in *Writings of John Leland,* 10.

66. Leland, "The History of Jack Nips," in ibid., 76–77.

67. See Leland's discussion of "The Right and Bonds of Conscience" in his pamphlet, *The Virginia Chronicle,* 45. "Conscience," Leland wrote in 1830, "is a court of judicature, erected in every breast, to take cognizance of every action in the home department, but has nothing to do with another man's conduct. My best judgment tells me that my neighbor does wrong, but my conscience has nothing to say of it. Were I to do as he does, my conscience would arrest and condemn me, but guilt is not transferable. Every one must give an account of himself" ("Transportation of Mail," in *Writings of John Leland,* 565).

68. Leland, *The Rights of Conscience Inalienable . . . or, The High-flying Churchman, Stript of his Legal robe, Appears a Yaho* (New London: Green, 1791), 8. Elsewhere Leland argued explicitly that truth would prevail in a free market of ideas: "Truth is not in the least danger of being lost, when free examination is allowed" (*The Bible-Baptist* [Baltimore, 1789], in *Writings of John Leland,* 78).

69. Leland, *The Rights of Conscience Inalienable,* 15–16. Three years later, in 1794, the Congregational minister Noah Worcester expressed the very stereotype of common folk that Leland rejected. In Worcester's view, the Baptists succeeded by their ability to engage that "class of persons . . . who possess weak judgments, fickle minds, and quick and tender passions." Worcester explained that such persons "are of such low understanding, that they are incapable of duly examining the force of arguments; and may be confounded by the length and multiplicity of them, while no real conviction is afforded to their minds." Worcester, *Impartial Inquiries Respecting the Progress of the Baptist Denomination* (Worcester, MA: L. Worcester, 1794), 11–12.

70. Leland's *Blow at the Root* was published in New London and Suffield, Conn. (1801), Bennington, Vt. (1801), Edenton, N.C. (1803), and Washington, Ga. (1805).

71. Errett Gates, *The Early Relation of Baptists and Disciples* (Chicago: R. R. Donnelley, 1904); David L. Rowe, *Thunder and Trumpets: Millerites and Dissenting Religion in Upstate New York, 1800–1850* (Chico, CA: Scholars Press, 1985).

72. Byron C. Lambert, *The Rise of the Anti-Mission Baptists: Sources and Leaders, 1800–1840* (Salem, NH: Ayer, 1980); Harold L. Twiss, "Missionary Support by Baptist Churches and Associations in Western Pennsylvania, 1815–45," *Foundations: A Baptist Journal of History and Theology* 10 (1967): 36–49; and James E. Tull, *A History of Southern Baptist Landmarkism in the Light of Historical Baptist Ecclesiology* (New York: Ayer, 1980).

73. Francis Wayland, president of Brown University and editor of the *American Baptist Magazine*, had hoped to transform the Triennial Convention of 1826 into a genuine instrument of Baptist polity. Instead, the convention was virtually dismantled. New England and New York delegates, led by Wayland, were effective in discrediting Luther Rice, whose base of operations was Washington, D.C. They concentrated power in their own hands and moved the headquarters of the missions board to Boston. For a full discussion of these developments, see Winthrop S. Hudson, "Stumbling into Disorder," *Foundations: A Baptist Journal of History and Theology* 1 (1958): 45–71.

6

Religion and Politics in the Antebellum North

DANIEL WALKER HOWE

Without an understanding of the religion of the middle period there can be no understanding of the politics of the time. This is the lesson of the historiography of the antebellum republic as it has evolved over the past two generations. Because the North and South display different patterns of political culture, this essay will deal only with the North. It will address its subject through a sequence of stages. The first step is simply learning to take religion seriously in the study of political history. The second is to comprehend the nature of the great evangelical movement of the age and its consequences for society. Third, I undertake to delineate the basic religious alignments that were reflected in the politics of the second party system. My goal is to reconceptualize the relationship between antebellum politics and religion in such a way as to make the best sense out of existing knowledge. If this goal is attained, it will also help focus our future inquiries.

Taking Religion Seriously

The modern historiography of middle-period politics begins with Arthur M. Schlesinger, Jr.'s *The Age of Jackson*, published in 1945. An instant classic, the book reinterpreted its subject for the generation shaped by the New Deal. Today it remains a readable and engaging account, for Schlesinger took the isues of the second party system seriously and wrote with a narrative verve that still conveys their excitement. It is, of course, a partisan account, and this partisanship is its strength. The book's weakness stems from its failure to take religion seriously as a social and cultural force. Schlesinger's own sympathies lay unashamedly with the anticlericals of the nineteenth century, and his discussions of religious ideas in this book registered nothing except the self-interested apologetics of employers. The transforming power of the great evangelical movement of the nineteenth century utterly escaped him. As a result, his book's ability to command our attention evaporates when its author turns from such economic issues as banking, currency, and the labor movement to the religiously oriented issues of temperance, nativism, Indian policy, and, most significantly, slavery.[1]

A round of criticism of Schlesinger's work reacted against his polarization of the Jacksonians and their Whig adversaries as good and evil, respectively. But this criticism—"consensus" historiography, as we call it—did not necessarily recognize the importance of religious history. Richard Hofstadter, in his brilliant collection of essays, *The American Political Tradition and the Men Who Made It*, scathingly criticized Andrew Jackson as a man-on-the-make but demonstrated the same secularist blind spot as Schlesinger. His admiring and admirable sketch of Wendell Phillips ignored the religious background of antebellum reform, and Hofstadter didn't find Jackson's Whig opponents even worthy of discussion.[2]

Richard P. McCormick, adopting a far more sophisticated methodology, studied the formation of the second party system as a problem of organization and voter turnout. Deliberately avoiding an examination of ideology, he addressed his subject using quantitative techniques.[3] Yet, in the long run, the careful reconstruction of the political system that the elder McCormick did so much to foster has revealed features demanding a reexamination of the hearts and minds of the voters. The parties of the antebellum era commanded extraordinary enthusiasm among the voters, to judge from their high turnout, as well as extraordinary party loyalty, to judge from the consistency of voting by both electors and elected. The "new political history," as it has come to be called, has borne out the observations of contemporary observers like Tocqueville: politics seems to have been centrally important to the average man in the pre–Civil War North. What was it that so captured the imagination of the public?

Recognition of the important role of religious and moral issues in the second party system begins with Lee Benson's reinterpretation, *The Con-*

cept of Jacksonian Democracy, published in 1961. Benson saw that many of the political issues of the Whig/Jacksonian era involved judgments of moral value. Different ethnocultural or religious communities made these judgments differently, and these communities became the building blocks of party. Benson also made a contribution of lasting worth by defining the role of "negative reference groups." Voters lined up with the party in opposition to the party of their principal negative reference group. Thus Irish Catholic immigrants voted Democratic while their despised competitors, the free blacks, voted Whig—prompting many Scots-Irish Presbyterian immigrants to vote Whig in reaction against the Irish Catholic Democrats.[4]

We can now say with confidence that issues of morality and religion were built into the second party system from its inception. It has been demonstrated that the moral issues of Sabbatarianism, anti-Masonry, and Indian removal all played important parts in the shaping of that system during the 1820s. (The white opposition to Jackson's Indian removal policy was led by Presbyterian missionaries.) As Richard Carwardine has recently shown, by the time of the classic Whig-Democratic confrontation of 1840, the evangelical community was active and prominent in the Whig campaign.[5]

Out of the approach pioneered by Benson has developed what is sometimes called the "ethnocultural" interpretation of antebellum politics. An outstanding example would be Robert Kelley's fascinating overview, *The Cultural Pattern in American Politics*. This interpretation has not simply replaced the economic interpretation, but has been synthesized with it in such works as Michael Holt's *Forging a Majority: The Formation of the Republican Party in Pittsburgh* and my own *The Political Culture of the American Whigs*. How the synthesis of cultural, moral, and economic elements can be integrated into a powerful narrative history is well displayed in W. R. Brock's *Parties and Political Conscience: 1840–1850*, a work by a leading British historian of the United States that deserves to be better known in this country.[6]

This enrichment of our understanding of antebellum politics has several consequences. In the first place, it underscores the practical effects of ideas and moral values, making American political history seem more ideological than it was once the fashion to admit.[7] Second, it demonstrates more clearly than ever the continuities between the second and third party systems, including those between Whigs and Republicans.[8] This awareness feeds into the third characteristic of recent scholarship, which is the new interest taken in the Whig party. Instead of being simply the conservative opponents of Jacksonian progress, the Whigs now are seen as frequently taking initiatives—evangelical, moral, and economic. Typical of the current respect for the Whigs is the following quotation from Louise Stevenson's fine new book, *Scholarly Means to Evangelical Ends*:

> Whiggery stood for the triumph of the cosmopolitan and national over the provincial and local, of rational order over irrational spontaneity, of school-based learning over traditional folkways and customs, and of self-control over self-expression. Whigs believed that every person had the potential to become moral or good if family, school, and community nurtured the seed of goodness in his moral nature. Richard Jensen identifies Whigs as the party of modernizers who promoted some aspects of the nascent middle-class economy and society while restraining others.[9]

In this new vision, party politics are seen to express deep conflicts over cultural values.

In developing this cultural perspective, historians have turned to their sister disciplines in the social sciences. Ironically—in view of the antireligious origins of much modern social science—historians have found in the social sciences tools to help them understand and appreciate the power of religion. Students of the early American republic have been learning much from sociologists like Robert Bellah, Peter Berger, John L. Hammond, and Gerhard Lenski, from political scientists like Michael Walzer, Samuel P. Huntington, and David Greenstone, as well as from anthropologists like Mary Douglas, Victor Turner, and the oft-quoted Clifford Geertz.[10]

Armed with this understanding, we are better able to appreciate ante-bellum political culture. From this perspective, we can see that issues of moral value did not arise in American politics only with the debate over slavery expansion and the birth of the Republican party. Moral issues were as characteristic of the second party system as they were of the third. (Therefore, it becomes harder to blame the Civil War on a "blundering generation" of fanatical agitators and irresponsible politicians in the 1850s.)[11] Nor can the *style* of antebellum campaigns be separated from their *substance* and made the explanation for popular involvement. The hullaballoo surrounding the political campaigns of the era—the torch-light parades, the tent pitched outside town, the urgent call for a commit-ment—was borrowed by political campaigners from the revival preachers. Far from being irrelevant distractions or mere recreation, the evangelical techniques of mass persuasion that we associate with the campaigns of 1840 and after actually provide a clue to the moral meaning of antebellum politics. Even the practice of holding national conventions

was borrowed by the parties from the cause-oriented benevolent associations. Anti-Masonry, which held the first presidential nominating convention in 1831, was both an evangelical reform movement (a "blessed
spirit" to its supporters) and a political party.[12]

But secular prejudice dies hard. Even though it is now admitted that
the voters were interested in religion, it is not universally admitted that
religion was a "real" issue. Sometimes historians have offered evidence of
ethnoreligious voting as an illustration of how little the ignorant masses
really understood politics. Other times, historians have refused to accept
the ethnoreligious interpretation because they feel it reflects badly on the
rationality of the electorate. And even a respected and thoughtful practi-
tioner of the "new political history" has expressed the fear that it has led
us into a blind alley by showing that nineteenth-century American voters
were concerned about something so politically irrelevant as religion![13] In
my opinion, a proper assessment of antebellum political life has to start
by admitting the legitimacy and relevance of religious and moral commitments to the politics of the age. Of course, all political issues didn't have a
religious dimension, but the ones that did—antislavery, Indian policy,
nativism, temperance, education, penal reform, treatment of the insane—
were no less momentous and worthy of attention (either from our point
of view or that of nineteenth-century contemporaries) than internal improvements, currency, and the tariff.

Revivalism and American Political Culture

The prominence of evangelical piety is one of the major continuities in
American life between colonial and national times. Indeed, for all the
attention that has been devoted to the so-called Great Awakening and its
effects, it seems likely that its nineteenth-century counterparts were even
"greater" in their impact on American culture and politics. John Murrin
once remarked that the Great Awakening and its legacy probably had
even more to do with the Civil War than with the Revolution, and it is a
perceptive comment.[14] The later evangelicals became more self-conscious
as shapers of society and opinion, for they attached increasing importance to subjecting social institutions and standards to divine judgment
and "reforming"—that is, reshaping—them accordingly.

In both the eighteenth and nineteenth centuries, revivalism and democracy were interrelated phenomena. Each asserted popular claims against
those of the elite, pluralism against orthodoxy, charisma against rationalism, competitiveness against authority, an innovative Americanism

against European tradition. Such is the thrust of a vast body of distinguished scholarship, from William Warren Sweet to Perry Miller, from Richard Bushman to Patricia Bonomi.[15] Indeed, the more active popular participation in American political life became, the more important moral and religious issues came to be in politics. It is no accident that religion was more potent a political factor in the second party system than it had been at the time of the adoption of the Constitution. It is a natural consequence of the increasingly democratic nature of American politics.[16]

Yet, the popular quality of the evangelical movement was only one side of it. Revivals did not spring forth from the populace spontaneously; they were "worked up." Terry Bilhartz has reminded us (if we needed reminding) that revivals took place not simply because there was a receptive audience, but because evangelists were promoting them.[17] These evangelists had on their agenda a reformation of life and habits, both individual and communal. They were demonstrating a continuation of the historic concern for church discipline so characteristic of the early Protestant Reformers. Voluntary discipline represented Protestantism's alternative to the authoritarianism of traditional society. If popular enthusiasm was the "soft side" of the great Evangelical Movement, the new discipline was its "hard side."

The new discipline of the evangelical movement had far-reaching consequences. Its reforms did no less than reshape the cultural system of the Victorian middle class in both Britain and America. We remember its morality as strict, and indeed it was—most notably in the novel restraints it imposed on the expression or even mention of sex and the use of alcohol. But even its most punitive severity was redemptive in purpose, as the words "reformatory" and "penitentiary" suggested. Put another way, the converse of Victorian discipline was the proper development of the human faculties. Education and self-improvement went along with discipline. The evangelical reformers characteristically opposed physical violence, campaigning against corporal punishment of children, wives, sailors, and prisoners, for example. They preferred mental coercion like solitary confinement to flogging and hanging. They were didactic modernizers and civilizers who embodied their values in such institutional monuments as schools, universities, hospitals, and insane asylums.[18] Most extreme in their espousal of Victorian modernization were the abolitionists and the feminists. They applied the principles of human self-development, the fulfillment of noble potential and the repression of base passions, to different races and sexes alike.[19]

The usefulness of evangelical moral reform to the new industrial capitalism of the nineteenth century has not escaped the notice of historians, and a vast literature has developed, analyzing it in terms of bourgeois "social control." Pro-Southern and anti-Whig historians have been using this approach to discredit abolitionists and other reformers for a long time.[20] But the interpretation has taken on new vigor with the reception of neo-Marxism and the social thought of Michel Foucault in the American academy during the past generation. Its recent advocates have included Michael Katz, David J. Rothman, Paul Johnson, and—in its most sophisticated and broadly ranging form—David Brion Davis. Davis's monumental volumes on slavery and antislavery in the modern world accord full respect to the moral integrity of the abolitionists and the justice of their cause. But they also portray the abolitionists as inadvertently promoting the hegemony of bourgeois capitalism. Through natural human limitations coupled with a measure of self-deception, the reformers were blind to the full implications of what they were doing. Without their being aware of it, the antislavery crusaders were providing a moral sanction for new capitalist methods of exploitation. Their critique of chattel slavery indirectly legitimated wage slavery. In this interpretation, social control, if no longer a conscious motive, is no less a consequence of the reformers' actions and helps explain their success.[21]

The interpretation of antebellum reform as social control, in both its pre-Marxian and neo-Marxian forms, has provoked an enormous critical reaction. Typically, this criticism has argued that the reformers were motivated by moral principle rather than ambition for worldly power.[22] Many critics of the social control thesis have sought to explain the evangelicals' behavior in psychological, frequently psychoanalytic, categories. In this view, the goal of evangelical commitment was a new personal identity, rather than class interest. The most sophisticated such analysis of antebellum reformers in terms of their quest for identity is Lawrence J. Friedman's *Gregarious Saints: Self and Community in American Abolitionism*.[23] Anthropological categories have also been offered as an alternative to Marxian class analysis, as William G. McLoughlin did when he adapted the "revitalization" theory of A. F. C. Wallace to his study *Revivals, Awakenings, and Reform*. When Wallace himself turned to antebellum history in his community study of Rockdale, Pennsylvania, however, he combined anthropological "thick description" with a crudely Marxist historical narrative featuring evil Christian Businessmen who first destroy their town's harmonious social relationships and then embark their section on a war of conquest over the South.[24]

The present state of historiography leaves unresolved two different perceptions of evangelical Christianity. The scholarship on the eighteenth century treats evangelical Christianity as a democratic and liberating force, whereas much of the literature on the evangelical movement of the nineteenth century emphasizes its implications for social control. Did some dramatic transformation of the revival impulse come about at the turn of the century? I would argue not; historians have concentrated on the "soft" and "hard" sides of evangelicalism in the eighteenth and nineteenth centuries, respectively, but both were consistently present. Evangelical Protestantism did not mysteriously mutate from a democratic and liberating impulse into an elitist and repressive one when it moved from the eighteenth to the nineteenth century. Austerity and self-discipline were present even in eighteenth-century evangelicalism; individual autonomy was asserted even in nineteenth-century evangelicalism. The problem is that our idea of "social control," implying *one* person or group imposing constraints on *another*, is appropriate for some aspects of the reform impulse, like the treatment of the insane, but not all. It does not take account of the embrace of *self*-discipline, so typical of evangelicals.

The essence of evangelical commitment to Christ is that it is undertaken voluntarily, consciously, and responsibly, by the individual for himself or herself. (That, after all, is why evangelicals, in any century, are not content to let a person's Christianity rest on baptism in infancy.) If we can substitute the more comprehensive category of "discipline" for that of "social control," we will be in a better position to understand the evangelical movement and the continuties between its colonial and antebellum phases. We will also be able to deal with the important psychological issues of personal identity that have been raised by the critics of the social control interpretation. Evangelical Christians were and are people who have consciously decided to take charge of their own lives and identities. The Christian discipline they embrace is at one and the same time liberating and restrictive. Insofar as this discipline is self-imposed it expresses the popular will; insofar as it is imposed on others it is social control.

The existing historical literature poses at least one other major problem. Conspicuously absent from the historiography until recently has been an approach that would acknowledge a relationship between evangelical reform and modern capitalism without using this connection to disparage reform. David Brion Davis, as we have seen, took the first step away from this, but he still regarded its connection with capitalism as a tragic limitation of nineteenth-century reform. A significant breakthrough has been achieved in this respect by Thomas Haskell. In a subtle and persuasive pair of articles, Haskell argues that nineteenth-century humanitarianism was the daughter of the capitalist system and a child of the market mentality *without* being an instrument of social control, intended or unintended. Haskell links humanitarian reform with the experience of the marketplace and the ideology of possessive individualism in two important ways: (1) the emphasis on covenants, or promise-keeping, and (2) the emphasis on causal perception, which encouraged people "to attend to the remote consequences of their actions." These two cultural traits, he argues, expanded the "cognition" of the people living in the new world of capitalism, heightening their moral sensitivity and producing humanitarian reform. Where Davis saw humanitarianism helping capitalism, Haskell sees capitalism fostering humanitarianism. And where Davis linked the two through the mechanism of unconscious motivation, Haskell links them through an expansion of conscious awareness.[25]

Haskell has connected the mentality of nineteenth-century reform to the political economy of capitalism. The moral philosophy of the age, within which political economy was originally a subdivision, also shows the connection between nineteenth-century reform and the disciplined development of human potential.[26] Overall, the new understanding of "cognitive style" supplied by Haskell would appear to supplement but not supplant "social control" as an aspect of nineteenth-century reform. Haskell looked primarily at abolitionism, but the element of social control is undeniable in movements more closely connected with party politics than abolitionism was, movements like temperance, penal reform, or asylums for the insane. The progression from self-discipline/ self-liberation to the benevolent discipline and liberation of others was natural and inevitable; indeed, the progression could also occur the other way around, notably in the case of women.[27] What needs to be found is a way of conceptualizing humanitarian reform that can subsume both social control and personal identity, as well as make profitable use of Haskell's discovery of the positive impact of modern capitalism on moral rationality and cognition. The study of "discipline" in the Puritan/ evangelical religious tradition could provide the answer.

The cultural impulse toward discipline manifested in evangelicalism can be viewed (as its contemporary practitioners did) as a positive and humanizing goal, especially when placed in the context provided by antebellum moral philosophy. The converse of liberating a battered wife in Victorian America might well be imposing discipline on her drunken husband. While compatible with a capitalist system, evangelical moral discipline was by no means equivalent to a desire to strengthen the hand of capitalists within that system. To escape from the dilemma of equating evangelicalism simply with capitalist social control, there is something to be said for looking at nineteenth-century reform as an example of "modernization" rather than of "capitalism." Socialist modernizing societies, after all, find it just as necessary as capitalist ones to impose new forms of discipline.[28]

Two works on the social history of Victorian Britain can provide models for an understanding of evangelical reform in America as well: Brian Harrison's study of temperance and Thomas Laqueur's study of Sunday schools. Both of them break free of the paradigm of social control, by showing how the movements in question transcended class lines. These evangelical reform causes were as much the product of working-class self-help and the voluntary pursuit of order, dignity, and decency as they were of middle-class paternalism.[29] Once the autonomy of evangelical reform and its supporters has been recognized, we can then see how, in the world of the nineteenth century, they would sometimes be found supporting or encouraging capitalism and other times criticizing it or counteracting its consequences.[30]

Haskell has shown that the capitalist rationality of the marketplace fostered humanitarian reform by enhancing the conscious powers of moral perception. The next step, if this conceptual breakthrough is to be properly exploited, will be to see how his analysis of the origins of humanitarianism relates to the Christian tradition. We will never understand nineteenth-century reform in *merely* humanitarian or political terms. We must link humanitarian reform with the Christian tradition and its discipline. For it was the explosive combination of humanitarianism plus Christianity that gave the world the evangelical movement and its attendant reforms. The evangelical emphasis on conscious, voluntary decision, and action represents a conjunction of Christianity with modernity. The new personal identity the evangelical attained was both follower of Christ *and* rational, autonomous individual—paradoxical as that may seem to some historians today. And in the America of the nineteenth century, it was the institutional and emotional resources of Christianity that typically empowered humanitarian reform.[31]

Ecumenicism versus Confessionalism

The evangelical movement of antebellum America was in many respects the functional equivalent of an established church. Although voluntary rather than compulsory in its basis, the evangelical movement shared with the traditional religious establishments of European countries the goal of a Christian society. For nineteenth-century evangelicals this goal was defined as something to be achieved rather than something to be maintained. To meet the goal entailed a gigantic effort of organization.[32] The revival established what contemporaries called "a benevolent empire": an interlocking network of voluntary associations, large and small, local, national, and international, to implement its varied purposes. The objectives of these voluntary societies ranged from antislavery to temperance, from opposing dueling to opposing Sunday mails, from the defense of the family to the overthrow of the papacy, from women's self-help support groups to the American Sunday School Union, from the American Bible Society to the National Truss Society for the Relief of the Ruptured Poor.[33]

This organizing process was the religious counterpart of the so-called American System, the political program of Henry Clay and the Whig party. Both wanted to impose system and direction upon the amorphousness of American society. Whether addressing religious and moral issues on the one hand, or banking, the tariff, internal improvements, and land sales on the other, the evangelical movement and the American System stood for conscious planning and uniformity rather than laissez-faire and diversity. What is more, both put their trust in the same leadership class of prosperous mercantile laity.[34] One reason why the Whigs may have been slower than the Democrats to accept the legitimacy of political parties is that the Protestant benevolent societies provided Whigs with an alternative mode of organizing in pursuit of their social objectives. Certainly the Whigs were no less "modern" than the Democrats in their outlook, no less "issue-oriented," and no less willing to make use of the new media of communication.[35] But the rise of political parties could only undercut the influence of the cause-oriented voluntary associations.

One of the features of the evangelical movement suggestive of an established church was its Protestant ecumenicism.[36] Led by laymen and, in a remarkable number of cases, laywomen, the evangelical movement was to a large degree emancipated from control by denominationally organized clergy. The laity was disposed toward interdenominational cooperation by considerations both practical and principled. In practical terms, ecumenicism made for efficiencies of scale. In ideological terms, it reflected a decline of interest in theological distinctions that had often formed the basis for denominational differentiation, accompanied by a rising sense of American nationality and national moral responsibility. For the American evangelical movement, the nation had taken on the character of a Christian community, within which members shared moral responsibility.

This ecumenicism, along with much else about the great revival, was controversial. The First Awakening had split Americans into New Lights and Old, and the Second was every bit as divisive. Just as there were people who objected to the imposition of political control by the Whig American System, there were those who objected to the imposition of the religious and moral discipline of the evangelical movement. If the evangelical movement was the American religious "establishment," its opponents were the American "dissenters." J. C. D. Clark has recently reinterpreted English politics of the early nineteenth century in terms of religious ideological conflict between Anglicans and Dissenters.[37] There is good reason to believe that a somewhat analogous religious conflict was almost as central to political life in the United States.[38]

The opponents of the revival may be characterized as "confessionalists," people who attached primary importance to bearing witness to the truth as they saw it. They did not share in the declining interest in theological distinctions, and they were unwilling to subsume their differences under the ecumenical banner of the revival. Often their religious loyalties were underscored by ethnic identifications. Among these confessionalists were Roman Catholics, Old School Presbyterians, Missouri Synod Lutherans, Dutch "True" Calvinists, Antimission Baptists, Latter-day Saints, and Orthodox Jews. (It is not entirely possible to define the opponents of the revival in denominational terms, since, as we have seen, its support was not defined in denominational terms either.) For our purposes, the handful of avowed freethinkers count as confessionalists, since they too were critics of the revival. What all these disparate groups had in common was a grim determination to preserve their independence in the face of the evangelical juggernaut.[39] To them, evangelical ecumenicism looked like religious imperialism. As the Jeffersonian Republicans had rallied deists and sectarians in opposition to the Anglican and Congregational establishments of the late eighteenth century, the Jacksonian Democrats became the party of those opposed to the ecumenical evangelical "establishment" of the antebellum era.[40]

Dedicated as they were to particularism and diversity, the confessional Democrats found doctrines of little government congenial. The natural rights philosophy of the Jacksonians asserted the individual's claims to be protected against interference from officious, ecumenical reformers. An emphasis on the separation of church and state was the logical complement of this philosophy, for it removed everything having to do with religion from the potential interference of government. The religious outgroups of the Jacksonian era were the heirs of the Jeffersonian Baptist John Leland. "Leland's legacy is an exaggerated opposition to official

Christianity," writes Nathan Hatch. "He articulated a twofold persuasion that operated powerfully in the hinterland of Baptist church life: an aversion to central control and a quest for self-reliance."[41]

On the whole, historians of the Democratic party have found less reason to discuss religion than historians of the Whig party. The political strategy of the Democrats—indeed, their very raison d'être—dictated a political secularism. Thus, for example, Jean H. Baker's fine study of the political culture of the antebellum Northern Democrats scarcely mentions religion. Had she looked into the subject, Baker would probably have been led to a conclusion similar to that of Sean Wilentz, in his study of the New York City Working Men's party. Stressing the diversity of religious opinion among his subjects, Wilentz concludes that "the artisans' disparate religious views provided a rough analogue to their democratic politics, opposed to all men of 'insolent morality' who would ratify their presumed social superiority with the Word of God."[42] When the Working Men's party did not succeed as a separate organization, it merged into the Democratic party. The freedom such people prized was "freedom from," while the goal of the Whigs was "freedom to."

The initiative in the great competition between ecumenicals and confessionals lay with the evangelicals. One of the differences between that America and our own was the dominant culture-shaping power of antebellum evangelical Christianity. It was the evangelicals who then formed what Ronald P. Formisano has termed the "core" of the national culture; the confessionalists occupied the "periphery."[43] The analogy already suggested with the Whig economic program continues helpful: Schlesinger interpreted the politics of the Jacksonian age in terms of a conflict between the powerful "business community" on the one hand and all the other interest groups in society on the other, forced to make common cause to protect themselves. In the cultural interpretation, the evangelicals become the counterparts of Schlesinger's business community, and the confessionalists, the alliance of outgroups. This analogy should not compel us to regard the confessionalists as the heroes of the story. But it should remind us not to focus exclusively on the evangelical core, that the religions of the periphery do have a fascinating cultural history (or, rather, histories) of their own. How several such bodies have reinforced their identity by using mainstream American society as a negative reference group is the theme of R. Laurence Moore's recent book, *Religious Outsiders*, a model study that avoids idealizing either side in the cultural conflict it portrays.[44]

The core/periphery metaphor has been applied to many other countries as well and lends itself to comparative study. One of the most interesting of the comparative treatments is Robert Kelley's *The Trans-atlantic Persuasion: The Liberal-Democratic Mind in the Age of Gladstone*. This work shows how the British Liberals, the Canadian Liberals, and the American Democrats were all parties of the ethnocultural periphery and therefore defenders of pluralism. Kelley's analogy between the American Whigs and the Anglo-Canadian Tory parties is less satisfactory, even though they did indeed all endorse national homogeneity. The difference is that in the British Empire, the evangelicals were part of the cultural periphery and aligned with the Liberal parties, whereas in the United States the evangelicals defined the cultural core.[45]

The second party system was not based in theological differences, and although the debate between Calvinism and Arminianism was one of the most interesting and sophisticated features of "high" intellectual history in nineteenth-century America, it did not define the distinction between Democrats and Whigs. Certainly, there were Calvinists and Arminians in both political parties. A theological development that was relevant, however, was the emergence of postmillennialism in American Christian thought. This doctrine taught that Christ's Second Coming will occur at the end of the thousand years of peace foretold in Scripture. The implication is that human efforts on behalf of social justice form part of the divine plan to bring about the day of the Lord. Postmillennialism became a prominent feature of the nineteenth-century evangelical movement.[46]

Of course, any major party in a two-party political system is bound to be a diverse coalition. The American Whig party included many voters who were not directly involved in the evangelical united front. Some of these Whigs shared in the perfectionist aspirations of the evangelicals but not in their creed—for example, Unitarians and Quakers. Sometimes excluded from evangelical organizations, these groups were particularly prominent in the more radical associations of the benevolent empire, addressing women's rights and antislavery. That such people became Whigs (and, later, Republicans) confirms that it was the perfectionism of the evangelicals rather than their theological orthodoxy that had political implications. Significantly, however, the heterodox perfectionists did not display as high a level of Whig party loyalty as the evangelicals, and they were often drawn into minor reform parties.[47]

The Whig party also included some people who were not evangelical even in a general sense of the term. Contemporaries were aware of this and took account of it; in the end it became the basis for the important distinction they drew between "Conscience" Whigs and "Cotton" Whigs in the North. Cotton Whigs included groups that identified with the cultural core of bourgeois British-American Protestantism but remained critical of evangelical didacticism, especially the crusade against slavery. Episcopalians and Princeton Old-School Presbyterians provide examples of this cultural conservatism. In general, such groups were not identified nearly as strongly with the Whig party as the revivalistic evangelicals were; many Episcopalians and Old School Presbyterians, for example, were Democrats. Some of them switched from Democratic to Whig affiliation only after large-scale Irish Catholic immigration had produced an important negative reference group for them.[48]

In the South things were different—which is why this paper can only deal with the North. In the South the evangelicals had never established themselves as the cultural core. Instead, the core position was occupied by the planters. Their culture, as it has been portrayed by such sensitive historians as Rhys Isaac, Eugene Genovese, Dickson D. Bruce, and Bertram Wyatt-Brown, emphasized premodern values like honor, patriarchalism, generosity, physical violence, and hedonism.[49] Evangelicalism took shape in large part as a critique of these traditional values. Conflict between the two rival value systems of the gentry and their evangelical critics has been a perennial theme of Southern cultural history, as Bertram Wyatt-Brown's chapter below describes at length. But the relative marginality of evangelical culture, like the relative marginality of the urban bourgeoisie in Southern society, left the Whig party weaker in the South than it was in the North. Furthermore, the increasing identification of the Second Great Awakening with Northern ecumenical didacticism in general and antislavery in particular alienated even devout pietists in the South. When secession finally came, it represented (as Joel Silbey has argued) the climax of Southern resistance against the threatened cultural hegemony of Northern Whig-Republicans.[50]

The most ambitious recent interpretation of the coming of the Civil War in terms of cultural conflict is that of the political scientist Anne Norton. Her book, *Alternative Americas: A Reading of Antebellum Political Culture*, emphatically affirms the centrality of the evangelical movement to Northern Whig-Republican political culture. The author demonstrates the importance of the Puritan tradition for Northern Whig-Republicans and shows the use they made of analogies with the English Civil War and the example of Cromwell. She also properly stresses the difference between North and South over the discipline and subordination of the human "passions." What was wholesome discipline to the Northern neo-Puritans represented tyranny to many white Southerners. By the time she is finished, Norton has made it very clear why seceding Southerners felt threatened by Yankee cultural imperialism.[51]

One of the most striking cultural contrasts between the sections in antebellum America lies in their receptivity to changing gender relationships. The Whig/Northern modernizing culture placed a higher value on female self-expression than the Democratic/Southern traditional one. Women played a much more active leadership role in the Northern evangelical movement than they did in the Southern resistance to it. (Conversely, the Southern cult of honor—among both the gentry and the common folk—placed more emphasis on the expression of physical "manliness" than Northern culture did.) Northern Whig women like Harriet Beecher Stowe and Sarah Josepha Hale made popular literature an instrument of evangelical didacticism—in their own expression, a "moral influence."[52] In fact, the relationship between the evangelical movement and the empowerment of women has been one of the most rewarding areas of historical research during the past generation.[53]

Conclusion: Culture and Personality

In the middle period of American history, as today, the goal of the evangelical Christian was to be born again in Christ, to become a new person. The tradition of the Reformation, which the antebellum Whig party carried on, was concerned not only with culture and politics, but also with personality and personal discipline. In this tradition, public policies were frequently reflections of private concerns. Legal prohibition of alcohol as a political issue, for example, was an outgrowth of an evangelical disciplinary impulse that was originally voluntary and individual. The only way we can understand antebellum humanitarian reform, in my judgment, is to approach it through the study of the interaction between culture and personality. In *The Political Culture of the American Whigs* I tried to show how the private struggles of prominent Whigs to shape their own personalities replicated the public conflicts of their time and the resolutions the Whig party offered for them. The model for this approach had been defined originally by Erik Erikson in his classic studies of Luther and Gandhi.[54] It is one more way in which historians of antebellum culture have drawn on the insights of the social sciences.

The values that the evangelical Whig tradition sought to implement in the antebellum North derived from the conjunction of ancient Christianity with the modern market society. As Ruth Bloch also points out in her essay in this volume, the Puritan/evangelical tradition did not simply adapt to, or borrow from, modernity and democracy; it actively helped form them. Individualism, voluntarism, and contractualism were features of the Puritan/evangelical religious tradition before they were taken over by the secular political philosophers of possessive individualism. In antebellum America, the evangelical tradition continued to contribute to shaping the culture of the modern world. As a social force, the revival worked largely through the organizations of the "benevolent empire" and party politics, but also through the media of print and lecture circuit.

The political culture formed by the clash between the evangelical movement and its adversaries was one that generated a high level of excitement and participation. Twentieth-century commentators have sometimes felt that it generated altogether too much fervor, blaming this for moving the country toward bloody civil war. In other moods, however, present observers sometimes look back nostalgically on a political system that engaged the involvement of the public so much more effectively than our own. Recently we have learned to attribute the public spirit of antebellum and colonial America to the classical republican tradition.[55] But this secular tradition was complemented in important ways by the Puritan/ evangelical religious tradition, which coexisted with it so often in the English-speaking world. Both traditions valued public virtue, private discipline, balanced government, and widespread participation.

As Tocqueville remarked, a host of issue-oriented voluntary associations connected individuals with public participation in antebellum America.[56] The evangelical benevolent empire was by far the largest network of these. It fostered a sense of active purposefulness among groups who had never experienced this before, notably women and free blacks. Whatever its implications for social control, evangelicalism also contributed to social empowerment, and the latter has been less thoroughly studied. Too often historians have taken it for granted that the Democratic party was the only agency for broadening popular participation in antebellum public life. An innovative essay by Carroll Smith-Rosenberg is an example of how historians are breaking free from this limitation. She uses anthropological theory to describe the ways in which the great revival provided religious forms for female self-assertion in early capitalist America.[57]

Today, many people have difficulty accepting the legitimacy of religion in politics. Reflecting this attitude, some historians cannot rid themselves of the feeling that if the politics of the antebellum period was religiously motivated, then it must have been irrational or reactionary. Yet one could argue that American party politics worked at its best during the second party system, when levels of voter participation were the highest in history, when religious issues and organizations were most salient, and when popular interest and involvement were thereby engaged. It was a time of social innovation, and religion was at the cutting edge of this innovation. Far from being reactionary, the religion of the great revival was an engine driving rational change, a force of modernization. If there is a special service that historians who are themselves Christians can bring to understanding the American past, if they have in fact a particular responsibility to the scholarly community, it might well be to affirm and explain the political rationality of religious commitment.

Notes

1. Arthur M. Schlesinger, Jr., *The Age of Jackson* (Boston: Little, Brown, 1945). The same blindness toward the significance of religion is apparent in Robert H. Walker, *Reform in America* (Lexington: University Press of Kentucky, 1985), the failure of which shows the hopelessness of trying to comprehend nineteenth-century reform in the terms of twentieth-century liberalism. On the other hand, what is enduringly valid in the progressive interpretation of the second party system may be seen in John Ashworth, *'Agrarians' and 'Aristocrats': Party Political Ideology in the United States, 1837–1846* (London: Royal Historical Society, 1983).

2. Richard Hofstadter, *The American Political Tradition and the Men Who Made It* (New York: Knopf, 1948), esp. chs. III and VI. The implications of this "consensus" approach were made explicit by Edward Pessen, who asserted that there was nothing to choose between the Whig and Democratic parties and dismissed their avowed programs as dissimulation. See his *Riches, Class, and Power Before the Civil War* (Lexington, MA: D. C. Heath, 1973); and *Jacksonian America: Society, Personality, and Politics*, rev. ed. (Homewood, IL: Dorsey, 1978), 197–260.

3. Richard P. McCormick, *The Second American Party System* (Chapel Hill: University of North Carolina Press, 1966). See also Robert E. Shalhope, "Jacksonian Politics in Missouri: A Comment on the McCormick Thesis," *Civil War History* 15 (1969): 210–225. For the current state of the "new political history," see Richard L. McCormick (son of Richard P.), *The Party Period and Public Policy* (New York: Oxford University Press, 1986); and Stephen Maizlish and John Kushma, eds., *Essays on American Antebellum Politics, 1840–1860* (Arlington: Texas A&M University Press, 1982). For a synthesis of the "new political history" with an interest in ideology, see Michael Holt, *The Political Crisis of the 1850s* (New York: Wiley, 1978).

4. Lee Benson, *The Concept of Jacksonian Democracy: New York as a Test Case* (Princeton: Princeton University Press, 1961). Reference group theory originated with the political scientist Herbert H. Hyman; see his "Reflections on Reference Groups," *Public Opinion Quarterly* 24 (1960): 383–396.

5. See Bertram Wyatt-Brown, "Prelude to Abolitionism: Sabbatarian Politics and the Rise of the Second Party System," *Journal of American History* 58

(1971): 316–341; Kathleen S. Kutolowski, "Antimasonry Re-Examined: the Social Bases of the Grass-Roots Party," *Journal of American History* 71 (1984): 269–293; David J. Russo, "Major Political Issues of the Jacksonian Period and the Development of Party Loyalty in Congress, 1830–1840," *Transactions of the American Philosophical Society* 62, 5 (1972): 3–51; Richard Carwardine, "Evangelicals, Whigs and the Election of William Henry Harrison," *Journal of American History* 17 (1983): 47–75.

6. Robert Kelley, *The Cultural Pattern in American Politics: The First Century* (New York: Knopf, 1979; Michael Holt, *Forging a Majority: The Formation of the Republican Party in Pittsburgh* (New Haven: Yale University Press, 1969); Daniel Walker Howe, *The Political Culture of the American Whigs* (Chicago: University of Chicago Press, 1979); William R. Brock, *Parties and Political Conscience: American Dilemmas, 1840–1850* (Millwood, NY: KTO, 1979). The ethnocultural interpretation is assessed and contextualized in several of the essays in Robert P. Swierenga, ed., *Beyond the Civil War Synthesis: Political Essays of the Civil War Era* (Westport, CT: Greenwood, 1975).

7. Contrast, for example, the recognition of ideology in Samuel P. Huntington, "Paradigms of American Politics," *Political Science Quarterly* 89 (1974): 1–26, with the celebration of the nonideological nature of America in Daniel Boorstin, *The Genius of American Politics* (Chicago: University of Chicago Press, 1953).

8. For example, William Gienapp, *The Origins of the Republican Party* (New York: Oxford University Press, 1986); and Joel Silbey, *The Partisan Imperative: The Dynamics of American Politics Before the Civil War* (New York: Oxford University Press, 1985).

9. Louise Stevenson, *Scholarly Means to Evangelical Ends: The New Haven Scholars and the Transformation of Higher Learning in America, 1830–1890* (Baltimore: Johns Hopkins University Press, 1986), 5–6. She makes reference to Richard Jensen, *The Winning of the Midwest* (Chicago: University of Chicago Press, 1971).

10. For example, Robert Bellah, *Habits of the Heart: Individualism and Commitment in American Life* (Berkeley: University of California Press, 1985); Peter Berger, *The Sacred Canopy: Elements of a Sociological Theory of Religion* (Garden City, NY: Doubleday, 1967); John L. Hammond, *The Politics of Benevolence: Revival Religion and American Voting Behavior* (Norwood, NJ: Ablex, 1979); Gerhard Lenski, *The Religious Factor: A Sociological Study of Religion's Impact on Politics, Economics, and Family Life*, rev. ed. (Garden City, NY: Doubleday, 1963); Michael Walzer, *The Revolution of the Saints* (Cambridge, MA: Harvard University Press, 1965); Samuel P. Huntington, *American Politics: The Promise of Disharmony* (Cambridge, MA: Harvard University Press, 1981); J. David Greenstone, "Political Culture and American Political Development," *Studies in American Political Development: An Annual* 1 (1986): 1–49; Mary Douglas, *Natural Symbols: Explorations in Cosmology* (New York: Pantheon, 1982); Victor Turner, *Image and Pilgrimage in Christian Culture: An Anthropo-*

logical Perspective (New York: Columbia University Press, 1978); Clifford Geertz, *The Interpretation of Cultures* (New York: Basic Books, 1973).

11. As the so-called revisionist historians of Civil War causation claimed; for example, James G. Randall, *Lincoln the Liberal Statesman* (New York: Dodd, Mead, 1947), 36–64.

12. Besides the Kutolowski article cited in n. 5, above, recent writings on anti-Masonry include: Ronald P. Formisano and Kathleen S. Kutolowski, "Antimasonry and Masonry: The Genesis of Protest," *American Quarterly* 29 (1979): 139–165; William P. Vaughn, *The Anti-Masonic Party in the United States* (Lexington: University Press of Kentucky, 1983); and Paul Goodman, *Towards a Christian Republic: Antimasonry and the Great Transition in New England* (New York: Oxford University Press, 1988).

13. For an example of the first, see Ronald P. Formisano, *The Birth of Mass Political Parties: Michigan, 1827–1861* (Princeton: Princeton University Press, 1971), 10–14; for the second, Eric Foner, *Politics and Ideology in the Age of the Civil War* (New York: Oxford University Press, 1980), 17–18. The third view is expressed by Richard L. McCormick in *Party Period and Public Policy*, ch. 1. Much of the secondary literature on the subject is characterized by an anti–anti-Masonic bias and/or an unwillingness to consider the anti-Masons rational.

14. John M. Murrin, "No Awakening, No Revolution? More Counterfactual Speculations," *Reviews in American History* 11 (1983): 161–171.

15. William Warren Sweet, *Religion in the Development of American Culture, 1765–1840* (New York: Scribner's 1952); Perry Miller, *The Life of the Mind in America: From the Revolution to the Civil War* (New York: Harcourt, Brace & World, 1965); Richard Bushman, *From Puritan to Yankee: Character and the Social Order in Connecticut, 1690–1765* (Cambridge, MA: Harvard University Press, 1967); Patricia Bonomi, *Under the Cope of Heaven: Religion, Society, and Politics in Colonial America* (New York: Oxford University Press, 1986). A somewhat different version of the argument is made in Alan Heimert, *Religion and the American Mind: From the Great Awakening to the Revolution* (Cambridge, MA: Harvard University Press, 1966), which interprets revivalism as democratic and communitarian rather than democratic and individualistic.

16. See Stephen Botein, "Religious Dimensions of the Early American State," in Richard Beeman, Stephen Botein, and Edward C. Canter II, eds., *Beyond Confederation: Origins of the Constitution and American National Identity* (Chapel Hill: University of North Carolina Press, 1987), 315–330.

17. Terry Bilhartz, *Urban Religion and the Second Great Awakening* (Rutherford, NJ: Fairleigh Dickinson University Press, 1986); cf. Richard Carwardine, "The Second Great Awakening in the Urban Centers," *Journal of American History* 52 (1972): 327–340.

18. For themes touched on in this paragraph, see the essays in Daniel Walker Howe, ed., *Victorian America* (Philadelphia: University of Pennsylvania Press, 1976); and Myra Glenn, *Campaigns Against Corporal Punishment: Prisoners,*

Sailors, Women, and Children in Antebellum America (Albany, NY: State University of New York Press, 1984).

19. On the abolitionists as modernizers opposed by traditionalists, see Leonard Richards, *"Gentlemen of Property and Standing": Anti-Abolition Mobs in Jacksonian America* (New York: Oxford University Press, 1970); on feminism as modernization, see Amy Dru Stanley, "Ideas and Practice of Freedom of Contract: Wage Labor and Marriage in Late 19th-Century America" (Ph.D. diss., Yale University, 1988).

20. For example, Avery Craven, *The Coming of the Civil War* (New York: Scribner's, 1942); Charles C. Cole, *The Social Ideas of the Northern Evangelists* (New York: Columbia University Press, 1954); and Clifford Griffin, "Religious Benevolence as Social Control," *Mississippi Valley Historical Review* 44 (1957): 423–444.

21. Michael Katz, *The Irony of Early School Reform* (Cambridge, MA: Harvard University Press, 1968); David J. Rothman, *The Discovery of the Asylum* (Boston: Little, Brown, 1971); Paul Johnson, *A Shopkeeper's Millennium* (New York: Hill and Wang, 1978); David Brion Davis, *The Problem of Slavery in the Age of Revolution* (Ithaca: Cornell University Press, 1975), esp. 251–254 and 346–357. See also Davis, *Slavery and Human Progress* (New York: Oxford University Press, 1984), 109.

22. An excellent introduction to this issue is Martin J. Wiener, ed., "Humanitarianism or Control? A Symposium on Aspects of Nineteenth-Century Social Reform in Britain and America," *Rice University Studies* 67 (1981): 1–84. See also Martin Duberman, ed., *The Antislavery Vanguard* (Princeton: Princeton University Press, 1965); Lois Banner, "Religious Benevolence as Social Control: A Critique of an Interpretation," *Journal of American History* 60 (1973): 34–41; and James B. Stewart, *Holy Warriors: The Abolitionists and American Slavery* (New York: Hill and Wang, 1976).

23. Lawrence J. Friedman, *Gregarious Saints: Self and Community in American Abolitionism, 1830–1870* (Cambridge, Eng.: Cambridge University Press, 1982). Other outstanding studies are Waldo E. Martin, Jr., *The Mind of Frederick Douglass* (Chapel Hill: University of North Carolina Press, 1984); Robert Abzug, *Passionate Liberator: Theodore Dwight Weld and the Dilemma of Reform* (New York: Oxford University Press, 1980); and Lewis Perry, *Radical Abolitionism: Anarchy and the Government of God in Antislavery Thought* (Ithaca: Cornell University Press, 1973).

24. McLoughlin, *Revivals, Awakenings, and Reform* (Chicago: University of Chicago Press, 1978); A. F. C. Wallace, *Rockdale: The Growth of an American Village in the Early Industrial Revolution* (New York: Knopf, 1978).

25. Thomas Haskell, "Capitalism and the Origins of the Humanitarian Sensibility," *American Historical Review* 90 (1985): 339–361 and 547–566. See also the illuminating "Forum" discussion among Haskell, Davis, and John Ashworth, ibid. 92 (1987): 797–878.

26. See Daniel Walker Howe, *The Unitarian Conscience: Harvard Moral Philosophy, 1805–1861*, rev. ed. (Middletown: Wesleyan University Press, 1988). All three participants in the "Forum" discussion just cited raise issues involving moral philosophy.

27. On the way evangelical benevolent societies developed women's sense of their own identity, see Nancy F. Cott, *The Bonds of Womanhood: "Woman's Sphere" in New England, 1780–1835* (New Haven: Yale University Press, 1977), 126–159; and Mary P. Ryan, *Cradle of the Middle Class: The Family in Oneida County, 1790–1865* (Cambridge, Eng.: Cambridge University Press, 1981).

28. Notwithstanding the criticism to which modernization theory has been subjected, historians of the nineteenth century continue to salvage and employ to advantage the concept of modernization. See Eric Foner, "The Causes of the Civil War: Recent Interpretations and New Directions," in Swierenga, ed., *Beyond the Civil War Synthesis*, 15–32; James M. McPherson, *Ordeal By Fire: Civil War and Reconstruction* (New York: Knopf, 1982), ch. 1; Daniel Walker Howe, "Victorian Culture in America," in his *Victorian America*, 3–28; and Richard D. Brown, *Modernization: The Transformation of American Life, 1600–1865* (New York: Hill and Wang, 1976).

29. Brian Harrison, *Drink and the Victorians* (London: Faber & Faber, 1971); Thomas Laqueur, *Religion and Respectability: Sunday Schools and Working Class Culture, 1780–1850* (New Haven: Yale University Press, 1976).

30. Timothy Smith's classic *Revivalism and Social Reform in Mid-19th-Century America* (New York: Abington, 1957) celebrates the autonomy of the evangelicals, though within the framework of a "consensus" approach to American history that now seems dated.

31. For example, there were virtually no white abolitionists for whom religion was not a central element in their rejection of slavery. Blacks could formulate an antislavery position without invoking religion, but whites could not. On the importance of the evangelical network of voluntary associations for empowering nineteenth-century reformers, see Bellah, *Habits of the Heart*.

32. See Donald G. Mathews, "The Second Great Awakening as an Organizing Process," *American Quarterly* 21 (1969): 23–44; and Robert Wiebe, *The Opening of American Society* (New York: Knopf, 1984), 229–232.

33. Besides works cited earlier, see Charles I. Foster, *An Errand of Mercy: the Evangelical United Front, 1790–1837* (Chapel Hill: University of North Carolina Press, 1960); Richard L. Power, "A Crusade to Extend Yankee Culture," *New England Quarterly* 12 (1940): 638–653; W. J. Rorabaugh, *The Alcoholic Republic* (New York: Oxford University Press, 1979); and Ronald G. Walters, *American Reformers, 1815–1860* (New York: Hill and Wang, 1978).

34. See Bertram Wyatt-Brown, *Lewis Tappan and the Evangelical War Against Slavery* (Cleveland: Case Western Reserve University Press, 1969); Peter Dobkin Hall, *The Organization of American Culture: Private Institutions, Elites, and the Origins of American Nationality* (New York: New York University Press,

1982); and Robert F. Dalzell, Jr., *Enterprising Elite: The Boston Associates and the World They Made* (Cambridge, MA: Harvard University Press, 1987).

35. See, for example, David Paul Nord, "Evangelical Origins of Mass Media in America, 1815–1835," *Journalism Monographs* 88 (1984): 1–30; and Gregory H. Singleton, "Protestant Voluntary Organizations and the Shaping of Victorian America," in Howe, *Victorian America*, 47–58.

36. Cf. Sidney Mead, *The Lively Experiment: The Shaping of Christianity in America* (New York: Harper & Row, 1963).

37. J. C. D. Clark, *English Society, 1688–1832: Ideology, Social Structure, and Political Practice During the Ancient Regime* (New York: Cambridge University Press, 1985).

38. Besides the works of Benson and Formisano already cited, see esp. Robert P. Swierenga, "Ethnocultural Political Analysis," *Journal of American Studies* 5 (1971): 59–79; and Kelley, *The Cultural Pattern*.

39. On the distinction between confessionalists and evangelicals, there is a substantial literature. For its origins, see esp. Benton Johnson, "Ascetic Protestantism and Political Preference," *Public Opinion Quarterly* 26 (1962): 35–46; Paul Kleppner, *The Cross of Culture: A Social Analysis of Midwestern Politics* (New York: Free Press, 1970); and Richard Jensen, "Religious and Occupational Roots of Party Identification," *Civil War History* 16 (1970): 325–343.

40. See William G. McLoughlin, *New England Dissent, 1630–1833: The Baptists and the Separation of Church and State*, 2 vols. (Cambridge, MA: Harvard University Press, 1970).

41. Nathan Hatch, "The Democratization of Christianity and the Character of American Politics," pp. 112–113 in this volume.

42. Jean H. Baker, *Affairs of Party: The Political Culture of the Northern Democrats in the Mid-Nineteenth Century* (Ithaca: Cornell University Press, 1983); Sean Wilentz, *Chants Democratic: New York City and the Rise of the American Working Class* (New York: Oxford University Press, 1984), 86.

43. Ronald P. Formisano, *The Transformation of Political Culture: Massachusetts Parties, 1790s–1840s* (New York: Oxford University Press, 1983).

44. R. Laurence Moore, *Religious Outsiders and the Making of Americans* (New York: Oxford University Press, 1986).

45. Robert Kelley, *The Transatlantic Persuasion: The Liberal-Democratic Mind in the Age of Gladstone* (New York: Knopf, 1969). Other important comparative works include Seymour M. Lipset and Stein Rokkan, eds., *Party Systems and Voter Alignments: Cross-National Perspectives* (New York: Free Press, 1967); and Michael Hechter, *Internal Colonialism: The Celtic Fringe in British National Development, 1536–1966* (Berkeley: University of California Press, 1975).

46. See Ernest L. Tuveson, *Millennium and Utopia* (Berkeley: University of California Press, 1949); and James Moorhead, *American Apocalypse: Yankee Protestants and the Civil War* (New Haven: Yale University Press, 1978).

47. Some historians use the words "pietism" or "devotionalism" to refer to the religious qualities that have such political implications, but I find these words too vague; as I understand the terms, confessionalists can be "pietists" and "devotionalists" too.

48. The writings of Robert Kelley are the best source for information on the politics of Old School Presbyterianism. For the impact of Irish Catholic immigration on Scots-Irish Old School Presbyterian voters, see Kelley, *The Cultural Pattern*, 170–174. See also Paul Kleppner, *The Third Electoral System, 1853–1892: Politics, Voters, and Political Cultures* (Chapel Hill: University of North Carolina Press, 1979), 164, 174, 177, 186.

49. Rhys Isaac, *The Transformation of Virginia, 1740–1790* (Chapel Hill: University of North Carolina Press, 1982); Eugene Genovese, *The Political Economy of Slavery* (New York: Pantheon, 1965); Dickson D. Bruce, *Violence and Culture in the Antebellum South* (Austin: University of Texas Press, 1979); Bertram Wyatt-Brown, *Southern Honor: Ethics and Behavior in the Old South* (New York: Oxford University Press, 1982).

50. See Bertram Wyatt-Brown, "The Antimission Movement in the Jacksonian South," *Journal of Southern History* 36 (1970): 501–529; Wyatt-Brown, *Yankee Saints and Southern Sinners* (Baton Rouge: Louisiana State University Press, 1985); Joel Silbey, "The Surge of Republican Power: Partisan Antipathy, American Social Conflict, and the Coming of the Civil War," in Maizlish and Kushma, *Antebellum Politics*.

51. Anne Norton, *Alternative Americas: A Reading of Antebellum Political Culture* (Chicago: University of Chicago Press, 1986).

52. On women and the moral goals of literary culture, see Jane Tompkins, *Sensational Designs: The Cultural Work of American Fiction* (New York: Oxford University Press, 1985); and William R. Taylor's enduring book, *Cavalier and Yankee: The Old South and American National Character* (New York: George Braziller, 1961). Ann Douglas, *The Feminization of American Culture* (New York: Knopf, 1977), argues that the rise of women's cultural power took place at the expense of the clergy.

53. Besides the books of Nancy Cott and Mary Patricia Ryan cited already in n. 28, see, for example, Carroll Smith-Rosenberg, *Religion and the Rise of the City* (Ithaca: Cornell University Press, 1971), 97–124; Ross Paulson, *Women's Suffrage and Prohibition* (Glenview, IL: Scott, Foresman, 1973); Ellen DuBois, *Feminism and Suffrage: The Emergence of an Independent Women's Movement in America* (Ithaca: Cornell University Press, 1978); and Blanche Hersh, *The Slavery of Sex: Feminist Abolitionists in 19th Century America* ((Urbana: University of Illinois Press, 1978).

54. Erik Erikson, *Young Man Luther: A Study in Psychoanalysis and History* (New York: W. W. Norton, 1958); Erikson, *Gandhi's Truth* (New York: W. W. Norton, 1969).

55. The seminal work is, of course, J. G. A. Pocock, *The Machiavellian Moment: Florentine Political Thought and the Atlantic Republican Tradition*

(Princeton: Princeton University Press, 1975). Republicanism and its relationship to liberalism have been more thoroughly explored by historians for the period before 1815 than after, but see Michael Holt, *The Political Crisis of the 1850s* (New York: Wiley, 1978); Howe, *Political Culture of the American Whigs*; Steven Watts, *The Republic Reborn: War and the Making of Liberal America, 1790–1820* (Baltimore: Johns Hopkins University Press, 1987); and Dorothy Ross, "Liberalism" in the *Encyclopedia of American Political History*, ed. Jack P. Greene (New York: Scribner's, 1984), I, 750–763.

56. Alexis de Tocqueville, *Democracy in America* (New York: Knopf, 1945), I, 198–205 and passim.

57. Carroll Smith-Rosenberg, "The Cross and the Pedestal: Women, Anti-Ritualism, and the Emergence of the American Bourgoisie," in her *Disorderly Conduct: Visions of Gender in Victorian America* (New York: Knopf, 1985), 129–164.

7

Ethnoreligious Political Behavior in the Mid-Nineteenth Century: Voting, Values, Cultures

ROBERT P. SWIERENGA

The most exciting development in American political history in the last twenty years is the recognition that religion was the key variable in voting behavior until at least the Great Depression. The move to restore religion to political analysis gained momentum slowly in the 1940s and 1950s through the work of the eminent scholars Paul Lazarsfeld, Samuel Lubell, and Seymour Martin Lipset, and it culminated in the 1960s when historians Lee Benson and Samuel Hays brought the new perspective to a generation of graduate students.[1] By the 1970s this so-called ethnocultural (or ethnoreligious[2]) interpretation of voting behavior had become the reigning orthodoxy, having supplanted the populist-progressive paradigm that "economics explains the mostest," to quote Charles Beard.[3] In recent years, a resurgent neoprogressive, or "new left," historiography, led by cultural Marxists, has challenged the ethnoreligious interpretation, but the edifice, which stands on solid research at the grass roots, remains largely intact.[4]

This essay summarizes the accumulated evidence in support of the thesis that religion was the salient factor in nineteenth-century voting behavior. How and why religion was at the center is extremely complex, as are the related issues of documentation and measurement. There were also regional and temporal variations in the role of religion in politics. Nevertheless, despite its limitations, a theological interpretation of voting behavior offers a refreshing new angle to our understanding of political culture in the eras of Andrew Jackson and Abraham Lincoln.

The Rediscovery of Religion

The revolution in American political history began when Lazarsfeld and his associates at the Bureau of Applied Social Research at Columbia University systematically surveyed voters during the 1940 presidential election campaign in Erie County, Ohio. To their surprise they found that voters were most influenced by their churches, or, in sociological jargon, their "social reference groups." Protestants and Catholics clearly differed in voting and party identification, even when "controlling" for socioeconomic factors.[5] In one giant step, Lazarsfeld and associates had brought into political analysis the religious variable that had been jettisoned by the first generation of professional historians and political scientists in the late nineteenth century. The prevailing wisdom was encapsulated in James Bryce's terse assertion in 1894: "Religion comes very little into the American party."[6] Sectional economic rivalries, class conflicts, and melting pot doctrines were the reigning orthodoxies following the influential historians Frederick Jackson Turner and Charles Beard. Why the rising professoriate was blind to expressions of religious values in politics is complex. Put simply, they were highly secularized and believed religion should be privatized and church and state kept totally separate. The doctrine of the melting pot, then dominant, also held that ethnic and religious differences were narrowing in society and politics.

So strong was this thinking in the twentieth century that political pollsters of the modern era never considered religious questions when gathering data on voting behavior. George Gallup, the first professional pollster and himself a Protestant churchgoer, did not ask respondents for their church affiliation until after Lazarsfeld published his 1940 study, *The People's Choice*, in 1944. Indeed, when Lazarsfeld told Gallup of his startling finding, Gallup expressed disbelief.[7] As late as 1959, during the Kennedy-Nixon presidential race, Elmo Roper, another leading pollster, challenged the "myth of the Catholic vote" and denied any connection between religion and voting.[8] The pollsters' skepticism gave way when Lipset, the prestigious director of the Institute of International Studies at the University of California, Berkeley, further documented the place of religion in American culture and politics. But Lipset still deferred to the long-dominant neo-Marxist paradigm then in its declension. Religion did not "explain everything," he allowed; class position was equally determinative.[9]

The next challenge to the liberal paradigm carried the day. In 1961 Lee Benson, a young historian who had studied nineteenth-century voting patterns at Lazarsfeld's Bureau in the mid-1950s, published one of the most significant books in American political history, *The Concept of Jacksonian Democracy: New York as a Test Case*. Benson began his research as a convinced economic determinist, but his analysis of group voting behavior led him to develop a sociological-psychological model based on ethnoreligious conflict. His key conclusion is the now classic statement: "At least since the 1820s, when manhood suffrage became widespread, ethnic and religious differences have tended to be *relatively* the most important source of political differences in the United States." Benson made no attempt to "prove" his proposition other than to demonstrate its validity in the 1844 presidential election in New York State. Intuitively, he felt that this theory conformed to common sense. "Since the United States is highly heterogeneous, and has high social mobility," he reasoned, "I assume that men tend to . . . be more influenced by their ethnic and religious group membership then by their membership in economic classes or groups."[10]

Within a decade, a host of historians led by Benson and Hays completed additional research for various Northern states that generally confirmed the religious dimension. These publications, which employed quantitative and social science methods and theories, demonstrated that religion and ethnicity were basic to American voting patterns.[11] This finding should not have been surprising. Foreign observers of America in the nineteenth century, such as Alexis de Tocqueville, had remarked often about the high religiosity of American society, especially after the Second Great Awakening filled empty churches with new converts. As Richard Jensen has stated: "The most revolutionary change in nineteenth century America was the conversion of the nation from a largely dechristianized land in 1789 to a stronghold of Protestantism by mid-century. The revivals did it." By 1890, church affiliation was above 70 percent in the Midwest, with the new revivalist sects and churches claiming over half. The revivals sparked confrontation in every denomination. Again quoting Jensen: "Until the mid-1890s the conflict between pietists and liturgicals was not only the noisiest product of American religion, it was also the force which channeled religious enthusiasm and religious conflicts into the political arena."[12] This was all the more true because the militant Evangelicals sought to link Christian reform and Republicanism into an unofficial Protestant establishment that virtually equated the Kingdom of God with the nation.[13]

From Religion to Politics: Values and Culture

The mechanism for translating religion into political preferences is complicated and much disputed. Lazarsfeld, Lipset, Lubell, Benson, and Hays all stressed the socialization process.[14] Individuals learned attitudes and values early in life from family, church, and community, which then shaped their perception of the larger world and gave them ethical values to live by. Persons, if you will, absorbed voting habits with their mother's milk, and these subconscious dispositions were later reinforced by the parson's sermons and the wisdom of the brethren. One political party was "right," the other "wrong." Parties were bound to conflict in a society flooded by wave after wave of immigrants. Each ethnoreligious group had its own social character, historical experience, and theological beliefs. Each had its friends and enemies, or, in Robert K. Merton's words, its positive and negative reference groups.[15] Irish Catholics, for example, reacted against hostile New England Protestants, who tended to be Whigs, by joining the Democratic party. Then, new British immigrants voted Whig because Irish Catholics voted Democratic, and so on.

The ethnoreligious thesis, on one level, shifted the focus from national to local issues and from elites to the behavior of voters at the grass roots. At a deeper level, it substituted religious culture for class conflict and sectionalism as a significant independent variable in voting choices. As Hays explained simply: "Party differences in voting patterns were cultural, not economic." "Ethnocultural issues were far more important to voters than were tariffs, trusts, and railroads. They touched lives directly and moved people deeply."[16] Instead of battles in Washington and statehouses over economic benefits and favors, ethnoreligionists stress fights over prohibition of alcohol, abolition of slavery, Sunday closing laws, parochial-school funding, foreign-language and Bible usage in public schools, anti-Catholic nativism and alien suffrage, sexual conformity and capital punishment, and a host of lesser crusades. The point of the new view is that moral rather than economic issues impelled nineteenth-century voters and produced the major political conflicts. Instead of being assimilated, ethnoreligious groups clung to their customs, beliefs, and identities for generations, and as they clashed over public policy at the polls, their values and attitudes were hardened, reshaped, or mellowed, depending on changing historical circumstances. Nevertheless, these structural differences remained deep-rooted. As Lipset noted, this made "religious variation a matter of political significance in America."[17]

Political socialization of individuals and structural conflict among social groups may explain how voters absorbed their values and prejudices and had them reinforced as groups fought to defend or advance their interests in the political arena; but this does not explain why particular ethnoreligious groups voted as they did. Why were Irish Catholics Democrats and New England Congregationalists Whig and Republican?

Ethnoreligionists have offered at least three distinct but often intertwined theories to explain how religious group impulses became political ones. Benson emphasized reference group theory, especially negative reactions. While valid in limited historical settings, such as Boston in the 1840s when Irish Catholic immigrants overran this Anglo-Protestant center, reference group theory is rather limited and simplistic, especially the notion that group members merely "absorb" political ideas and "react" to other groups. Hays added a refinement, that of group hegemonic goals, which he called the "social analysis of politics."[18] Ethnoreligious groups use political means to try to extend the domain of their cultural practices or, conversely, to protect themselves from legal or legislative attacks. As Catholic Irish and German immigrants seemed to inundate the United States, for example, native-born Protestants turned to nativist laws to keep Catholic Sabbath desecration or beer drinking in check. Again, this social approach begs the question of the sources of differing lifestyles. If groups clashed because of historic antagonisms and conflicting cultural traditions, it was because their religious roots differed.[19]

This led to the third theory, that "theology rather than language, customs, or heritage, was the foundation of cultural and political subgroups in America," to quote Richard Jensen.[20] "Political choices were thus derived from beliefs about God, human nature, the family, and government. Citizens were not robots, but reflective beings whose value system had been 'sanctified' by their family, friends, and congregations."[21] Different ways of living and voting derive from different ways of believing. Moral decision-making rests on religious values, theological distinctions, or, more broadly, worldviews.[22]

Kleppner cogently explained the nature of belief. Religion "involves a rationale for existence, a view of the world, a perspective for the organization of experience; it is a cognitive framework consisting of a matrix within which the human actor perceives his environment." Although it is not the only perspective, it "penetrates all partial and fragmentary social worlds in which men participate; it organizes and defines how they perceive and relate to society in general." Religiosity, Kleppner continues, comprises five core dimensions: belief, knowledge, practice, experience, and consequences. Various denominations emphasize different dimensions and their linkages, and out of this come behavioral differences. Historically, the two broad clusters of denominations were the pietists, who went from belief to experience and consequences, and the liturgicals, who tied belief to knowledge and practice.[23]

It must be admitted that any attempt to explain voting behavior on the basis of Christian theology, liturgy, or lifestyle is a sticky wicket. Voters, because their minds and wills are innately flawed, do not *always* act consistently with their ultimate beliefs. They may be cross-pressured by competing and conflicting religious "oughts." Finney evangelicals, for example, worked to free slaves but not women. Voters may delude themselves and vote their pocketbook while claiming to follow ethical principles. Churches and historical issues and pressures also changed over time, and generalizations are thus necessarily limited in time and place.[24] Scholars have also struggled with theological typologies that can adequately categorize the many denominations according to their various belief systems.

The Liturgical-Pietist Continuum

Kleppner and Jensen offered the first sophisticated religious theory of American voting in the nineteenth century. Based on a wide reading in the sociology of religion and the history of individual denominations and groups, they developed the ritualist-pietist, or liturgical-pietist, continuum, which locates ethnoreligious groups and denominations along a single dimension based on the central tendency of their theological orientation.[25] On the one side were ecclesiastical, ritualistic, and liturgically oriented groups; and on the other were the sectlike evangelicals or pietists who stressed a living, biblical faith and the imminent return and rule of the Messiah. The liturgical churches (such as the Roman Catholic, Episcopal, and various Lutheran synods) were credally based, sacerdotal, hierarchical, nonmillennial, and particularistic. These ecclesiasticals were ever vigilant against state encroachment on their churches, parochial schools, and the moral lives of their members. God's kingdom was otherworldly, and human programs of conversion or social reform could not usher in the millennium. God would restore this inscrutable, fallen world in His own good time and in His own mighty power.

The pietists (Baptists, Methodists, Disciples, Congregationalists, Quakers) were New Testament–oriented, antiritualist, congregational in governance, active in parachurch organizations, and committed to individual conversion and societal reform in order to usher in the millennial reign of Jesus Christ. Pietists did not compartmentalize religion and civil government. Right belief and right behavior were two sides of the same spiritual coin. The liturgicals excommunicated heretics, the pietists expelled or shunned sinners.

These theological differences directly affected politics in the Jacksonian era because the Yankee pietists launced a crusade to Christianize America and the liturgicals resisted what they viewed as an enforced Anglo-conformity.[26] The pietists staged a two-pronged public program. First they created the "benevolent empire" in the 1810s to spread the gospel and teach the Bible. Then, in the 1820s, they established reform societies to eradicate slavery, saloons, Sabbath desecration, and other social ills. Finally, in the 1830s, they entered the political mainstream by joining the new Whig party coalition against the Jacksonian Democrats. By the 1840s, in fear of the growing Catholic immigrant menace, they added nativist legislation to their agenda, especially extending the naturalization period from five to fourteen years. As the reformed-minded Yankees threatened to gain control of the federal and state governments through the Whig party and, after 1854, the Republican party, the liturgicals, who were mainly immigrants, fought back through the Democratic party.

Why the liturgicals joined the Democracy and the more pietist Christians gravitated to the Whig and Republican parties requires a brief explanation of party ideologies and programs. With Thomas Jefferson as its patron saint and Andrew Jackson as its titular head, the Democratic party from its inception in the 1820s espoused egalitarian, libertarian, and secularist goals.[27] The Democrats were social levelers who believed in a limited, populistic government and a society rooted in self-interest and individual autonomy. They sought a secular state that did not try to legislate social behavior and was free of church control.[28] An editorial in an Ohio Democratic newspaper condemned all reform movements that were motivated by "ascetic law, force, terror, or violence," and a

Michigan editor declared: "We regard a man's religious belief as concerning only himself and his Maker." Government must thus restrain all economic power brokers and promote a laissez-faire society. Democratic theorists like George Bancroft believed that "the voice of the people is the voice of God."[29] The highest good was universal manhood suffrage, majoritarian rule, a nonexploitative society, and a government that granted no undue favors. The Democrats easily attracted immigrants from the beginning and always stood for cultural and ethnic diversity.[30]

The opposition Whig party was more elitist, parternalistic, cosmopolitan, entrepreneurial, and legalistic.[31] This "Yankee Party" viewed government positively, trusted the governors more than the governed, and believed in absolute law based on eternal verities. The goal of the Northern Whigs was to enlist all Christians and their clerical leaders who sought collectively to promote moral behavior and social harmony.[32] The Whigs, said Robert Kelley, were "the party of decency and respectability, the guardians of piety, sober living, proper manners, thrift, steady habits, and book learning."[33] The Whig agenda of building a "righteous empire" (to use the apt title of Martin Marty's book) received a tremendous boost initially from the Second Great Awakening. Indeed, without the spiritual revivals, the Whig leaders could not have built a viable mass party. Later in the 1840s the backlash against mass immigration and the perceived Irish menace further strengthened the Anglo-Whig party. When Bishop John Hughes of New York City objected to the reading of the King James Bible in the public schools as an attempt to proselytize Catholic children, and tried to obtain public funding for Catholic schools, Protestant leaders became alarmed and worked through the Whig party to enact nativist laws to weaken or contain the Catholic threat.[34] To Yankees, the Irish were English "blacks," social pariahs who were now infesting Protestant America.[35]

Given these opposing ethnoreligious groups, it is not surprising that historians find many links between religion and politics. Liturgicals demanded maximum personal freedom and state neutrality regarding personal behavior. They tended to find a congenial home in the Democratic party. But pietists, who felt an obligation to "reach out and purge the world of sin," found in the Whigs a vehicle to accomplish this.[36] Paul Kleppner's generalization is the standard summary of the ethnoreligious thesis: "The more ritualistic the religious orientation of the group, the more likely it was to support the Democracy; conversely, the more pietist the group's outlook the more intensely Republican its partisan affiliation."[37] In short, "the primary cleavage line of party oppositions . . . pitted evangelical pietistics against ritualistic religious groups."[38]

Was this political and social conflict between religious groups rooted in simple ethnic and religious prejudices and differing lifestyles, or did a theological cleavage underlay the behavioral distinctions? Some scholars (Benson and Formisano, for example) stress the clash of cultures, the historic reference group hatreds and prejudices, the group defenses and hegemonic goals. Although there is no dearth of historical evidence for such a pattern of brokenness in American history, it does not mean that human behavior is usually (or always) unthinking, reactive, and culturally determined. As noted earlier, to explain that German Catholics supported the Democrats because that party opposed prohibition and Quakers voted Whig and Republican because that party favored prohibition is not to explain the behavior at all. To claim that Irish Catholics voted Democratic because they hated Yankee Whigs does not explain the source of the prejudice. The reason that people voted this way ultimately lies deeper than symbols or culture; it is rooted in religious worldviews.[39] People act politically, economically, and socially in keeping with their ultimate beliefs. Their values, mores, and actions, whether in the polling booth, on the job, or at home, are an outgrowth of the god or gods they hold at the center of their being.

In a nation of immigrants, where members of ethnoreligious groups often lived out their daily lives together in churches, schools, societies and clubs, work and play, and in marriage and family life, group norms were readily passed from parents to children, along with a strong sense of identity and a commitment to their political and social goals. Such groups were understandably ready to promote or defend their beliefs when public policy issues arose that touched their lives directly. Religious issues, more than social class, status, or sectional interests, were at the crux. As Kleppner asserts: "Attachments to ethnoreligious groups were *relatively* more important as determinants of nineteenth-century social-group cohesiveness and party oppositions than were economic attributes or social status." Notice the word "relatively." Ethnoculturalists have not claimed that their findings *exclusively* explain mass voting patterns, only that differing religious beliefs *best* explain that behavior.[40] They also recognize that in the South the race issue was paramount.

Ethnoculturalists also recognize that cross-pressures and particular historic contexts may change patterns or create unique situations.[41] The Pella (Iowa) Dutch pietists continued to vote Democratic after the Civil War when other Dutch Reformed colonies in the Midwest switched en masse to the Republicans. The nativist attacks on the community in the 1850s had been too strong and bitter to forget.[42]

Measurement Problems

Having explained the religious roots of voting behavior, I now turn to the pithy question Lee Benson first posed in 1957: "Who voted for whom, when?"[43] How ethnoreligious group members voted is a factual question that requires an empirical answer.[44] While the question is straightforward, finding the answers have been very difficult. Two basic measurement problems keep cropping up. The first is to determine the religious affiliation of party members and voters, and the second is to measure the extent to which religious values acted in conjunction with socioeconomic and other factors to determine voting behavior.

Identifying the religion of voters is by far the more difficult problem. Federal census publications did not report the number of church members or communicants until the 1890 census. Beginning in 1850, however, the census enumerated church seating capacity per community. Since "sittings" were not directly proportionate with membership, particularly in the Catholic church, some scholars estimated pre-1890 membership by assuming that the 1890 ratio of members to sittings was a reasonable approximation of the earlier ratio.[45] Some scholars simply used sittings, or an even cruder measure, the number of church buildings.[46] It is also recognized that church attendance consistently exceeded membership, but nominal and occasional members likely shared the values and worldviews of full members.[47]

In some areas, local sources such as county biographical directories occasionally state the religious affiliation of family heads.[48] But one had to pay to be listed in these "mug books," so they do not include all potential voters. Poll books of active voters survive in some counties and when they are collated with church membership records, it is possible to determine precisely the religion of voters.[49] Such individual-level data are ideal, but rare. One scholar estimated Catholic strength in minor civil divisions by collating the names of fathers and godfathers listed in baptism records with names in federal census records, multiplying by the ratio of births per adult member (15:1 in 1860), and thus determining the Catholic population per ward.[50]

Another common method of estimating religion was to note the state or country of birth in the manuscript censuses (recorded from 1850 on) as a proxy for ethnoreligious identity, and then to locate "homogeneous" counties or preferably townships and wards, that is, communities that were predominantly German Lutheran, Dutch Reformed, Swedish Lutheran, New England Yankee, and so on. The voting behavior in these homogeneous townships is then taken to represent the voting of the entire group in a state or region.[51] Critics charged that such communities were atypical, because group pressures would be unduly strong there. Would a German Lutheran living in a largely German village in Wisconsin vote differently than a fellow church member who was living among Irish Catholics in Chicago?

The alternative to finding homogeneous areas is to estimate the relative proportion of ethnoreligious groups per county for an entire state or section of the country, either in whole or by sampling. The ideal, which no one has yet attempted, is to draw a random township and ward sample of the northeastern United States, compile township-level aggregate data on religion, ethnicity, occupation, wealth, and other pertinent variables in the period 1850–1900, and then, using multiple regression analysis, determine the relative relationships between religion and voting, taking into account the effects of all of the other variables.[52] Until such a large project is undertaken, we must rely upon the several dozen case studies at the state and local level completed in the last twenty years. These studies cover the years from 1820 to 1900 in the Northeastern and Midwestern states.[53]

Ethnoreligious Groups

Although regional variations existed, the findings generally agree in the political categorization of the major ethnoreligious groups. The various groups can best be arranged in four categories: strongly Democrat (75+ percent), moderately Democratic (50–75 percent), moderately Whig or Republican (50–75 percent), and strongly Whig or Republican (75+ percent) (see Table 7-1). Strongly Democratic groups were all Catholics (Irish, German, French, French Canadian, Belgian, Bohemian, etc.), and Southern Baptists and Southern Methodists. Moderately Democratic groups were Old (i.e., colonial) German Lutheran, Old German and Old Dutch Reformed, Old British Episcopalians, New England Universalists, and Southern Presbyterians and Disciples of Christ. Moderately Whig and Republican in their voting were the German pietist sects (Brethren, Mennonites, Moravians, Amish), New German and Danish Lutheran, New Dutch Christian Reformed, Old School Presbyterians, Regular and

Table 7-1. Political Orientation of
Major Ethnoreligious Groups, 1830-1890

Strongly Whig/Republican 75-100%	Moderately Whig/Republican 50-75%
Quaker	Christian Church - Disciples
Scotch-Irish Presbyterian	Missionary Baptist
Free Will Baptist	Regular Baptist
Congregationalist	Universalist (Midwestern)
New School Presbyterian	Old School Presbyterian
Unitarian	New German Lutheran
Northern Methodist	Danish Lutheran
Irish Methodist	German Pietist Groups
Cornish Methodist	Amish
Welsh Methodist	Brethren
Swedish Lutheran	Mennonite
Norwegian Lutheran	Moravian
Haugean Norwegian	New Dutch Christian Reformed
English Episcopal	
Canad'an English Episcopal	
New Dutch Reformed	
French Huguenot	
Black Protestants	

Strongly Democratic 75-100%	Moderately Democratic 50-75%
Irish Catholic	Old British Episcopal
German Catholic	Southern Presbyterian
French Catholic	Universalist (New England)
Bohemian Catholic	Southern Disciples of Christ
French Canadian	Old German Lutheran
French	Old German Reformed
Southern Baptist	Old Dutch Reformed
Southern Methodist	

Source: Works cited in notes 10 and 45, especially Kleppner,
Cross and Third; Jensen, Winning; and Formisano, Birth.

Missionary Baptists, Midwestern Universalists, and the Christian Church. Strongly Whig and Republican were Northern Methodists (including Irish and Cornish Methodists), Free Will Baptists, Congregationalists, New School Presbyterians, Unitarians, Quakers, French Huguenots, Swedish and Norwegian Lutherans, Haugean Norwegians, New Dutch Reformed, Canadian English and New England Episcopalians, and blacks. (Groups designated "Old" immigrated prior to the American Revolution; "New" arrived afterwards.)

The ethnoreligious specialists deserve credit for discovering these group voting patterns. Some distinctions are extremely subtle. For example, among Michigan's Dutch Calvinist immigrants of the mid-nineteenth century, the majority group affiliated with the largely Americanized Old Dutch Reformed Church in the East in 1850, but a minority opposed the union, seceded, and formed an independent immigrant church, the Christian Reformed Church. One of the major doctrinal issues in the split was the conviction of the seceders that the Dutch Reformed espoused a revivalist free-will theology and used evangelical hymns and other "tainted" aspects of Yankee pietism.[54] In their politics, Kleppner found that the Dutch Reformed after the Civil War consistently voted Republican more strongly than did the Christian Reformed (66 percent versus 59 percent).[55] Even among a homogeneous immigrant group like the Dutch Calvinists, the inroads of revivalism strengthened commitments to the Yankee political party.

Religion and Politics

Not only for the Dutch Calvinists but for all ethnoreligious groups, revivalism was the "engine" of political agitation.[56] Evangelist Charles G. Finney began preaching revival in the mid-1820s throughout New England and its Yankee colonies in western New York. By 1831 religious enthusiasm had reached a fever pitch in Yankeedom and mass conversions swept town after town. Church membership doubled and tripled and large portions of the populace were reclaimed for Protestantism. Finney challenged his followers to pursue "entire sanctification" or perfectionism and to become Christian social activists. The converts first entered politics in the anti-Masonic movement in New York in 1826–27. By the mid-1830s the evangelicals entered national politics by opposing slavery, alcohol, and other social ills that they believed the Jackson administration condoned. Converts such as Theodore Dwight Weld became leaders in the antislavery movement. And in the 1840s and 1850s, revivalist regions of the country developed strong anti-slavery societies and voted Liberty, Whig, and later Republican.[57] Ultimately, the allegiance of pietists to the Whig party led to its demise because the pietists put ethical goals, such as abolition of slavery, above party loyalty. The idea of a party system built on patronage and discipline was much stronger in Democrat than in Whig ranks. Evangelicals had a disproportionate share of antiparty men. In their estimation, Popery, Masonry, and Party were all threats to freedom of conscience and Christian principles.[58]

The disintegration of the Whig party in the early 1850s, followed by the brief appearance of the Know-Nothings and then of the new Republican party, and the fissure of the Democratic party in 1860 were the main components of the political realignment of the decade. The Second Electoral System gave way to the Third System. But "Yankee-cultural imperialism" now expressed through the Republican party continued as the dynamic force, carrying out God's will against racists and other sinners in the Democratic party. Broadly speaking, in the third electoral era pietist religious groups, both native-born and immigrant, led the Republican party against antipietist Democrats.[59]

The 1860 presidential election signaled the future direction of the social bases of partisanship. Catholic voter groups of all ethnic backgrounds and across all status levels voted more solidly Democratic than ever before. Meanwhile some former Democrats moved toward the Republicans, notably Yankee Methodists and Baptists, and pietistic Norwegians, Dutch Reformed, and Germans.[60] The increasingly Catholic character of the Democracy, as well as that party's presumed responsibility for the Civil War, drove these Protestants away.

The impact of religious conflict on voting behavior in the 1860 Lincoln-Douglas election is illustrated in Cleveland, Ohio, in a study by Thomas Kremm.[61] Although founded by New England Yankees, Cleveland lay astride the immigrant route from New York to points west, and by 1860 the majority of the population was foreign-born. Roman Catholic immigrants, mainly German and Irish, comprised 30 percent of the population in 1860. Catholics numbered more than half the population in two wards (out of eleven in the city) and just under half in another ward.

The influx of Catholics in the 1840s and 1850s led to a nativist backlash. To the Protestant majority, Catholics were un-American; they rejected the "public religion" of the republic. Moreover, the Catholic church was an "undemocratic engine of oppression." As the editor of the Cleveland *Express* declared: "Roman Catholics, whose consciences are enslaved, . . . regard the King of Rome—the Pope—as the depository of all authority." [62] Religious tensions were also stirred by Catholic opposition to public-school tax levies, by their "European" use of the Sabbath for recreation, and by their consistent bloc voting for the Democrats. Irish Catholics, charged the editors of the Cleveland *Leader*, "were sots and bums who crawled out of their 'rotten nests of filth' on election days to cast 'ignorant' ballots for the candidates of the 'slavocracy.' These 'cattle' lured to the polls by huge quantities of whisky, worshipped the three deities of the Ruffian Party—the Pope, a whisky barrel, and a nigger driver.'"[63]

This level of invective suggests that the Cleveland electorate divided along Catholic versus non-Catholic lines, rather than over slavery extension. Voting analysis of the 1860 election proves this. The percentage of Catholic voters per ward and the Douglas vote were almost perfectly correlated. Similarly, the percentage of non-Catholic voters and the Lincoln vote were almost perfectly correlated. Even when removing the effects of ethnicity, occupation, and wealth, religion explains over 80 percent of the variation across wards in the Republican and Democratic percentages. Religion, Kremm concluded, was the "real issue," the "overriding factor determining party preference in 1860." Catholics voted for the Democratic candidate, Stephen Douglas, and non-Catholics, irrespective of other socioeconomic factors, voted for Lincoln.[64]

The rise of the Republican party in Pittsburgh in the 1850s is similar to the Cleveland story. As Michael Holt discovered, the Republican coalition rose on a wave of anti-Catholic sentiment among native-born Protestants, which flared on issues of Sabbatarian laws and parochial schools. The growing Irish and German Catholic population increasingly voted the Democratic ticket. Holt's careful statistical correlations between voting patterns and ethnoreligious and economic characteristics of the city's wards revealed that "economic issues made no discernible contribution to Republican strength. . . . Instead, social, ethnic, and religious considerations often determined who voted for whom between 1848 and 1861. Divisions between native-born Americans and immigrants and between Protestants and Catholics, rather than differences of opinion about the tariff or the morality of slavery, distinguished Whigs and Republicans from Democrats."[65]

The temperance issue and other social concerns, except abolition of slavery, lessened during the war years, but in the early 1870s legal moves against alcohol and saloons resurfaced. The Republicans, who were generally supportive, lost voting support over temperance agitation. The Yankee party also had a negative fallout from the economic depression set off by the financial panic of 1873.[66] The Democrats, meanwhile, benefited from the Catholic fertility "time bomb" that exploded in the 1870s. The relative strength of the ritualists thus grew at the expense of the pietists. In 1860, pietists outnumbered ritualists nationwide by 21 percentage points (50 to 29 percent), but by 1890 pietists led by only 5 percent (40 to 35). The population increase among pietist groups averaged 2.4 percent per year, compared with 5.3 percent among liturgicals (and 6.2 percent among Catholics).[67]

Out of political desperation, as well as concern for the moral decline in American society, the Republican pietists in the 1870s and 1880s revived the "politics of righteousness"—Sabbatarian and temperance laws, anti-Catholic propaganda, and defense of Protestant public schools and

English-only language instruction. Despite these efforts, the Democrats, bolstered by the "solid South," surged after 1876, winning three of four presidential elections by close margins. In effect, the Northern supporting groups held steady in both camps for several decades until the major realignment of the 1890s caused a "cross of culture." In the political unheaval of the nineties, William Jennings Bryan molded the old Democracy into a new "party of reform" and William McKinley redirected the Republicans into a middle-of-the-road position that fought against silver coinage rather than alcoholic beverages.[68]

Contributions and Critique

There are many positive results of the ethnoreligious interpretation of American voting behavior. Most important is the realization that religious beliefs significantly affected mass voting behavior. Religious groups and political parties had a symbiotic relationship. Churches influenced political agenda by determining that slavery or alcohol or some other moral problem required legislative action.[69] Parties, in turn, built constituencies from various religious groups whose worldviews jibed with the party's programs and goals. The relationship between religion and politics was so close in the nineteenth century that Kleppner rightly calls the parties "political churches" and their ideologies "political confessionalism."[70]

The ethnoreligionists had made their case convincingly, even to the point of "boredom and hostility," in the words of a Marxist reviewer. By 1970 religion had become the new orthodoxy in voting studies. As critic James Wright admitted, the new school had "done their work well. It is virtually impossible to avoid their frame of reference."[71] Since the mid-1970s political historians have had to *disprove* the salience of religion and culture as major explanations of voting patterns. Even the cultural Marxists have factored religious forces into their economic models.[72]

Second, the ethnoreligious research shifted attention from the national to the local level, from political elites to voters at the grass roots. The radically different perspective, working "from the bottom up," brought great excitement to the new political history in the 1960s and 1970s and sparked many new studies.[73]

Unfortunately, the momentum slipped in the 1980s. There has been no major research study since Kleppner's *Third Electoral System* appeared in 1979 and Formisano's *Transformation of Political Culture* in 1983. Must we agree with Jean Baker that "the limits have been reached," or

with Richard McCormick that ethnoreligious political analysis "as originally conceived, was at a dead end" by the late 1970s?[74] I think not, and
neither does McCormick, who has been a cogent critic. The ethnocultural
interpretation received a boost from new scholarship in the 1980s, which
blended the political ideology of republicanism and the rising forces of
capitalism with the social analysis of politics.[75] Moreover, the best work
since the mid-1970s has incorporated more sophisticated statistical techniques (multivariate correlation and regression analysis, partialing, path
analysis) that explain the relationship between voting choices and occupation, wealth, status, religion, and ethnicity. These studies proved again
that the politics of "'Amens' and 'Hallelujahs'" determined voting more
than class and status variables.[76]

Critics have leveled against the ethnoreligionists many charges, a few
of which are valid but most are not. Unsubstantiated charges are that
they are monocausalists who have exaggerated the religious variable to
the point of "religious determinism," that they have a "fixation" with
vague "symbolic" aspects of politics while ignoring concrete issues, that
they are ahistorical in treating religion independently of time and place,
that they ignored the unchurched or nominally churched half of the
population, that their statistical methods were weak and misguided, and
that their case study approach was not representative of the nation at
large.[77] The cultural Marxists have also reiterated their a priori assumptions about the centrality of economic factors.[78]

There are two valid criticisms—one relates to the religious model and
the other involves research design. Most important is the pietist-liturgical
continuum, which predicted how doctrinal beliefs were translated into
voting patterns. It is inadequate not because religious beliefs were "seldom dominant" in voting decisions, as one critic charged, but because
ultimate values and beliefs, which are always dominant in human
decision-making, are too complex for a one-dimensional, "either-or"
scale. In his 1979 book Kleppner offered a more complex model that
treated the pietistic and ritualistic perspectives as "more-or-less" characteristic of the various denominations rather than divided into two mutually exclusive types. He also drew distinctions among pietists between
Northern "evangelicals" and Southern "salvationists," and among ritualists between Lutherans and Catholics, centering on the extent to which
these groups compartmentalized the sacred from the secular. The sharper
the division, the less moral legislation.[79]

But this more sophisticated model still fails to incorporate necessary
distinctions among Northern evangelical pietists between mainline denominations such as Congregationalists, perfectionist denominations

such as Wesleyan Methodists, primitivist denominations such as the Churches of Christ, and separatists such as the Amish.[80] Issues of theology, polity, and praxis separated these groups, and we still need a model that incorporates these complexities and yet is sufficiently simple to be useful in research (the jargon word is "operational"). Kleppner's newer model points in the right direction. The relationship of the church to the world is crucial, as H. Richard Niebuhr explained in his book *Christ and Culture*.[81] Niebuhr identified five historic views: Christ *against* culture, Christ in *agreement* with culture, Christ *above* culture, Christ in *tension* with culture, and Christ *transforming* culture. While Niebuhr's categories need revision, especially since the current religious Right has made a shambles of the opposition view which stressed separation from culture, yet the key issue remains: how do persons of faith relate to the political world. Specialists in American religious history could make a major contribution to political history by developing a usable theological topology.

The other challenge is for energetic political historians with good statistical skills to undertake the massive study Kousser called for in 1979.[82] This is to validate the ethnoreligious interpretation by drawing random areal samples of rural townships and city wards, gathering all relevant socioeconomic facts for several decennial census years in the nineteenth century for these areas, and then making multivariate statistical tests to uncover the key determinants of voting behavior. Such a study might well yield a more generalized model of American voting behavior. It might even convince skeptics that religious institutions and values counted heavily in American politics and American history generally.

Religion, we now know, was the "stuff of political choice" in the last century, shaping the issues and rhetoric and determining party alignments.[83] Churches were primary value-generating institutions and religious beliefs inevitably affected political choices and goals. Voters responded to the theological outlook toward culture of their particular denominations, encouraged by in-group pressures and the influence of pastors and teachers. For opening this long-overlooked component of American political history, the ethnoreligious scholars deserve accolades. Until proven otherwise by new research, the legacy of their work stands.

Notes

1. Joel H. Silbey, Allan G. Bogue, William H. Flanigan, eds., *The History of American Electoral Behavior* (Princeton, NJ: Princeton University Press, 1978), 3–27, and references cited therein; Allan G. Bogue, "The New Political History of

the 1970s," in Bogue, *Clio and the Bitch Goddess: Quantification in American Political History* (Beverly Hills: Sage, 1983), 113–135. See also Bogue, "Inside the 'Iowa School'," in ibid., 19–50, esp. 22–24; Seymour Martin Lipset, "Religion and Politics in the American Past and Present," in Robert Lee and Martin E. Marty, eds., *Religion and Social Conflict* (New York: Oxford University Press, 1964), 69–126; Samuel Lubell, *The Future of American Politics* (Garden City, NY: Doubleday Anchor, 1956), 129–157; Lee Benson, "Research Problems in American Political Historiography," in Mira Komarovsky, ed., *Common Frontiers of the Social Sciences* (Glencoe, IL: Free Press, 1957), 113–183; Benson, *The Concept of Jacksonian Democracy: New York as a Test Case* (Princeton, NJ: Princeton University Press, 1961); Samuel P. Hays, "History as Human Behavior" [1959] and "New Possibilities for American Political History: The Social Analysis of Political Life" [1964], reprinted in Samuel P. Hays, *American Political History as Social Analysis* (Knoxville: University of Tennessee Press, 1980), 51–65, 87–132; Richard L. McCormick, "Ethnocultural Interpretations of Nineteenth Century American Voting Behavior" [1974], in Richard L. McCormick, *The Party Period and Public Policy: American Politics from the Age of Jackson to the Progressive Era* (New York: Oxford University Press, 1986), 29–63.

2. Lawrence H. Fuchs coined the term "ethnoreligious" in 1956 because of its "inclusive quality"; it incorporated ethnic groups such as the Irish, religious groups such as Jews and Quakers, and even racial groups such as blacks. See Fuchs, *The Political Behavior of American Jews* (Glencoe, IL: Free Press, 1956), 13. Another early analysis of the influence of religion in American voting is Benton Johnson, "Ascetic Protestantism and Political Preference," *Political Science Quarterly* 26 (Spring 1962): 35–46.

3. Silbey et al., *American Electoral Behaivor*, 20, 253–262; Robert P. Swierenga, "Ethnocultural Political Analysis: A New Approach to American Ethnic Studies," *Journal of American Studies* 5 (April 1971): 59–79; Samuel T. McSeveney, "Ethnic Groups, Ethnic Conflicts, and Recent Quantitative Research in American Political History," *International Migration Review* 7 (Spring 1973): 14–33; McCormick, "Ethnocultural Interpretations." A perceptive analysis of the evolving ethnic component of religion is Harry S. Stout, "Ethnicity: The Vital Center of Religion in America," *Ethnicity* (April 1975): 204–224.

4. The best summary of the literature is Richard L. McCormick, "The Social Analysis of American Political History—After Twenty Years," in McCormick, *Party Period*, 89–140.

5. Lipset, "Religion and Politics," 70; Silbey et al., *American Electoral Behavior*, 12–13.

6. Quoted in Richard Jensen, "The Religious and Occupational Roots of Party Identification: Illinois and Indiana in the 1870s," *Civil War History* 16 (December 1970): 325.

7. Lipset, "Religion and Politics," 120, n. 2.

8. Elmo Roper, "The Myth of the Catholic Vote," *Saturday Review of Literature*, October 31, 1959, p. 22.

9. Lipset, "Religion and Politics," 71, 120–121.

10. Benson, *Concept*, 165.

11. The core studies are: Paul Kleppner, *The Cross of Culture: A Social Analysis of Midwestern Politics, 1850–1900* (New York: Free Press, 1970); Richard J. Jensen, *The Winning of the Midwest: Social and Political Conflict, 1888–96* (Chicago: University of Chicago Press, 1971); and Ronald P. Formisano, *The Birth of Mass Political Parties: Michigan, 1827–1861* (Princeton, NJ: Princeton University Press, 1971). Recent major additions are: Paul Kleppner, *The Third Electoral System, 1853–1892: Parties, Voters, and Political Cultures* (Chapel Hill: University of North Carolina Press, 1979); and Ronald P. Formisano, *The Transformation of Political Culture: Massachusetts Parties, 1790s–1840s* (New York: Oxford University Press, 1983). Although omitted in this paper, Jews also had block voting for Jeffersonian Republicans and Jacksonian Democrats in the early republic, and after the 1840s they switched and became solidly Republican until the New Deal. See Wm. Ray Heitzmann, *American Jewish Voting Behavior: A History and Analysis* (San Francisco: R & E Research Associates, 1975).

12. Jensen, *Winning*, 62, 63–64. The exceptional religiosity of American life is also described in Seymour Martin Lipset, *The First New Nation* (New York: Basic Books, 1963), ch. 4, "Religion and American Values," 140–169.

13. George M. Marsden, *The Evangelical Mind and the New School Experience* (New Haven: Yale University Press, 1970), 239–242, relying on Perry Miller.

14. Benson, *Concept*, 281–287; Hays, "New Possibilities," 104–116; Hays, *American Political History*, 13–36, 132–156; Lipset, "Religion and Politics," 21, 111–120.

15. Derived from Merton's observation that "men frequently orient themselves to groups *other than their own* in shaping their behavior and evaluations," in *Social Theory and Social Structure* (Glencoe, IL: Free Press, 1957), 288.

16. Hays, "History as Human Behavior" [1959], in Hays, *American Political History*, 54; and Hays, "Political Parties and the Community—Society Continuum" [1967], in ibid., 300.

17. Lipset, "Religion and Politics," 71.

18. Benson, *Concept*, 27, 281–287; Hays, "History," in Hays, *American Political History*, 66, 87, and passim.

19. McCormick, "Ethnocultural Interpretations," 39–47, perceptively explains that the ethnocultural scholars somewhat carelessly intermixed these three theories.

20. Jensen, *Winning*, 82, 89.

21. Kleppner, *Cross*, 37, 75; Kleppner, *Third*, 183–197; Formisano, *Birth*, 102, 55; Jensen, *Winning*, 58, 88.

22. Kleppner, *Third*, 183, following Milton Rokeach, J. Milton Yinger, Rodney Stark, Charles Glock, Peter Berger, and other psychologists and sociologists of religion. While acknowledging religious values, some scholars believe that

political parties took shape independently and then they either attracted or repelled religious groups, depending on their platforms and programs. This is only a variant on the interest group interpretation. See John Ashworth, *'Agrarians' and 'Aristocrats': Party Political Ideology in the United States, 1837–1846* (London: Royal Historical Society, 1983), 219–221. Churches preceded parties in America and it is also logical to assume that religious preference preceded partisan preference. Cf. Jensen, *Winning*, 59.

23. Kleppner, *Third*, 183–185.

24. Kleppner, makes this point forcefully in ibid., 357–382.

25. Kleppner, *Cross*, 71–72; Kleppner, *Third*, 185–189; Jensen, *Winning*, 63–67. A contemporary scholar, Robert Baird, in *Religion in America* (New York: Harper & Row, 1844), divided all denominations into "Evangelical" and "Unevangelical" (p. 220). Scholars have struggled with other terms to identify the same distinction: Benson, puritan/nonpuritan (*Concept*, 198); Formisano, evangelical/anti-evangelical (*Birth*, 138) and center/periphery (*Transformation*, 5–7, passim); Philip R. VanderMeer, church/sect ("Religion, Society, and Politics: A Classification of American Religious Groups," *Social Science History* 5 [February 1981]: 3–24); Roger D. Peterson, traditionalist/pietist ("The Reaction to a Heterogeneous Society: A Behavioral and Quantitative Analysis of Northern Voting Behavior, 1845–1870, Pennsylvania a Test Case" [Ph.D. diss., University of Pittsburgh, 1970]; Edward R. Kantowitz, insider/outsider and dogmatist/pietist ("Politics," in Stephan Thernstrom, Ann Orlov, and Oscar Handlin, eds., *Harvard Encyclopedia of American Ethnic Groups* [Cambridge, MA: Harvard University Press, 1980], 803–804). Benson and Formisano are more reluctant than the other scholars cited to associate liturgical and pietist values with theology rather than to offer sociological explanations. See McCormick, *Party Period*, 48.

26. Alternatively, some have argued that the Jacksonians were rationalistic, republican nation-builders who enlisted Protestant imagery and symbols in order to legitimate and unify the "new experiment in self-government" and create a "public religion," to use Benjamin Franklin's phrase. Sidney Mead argues that in the second half of the nineteenth century, Protestantism was amalgamated with "Americanism" to form an all-encompassing "civil religion," the "Religion of the Republic." See Martin E. Marty, *Pilgrims in Their Own Land: Five Hundred Years of Religion in America* (New York: Viking Penguin, 1984), 154–166; Sidney E. Mead, *The Lively Experiment: The Shaping of Christianity in America* (New York: Harper & Row, 1963), 134–187; and Marsden, *Evangelical Mind*, 239–241.

27. This paragraph and the following rely heavily on Robert Kelley, *The Cultural Pattern in American Politics: The First Century* (New York: Knopf, 1979), ch. 5–8, esp. 160–170, 223–227; and Ashworth, *'Agrarians'*.

28. Georgetown *Democratic Standard*, September 12, 1843, as quoted in Stephen C. Fox, "The Bank Wars, The Idea of 'Party,' and the Division of the Electorate in Jacksonian Ohio," *Ohio History* 88 (Summer 1979): 257; Ann Arbor *Michigan Argus*, February 1, 1843, quoted in Formisano, *Birth*, 110.

29. See Bancroft, "The Office of the People in Art, Government and Religion," *Literary and Historical Miscellanies* (New York, 1855), 408–435, excerpted in Joseph L. Blau, *Social Theories of Jacksonian Democracy: Representative Writings of the Period, 1825–1850* (Indianapolis: Bobbs-Merrill, 1954), 263–273; and quotes in Arthur M. Schlesinger, Jr., *The Age of Jackson* (Boston: Little, Brown, 1945), 419.

30. Kelley, *Cultural Patterns*, 147; Ashworth, *'Agrarians'*, 178.

31. The best analysis of Whig culture and ideology is Daniel Walker Howe, *The Political Culture of the American Whigs* (Chicago and London: University of Chicago Press, 1979).

32. The Reverend Ezra Stiles Ely, pastor of Philadelphia's Third Presbyterian Church, was one such cleric who called for a Christian citizens movement, a loosely organized *"Christian party in politics,"* to influence Christians to vote for avowed Christian candidates. Ezra S. Ely, *The Duty of Christian Freeman to Elect Christian Rulers* (Philadelphia, 1827), cited in John R. Bodo, *The Protestant Clergy and Public Issues, 1812–1848* (Princeton: Princeton University Press, 1954). See also Benson, *Jacksonian Democracy*, 199–200.

33. Kelley, *Cultural Patterns*, 160–169.

34. Sydney E. Ahlstrom, *A Religious History of the American People* (New Haven: Yale University Press, 1972), 559–563.

35. Kelley, *Cultural Patterns*, 172.

36. Jensen, *Winning*, 67–68.

37. Kleppner, *Cross*, 72–75; and *Third*, 74, 360–363; cf. Jensen, *Winning*, 69; Formisano, *Birth*, 128, 324, 330; and Benson, *Concept*, 198–207.

38. Kleppner, *Third*, 363.

39. Ibid., 363–364. McCormick allows that religious beliefs explain the political behavior of pietists but not liturgicals, who simply acted in self-defense. Their worldview, says McCormick, had "no political significance until they were assaulted by pietists" (*Party Period*, 367). But it is illogical to hold that pietist theology was intrinsically political and liturgical theology was intrinsically apolitical. Liturgicals were on the defensive in the antebellum era because the Great Awakening impelled revivalists toward social activism. In the progressive era, however, pietist fundamentalists made the "great reversal" and withdrew from political life, while the liturgicals launched the social gospel movement. See David O. Moberg, *The Great Reversal: Evangelicalism versus Social Concern* (Philadelphia: Lippincott, 1972).

40. Kleppner, *Third*, 371, 359–361. Kelley, *Cultural Patterns*, 164, speaks of a "marginal preponderance."

41. Kleppner, *Third*, 363.

42. Ibid., 363–371, 167–168; Robert P. Swierenga, "The Ethnic Voter and the First Lincoln Election," *Civil War History* 11 (March 1965): 27–43, reprinted in Frederick C. Luebke, ed., *Ethnic Voters and the Election of Lincoln* (Lincoln: University of Nebraska Press, 1971), 129–150.

43. Benson, "Research Problems," 122.

44. See Kleppner, *Third*, 9–15, 322–331, 355–373, and passim for a discussion of the concept of social group.

45. Kleppner, *Third*, 204–205; Jensen, *Winning*, 85–87. Dale Baum, "The 'Irish Vote' and Party Politics in Massachusetts, 1860–1876," *Civil War History* 26 (June 1980): 120, argues that systematic underenumeration in counting "seats," especially for Catholic churches, which served several groups of parishioners, would "make no difference" in statistical analyses. Formisano is unduly pessimistic when he says: "religion counted for very much in politics, [but] it is almost impossible to measure precisely religious affiliation among the electorate" (*Transformation*, 289–290). Formisano was more favorable earlier. See his "Analyzing American Voting, 1830–1860: Methods," *Historical Methods Newsletter* 2 (March 1969): 1–12. The censuses of "Social Statistics" from 1850 list each church by denomination in every town and give the number of "accommodations" or "seats" in each building. The percentage of each denomination's seats of the total seats indicates the "religious preferences" of each township.

46. Peterson, "Reaction."

47. Lipset, "Religion and Politics," 101–102.

48. Jensen, "Religious and Occupational Roots," 168–169; Jensen, *Winning*, 325; Peterson, "Reaction," 263–269.

49. Formisano, *Birth*, 297–298, 318–323, 346–348, found voter lists for Lansing, Detroit, and Ingham County in the 1850s. Melvyn Hammarberg, *The Indiana Voter: The Historical Dynamics of Party Allegiance During the 1870s* (Chicago: University of Chicago Press, 1977), 107–108, found *People's Guides* in Indiana in the 1870s that specified religion. See also: Kenneth J. Winkle, "A Social Analysis of Voter Turnout in Ohio, 1850–1860," *Journal of Interdisciplinary History* 13 (Winter 1983): 411–435; Paul F. Bourke and Donald A. DeBats, "Individuals and Aggregates: A Note on Historical Data and Assumptions," *Social Science History* 4 (May 1980): 229–250; John M. Rozett, "Racism and Republican Emergence in Illinois, 1848–1860: A Re-Evaluation of Republican Negrophobia," *Civil War History* 22 (June 1976): 101–115, based on Rozett, "The Social Bases of Party Conflict in the Age of Jackson: Individual Voting Behavior in Greene County, Illinois, 1838–1848" (Ph.D. diss., University of Michigan, 1974); David H. Bohmer, "The Maryland Electorate and the Concept of a Party System in the Early National Period," in Silbey et al., *History of American Electoral Behavior*, 146–173.

50. Thomas A. Kremm, "Cleveland and the First Lincoln Election: The Ethnic Response to Nativism," *Journal of Interdisciplinary History* 8 (Summer 1977): 77–78. This article is based on Kremm, "The Rise of the Republican Party in Cleveland, 1848–1860" (Ph.D. diss., Kent State University, 1974).

51. Lee Benson and Samuel Hays pioneered this technique. See Benson, *Concept* (paperback ed., 1963), ix–x, 165–207; and Hays, *American Political Analysis*, 10–12. J. Morgan Kousser, "The 'New Political History': A Methodological Critique," *Reviews in American History* 4 (March 1976): 1–14, harshly

castigates this approach as "gestalt correlation," and "proving correlation by intimidation" (5-6). McCormick is also critical; see "Ethnocultural Interpretations," 41.

52. Kousser, "'New Political History,'" 10-11.

53. In addition to the studies already cited, see: Michael F. Holt, *Forging a Majority: The Formation of the Republican Party in Pittsburgh 1848-1860* (New Haven: Yale University Press, 1969); William E. Giennap, *The Origins of the Republican Party, 1852-1856* (New York: Oxford University Press, 1987); William G. Shade, *Banks or No Banks: The Money Issue in Western Politics* (Detroit: Wayne State University Press, 1972); Samuel McSeveney, *The Politics of Depression: Political Behavior in the Northeast, 1893-1896* (New York: Oxford University Press, 1972); John L. Hammond, *The Politics of Benevolence: Revival Religion and American Voting Behavior* (Norwood, NJ: Abbey, 1979); Frederick C. Luebke, *Immigrants and Politics: The Germans of Nebraska, 1880-1900* (Lincoln: University of Nebraska Press, 1969); Philip R. VanderMeer, *The Hoosier Politician: Officeholding and Political Culture in Indiana 1896-1920* (Urbana: University of Illinois Press, 1985); Dale Baum, *The Civil War Party System: The Case of Massachusetts, 1848-1876* (Chapel Hill: University of North Carolina Press, 1984); Joel H. Silbey, *The Transformation of American Politics* (Englewood Cliffs, NJ: Prentice-Hall, 1967); Jed Dannenbaum, *Drink and Disorder: Temperance Reform in Cincinnati from the Washingtonian Revival to the WCTU* (Urbana: University of Illinois Press, 1984); Walter D. Kamphoefner, "Dreissiger and Forty-Eighter: The Political Influence of Two Generations of German Political Exiles," in Hans L. Trefousse, ed., *Germany and America: Essays on Problems of International Relations and Immigration* (New York: Brooklyn College Press, 1980), 89-102; Stephen C. Fox, "The Group Bases of Ohio Political Behavior, 1803-1848" (Ph.D. diss., University of Cincinnati, 1973); Fox, "Politicians, Issues, and Voter Preference in Jacksonian Ohio: A Critique of an Interpretation," *Ohio History* 86 (Summer 1977): 155-170; Roger E. Wyman, "Wisconsin Ethnic Groups and the Election of 1890," *Wisconsin Magazine of History* 51 (Summer 1968): 269-293, reprinted in Robert P. Swierenga, ed., *Quantification in American History: Theory and Research* (New York: Atheneum, 1970), 239-266.

54. The leader of the Holland colony, Albertus C. Van Raalte, who had led the affiliation with the Reformed Church in the East, was accused of promoting the Arminian theology of the Reverend Richard Baxter, found in his booklet "Call to the Unconverted." See *Classis Holland Minutes, 1843-1858* (Grand Rapids: Eerdmans, 1950), 144-145, 181-182, 227-228, 240-243, 246.

55. Kleppner, *Third*, 166-169.

56. Formisano, *Birth*, 104.

57. Hammond, *Politics*, ch. 4-5, esp. 75-76, 124-133.

58. Formisano, *Birth*, 58, 79.

59. Kleppner, *Third*, 59, 73, citing Richard L. Power, *Planting Cornbelt Culture* (Indianapolis: Indiana Historical Society, 1953).

60. Ibid., 74.

61. Kremm, "First Lincoln Election," 69–86.

62. Ibid., 82, citing the January 30, 1855, issue of the Cleveland *Express*.

63. Ibid., 83–85, quote on 85, citing various articles of the Cleveland *Leader*.

64. Ibid., Table 6, 76, 80–81.

65. Holt, *Forging*, 218, quote on 7, 9.

66. Kleppner, *Third*, 136–140.

67. Ibid., Table 6.3, 205–206.

68. Kleppner, *Cross*, 316–368.

69. VanderMeer, "Religion," 18. Other positive comments are in VanderMeer, "The New Political History: Progress and Prospects," *Computers and the Humanities* 11 (September–October, 1977): 267.

70. Kleppner, *Third*, 196.

71. Sean Wilentz, "On Class and Politics in Jacksonian America," *Reviews in American History* 10 (December 1982): 47–48; James E. Wright, "The Ethnocultural Model of Voting: A Behavioral and Historical Critique," in Allan G. Bogue, ed., *Emerging Theoretical Models in Social and Political History* (Beverly Hills: Sage, 1973), 40.

72. See, for example, Paul E. Johnson, *A Shopkeeper's Millennium: Society and Revivals in Rochester, New York, 1815–1837* (New York: Hill and Wang, 1978). An excellent review of the Marxist social historians of American politics is McCormick, "Social Analysis," 98–115.

73. Allan G. Bogue, "The New Political History in the 1970s," in Bogue, *Clio and the Bitch Goddess*, 116.

74. Jean H. Baker, *Affairs of Party: The Political Culture of Northern Democrats in the Mid-Nineteenth Century* (Ithaca: Cornell University Press, 1983), 11; McCormick, "Social Analysis," 95.

75. McCormick, "Social Analysis," 96–97.

76. Kleppner, *Third*, 326–328, 361–363.

77. Allan G. Bogue, "The New Political History," *American Behavioral Scientist* 21 (November–December 1977), 203 (but Bogue withdraws the charge of monocausality in "New Political History in the 1970s," 122); Richard B. Latner and Peter Levine, "Perspective on Antebellum Pietistic Politics," *Reviews in American History* 4 (March 1976): 19, and Eric Foner, "The Causes of the American Civil War: Recent Interpretations and New Directions," *Civil War History* 20 (September 1974): 200, make the charge of religious determinism; Edward Pessen, review of Kelley, *Cultural Pattern*, in *Civil War History* 25 (September 1979): 281, for the fixation charge; Latner and Levine, "Perspectives," 17, Foner, "Causes," 200, and Wright, "Ethnocultural," 46, for the ahistorical charge; Hammarberg, *Indiana Voter*, 116, for ignoring unchurched; Kousser, "'New Political History,'" 1–14, and A. J. Lichtman and L. I. Langbein, "Ecological Regression Versus Homogeneous Units: A Specification Analysis," *Social Science History* 2 (Winter 1978): 172–193, for methodological critiques (but for a rebuttal, see William G. Shade, "Banner Units and Counties: An Empirical

Comparison of Two Approaches," unpublished paper); Bogue, "New Political History," 209, for the case approach comment.

78. Kleppner, *Third*, 376; McCormick, "Social Analysis," 98–115. The strongest voting study from an economic perspective is Baum, *The Civil War Party System*.

79. Kleppner, *Third*, 186–188.

80. VanderMeer, "Religion," 10–16.

81. Niebuhr, *Christ and Culture* (New York: Harper, 1951), 39–44.

82. Kousser, "'New Political History,'" 10–11.

83. Silbey et al., *American Political Behavior*, 23.

8

Religion and the "Civilizing Process" in the Early American South, 1600–1860

BERTRAM WYATT-BROWN

The Southern mind has always been divided between pride and piety. Despite the significance of that dichotomy, no historian, theologian, or sociologist has yet portrayed the tortured relationship between Protestantism and popular ethics—what people, churched and unchurched, thought and practiced rather than what they proclaimed. Among the reasons for the neglect is the fact that some scholars deny the reality of a Southern identity and unique set of values.[1] Moreover, such church historians as Sidney Mead have fixed on the role of denominational rivalry in creating the voluntary and democratic character of the young republic rather than upon problems of religious and social change.[2] Above all, the ethical foundations of the white South have not been well enough understood for the question to be properly posed.

One of the basic factors of Southern moral experience was the code of honor, an ideology and mode of discourse that contended with Christianity for mastery of the soul of the South. Preachers and ministers not only had to fight "sin"—that is, those basic faults to which all mankind is subject—they also had to confront a system of rigid and sacralized customs that stressed manhood over effeminacy, patriarchal over companionate marital life, and other formulations that separated what we might call Christian modernity from ancient male privilege. A proper understanding of that conflict helps to reveal the distinctiveness of Southern politics, which was as distinctive as the region's religious system—rationalistic in the eighteenth century but thereafter evangelical and revivalistic. The rhetoric and even goals of Southern politics, as defense of white supremacy, conservative economics, and limited government, rested, Southerners thought, upon Christian concepts of order and conduct, but also upon honor, a marital ethic originating in pre-Christian Europe. An examination of these often competing forces, while not a narrowly political or narrowly religious exercise in itself, is in fact a necessary precondition for understanding the singular unfolding of both religion and politics in Southern history.

As a moral construction, honor has a singular and tragic defect. According to Julian Pitt-Rivers, the well-known anthropologist, the ethic "stands as a mediator between individual aspirations and the judgment of society," a standard less than lofty. The elements that compose honor, he further explains, "may be viewed as related in the following way: honor felt [in the individual aspirant] becomes honor claimed, and honor claimed becomes honor paid. . . . Public opinion, in its sympathy for the successful [and sometimes charismatic], betrays the notion of honor as a purely moral concept."[3] Although dedicated to the higher criteria of Christian conduct, clergy and pious laymen were themselves part of the social regime that upheld the regional conventions and mores. The divergences between Christian principle and honor could often be reconciled. After all, codification of honor could be located in Scripture itself. Middle Eastern cultures, then and now, have been partly based upon a rigid code of honor and heightened fear of shame. The worship of God was itself an act conceptualized in terms of that code. The prophets' jeremiads denounced the wayward Israelites for the dishonoring offense of impugning the blamelessness of God. They took from God due honor and glory—two interconnected modes of praise rendered in the one Hebrew word *KABOD*. Even the commandment "Love thy neighbor as thyself," meant, according to rabbinic tradition, to hold others—their properties and families—in honor as you would have them respect you, your relations, and your possessions. Southern Protestants had no difficulty adopting such an approach to divine understanding.[4] Ancient honor of this kind, as the classicist Paul Friedrich observes, could "'look back' at what it presupposes and 'look ahead' to what it enjoins." Thus magnanimity, a prime virtue in the code of honor in which the power to give was displayed, resembled Christian charity in appearance if not in motive. Southern hospitality sometimes involved both ethical modes. In sum, the biblical rendering of honor endured among Southerners accustomed to face-to-face, small-scale, family-oriented usages that bore analogy with the pastoral society that produced the Holy Word.[5]

Other aspects of honor, however, were clearly anti-Christian, though stubbornly adhered to, even by Christians themselves. These factors involved issues of precedence—race, blood lineage, appearance, inherited wealth—matters that underlined inequalities in the social order. Old Testament vengeance against those dishonoring Jehovah certainly gave scriptural justification to acts of violence and feuding. But on a more secular, even pagan level, an insistence upon the equality of all Southern white men to strive for honors was itself an invitation to aggression. As Edward Ayers puts it, "Honor was the catalyst necessary to ignite the South's volatile mixture of slavery, scattered settlement, heavy drinking, and ubiquitous weaponry."[6]

The topic is broad and the concepts involved elusive. Terms like "honor," "shame," "conscience," and "guilt" are merely glosses for much more discrete actions and attitudes which may contradict, overlap, or reinforce each other.[7] Yet a shorthand is necessary, as well as a division of the topic into chronologically manageable parts. To that end the ethical/ social development of the white South may be separated into three eras of relative dominance over the popular mind. The first is labeled the Age of Custom, a time marked by a continuation of English tradition along with a fragile but growing social and moral consolidation toward an American synthesis, roughly 1600–1760. During this period, the ascriptive character of Southern—or, more precisely, Chesapeake and Carolinian—life was much more evident than any religious set of prescriptions governing behavior, a contrast with the Puritan settlements of New England and the Quaker province of Pennsylvania. The second era, to be called the Age of Fervor, represented a sharp break with the past, 1760–1840. During this interval a Christian consensus gradually emerged to challenge or at least coexist with the older tradition. As the church in the slave South grew more self-confident, the region entered what is designated here as the Age of Ambivalence, a short span of still greater change that ended in 1861 with the establishment of a confederacy based on a paradoxically dissonant union of honor and the cause of God.

With reference to the first of the stages in social and religious development, early Southern society was crude, hierarchic, racialist, and communally mistrustful. Only gradually was a sense of helplessness and pagan fatalism shed. The unpredictability of life and fortune in the malarial semitropical climate of the South was responsible. In addition, as Jon Butler has proposed, ancient notions of magic persisted in all sections of early America, but most especially in the Southern colonies. For substantial numbers of Southern Christians, institutional religion and white magic were so intermingled that "the prayers of the common people were more like spells and charms than devotions," observed Sir Benjamin Rudyerd in 1628 with regard to his English contemporaries. Such incantations, argues the historian Darrett Rutman, gratified "the thirst to systemize the unknown." Early Virginia planters placed books on the occult next to bound sermons and weighty political treatises.[8] "Witchmasters" and cunningmen, that is, individuals paid to mediate between unseen forces and their victims, served public needs as readily as did the Anglican clergy. Indeed, witchcraft and pagan divinations were as popular in Virginia as they were in the rural districts of Old England. By such means men sought control over their environment and prospects with the same hope of success as they might beseech divine favor in a more institutional setting. Such patterns of thought encouraged the old belief that a person's honor was more valuable than his life and that to place survival above honor was to be degraded.[9]

The church was not in the best position to alter supernatural belief and practice or to challenge the salience of honor and shame. Patricia Bonomi argues that colonial Americans worshiped regularly. Southern churchmanship, however, did not match the national standard, which was itself low enough.[10] In addition, Southern church attendance was often spotty. On the one hand, in Middlesex, Virginia, in 1724, roughly a third of the white, adult citizenry were communicants, a total of 230. On the other hand, in that same year, Baltimore's St. Paul's, the "mother church" of Maryland, counted only 25 communicants in a settlement of nearly 400 families.[11] Moreover, Sabbatarian enforcements by law guaranteed only physical presence, not mental attentiveness. The program for Southern evangelization that the Society for the Propagation of the Christian Gospel began at the close of the seventeenth century made remarkable strides forward during the next half-century, but still left pulpits unfilled, churches unbuilt, and white settlers—as well as vast numbers of the Southern slaves—unchurched. All too often the church functioned in ways that combined secular needs with spiritual ones in a traditional English fashion that enhanced social life but not necessarily religious aims. Families gathered at church to gossip, display power and wealth, or make plans for business or entertainment.[12] Furthermore, the

Anglican church in the South upheld the system of honor, particularly with regard to political power. Parishioners elected gentlemen of standing to the vestry or vestrymen themselves filled vacancies with friends, but by one means or another the same end was reached: the confirming of the new vestryman's prestige in the community at large.[13]

Most important of all, the established church served as guardian of social order in a coarse, undereducated, and rather institutionless society which recognized moral claims largely on the basis of assertions of power. Clerical leaders urged the maintenance of law, but the law was weakly enforced since household or patriarchal autonomy—freedom from outside control and from dependency—was the essence of all men's honor, regardless of individual social standing. Ceremony, draconian penalties, and clerical admonition could not master a people still living by an ethic of honor. In 1676, the Rev. John Yeo lamented that in his part of southern Maryland "the lords day is prophaned, Religion despised, and all notorious vices committed soe th[a]t it is become a Sodom of uncleanness and a Pest house of iniquity." Just or not, his complaint indicated that the church's mission almost had to be the upholding of public order rather than the saving of souls. After all, 1676 was the year of Bacon's rebellion, one of several outbreaks that the traditional code had long encouraged in England as well as early America.[14] Nor had the moral climate greatly improved some fifty years later. Governor William Gooch in 1735 confided to Edmund Gibson, Bishop of London, that "gross Ignorance, an heathenish Rudeness, and an utter unconcernedness for the Things of God" were so prevalent that "many Parishes are even at this day, like churches newly Planted, but not well formed." Commenting on life in the mid-eighteenth-century Shenandoah Valley, Samuel Kercheval declared that "neither law nor gospel" domesticated a population both "illiterate" and "rough and tumble."[15]

Bearing these circumstances in mind, we can appreciate the insights of German sociologist Norbert Elias, who sees a close connection between the way people in the past behaved and the material circumstances and social structures to which they were accustomed. According to Elias, central to the "civilizing process" was the development of an ever greater complexity of forms. Advances in the goods people owned and the specializations of work produced required an ever higher "threshold of shame" and tended toward the repression of sheer natural, childlike impulse. Yet, so long as material circumstances provided little sense of privacy and self-differentiation, more primitive habits could not easily be reformed.[16]

In early modern times, men, women, and children—even stranger-guests—customarily slept in the same bed or at least the same room. Elias argues that people so disposed "stood in a different relationship with each other" from that to which we are accustomed. Men and women were much less conscious of those proprieties which create and express the notion of individual privacy and autonomy. They lacked that uncalculated social trust in the self-restraint of others that is the hallmark of the notion of individual privacy. That development was slow to arrive in the early South, owing in part to the harshness of material life and the impulsive character of its settlers.[17]

Living conditions in Virginia resembled the largely untamed state of life in southern England from which, according to linguistic evidence, the Chesapeake inhabitants had migrated.[18] As in the southern districts of England, seventeenth-century Southern houses were public, cramped, and uncomfortable. "Crowding people into a single room—sometimes as small as ten by twelve feet—made for a communal style of life," observes the colonial historian Rhys Isaac. "With so little specialization of space there could be only minimum differentiation of functions. Persons growing up in such an environment would not develop a sense of segregated self with a need for privacy."[19]

By the mid-eighteenth century housing, furnishings, and amenities (such as tea and coffee) had improved considerably. Both taste and means had improved throughout the Chesapeake, argue two noted economic historians, but possibly as many as the entire bottom third of whites escaped their calculations, which are drawn from tax lists and will inventories. In any event, if Middlesex County, Virginia, was representative, most habitations were not much larger than they had been eighty or more years before. They were still, say the Rutmans, "'Virginia common built' houses, more often than not one or two rooms and a loft, of weathering wood and inevitably in some degree of disrepair."[20] Crowding was unavoidable, even with blankets (though needed for warmth) to partition rooms. As late as 1776, Francis Asbury complained about living in a house in Virginia only "twenty feet by sixteen," with "seven beds and sixteen persons therein, and some noisy children."[21] Given these conditions, a rigorous sense of shame and self-control—as well as sense of humanity and individuality—could not develop swiftly.[22]

The concept of private shame which could undermine the psychology of public honor grew fitfully in the South, partly, too, because of the rapid growth of slavery. Bondage permitted a raw, institutionless society to reproduce the kind of untrammeled power that once had been the sole prerogative of the medieval nobility. Slavery encouraged vanity, one might even say vulgarity. Just as social hierarchy permitted a medieval lord's shamelessness in front of his valet or housemaid, such immodesty was accepted in the slave South. Frances Trollope, the caustic English observer of the American scene, reported as late as the 1820s how a young lady, so modest that she went out of her way to avoid touching the elbow of a male dinner partner on one occasion, laced her corset stays sometime later "with the most perfect composure before a negro footman." Even later still—in the 1850s—a Northern woman, newly married to a North Carolina planter, remarked that maidservants came and went through boltless bedroom doors as if it scarcely mattered what scene they might come upon.[23]

The reverse order of immodesty also applied: black nakedness apparently violated no white propriety. In 1781, William Feltman, a Pennsylvania Revolutionary officer, reported in his diary that young slave boys waited on plantation dining guests in clothing that left nothing to the imagination. "I am surprized," he said, "this does not hurt the feelings of this fair Sex to see these young boys of about Fourteen and Fifteen years Old to Attend them. these [sic] whole nakedness Expos'd and I can Assure you It would Surprize a person to see these d--d black boys how well they are hung."[24] Indeed, slaves were almost universally whipped unclothed and were customarily forced to disrobe for buyers' inspection. Slaves, argued Dr. Benjamin West, often showed "courage, resolution and genious" far above the ordinary, but "a [white] man will shoot a Negro with as little emotion as he shoots a hare."[25] Such a bestial view of slaves encouraged a coarseness of sensibility. In some instances even ministers treated slaves with unconscionable brutality. After supervising the fatal beating of his slave for running away, an Anglican divine of seventeenth-century Virginia remarked, "Accidents will happen now and then."[26]

Behind the clergyman's uncontrolled passions there lay a style of acting that betrayed the sense of helplessness, even hopelessness, which adherents to the code of honor sought to hide from themselves and others. Malignity was a function of an unrecognized sense of impotence—an emptiness that religious faith was supposed to fill. But under the hierarchies of race and class, honor, not Christian practice, provided the psychological framework in an unreliable world.[27] Thus, the purpose of the code was to unite the internal man and the external realities of his existence in such a way that the aspirant to its claims knew no other good or evil except that which the community designated.[28] The white Southerner's lack of self-restraint was a way of asserting power to be publicly admired and to cast off any doubt of cowardice or deception. Brutal fights in which a man might lose an eye, ear, lip, or nose erupted over the pettiest of quarrels. Rivalry for public esteem lay behind most of them.[29]

During the second era in the "civilizing process," the Age of Fervor, circumstances improved dramatically. The hard code of family-based honor gradually softened as piety became a prerequisite for the determination of respectability. Living conditions for slaves—and for whites—also improved under the reign of King Cotton, whose profits financed improved shelter, diet, and clothing, as Robert Fogel and Stanley Engerman persuasively argue.[30] Greater privacy and self-respect for slaves not only benefited life in the quarters but gave whites a greater sense of order. Acculturated and Christian blacks were unlikely to rebel; masters would have less occasion to be themselves disorderly in slave management; and the white children would not witness and emulate displays of white adult ill temper and arrogance, as they often did. Moreover, in over greater numbers slaves were drawn into the Christian fold and even helped to shape the spiritual understandings of whites, a development which, as historian Mechal Sobel has so thoughtfully argued, began in the eighteenth century.[31]

Religious advances also aided a quickening pace of social amelioration, largely through the development of the dissenting faiths. Bitter for both social and religious reasons, leaders of the Baptist yeomanry in Virginia and elsewhere during the First Awakening sought to counter the example that the gentry class had set before the public. Declared David Thomas, a Virginia Baptist, "Riches and honor and carnal wisdom are no badges of the Christian Religion."[32] As Philip Fithian, the Yankee tutor in Virginia, noted, they were "quite destroying pleasure in the country" with their fervent prayer and "an entire Banishment of *Gaming, Dancing,* and Sabbath-Day Diversions."[33] On such grounds, Baptists as well as early Methodists did effect a major social revolution in the late eighteenth and early nineteenth centuries as their numbers grew. Although opposed to the blood sports, races, and other games because of their long association with gambling, drinking, and similar male vices, the regenerates used physicality in what they called Christian ways. Thus, the pleasures of motion in dancing and sports found expression in the movements and touching of converts that characterized the revival experience. Both Baptists and Methodists created new emotional ties among their members with rituals of embrace that made use of the older, uninhibited impulsive habits.[34] By giving them a more instrumental, democratic purpose, they not only changed men's habits but also reshaped the meaning of respectability. Honor's value had depended upon its exclusivity; the Christian gospel, as the dissenters interpreted it, in effect devalued honor by making salvation available to all regardless of place in the social order.[35] In addition, the dissenters replaced the ineffective Anglican reliance upon public law for policing local morals with inner church discipline. As early as the mid-eighteenth century and throughout the greater part of the nineteenth, expulsion or even reprimand by one's brethren in church often shamed culprits into conformity, sporadic or permanent.[36]

In the antebellum period, members of the Baptist and Methodist faiths, however, grew wealthier and more sophisticated with each generation. Despite former convictions about the sins of Mammon and love of ease, Baptists were more likely than any others to own slaves, a form of property which encouraged luxury, license, and other violations of God's law. Their religious life became more sedate. Yet their adherence to the newly acquired honor of slaveholding respectability increased. The sensibilities of antique honor and shame—polarities of the old faith in the world of the unprivate self—began to weaken and merge into the new individualized order of conscience and guilt.

Other aspects of the older ethic underwent change, too. With inebriation a chief offense in church courts, sobriety became a more widely approved personal virtue (although alcoholic consumption actually increased until 1835, when a slow decline began).[37] Earlier, in eighteenth-century South Carolina, for instance, Carolinian diners at hunt-club feasts would allow no member "to go home sober," an affront, recalled William J. Grayson, "to good manners."[38] Piecemeal or in whole, antebellum Southerners were adopting the restrictive proprieties that the more economically advanced parts of the Western world had already established as conventions.

The story of the Second Great Awakening and its successes needs no retelling here; the focus must be upon factors inhibiting its impact.[39] First, an eroding but still lively sentiment thrived that male participation in church life was unmanly.[40] Part of the problem was men's growing wariness about women's growing role in religion and their tacit or overt disapproval of male associations outside the home. Stimulated by revivals and clerical admonitions to guard the house from sin, women exploited the changing ethical landscape to grasp for domestic power with claims of high religious motives in the eternal battle between the sexes. Quarrels and smoldering enmities sometimes arose from the struggles between pious women and husbands accustomed to "dissipating at the Races and Theatres; every day dining out," as one antebellum Southern matron complained.[41]

In Southern society the parallels between the kind of church system that developed and the precepts of the old ethic were rather remarkable.

The pagan fatalism of honor had its counterpart in the predestinarianism of the Southern denominations. The Manichaean distinction of good and evil, hero and coward, resembled the Christian doctrines of heavenly reward and hellfire punishment. The camaraderie of the militia muster had its echo in the right hand of fellowship of the Wesleyan and Baptist faithful. As the historian Johann Huizinga noted some years ago, sports like cockfighting and horse-racing often involved a kind of oneness of man and beast in a "sacred identity . . . a mystic unity. The one has *become* the other."[42] The dejection of the gambler at loss and his ecstasy on winning mocked, in a sense, the Christian experience of alienation and conviction, for the polarities of victory and loss at games had their popular appeal. Rather than trust God's providence, the gambler and sportsman venerated a pagan fate in whose hands the bettor surrendered his hopes for the sake of virile self-regard rather than for a Christian humility and a pride in hard work.[43] "Those who participated in the emotional fervor of the revival meetings," historian Ted Ownby declares, "were rarely the same people enjoying the hot-blooded competitions of male gatherings." The tension, he argues, between "the extremes of masculine aggressiveness and homecentered evangelicalism" endowed "white Southern culture" with its paradoxical and passionate character.[44]

By no means did the Christianization of the South in the nineteenth century, either before or after the Civil War, bring an end to the impulsive habits of Southern violence. The church leaders only imperfectly channeled aggression into revival ecstasies. Sometimes they even provided a subtext of hatred against nonbelievers and perceived community enemies. One Southern church historian has observed that in the absence of other institutions, the churches were "practically the only agency for the improvement of the people."[45] But so solitary a force could not meet the challenge under the changed conditions of flux, secular forces, and declining use of church discipline which had depended upon intensely familial social relations. In a Tennessee-Kentucky border district in the late nineteenth century, the six local churches "were unsuccessful as agents of social change" and sometimes had to face the taunts of invading bullies during services. A mountaineer, arrested in 1905, interrupted worship by accusing the church folk of "stealing stove caps from women's cook-stoves, fornications, stealing hog heads and hog faces, laundered shirts etc." Such scenes had marked the experiences of missionaries and preachers in the Southern wilderness as early as the days of the Reverend Charles Woodmason in colonial North and South Carolina. With only a few exceptions church leaders, even in sophisticated areas, seldom treated violence as a regional or even local social problem.[46]

To control passions effectively, a transformation of the whole social and ethical order would have had to emerge. The church was not strong enough to speed the trend. Prohibitions against gaming, drink, and dueling, for instance, were all but unenforceable given the restrictive technicalities of the court system and the reluctance of juries to convict when communities and states attempted such approaches.[47] First there was the institutional inadequacy of the churches. Ministers continued to be in short supply throughout the antebellum period.[48] Southern church goers and their leaders showed a number of negative reactions: suspicion of new ways, defense of noblesse oblige, dread of outside encroachment upon male and family prerogative, fear of effects upon the racial order, concern over the theological correctness of using human agencies for spiritual ends in the fashion of the Northern Whig/evangelical culture that Daniel Walker Howe has described. A deep-seated pessimism about the reformability of man conspired against participation in voluntary associations for moral purposes. In the 1820s and 1830s, missionaries from Northern benevolent societies met stiff resistance and sometimes ridicule. Voluntarism, declared suspicious Antimission Baptists—and others as well—was merely a "Money Making Scheme of less Public utility than common Lotteries."[49] One Pennsylvania missionary found Arkansas, his newly assigned district, so hostile that he called the new district *"heathen country"* compared with his itinerancy in Indiana, a truly *"Christian land."*[50]

Among the many problems was the difficulty of finding male lay leaders to sponsor the new measures of voluntarism and clerical professionalism. Helping a pious itinerant stranger brought local laymen no particular community prestige. He might disseminate dangerous notions.[51] Moreover, in terms of reaching the young with the Christian message, the lack of common schools ill prepared both pupils and local teachers for Christian study. Old attitudes about child-rearing worked against efforts to reach the young through the innovation of Sunday schools. Sheldon Norton, another Northern missionary, discovered in Alabama that parents wished their offspring to be "unrestrained," as childhood was thought to be "a season which should be left run to waste."[52] (For church folk as well as the unchurched, aggressiveness in male children was not to be discouraged for fear of effeminacy.)

Finally, most evangelical clergy, even Methodist bishops, were, in a sense, part-time ministers. By necessity of low salaries, they devoted most weekdays to farming or business, not to church activities or pastoral visits. In contrast, Northern and Western churchmen, whose stipends largely permitted full-time work, adopted modes of "associationism" and voluntary action with remarkable results both for religion and for "the civilizing process." Don Doyle, the urban historian, has pointed out that in antebellum Jacksonville, Illinois, a typical Midwestern town, the voluntary association offered participants social and ethical advantages. Active members were likely to appear in the local paper, no mean advantage in "a young community of newcomers." Furthermore, benevolent societies served to "integrate sectional, religious, or political factions within the middle class." For ambitious young mechanics and craftsmen who found "card tables and billiard saloons" distasteful, the voluntary society was a more agreeable organization to join than the militia, the Southern ladder to social and political success.[53] Evidence indicates that the urban South lagged only slightly behind the advance of benevolent agencies in the free states. Yet, most Southerners lived in tiny hamlets and rural districts where civic or charitable activity was bound to be less welcome, less organized, less sustainable.[54] In those locations, especially, the kinship bond was the chief foundation of church life, just as it was for most other social events in the South.[55]

The maintenance of Southern familial and community honor had traditionally involved the use of informal, extralegal modes of surveillance and control. To attack crime or wrongdoing required neither the forming of a moral reform society nor Whiggish calls for laws to be strictly enforced, but rather the assembling of a community-based charivari. In Mississippi, a woman who conspired with her lover to kill her husband received a severe whipping at the hands of irate citizens. On the basis of a coerced confession, she was tried at the bar and convicted as an accessory to murder. Petitioners to Governor Hiram G. Runnels urged clemency, not because her rights had been violated but because the community penalty abrogated the need for any further punishment.[56] In the North such Federalist church leaders as those whom Harry Stout has portrayed promptly denounced the "people in the streets" when riots or vigilantism arose. In the antebellum South their clerical counterparts were mute. Churchmen rationalized their silence as a worthy insusceptibility to the clamors of political warfare. For Methodists, most especially, the "family" of the faithful were to be kept separate from the world or else become contaminated by it.[57]

Yet Southern ministers were not altogether consistent about the handling of political agitations. During the Nullification Crisis, some South Carolinian clergymen spoke out pro and con. The fire-eating Rev. Thomas Goulding of the Presbyterian Theological Seminary in Columbia declared that "Disunion would be, in national politics, to prefer weakness to strength—degradation to honorable rank." On the other

hand, at Pendleton Village, Richard P. Cater invested the Nullifiers' case
with biblical significance, likening South Carolina to the King of Israel in
dealing with the "Princes of Ammon." Linking Carolina's honor with
Christian zeal, he urged churchgoing freemen to repudiate the Union and
thus to "prefer the stillness and silence of the grave, to the heart chilling
clangour [sic] of the chains of slavery." Such outspokenness threatened
congregational schisms. By and large, clergymen preferred a more tran-
quil gaze on the political scene, reserving their anger for such uncontro-
versial targets as the abolition menace.[58] Otherwise, the antebellum
Southern divines guarded their reputations with care.[59] Their position,
church historian Samuel S. Hill explains, was that religion should be
largely "a matter of the individual's standing before God, who would
grant or withhold pardon of sins and the reward of everlasting life, and of
the sinner's relationship with the Lord, emanating in assurance and
consolation." As a result, he concludes, "responsibility for the public
order or for prophetic scrutiny into society's ways" played little role in the
life of the Southern church.[60]

Between 1840 and 1861, the Age of Ambivalence, church power had
developed to a point that jeopardized the rule of honor. Churches and
church wealth were growing at the rate of 20 to 50 percent from 1850 to
1860 in Virginia. Other states showed similar advances. Colleges and
seminaries sprouted even in denominations formerly opposed to secular
and even theological learning. By the end of the revival era, the Christian
ethos had won official preeminence as the arbiter of "civil religion" for
the South. In the upper reaches of society the "infidel" stood outside the
charmed circle of gentility.[61] In less refined sectors of the region, Christian men professed their faith in Jesus Christ without the fear of ridicule
that in colonial Virginia, for instance, had dismayed the faithful.[62]
Strengthened by the successful planter-led Mission to the Slaves, the
proslavery argument gave "divine sanction" to the region's economic and
social foundation. A few churchmen openly advocated sanctified mar-
riages and instruction to enable slaves to read the Bible. The intellectual
rigor of the proslavery defense and mission efforts benefited enormously
from the participation of Northern clergy in Southern parishes and
Southern clergy trained at Northern seminaries.[63]

Nonetheless, the legacy of the past held back advances in the "civilizing
process." First, the concepts of privacy and individuality were still under-
developed as periodic mob actions continued to suppress deviancies.
Whereas in the North families retreated into what Mary Ryan calls "a
narrowing social universe, one even more solitary than privacy—the

domain of the self, the individual, of 'manly independence.'"[64] The latter term had a different meaning from that of the white Southerner. For Northern church people it meant a relative indifference to public conventions because virtue was self-generated, self-induced, not dependent upon fears of public disapproval and shame. Privacy in the North implied a yearning for immunity from the influences of the street, a segregation from lower-class vices and crudeness. Such contaminations were thought especially harmful in the upbringing of children.

In the rural South, however, segregation of rich from poor was impossible. Plantation whites were in constant contact with slaves. Towns were too small and familial to permit the isolation available in the anonymity of city life. The same enraged impotence that sometimes led to cruelty toward slaves could affect the recipients as well, leading to a general meanspiritedness. While acknowledging the universal piety of Huntsville, Alabama, the writer Anne Royall was nonetheless horrified at the churlishness of both whites and blacks. "I have never looked into the streets," she wrote, "but I see those brutal negroes torturing and wounding poor innocent cats, dogs, hogs, or oxen, and no one interferes." She concluded: "A curse must fall on a land so lost to feeling."[65]

Furthermore, a sanctioned virility remained so powerful a force in Southern culture that the church remained circumspect and ambivalent in dealing with those conventions that still had important social functions. Only one of the leading moral issues can be touched upon here: the dram. In the antebellum period, Southern teetotalers tried to persuade churches to expel liquor dealers, excommunicate habitual drinkers, and press for total statutory prohibition, at home and in the tavern. Yet the movement failed, largely for four reasons. First, in areas where transportation was poor, it was more economical and efficient to distill grain than to ship in bulk. As a result, farmers were not eager to relinquish the option. Reflecting their constituency, politicians and publicans had little reason to encourage sobriety when a thirsty public still demanded the old custom of largess at election time. Second, churchmen were themselves divided. In some quarters, both Baptist and Methodist congregations split over the issue of antialcohol and the expulsion of intemperates.[66] For some Christians the question also raised issues of class. Most alarmed were the "hard-rined" Antimission Baptists who saw in temperance the intrusions of educated snobs whose moral societies were themselves unsanctified in their use of rationalistic, noncommunal methods.[67]

Third, there was the outside pressure of ridicule from the mouths of the unchurched. That was particularly so in the Southern river and coastal ports. For instance, no clergyman, not even Benjamin M. Palmer, the prominent Presbyterian divine, could puritanize the New Orleanians. Their bibulous tendencies, shuddered a pious Yankee businessman, were "perfectly chilling." On a single Sabbath, one New Englander counted some twenty profane events in the city, including two circuses, a French opera, duel, boxing match, cockfight, masquerade ball, waxwork exhibition, and countless dinner parties.[68]

Finally, traditions of both church and state upheld local autonomy of congregation, county, and family to oppose any scheme that implied a central authority, especially one with a Yankee odor about it. A stern temperance leader, General John Hartwell Cocke, lamented that his fellow Virginians would discountenance any law that barred "a man [from] furnishing himself and getting drunk in his own House. This would be invading a privilege held sacred with us at present."[69] Likewise, not until 1886 did the Southern Baptist Convention officially commit itself to total abstinence, leaving such matters to local churches and state assemblies. Even so there were doubts about the efficacy of intruding into the dangerous waters of politics and personal decision-making on questions of a public character. Sophisticated churchmen like James Henry Thornwell, the South Carolina Presbyterian leader, worried—as did the "Primitive Baptists"—that reliance on human instrumentalities of enforced prohibition endangered personal piety and family responsibility.[70] Reluctance to speak out on matters of general reform did not mean that religion played no role in politics, but only that the clergy had to restrict themselves to those issues about which there was no disagreement at all.

The struggle against the traditional ethic of the South had always been piecemeal and ambivalent. As a codification of rules whereby Southerners justified the use of force, honor could not be wholly relinquished unless they were ready to accept women and blacks, most particularly, on a level of equality. Since that proposition was beyond imagining, the hard code of masculinity pervaded all the social classes. White supremacy, the centrality of family loyalty, the hierarchy of ascriptions, the primacy of public reputation over individual conscience, and the retributive nature of justice were presuppositions and enjoinings that the churched and unchurched shared and gave political voice in one form or another. Dissent on these matters was not to be countenanced at any time or place. For instance, as late as June 1865, both slavery and Southern independence lay in ruins, but the Methodist minister John H. Caldwell outraged his Newnan, Georgia, congregation when he argued from the pulpit that God had punished the South for its sins against the slave. "If our practice had conformed to the law of God, he would not have suffered the institution to be overthrown," he concluded. Caldwell lost his church and was reassigned to a rough district, a position he declined out of fear for his life.[71]

Despite the heavy hand of white conformity, the definition of the Southern ethic was itself undergoing transformation along Christian lines. Self-restraint had become part of the way men strove to behave, not always with success, as Northern and English visitors to the South were often quick to notice.[72] However slow was the advance, overdrinking, male sexual license, and other sins of the flesh did arouse public criticism that eventually hardened into Victorian repressiveness. In the meantime, the two ethical systems coexisted in uncertain balance.[73] For all their vexation over selected aspects of male liberties of behavior which the code of honor permitted, the Southern evangelicals were as loyal to the cause of sectional vindication as the political "Fire-eaters." By such means the clergy pledged loyalty to community values. In urging the cause of secession, preachers sometimes employed the same language as the politicians. Samuel Henderson, an Alabama Baptist editor, for instance, argued that his state "owes it to her own honor . . . to secede from the Union."[74] How easy it was to merge sentiments of honorable retribution with righteous indignation against abolitionist and black Republican malevolence. They became one.

Because honor to God and honor to self in this Southern discourse were so closely bound together, it was possible for churchgoers to reconcile the traditional ethic and evangelical belief. Sarah Dorsey, a wealthy plantation mistress of Louisiana, presented Confederate General Leonidas L. Polk, prewar Episcopal bishop of Louisiana, a battle flag upon which she had emblazoned the Cross of Constantine. "We are fighting the Battle of the Cross against the Modern Barbarians who would rob a Christian people of Country, Liberty, and Life," she wrote him. "Never defeated, annihilated, never conquered. While a single Southern heart beats in the breast of man woman or child, there will live defiance and resistance to those who would tread us beneath their feet." As Mrs. Dorsey's words suggest, romantic heroism and Christian zeal were congenially united. Robert E. Lee, Stonewall Jackson, and Jefferson Davis epitomized in Southern terms both the Christian gentleman and the man of honor.[75]

Under such circumstances, neither honor nor evangelicalism wholly triumphed. Instead, the South would have to live thereafter with a divided soul, a dissonance seldom acknowledged. The dichotomy that endured to affect the politics and history of the region well into the present century recognized no need to make choices between honor and Christianity, between Athens and Jerusalem. The white Southerners' deity could be worshiped not only as a saving Christ but as the Ruler of Honor, Pride, and Race. At one time such a God was Gail Hightower's object of reverence, but by the end of Faulkner's *Light in August*, Hightower realizes that the churches' steeples as representations of that divinity were "empty, symbolical, bleak, sky-pointed not with ecstasy or with passion but in adjuration, threat, and doom."[76] Yet, for all the tragedy that came from the fusion of honor and piety in early Southern culture, the result was a lightening of the load of human care in peace and an inspiration for many to nobility in war, albeit in a doubtful cause.

Notes

1. See Jon Butler, "Magic, Astrology, and the Early American Religious Heritage, 1600–1760," *American Historical Review* 84 (1979), 318. Cf. James Oakes, *The Ruling Race: A History of American Slaveholders* (New York: W. W. Norton, 1982), 34, 134, 227; Richard Gray, *Writing the South: Ideas of an American Region* (Cambridge, Eng.: Cambridge University Press, 1986); Michael O'Brien, *The Idea of the American South, 1920–1941* (Baltimore: The Johns Hopkins University Press, 1979).

2. Sidney E. Mead, *The Lively Experiment: The Shaping of Christianity in America* (New York: Harper & Row, 1963), 113–115.

3. See George Fenwick Jones, *Honor in German Literature* (Chapel Hill: University of North Carolina Press, 1973 [1956]), 40; essays in J. G. Peristiany, ed., *Honour and Shame: Contributions to Mediterranean Sociology: Mediterranean Rural Communities and Social Change* (Paris: Mouton, 1967); Julian Pitt-Rivers, "Honor," in David L. Sills, ed., *International Encyclopedia of the Social Sciences* (New York: MacMillan, 1968), 503–504; Michael Herzfeld, "Honour and Shame: Problems in the Comparative Analysis of Moral Systems," *Man* 15 (1980), 339–351. For a theological approach to honor, see Evertt W. Huffard, "Thematic Dissonance in the Muslim-Christian Encounter: A Contextualized Theology of Honor" (unpublished Ph.D. diss., Fuller Theological Seminary, 1985).

4. Evertt W. Huffard, "Biblical Word Study KABOD: 'Honor'," *The Exegete* 3 (1983): 1–5, esp. 3; Johannes Pederson, *Israel, Its Life and Culture I–II* (London: Oxford University Press, 1926).

5. Paul Friedrich, "Sanity and the Myth of Honor: The Problem of Achilles," *Ethos* 5 (1977): 285.

6. Edward L. Ayers, *Vengeance and Justice: Crime and Punishment in the Nineteenth-Century American South* (New York: Oxford University Press, 1984), 33.

7. See Rina Palumbo, "Religious Declension, Psychic Discontinuity and Guilt: Perspectives in Nineteenth-Century American Revivalism," an unpublished seminar paper, Department of History, Queen's University, Kingston, Canada, kindly lent by the author.

8. Sir Benjamin Rudyerd (1628) quoted in Mervyn James, *Family, Lineage, and Civil Society: A Study of Society, Politics, and Mentality in the Durham Region, 1500–1640* (Oxford: Clarendon, 1974), 125 (first quotation). Second quotation from Darrett B. Rutman, "The Evolution of Religious Life in Early Virginia," *Lex et Scientia: The International Journal of Law and Science* 14 (1978): 192, 196; Butler, "Magic, Astrology," 317–346.

9. On witchcraft and witch trials, see Richard Beale Davis, "The Devil in Virginia in the Seventeenth Century," *Virginia Magazine of History and Biography* 65 (1957): 131–149; Raphael Semmes, *Crime and Punishment in Early Maryland* (Baltimore: Johns Hopkins University Press, 1938), 168–169; Samuel Kercheval, *History of the Valley of Virginia* (Strasburg, VA: Shenandoah 1925 [1833]), 280–283; Rutman, "The Evolution of Religion in Early Virginia," 193–194, 196; Keith Thomas, *Religion and the Decline of Magic* (New York: Scribner's, 1971), 536–583.

10. Cf. Patricia Bonomi, *Under the Cope of Heaven: Religion, Society, and Politics in Colonial America* (New York: Oxford University Press, 1986), esp. 91–102; Patricia U. Bonnomi and Peter R. Eisenstadt, "Church Attendance in the Eighteenth-Century British American Colonies," *William and Mary Quarterly*, 3rd ser., 39 (1982): 245–286, should be judged in light of Rodney Stark and Roger Finke, "American Religion in 1776: A Statistical Portrait," in *Sociological Analysis* 49, 1 (1988): 39–51. Stark and Finke found that white Southern churchmanship (Virginia, North Carolina, South Carolina, and Georgia) came to 6.2 percent of population (partly because slaves were yet to be converted in great numbers) when a national average, excluding blacks, came to 12 percent.

11. See Darrett B. Rutman and Anita H. Rutman, *A Place in Time: Middlesex County, Virginia, 1650–1750* (New York: W. W. Norton, 1984), 125; Jon Butler, "Enlarging the Bonds of Christ: Slavery, Evangelism, and the Christianization of the White South, 1690–1790," in Leonard I. Sweet, ed., *The Evangelical Tradition in America* (Macon, GA: Mercer University Press, 1984), 96; Ralph Emmett Fall, ed., *The Diary of Robert Rose: A View of Virginia by a Scottish Colonial Parson, 1746–1751* (Verona, VA: McClure, 1977).

12. Rutman, "Religious Life in Early Virginia," 198, 204.

13. Rutman and Rutman, *Place in Time*, 143; Philip Alexander Bruce, *Social Life in Old Virginia: From the 'Institutional History of Virginia in the Seventeenth Century'* (New York: Capricorn, 1965 [1910]), 65–72.

14. Winton U. Solberg, *Redeem the Time: The Puritan Sabbath in Early America* (Cambridge, MA: Harvard University Press, 1977), 85–106 (quotation, 103).

15. William Gooch to Edmund Gibson, July 20, 1735, in Rev. G. McLaren Bryden, ed., "The Virginia Clergy: Governor Gooch's Letters to the Bishop of

London, 1727–1749 from the Fulham Manuscripts," *Virginia Magazine of History and Biography* 32 (1924): 333; Kercheval, *History of the Valley of Virginia*, 284, 290.

16. Norbert Elias, *The Civilizing Process: The Development of Manners, Changes in the Code of Conduct and Feeling in Early Modern Times*, trans. Edmund Jephcott (New York: Urizen, 1978 [1939]); Patrick H. Hutton, "The History of Mentalities: The New Map of Cultural History," *History and Theory* 20 (1981): 237–259. See also Georges Duby, ed., *A History of Private Life*, Vol. II: *Revelations of the Medieval World*, trans. Arthur Goldhammer (Cambridge, MA: Harvard University Press, 1987), esp. Phillippe Braunstein, "Towards Intimacy," 535–630.

17. Elias, *Civilizing Process*, 63–68.

18. See David Hackett Fischer, *Britain in America* (tentative title) (New York: Oxford University Press, forthcoming), on origins of Virginians; see Cleanth Brooks, *The Language of the American South* (Athens: University of Georgia Press, 1985), 8–15, and idem, *The Relation of the Alabama-Georgia Dialect to the Provincial Dialects of Great Britain* (Baton Rouge: Louisiana State University Press, 1935).

19. Rhys Isaac, *The Transformation of Virginia: 1740–1790* (Chapel Hill: University of North Carolina Press, 1982), 72.

20. Rutman and Rutman, *A Place in Time*, 235–236; Harold Robert Shurtleff, *The Log Cabin Myth: A Study of the Early Dwellings of the English Colonists in North America* (Cambridge, MA: Harvard University Press, 1967 [1939]), 127–162; Lois Green Carr and Lorena S. Walsh, "Inventories and the Analysis of Wealth and Consumption Patterns in St. Mary's County, Maryland, 1658–1777," *Historical Methods* 13 (1980): 81–104; and idem, "The Standard of Living in the Colonial Chesapeake," *William and Mary Quarterly*, 3rd ser., 45 (1988): 135–159; and Billy G. Smith, "Comment," ibid., 163–166.

21. Isaac, *Transformation of Virginia*, 72–73. The blanket as partition is discussed in David H. Flaherty, *Privacy in Colonial New England* (Charlottesville, VA: University Press of Virginia, 1967), 36 (although a reference only to New England, such an obvious expediency must have been used in Virginia); Francis Asbury, *The Journal and Letters of Francis Asbury*, 3 vols., ed. Elmer T. Clark, J. Manning Potts, Jacob S. Payton (Nashville: Abingdon Press, 1958), I, August 12, 1776, 197 (quotation). See also A. A. Parker, *Trip to the West and Texas . . . in the Autumn and Winter of 1834–35* (Concord, NH: White & Fisher, 1835), 112–115.

22. See Erik H. Erikson, *Identity and the Life Cycle* (New York: W. W. Norton, 1959), 65–74; Helen M. Lynd, *On Shame and the Search for Identity* (New York: Harcourt, Brace, 1958).

23. Frances Trollope, *Domestic Manners of Americans*, ed. Donald Smalley (New York: Random House, 1960), 249–250; Sarah Hicks Williams to Sarah and Samuel Hicks, October 10, 1853, in James C. Bonner, ed., "Plantation Experiences of a New York Woman," *North Carolina Historical Review* 33 (1956): 389.

24. Entry for June 22, 1781, "Military Journal of Lt. William Feltman, May 26, 1781 to April 25, 1782," in Historical Society of Pennsylvania, *Collections*, I (1853), 305; but for quotation, see Winthrop Jordan, *White over Black: American Attitudes toward the Negro, 1550–1812* (Chapel Hill: University of North Carolina Press, 1968), 195. (Passage deleted in published version of diary.)

25. See Keith Thomas, *Man and the Natural World: A History of the Modern Sensibility* (New York: Pantheon, 1983), 44–46; Jordan, *White over Black*, 230–234, 493–494; Benjamin West to the Rev. Samuel West, July 23, 1778, in James S. Schoff, ed., *Life in the South, 1778–1779: The Letters of Dr. Benjamin West* (Ann Arbor: University of Michigan Press, 1963), 32–33.

26. Rutman and Rutman, *Place in Time*, 171.

27. The differences between and interconnections of honor and shame and conscience and guilt are discussed in Bertram Wyatt-Brown, *Southern Honor: Ethics and Behavior in the Old South* (New York: Oxford University Press, 1982), 145–155 and passim.

28. Ibid., 15. See also 3–87.

29. Eliott J. Gorn, "'Gouge and Bite, Pull Hair and Scratch': The Social Significance of Fighting in the Southern Backcountry," *American Historical Review* 90 (1985): 18–43; Tom Parramore, "Gouging in Early North Carolina," *North Carolina Folklore Journal* 22 (1974): 55–62; Jennie Holliman, *American Sports (1785–1835)* (Durham: Seeman, 1931), 138–139; Jane Carson, *Colonial Virginians at Play* (Williamsburg, VA: Colonial Williamsburg, 1965), 164–166; Henry Benjamin Whipple, *Bishop Whipple's Southern Diary, 1843–1844*, ed. Lester Burrell Shippee (Minneapolis: University of Minnesota Press, 1937), 26–27; Merrill E. Gaddis, "Religious Ideas and Attitudes in the Early Frontier," *Church History* 2 (1933): 152–170, a surprisingly realistic exposition.

30. Robert Fogel and Stanley L. Engerman, *Time on the Cross: The Economics of American Slavery* (Boston: Little, Brown, 1974); Stanley L. Engerman, "A Reconsideration of Southern Economic Growth, 1770–1860," *Agricultural History* 49 (1975): 343–361.

31. See, for instance, on slavery's corruptiveness, William Byrd II, in Marion Tinling, ed., *The Correspondence of the Three William Byrds*, 2 vols. (Charlottesville: Virginia Historical Society, 1977), II, 488; Mechal Sobel, *The World They Made Together: Black and White Values in Eighteenth-Century Virginia* (Princeton: Princeton University Press, 1988).

32. Quoted in Garnett Ryland, *The Baptists of Virginia, 1699–1926* (Richmond: Baptist Board of Missions and Education, 1955), 24.

33. Hunter Dickinson Farish, ed., *Journal and Letters of Philip Vickers Fithian, 1773–1774: A Plantation Tutor of the Old Dominion* (Williamsburg: Colonial Williamsburg, 1957), March 6, 1774, 72.

34. See Nancy L. Struna, *The Cultural Significance of Sport in the Colonial Chesapeake and Massachusetts* (Eugene, OR: Microform Publications, College of Health, Physical Education and Recreation, 1981 [Ph.D. diss., University of Maryland, 1979]), 155.

35. As F. G. Bailey, *Stratagems and Spoils: A Social Anthropology of Politics* (New York: Schocken, 1969), 21, points out "Honour has meaning only when some people are without honour; power and wealth are got at the expense of other people. People compete only because the prizes are in short supply."

36. See Waldrep, "The Decline of Religious Discipline"; Richard R. Beeman, *The Evolution of the Southern Backcountry: A Case Study of Lunenburg County, Virginia, 1746–1832* (Philadelphia: University of Pennsylvania Press, 1984), 108; W. D. Blanks, "Corrective Church Discipline in the Presbyterian Churches of the Nineteenth Century South," *Journal of Presbyterian History* 44 (1966): 89–105.

37. W. J. Rorabaugh, *The Alcoholic Republic: An American Tradition* (New York: Oxford University Press, 1979), 8, 9, Charts 1.1 and 1.2.

38. Samuel Gaillard Stoney, ed., "The Autobiography of William John Grayson," *South Carolina Historical and Genealogical Magazine* 49 (1948): 25–26.

39. John B. Boles, "Evangelical Protestantism in the Old South: From Religious Dissent to Cultural Dominance," in Charles Reagan Wilson, ed., *Religion in the South* (Jackson: University Press of Mississippi, 1985), 13–34. See also Jon Butler, "Enthusiasm Described and Decried: the Great Awakening as Interpretive Fiction," *Journal of American History*, 69 (1979): 305–325.

40. Ann Douglas, *The Feminization of American Culture* (New York: Knopf, 1978); Rev. Walter C. Whitaker, "Bishop Richard Hooker Wilmer," *Transactions of the Alabama Historical Society, 1899–1903*, IV (Montgomery, 1904), 23; Sarah McCulloh Lemmon, *Parson Pettigrew of the 'Old Church': 1744–1807* (Chapel Hill: University of North Carolina Press, 1970), 23; Lida Bestor Robertson, Diary, September 14, 1851, Alabama State Department of Archives and History.

41. Steven M. Stowe, *Intimacy and Power in the Old South: Ritual in the Lives of the Planters* (Baltimore: Johns Hopkins University Press, 1987), (quotation) 151.

42. Johann Huizinga, *Homo Ludens: A Study of the Play-Element in Culture* (Boston: Little, Brown, 1955 [1949]), 25. For instance, take the gamester William Byrd III; see David Meade, recollections, in "Letters of William Byrd III," *Virginia Magazine of History and Biography* 37 (1929): 310–311.

43. Shippee, ed., *Bishop Whipple's Southern Diary*, 101.

44. Ted Ownby, "Evangelicalism and Male Culture: Recreation and Religion in the Rural South, 1865–1920," (unpublished Ph.D. diss., Johns Hopkins University, 1986), 20–21. There were, of course, conversions of tavern-keepers, gamesters, and horsemen. See, for instance, "The Autobiography of Rev. Robertson Gannaway," *Virginia Magazine of History and Biography* 37 (1929): 316–320.

45. George Washington Paschal, *History of the North Carolina Baptists* 2 vols. (Raleigh: General Board of the North Carolina Baptist State Convention, 1955), II, 238.

46. William Lynwood Montell, *Killings: Folk Justice in the Upper South* (Lexington: University Press of Kentucky, 1986), 36–37; The Rev. Charles Wood-

mason, *The Carolina Backcountry on the Eve of the Revolution*, ed. Richard J. Hooker (Chapel Hill: University of North Carolina Press, 1953). On the church and violence, see, however, the Rt. Rev. B. B. Smith, Bishop of the Episcopal Diocese of Kentucky, as quoted in Theodore Dwight Weld, *Slavery as It Is: Testimony of a Thousand Witnesses* (New York: American Anti-Slavery Society, 1839), 204–205.

47. See especially, Waldrep, "The Decline of Religious Discipline."

48. Anne C. Loveland, *Southern Evangelicals and the Social Order, 1800–1860* (Baton Rouge: Louisiana State University Press, 1980), 52–64. One minister in 1300 in the slave states and 1 minister in 900 in the free states were estimates of the Southern Aid Society. See Frederick Law Olmsted, *The Cotton Kingdom*, ed. Arthur M. Schlesinger, Sr. (New York: Random House, 1984), 203.

49. "Conditions of American Baptists" (reprint from *Baptist Repository*), *Baptist Weekly Journal of the Mississippi Valley* (Cincinnati), March 15, 1832; Christopher MacRae et al. to Frederick Porter, March 16, 1827, American Sunday School Union Papers, Presbyterian Historical Society, Philadelphia, hereinafter ASSU. See David Edwin Harrell, Jr., "The Evolution of Plain-Folk Religion in the South, 1835–1920," in Samuel S. Hill, ed., *Varieties of Southern Religious Experience* (Baton Rouge: Louisiana State University Press, 1988), 24–51.

50. Quoted from Ralph R. Smith, "'In Every Destitute Place': The Mission Program of the America Sunday School Union, 1817–1834" (unpublished Ph.D. diss., University of Southern California, 1973), 94, n.33; see also ASSU, Samuel P. Barton to Porter, June 28, 1835, and James W. Douglass to Porter, June 27, 1836.

51. ASSU: Richard Hooker to Porter, May 19, June 19, 1830; W. A. N. Campbell to Porter, January 18, 1828; John Endith to Porter, February 20, 1828.

52. Norton quoted by Smith, "'In Every Destitute Place,'" 163; see also ASSU, Hooker to Porter, May 31, 1830; Joseph Miller, "Travelling Preacher and Settled Farmer," *Methodist History* 5 (1967): 3–14.

53. Don H. Doyle, "The Social Functions of Voluntary Associations in a Nineteenth-Century American Town," *Social Science History* 1 (1977): 333–355, quotations, 338, 342, 349, 350; Richard D. Brown, *Modernization: The Transformation of American Life, 1600–1865* (New York: Hill and Wang, 1976), 147.

54. Donald G. Mathews, *Religion in the Old South* (Chicago: University of Chicago Press, 1978), 88; Suzanne Lebsock, *The Free Women of Petersburg: Status and Culture in a Southern Town, 1784–1860* (New York: W. W. Norton, 1984), 216–225. Opposition to women's activism hindered female voluntary work in the South. See Jean Friedman, *The Enclosed Garden: Women and Community in the Evangelical South, 1830–1900* (Chapel Hill: University of North Carolina Press, 1985), 19. On Southern weakness of organization, see Edmund Ruffin Diary, "Cassandra Warnings," in William Scarborough, ed., *The Diary of Edmund Ruffin*, 2 vols. (Chapel Hill: University of North Carolina Press, 1972), I, Appendix D, 630.

55. See Friedman, *The Enclosed Garden*, 9–11; Gwen Kennedy Neville, *Kinship and Pilgrimage: Rituals of Reunion in American Protestant Culture* (New York: Oxford University Press, 1987), 94–104.

56. Clanton W. Williams, "Early Ante-Bellum Montgomery: A Black Belt Constituency," *Journal of Southern History* 7 (1941): 502. *State v. Mary DuBois*, Citizens of Warren County to H. G. Runnels, Governors Papers (RG 27), n.d. [1833], Mississippi State Department of Archives and History.

57. See Donald G. Mathews, "North Carolina Methodists in the Nineteenth Century: Church and Society," in O. Kelly Ingram, ed., *Methodism Alive in North Carolina* (Durham: Divinity School of Duke University, 1976), 59–74.

58. Goulding and Cater quoted from Mitchell Snay, "Gospel of Disunion: Religion and the Rise of Southern Separatism, 1830–1861" (unpublished Ph.D. diss., Brandeis University, 1984), 14–19; see also, for instance, Saranne E. Crabtree, "*South Western Baptist*, 1850–1860: Defender of Southern Rights" (unpublished M.A. thesis, Auburn University, 1973), 82 (on Charles Sumner's caning).

59. See Snay, "Gospel of Disunion," 34.

60. Miller, "Travelling Preacher and Settled Farmer," 3; Samuel S. Hill, Jr. *The South and the North in American Religion* (Athens, GA: University of Georgia Press, 1980), 73–74.

61. C. C. Pearson and J. Edwin Hendricks, *Liquor and Anti-Liquor in Virginia, 1619–1919* (Durham: Duke University Press, 1967), 147; Clement Eaton, *Freedom of Thought Struggle in the Old South* (New York: Harper & Row, 1964), 300–301.

62. See, for an example of common talk about religion among men, Olmsted, *The Cotton Kingdom*, 204–205; William Warren Sweet, "The Churches as Moral Courts of the Frontier," *Church History* 2 (1933): 4.

63. Loveland, *Southern Evangelicals and the Social Order*, 210–212; Reuben Edward Alley, *A History of Baptists in Virginia* (Richmond: Virginia Baptist General Board, 1973), 230–232; Donald G. Mathews, *Slavery and Methodism: A Chapter in American Morality, 1780–1845* (Princeton: Princeton University Press, 1965); idem, "Charles Colcock Jones and the Southern Evangelical Crusade to Form a Bi-Racial Community," *Journal of Southern History* 41 (1975): 299–320; Eugene D. Genovese and Elizabeth Fox-Genovese, "The Divine Sanction of Social Order: Religious Foundations of the Southern Slaveholders' World View," *Journal of the American Academy of Religion* 55 (1987): 211–233; idem, "The Religious Ideals of Southern Slave Society," *Georgia Historical Quarterly*, 70 (1986): 1–16; Larry E. Tise, *Proslavery: A History of the Defense of Slavery in America, 1701–1840* (Athens, GA: University of Georgia Press, 1988), 308–346.

64. Mary P. Ryan, *Cradle of the Middle Class: The Family in Oneida County, New York, 1790–1865* (Cambridge, MA: Cambridge University Press, 1981), 147 (quotation), see also 48–49.

65. "Letter L," June 8, 1822, in Anne Newport Royall, *Letters from Alabama, 1817–1822*, ed. Lucille Griffith (University: University of Alabama Press, 1969), 248–249.

66. Daniel Jay Whitener, *Prohibition in North Carolina, 1715–1945* (Chapel Hill: University of North Carolina Press, 1946), 17; Loveland, *Southern Evangelicals and the Social Order,* 142–158; Sweet, "The Church as Moral Courts of the Frontier," 14.

67. Bertram Wyatt-Brown, "The Anti-Mission Movement in the Jacksonian South: A Study in Folk Culture," *Journal of Southern History* 36 (1970): 501–529; Harrell, "The Evolution of Plain-Folk Religion in the South, 1835–1920," 24–31.

68. Dale A. Somers, *The Rise of Sports in New Orleans, 1850–1900* (Baton Rouge: Louisiana State University Press, 1972), 12 (quotation), 13–14; and [Joseph Holt Ingraham], *The South-West; by a Yankee . . . ,* 2 vols. (New York: Harper Bros., 1836), I, 219; Whipple, *Southern Diary,* 117–120.

69. John Hartwell Cocke to Joseph C. Cabell, June [?], 1852, John Hartwell Cocke MSS, Alderman Library, University of Virginia, as quoted in Pearson and Hendricks, *Liquor and Anti-Liquor in Virginia,* 130, n. 64; see also, on state-rights reactions to temperance, Whitener, *Prohibition in North Carolina,* 43.

70. John Lee Eighmy, *Churches in Cultural Captivity: A History of the Social Attitudes of Southern Baptists* (Knoxville: University of Tennessee Press, 1972), 52; Loveland, *Southern Evangelicals and the Social Order,* 145–158.

71. John H. Caldwell, *Slavery and Southern Methodism: Two Sermons Preached in Newnan, Georgia* (n.p., 1865), 20–21. See also Daniel W. Stowell, "John H. Caldwell: Anti-Slavery Conscience of Southern Methodism" (unpublished seminar paper December 9, 1986, University of Georgia). "Who among us has ever lifted up a true, manly, martyr-like remonstrance against the crying evils of slavery? There has not been one martyr to the principles of true conservatism," he told his congregation (Caldwell, *Slavery and Southern Methodism,* 69).

72. See, particularly Grady McWhiney, *Cracker Culture: Celtic Ways in the Old South* (Tuscaloosa, AL: University of Alabama Press, 1988), 171–192.

73. Ownby, "Evangelicalism and Male Culture," 20–21.

74. Jon G. Appleton, "Samuel Henderson: Southern Minister, Editor, and Crusader, 1853–1866" (unpublished M.A. thesis, Auburn University, 1968), 8.

75. Sarah A. Dorsey to Leonidas L. Polk, February 20, 1862, Leonidas L. Polk Papers, Jessie Ball DuPont Memorial Library, University of the South, Sewanee, Tennessee. Mrs. Dorsey was Jefferson Davis's greatest admirer, bequeathing him "Beauvoir," her Biloxi, Mississippi, residence. A novelist and wealthy plantation mistress, she was also an early student of comparative religion, especially Hinduism and Anglican theology. She became an archdeaconness, founding a Louisiana order of Episcopal nuns under Bishop Polk.

76. William Faulkner, *Light in August* (New York: Modern Library, 1950 [1932], 426.

COMPARATIVE THEMES

9

Beyond Commonality and Plurality: Persistent Racial Polarity in American Religion and Politics

DAVID W. WILLS

Some fifteen years ago, at a conference on Robert Bellah's then relatively fresh concept of an American civil religion, Charles Long complained that "a great deal of . . . discussion on the topic of American religion has been consciously or unconsciously ideological, serving to enhance, justify and render sacred the history of European immigrants in this land." "From a black point of view," he suggested, it did not make a great deal of difference whether one made much or little of the notion of civil religion, for either way "the crucial issue" remained "the overwhelming reality of the white presence." To understand the meaning and reality of that presence, he suggested, one had to get behind the "hermeneutics of conquest and suppression," "the telling and retelling of the mighty deeds of the white conquerors," and learn to see as problematic that which our national cosmogony was intended precisely to render unproblematic, that is, the reality of white power. That could only be done by rendering

visible what our familiar narratives rendered invisible, the crucially important presence in our past—*from the beginning*—of nonwhite peoples.[1]

One would like to think, at this late date, that such a thoroughgoing
critique of the scholarly study of American religion no longer had much
relevance, but the evidence suggests otherwise. No doubt, there has been
in the last fifteen years an enormous increase in the amount of scholarly
attention given to the religious life in North America of people of color.
There has also been, surely, a widespread sense that the story of religion
in America must now be told in a far more inclusive way than in the past.
Still, certain intellectual habits are very hard to break. Probably no work
significantly concerned with American religion has received more public
attention in the last few years than Robert Bellah et al.'s *Habits of the
Heart*.[2] For all its many virtues, this book seems to rest on the premise
that it is possible to talk about the essence of the American experience—
both in the past and in the present—without speaking in more than a
passing way about the fateful realities of race. Bellah and his coauthors
do include Martin Luther King, Jr., in their pantheon of American
heroes and they praise the civil rights movement as the kind of public-
spirited social movement contemporary America so badly needs. But, as
Vincent Harding has observed, the Afro-American religious tradition is
so entirely invisible in the book that the King they present seems to
appear from nowhere.[3] The civil rights movement as they recall it also
seems far more a matter of consensus and less a matter of conflict than
the historical record would suggest. In any case, the realities of race
clearly lie at the margins and not at the center of *Habits of the Heart*.

What does lie at the center of the book is a very familiar theme in the
study of American religion—the tension between commonality and plurality, between those cultural forces that draw us together around some
common purpose and those tendencies that make us go our separate
ways. As the authors of *Habits of the Heart* tell the story, we need to
recover the wisdom of the former (for them "the biblical tradition" and
"civic republicanism") in order to restrain the excesses of the latter
("utilitarian" and "expressive individualism"). But it is easy enough, as
many historians of American religion have shown, to tell essentially the
same tale with a different ending—that is, to speak in a more positive way
about how we have blessedly escaped our early heritage of religious
uniformity and moved to affirm an ever more expansive plurality of
religious options. In either version, however, the often bitter and always
difficult encounter of black and white is almost inevitably displaced from
the center of the story. The enduring racial polarity in American life is
just that—a polarity—and it is very difficult to take it adequately into

account in a story that centers on either commonality or plurality or both. This is painfully evident in *Habits of the Heart*.

It is equally evident in some recent general discussions of religion in American politics. Consider, for example, A. James Reichley's *Religion in American Public Life*, a book I choose not because it is in this respect unusual but precisely because it is not.[4] As Charles Long reminded historians of American religion fifteen years ago, how we begin our stories is fundamentally important. Where we begin them can be equally decisive. Reichley begins his historical narrative in New England, with a discussion of "the single most influential cultural force at work in the new nation," Puritanism, and then proceeds to discuss the "practice of American pluralism" as this "originated in the middle colonies, particularly in New York, Pennsylvania and Maryland."[5] The themes of commonality and plurality firmly in place, Reichley touches lightly on the history of the Anglican establishment and the rise of religious toleration in Virginia and then proceeds to a careful examination of the religious settlement wrought by the Founding Fathers and an extended treatment of the judicial history of the First Amendment. Constitutional battles over church-state questions are, of course, relatively easy to construe as a working out of the tension between Puritan corporatism and the impulse to pluralism and toleration. The same can be said about cultural conflicts institutionalized in the various American party systems. Reichley provides a long narrative account of religion's important place in American electoral politics, organizing his discussion around the enduring ethnocultural conflict between "the party of order" (the Whigs and then the Republicans) and "the party of equality" (the Democrats). The connection to the original themes of commonality and plurality is even closer if one adopts the language employed years ago by Seymour Martin Lipset and speaks of a historical contest between "the party of Protestant moralism" and "the party of cultural pluralism."[6]

On any of these points, Reichley's account could no doubt be criticized by specialists far more attentive than he to the nuances of colonial religious history, the complications of constitutional law, and the intricacies of partisan coalitions. My concern here is only with the most general outline of his story. What is missing in this regard is, of course, sustained attention to the theme of racial polarity. The disruptive effects of the slavery issue on the second American party system are duly noted and, as in *Habits of the Heart*, attention is given to Martin Luther King, Jr., and the civil rights movement. But up until the mid-twentieth century, black people themselves are almost entirely absent from his narrative, and race is treated throughout as an episodically rather than a continuously important feature of American public life. That this would be the case was virtually guaranteed, I would suggest, by the geography of his beginning. However much work is done on religion in the colonial South, it nonetheless still tends to be left out of account when it comes time to set the plot for the whole story. Reichley follows this unspoken consensus that the South provides no motif as central to our religious history as the stories of Puritanism or religious pluralism. This seems to me a truly fundamental error. Only if we think of the colonial South solely as the white South can we reasonably come to this conclusion—and, surely, to think of the colonial South as less than a biracial reality is itself unreasonable. However much neglected or denied, there is indeed a Southern theme in our religious history, and it is equally foundational with the themes of commonality and plurality. It is the theme of racial polarity. It was there at the beginning and it has been with us ever since. And it is particularly important for understanding the relation of religion and politics in America.[7]

To ask about religion and politics is to ask, as much as anything else, about the way the exercise of power in America has been given meaning. Particularly important here is the way the exercise of coercive power has been understood. Nowhere has the exercise of this kind of power been more widespread and problematic in America than in the relation of blacks and whites. Slavery was a thoroughly coercive institution and an institution that could survive only when more or less unhesitatingly supported by the coercive apparatus of the state. The same was true of segregation. For most of our history, most white Americans have agreed that this unique exercise of power was legitimate—religiously legitimate. Most black Americans have not. The issue in America between blacks and whites has therefore most essentially always been one of power—its exercise and meaning—not prejudice. It has also always been a central issue in our politics as a whole, for it touches on the very way American social reality was constituted—*at the beginning*—and maintained ever since by the exercise of power. To ask about the relation of religion and politics in Afro-American history is therefore scarcely a matter of wandering off to the edges of our history. It is rather to ask how black people have attempted to come to terms with one of the foundational realities of American life, the exercise of white power—what Charles Long called "the overwhelming reality of the white presence."[8]

African slavery endured in North America for two and a half centuries, and during that entire period the vast majority of Afro-Americans were slaves. To ask about black religion and politics is therefore in the first instance to ask about the religion and politics of the slaves. Politics here cannot of course mean electoral politics in any conventional sense. Nor can religion be taken to mean, for much of this period, the kind of black evangelical Protestantism that eventually became quite familiar in America. The mass conversion of the slave population to Christianity is a relatively late feature of the slavery period, beginning only in the mid-eighteenth century and culminating in the three decades immediately preceding the Civil War. Prior to that, Afro-American religion presumably consisted primarily of a rather open-ended syncretism of varied African traditions, with considerable local variation depending on the areas in Africa from which the slaves had primarily been drawn, the circumstances surrounding their importation, and the demographic balance and characteristic patterns of interaction between blacks and whites. Where Euro-American patterns had been assimilated, they were more likely to have been drawn from the realm of popular religion than the more institutionalized forms of Euro-American Christianity. About both the religion and the politics of these people we still know relatively little.

Much more is known, of course, about the religion of the slave Christians of the last century of the slavery era. Afro-American Protestantism emerged in eighteenth-century America out of the encounter between an expansive Euro-American evangelicalism and people of African descent. Sparked initially by the efforts of white Presbyterian, Baptist, and Methodist preachers, evangelicalism spread among the slaves in large measure because it was passed from black to black. In the hands of the slave preachers and their early converts, Euro-American evangelicalism became indigenized in Afro-American forms—especially in the African-influenced performance styles evident in preaching, song, and ecstatic worship. It is this tradition in its myriad forms that came to dominate Afro-American religious life in the nineteenth century and remains today the single most powerful religious force among black Americans.[9]

What, in its origins under the condition of slavery, was the predominant politics of this religious tradition? The question is by no means a simple one and it deserves a far more complicated answer than it can receive here. To put the matter as simply and concisely as possible, it can be said that most slave Christians practiced a politics of cultural resistance. To say this is to set aside two other interpretations of the politics of slave religion. It is, for one thing, to reject the idea that slave Christianity was apolitical, that it had no concern whatsoever with the exercise of worldly power. It has sometimes been suggested, of course, that slave religion was just that—an escapist, otherworldly piety that made the slaves so much psychological putty in their masters' hands. But this view is now widely regarded—and rightly so—as a gross caricature. It will also not do, however, to characterize the politics of slave religion as primarily the politics of active, physical resistance. Afro-American Christianity (like more entirely African-based forms of slave religion) did produce during the slavery era militant leaders who were ready to contest the organized, violent, coercive power of the slavery system with organized, violent, coercive power of their own. But they were the exceptions rather than the rule. The predominant pattern was one of accepting the power realities of the slavery system as a matter of fact but refusing to assent to them as a matter of right. This is essentially what I mean by the politics of cultural resistance.[10] This, no doubt, can seem from some points of view a very insubstantial politics indeed. Eugene Genovese in *Roll, Jordan, Roll* ends his generally sympathetic chapter on the religion of the slaves with these words:

> The synthesis that became black Christianity offered profound spiritual strength to a people at bay, but it also imparted a political weakness, which dictated, however necessarily and realistically, acceptance of the hegemony of the oppressor. It enabled the slaves to do battle against the slaveholders' ideology, but defensively within the system it opposed; offensively, it proved a poor instrument. The accomplishment soared heroically to great heights, but so did the price, which even now has not been fully paid.[11]

Such a critique makes many assumptions, among them, it would appear, the assumption that there are ordinarily political solutions to our most pressing collective problems. Perhaps it has been a characteristic or at least widespread pattern in American religious life to assent to this proposition, whether in its more radical or in its more conventional forms. If so, it is not the least important thing about the experience of Afro-Americans that through most of their history this kind of faith in the transformative efficacy of human action has not been readily available. It may be, as Genovese suggests, that this has made the descendants of the slaves slower than they might otherwise have been to seize the opportunities for forceful collective action that have eventually lain open to them in the United States. But if so—and it is a generalization to be treated with caution—a good Calvinist might judge that black evangelicals in America had wisely retained a living faith in the sovereignty of God long after their white counterparts had drifted off into an unwarranted confidence in the human will. Or, as Charles Long has suggested, the very intractability of their social circumstances may have rendered more accessible to black Americans the experience of what Rudolf Otto called the *mysterium tremendum*, the wholly-otherness that lies at the heart of the experience of the sacred.[12]

However important in itself and foundational for much of what follows, the religion and politics of the slaves is not the primary concern of this essay. My focus here is rather on Afro-American religion and politics as these have developed in the context of black Americans' painfully slow and not yet complete inclusion into the political system of the United States. This inclusion has occurred in four stages: (1) the period from the "First Emancipation" to the Civil War; (2) the period from Reconstruction to World War I; (3) the period from World War I to the civil rights movement; and (4) the years since the Voting Rights Act of 1965. Since the story as a whole is one of increasing black access to the franchise and other forms of political participation, it is tempting to see in it evidence of a more or less inevitable progress in America toward overcoming racial injustice. That is a temptation largely to be resisted. In none of these periods has the movement of blacks into the electorate been straightforward and without reversals. In every case, an initial inclusion of blacks in the political process has been followed by an at least partially successful effort to reverse any apparent tendency of blacks to develop genuinely effective political power.

In the years of the Revolutionary and early national period, the same developments that began to eliminate slavery from the North and seemed to put it on the road to extinction everywhere also created a new black electorate. With the exception of Connecticut, the New England states gradually extended the franchise to their black male citizens. By the early 1800s, free black men were also voting in New York, Pennsylvania, Maryland, North Carolina, and Tennessee. In 1810, however, Maryland withdrew the ballot from its black voters and by 1838 every state south of New England had followed suit. Pennsylvania, for example, in that year revised its constitution to restrict the suffrage to white males. Even at its peak, of course, the black electorate of the antebellum period included only a tiny minority of the Afro-American population, the overwhelming majority of whom were Southern slaves.[13]

It was precisely the attempt to enfranchise these slaves that lay at the political center of the Reconstruction era. The Fifteenth Amendment, added to the Constitution in 1870, declared that "the right of citizens of the United States to vote shall not be denied or abridged . . . on account of race, color, or previous condition of servitude." The potential impact of this amendment is readily apparent when one recalls that at the time of its adoption South Carolina, Mississippi, and Louisiana had black majorities, while the black proportion of the population of Florida, Alabama, and Georgia exceeded 45 percent.[14] That such an immense shift in the balance of political power between the two races in the South was even attempted is, of course, extraordinary and note must be taken of the significant degree of black electoral empowerment that did in fact occur. But the central truth remains that the Fifteenth Amendment was never fully and effectively implemented even in the Reconstruction era itself. When other methods failed, white Southerners who had gone to war in 1861 because they were unwilling to accept the election of Lincoln at times resorted to clandestine violence to avoid the triumph of black power at the polls. Already by the mid-1870s, it was clear that the federal government would not respond to this use of force as it had to secession.[15] By the end of the century, moreover, what had initially been accomplished by force and intimidation was more thoroughly and peacefully achieved by constitutional reform. The case of Louisiana provides a graphic example. In 1896, 44.8 percent of the duly registered Louisiana electorate was black. By 1900, two years after the adoption of a new state constitution that put literacy tests, property qualifications, and a poll tax as barriers between blacks and the ballot, blacks constituted only 4 percent of the state's electorate. More than 121,000 black Louisianans had lost their vote.[16] The enduring effects of the Fifteenth Amendment were actually felt primarily in the North. Even at the height of Reconstruction, Northern white electorates, voting largely along party lines, repeatedly refused to expand their states' franchise to include blacks. In the fall of 1865, for example, constitutional amendments to extend the suffrage to black adult males were defeated in Connecticut, Minnesota, and Wisconsin. In eleven of the twenty-one Northern states—and in all the nonseceding border states—black men received the vote only as a result of the Fifteenth Amendment. The enduring effect of the Civil War and Reconstruction on black electoral politics was, then, the enfranchisement of the Northern black male.[17]

The full consequence of this development was not felt, however, until long after it had occurred. In 1870, when the Fifteenth Amendement was adopted, only a small percentage of the potential black electorate—around 10 percent—resided outside the South, a circumstance that persisted for most of the ensuing half-century. Beginning in 1910, however, the steadily increasing outmigration of Southern blacks, greatly accelerated by World War I, began to swell the numbers of Northern—and therefore voting—blacks. The immediate effect of this Great Migration, which involved around 450,000 blacks in the century's second decade and some 750,000 in its third decade, was compounded, as Evelyn Brooks has recently reminded us, by the effect of the Nineteenth Amendment enfranchising women. Northern black voters tended, moreover, to live primarily in cities, and this residential concentration further enhanced the potential power of the black electorate. The new political possibilities which the migration created were most fully realized in Chicago, where black voters became an integral part of the Republican machine of Mayor William Hale Thompson and in 1928 elected to Congress the first black to represent a Northern district, Oscar DePriest. (He was also, at that time, the only black member of Congress.) But what the North gave with one hand, it often took away with the other. At-large elections, gerrymandering, and like devices were used to dilute the power of the newly enlarged black electorate, while urban machines that had welcomed all manner of European immigrants went out of their way to freeze out black politicians. Meanwhile, though many blacks had left the South, most had not. As late as 1960, 60 percent of all black Americans resided in the South (as defined by the United States Bureau of the Census to include Delaware, Maryland, the District of Columbia, West Virginia, Kentucky, and Oklahoma as well as the states of the Confederacy). By 1970, the figure still stood at 53 percent.[18]

Southern blacks did make some progress in the first two-thirds of the twentieth century in their struggle to regain the vote, especially in urban areas. The most notable example of their success occurred in Memphis, where black voters, allying themselves with the white political machine of "Boss" Edward Crump, were an important force in city elections. As the legal structure of black disfranchisement was slowly eroded, as, for example, in federal and state decisions outlawing the white primacy, the gradual reemergence of the Southern black electorate became more widespread. It was, however, only the Voting Rights Act of 1965 that finally broke through the white South's century-long resistance to granting the suffrage to the black South. And still today, of course, the question of how fully political power in all its forms will be shared across racial lines remains unanswered. The new black voters of the South, like their Northern counterparts of an earlier day (and sometimes of the present as well), complain that district lines are drawn and electoral rules set in ways that minimize the effect of their votes. And every time the Voting Rights Act comes due for renewal, there are efforts in one way or another to weaken it. There is nothing in our history, moreover, that suggests that we are incapable of serious backsliding in this matter. The saints may persevere, but it would appear that the will of the American people to maintain a racially equal franchise does not.[19]

This long and difficult history of blocked access to the franchise (and enduring exclusion from other central aspects of the political process) provides the context in which the religious institutions of legally free blacks have undertaken political action. There is no need to labor the point that no other American religious group (with the possible exception of Native Americans) has faced such a persistently hostile political environment. My concern is rather to sketch the encounter between the more institutionalized forms of black religious life—and here I refer primarily to the black Protestant churches—and the more institutionalized forms of American politics. This is not to say there are not other areas equally worth considering. It would be well worth asking, for example, about the continuing place in post-Emancipation black life of the politics of cultural resistance developed during the slavery era. The political strategy of resisting imaginatively a white power that could not be overturned literally did not end when slavery ended. James M. Washington has emphasized how the common worship style that one finds broadly among the black churches provides "a spiritual praxis that nurtures and supports the psychic infrastructure of black America." "The positivistic obsession of the social sciences," he contends, has often led them unduly to neglect "the politics of spirituality."[20] One could also fruitfully examine the long tradition of black freedom celebrations, a tradition reaching from the earliest celebrations to mark the end of the slave trade right down to contemporary observance of the national holiday in honor of Martin Luther King, Jr. This liturgical tradition has been public and communal and has provided an important setting in which black religious and political leaders have sought to articulate a compelling vision of Afro-American destiny.[21] As such, it could fruitfully be studied in relation to the practice of "civil religion" among whites. Relevant here also is Randall Burkett's important contention that the Universal Negro Improvement Association in part succeeded in becoming the largest mass organization in Afro-American history because its leader, Marcus Garvey, so skillfully developed a kind of black civil religion that allowed him to mobilize the energies of a wide range of black religious groups without becoming the prisoner of any one of them.[22] But I turn aside here from all these important topics in order to focus more narrowly on the political role of the black churches.

If power is defined not competitively, as coercive power, but more collaboratively, as "the capacity to participate in making social decisions," then the black churches have been the major vehicle for the development of black power in America.[23] More than any other institution, the churches have provided a place where black Americans could collectively order their own lives—and also a kind of institutional beachhead on the decision-making terrain of the wider society. That these black churches—and the network of voluntary associations closely connected with them—have existed at all is in large measure a result of the widespread institutionalization of religious and associational freedom in the Revolutionary and early national periods. Without religious liberty, there would have been no black church—not, at least, in the sense that we have known it. But, as Will Gravely has pointed out, in an especially apt phrase, the black church was "an *unforeseen* consequence of religious freedom."[24] Those responsible for shaping the American pattern of religious voluntarism were not, we may assume, largely motivated by any concern to create organizational opportunities for the black people in their midst. Indeed, it is readily apparent that no other group has had its rights to religious liberty so often curtailed by the excercise of state power as Afro-Americans have. Discussions of church-state relations in America very frequently leave entirely out of account the police laws of the slave states restricting the hours at which slaves could hold religious meetings, the number of slaves who could be present, the kind of meetings that could be held, and so forth. But it is clear that these provisions, however unevenly enforced, are telling evidence that "the free exercise" of religion, unimpeded by state interference, was scarcely a reality for the antebellum black slave.[25] It was for free blacks, however, and that fact was of critical importance for the rise of the independent black churches.

Formed in the late eighteenth and early nineteenth centuries, mostly through a process of extended and painful separation from biracial evangelical congregations and denominations, the independent black churches were first a local and then a regional phenomenon. At the local level, the initial impulse of many black Protestants seems to have been to secure religious independence by forming themselves into interdenominational African churches, but the rising tide of denominationalism soon swamped most of these efforts at union churches. The resulting religious division of the black community locally was balanced by the promotion of regional solidarity among black believers with shared denominational loyalties. In some cases, as among the Presbyterians and Congregationalists, no independent black denominational structures ever emerged. But even here translocal links were forged, that is, in the 1840s and 1850s, when the black leaders of these churches formed evangelical associations and conventions that were in many ways forerunners of the Black Caucus of the late 1960s and 1970s. More notable, of course, were the pioneering efforts of the independent black Methodist denominations. Established in 1813, the African Union Church, centered in Wilmington, Delaware, was just barely more than a local organization. But the African Methodist Episcopal Church (1816) and the African Methodist Episcopal Zion Church (1821) were organized broadly across the free states and to some extent along the periphery of the South as well. (A fourth black Method-ist denomination, the Colored—later Christian—Methodist Episcopal Church, was exclusively Southern in its origins, but it was established only in 1870.) Baptists organized more slowly, but the American Baptist Missionary Convention, founded in the North in 1840, was the first major step down a long road of national denominational organizations that culminated in 1895 with the formation of the National Baptist Conven-tion, U.S.A., Incorporated. (Schisms from that body later produced, in 1915, the National Baptist Convention of America and, in 1960, the Progressive National Baptist Convention.)[26]

Because of both the legal and more informal impediments that effec-tively barred them from the slave South, none of these black denomina-tions was a truly national church in the antebellum period. But during the years of the Civil War and Reconstruction, these black denominations competed quite successfully with the biracial denominations for the loyalties of the vast body of Christian freedmen—and thereby secured for themselves a place at the organizational center of black religious life from which they have yet to be dislodged. The rapid growth in the twentieth century of the Black Holiness and Pentecostal denominations (above all the Church of God in Christ, organized initially in 1897), the rapid increase in the middle of the century of the number of black Catholics, and the emergence of major non-Christian challengers, such as the Na-tion of Islam (and its main successor organization, the World Community of Al-Islam in the West), has no doubt significantly reduced the "market share" of the old-line black religious establishment. But the great black Baptist and Methodist denominations still remain the most prominent and powerful religious organizations in the black community, and it is therefore predominantly upon them that my attention will be focused.[27]

For all that has been said and written about the important role of these churches in black politics, we actually have a much less clear picture of its overall historical development than might be supposed. A major part of the problem is that our understanding of the black churches' actual role in the political process has been significantly obscured by the presence of two recurring generalizations that are as unproven as they are familiar. I refer here to what can be termed the twin myths of "modernization" and "the fall" of the black church. I use the term "myth" here with a certain degree of seriousness. Both of the views I mean to challenge embed specific historical judgments about the black churches and politics in the context of broad, meaning-giving visions about some larger historical process—and by so doing obscure as much as they reveal. In the space that remains, my task is to characterize these two myths, to suggest why I find them misleading, and to offer some provisional generalizations of my own to be explored in future research.

By the "myth of modernization," I refer to the application to Afro-American religion and politics of the very general idea that such social processes as urbanization and industrialization are steadily producing across the globe a "modern" social order with certain more or less invariant characteristics.[28] Among these is the increasing "differentiation" of the various social institutions, for example, family and work, economic and political power, and—most important for our purposes—religion and politics. From this standpoint the story of the black church and politics can easily be told as the story of an increasing differentiation of religious and political life or, to put it more sharply, the ever increasing loss of political function by black religious institutions and their leaders. Once upon a time, it has been suggested, when slavery and then segregation blocked Afro-Americans' access to the most modernized sectors of American life and kept them in a traditionalistic enclave, the church and the clergy performed those limited political functions available to the black community. But the cumulative effect of the increasing integration of blacks into the nation's modern, democratic polity, first through the migration and then through the successes of the civil rights movement, has been a decline in the influence of black religion in black politics. The political scientist Adolph L. Reed, Jr., for example, concluded in 1986 that "the development of a new context of political authority in the aftermath of the civil rights movement [has] deemphasized the church's role in political spokesmanship. . . . By the 1980s, [W. E. B.] DuBois' 1903 prediction of the supercession of a clerically grounded leadership appeared to have reached fruition."[29]

Reed's work, however, is also a very good example of a certain ambiguity that appears in much of this kind of analysis, a certain equivocation about whether the central point being made is primarily descriptive or prescriptive. Reed's highly polemical book, *The Jesse Jackson Phenomenon*, might be not unfairly described as an outraged attack on Jackson for not having grasped the message of history—and acted accordingly. As Reed declares, "the Jackson phenomenon . . . represents a resurgence of the principle of clerical political spokesmanship." As such, it is historically regressive and ought not to be occurring. As we all know, however, Reed's critique did not prevent the Jackson phenomenon from recurring yet again in 1988, this time with most black elected officials—the advance of modernity notwithstanding—lining up behind the clergyman-candidate. There is a very considerable irony here. Reed, in his own analysis of the political role of the black churches, draws heavily on the work of "the generation of functionalist sociologists and social psychologists who studied the Afro-American community in the 1930s and 1940s," above all on the work of E. Franklin Frazier. These social scientists, most of whom were supremely confident that the migration-launched urbanization of black Americans was already undermining the hold over them of their religious institutions, saw traditional black faith as thoroughly compensatory—as offering to blacks a fulfillment in fantasy that they could not achieve in fact. The same might be said of some of their own works. Secular black intellectuals have overthrown in print a rival clerical elite that they could not displace in practice. Adolph Reed's critique of Jesse Jackson is from this perspective the academic equivalent of "getting happy," a cathartic encounter with the spirit of secular modernity that, however, in the end leaves the realities of black clergy political power just exactly as they were.[30]

At the risk of going to the other extreme from those who have emphasized the "myth of modernization," I want to suggest that the story of the black church and clergy in black politics is a tale of continuity rather than change. From the earliest stages of black inclusion in the political process in the antebellum North down to the present, black religious institutions and their leaders have played a central but never dominant role in black electoral politics. There is not space here to argue this point in any detail. All I can offer is a pair of illustrations that suggest the kind of evidence that might be considered.

One of the earliest forms of black community organization, reaching well back into the colonial period, was what was known as "Negro Election Day."[31] Occurring mostly in New England, it took a wide variety of forms. In Salem, Massachusetts, for example, where it can be traced back to the 1740s, "Negro Election Day" seems merely to have been a time of black communal festivity—there was fiddling, dancing, and "playing with pennies"—that coincided with Massachusetts Election Day. But in many other New England towns, blacks elected officials of their own on "Negro Election Day"—governors and kings, for example—who in a few instances actually did some governing within the black community. In Newport, Rhode Island, for example, the black "Governor, Deputy Governor and their assistants . . . exerted judicial responsibilities. . . . Magistrates, appointed by the Governor, tried all cases brought against any black, whether by a white or a black, and punished at their discretion."[32] Where, in the Revolutionary and early national period, New England blacks received the franchise, "Negro Election Day" generally atrophied. But it endured in Connecticut (where blacks did not vote) well into the nineteenth century. In New Haven, William Lanson, "contractor and owner of the Negro vice section, hardheaded man of affairs, and elected 'African King,'" was still the preeminent figure in the city's black community when his leadership was challenged in the 1830s by black Congregationalist pastor Amos G. Beman.[33] The main point here, as mention of the contest between Lanson and Beman suggests, is that "Negro Election Day" represents an early form of political organization among blacks that antedated the black church and in some cases gave way to it only grudgingly. From the beginning, then, there has been a rivalry between church-based and non-church-based elites for political leadership in the black community.

The second bit of illustrative evidence I can offer here to support my broad thesis of continuity in the relation of the black church and black politics concerns the election of black clergymen to the U.S. Congress. Mary R. Sawyer has done a comparative study of blacks elected to Congress during the First Reconstruction and those elected between 1950 and 1980.[34] Biographical information on some of the twenty-two blacks elected to Congress between 1870 and 1900 is hard to obtain, but the evidence is that two and possibly three of them were ordained ministers: Hiram Revels, Richard Harvey Cain, and Jeremiah Haralson. Among the thirty blacks who served in Congress between 1950 and 1980, there were four clergymen: Adam Clayton Powell, Jr., Andrew Young, Walter Fauntroy, and William H. Gray III. It is certainly hard to see in this comparison any evidence of a major shift in the political role of the black clergy. This in and of itself of course *proves* nothing. But it may nonetheless indicate something quite fundamental.

The second myth I want to address is that of the fall of the black church. If the modernization myth looks forward to the time when black politics will be more or less entirely delivered from the taint of religiosity, the myth of the fall of the black church looks back to an Edenic period when the black church was the more or less uncompromised bearer of the Afro-American quest for peoplehood and freedom—a status of political sinlessness from which it somehow subsequently fell. If the modernization myth is propounded mostly by social scientists of a secularist persuasion, the myth of the fall of the black church is the handiwork of militant black churchmen. It is a general rule that no one speaks of a fall unless he (or she) hopes for a redemption—and those who have spoken of the fall of the black church are no exception to this general rule. To speak of a fall is to call sinners to repentance—and this is exactly how such rhetoric has functioned with regard to the black church and politics. But here again there is an irony. Those who see the black church as having fallen sometimes accuse it of having lapsed into escapist otherworldliness. Yet the myth of the fall of the black church is itself in some respects an escape from the obviously compromised world of the present into a prefall past where such painful realities are imagined to have been largely absent. Is it too much to suggest that radical black churchmen have sometimes achieved through an act of historical fantasy something they have been generally unable to accomplish in fact—a marshaling of the entire collective force of the black churches behind a militant political agenda?

James Cone, for example, in his important early manifesto of the black theology movement, *Black Theology and Black Power*, lamented an alleged post-Reconstruction decline in black church militancy. "The black church lost its zeal for freedom," he declared, "in the midst of the new structures of white power. . . . The passion for freedom was replaced with innocuous homilies against drinking, dancing and smoking; and injustices in the present were minimized in favor of a Kingdom beyond this world." This condemnation of the post–Civil War black church depended, of course, on a romanticization of its prewar predecessor. Cone had conceded, in discussing the earlier period, "that some black ministers preached that Christianity was unrelated to earthly freedom." But his overwhelming emphasis was on the political thrust of the early black church. "The birth of the independent black churches and the teaching of the free black preachers show clearly that Christianity and earthly freedom were inseparable for the black man," he reported. "The black church was born in protest . . . protest and action were the early marks of its uniqueness." It is no denigration of the important element of truth in these assertions to say that they are nonetheless exaggerated. Homilies against drinking, dancing, and smoking do not appear in the black pulpit only after Reconstruction. There was a strong moralistic strain in precisely some of those black churchmen who were the most strongly antislavery—a moralism that included all the bourgeois virtues, including economic asceticism.[35] The black church, moreover, was not always willing to place the antislavery witness ahead of all other concerns. One example will have to suffice.

In 1856, the General Conference of the A.M.E. Church debated the question of whether to strengthen the provision in its discipline against slaveholding. There were, among the church members in the South and the border states, some slave owners. Some of their slaveholding may have served as a kind of legal fiction to allow actual freedom to slaves in states where laws preventing manumission precluded legal freedom. In other instances, black owners may have retained title to slaves they had purchased with an intent to free while the slaves were working off the purchase price. In any case, some of the more militant members of the church insisted in 1856 that the church no longer retain or accept as members anyone who owned a slave under any circumstances or for whatever reason. Their proposal was defeated 40 to 12. One of the concerns raised by the majority was that the adoption of this proposal might hamper the church's missionary efforts along the Southern periphery.[36] What this incident suggests is that the leaders of the antebellum black church, like their successors, were animated by a wide range of concerns. Some of them, all of the time, and others, part of the time, put protest and political action against slavery at the head of their agendas. But others were apparently disinterested in organized protest activities and some who were interested were nonetheless willing to subordinate their concern to other goals on particular occasions. This is scarcely surprising if one assumes, as I think we should, that the black churches have never been politically monolithic.

One more instance of a belief in the fall of the black church is worth noting before drawing conclusions about the enduring continuities in the relation of the black church to politics. Gayraud S. Wilmore's *Black Religion and Black Radicalism* is the closest thing to a survey history of Afro-American religion that has been published in the last quarter-century. Wilmore tells a far more nuanced story then Cone, yet in the end his account also turns on a tale of the fall of the black church. Wilmore speaks of this fall as "the deradicalization of the black church" and dates it roughly to the era of World War I and the 1920s. Its onset is for him symbolized by the death, in 1915, of the aggressively nationalist and emigrationist A.M.E. bishop Henry McNeal Turner. After Turner had left the scene, Wilmore declares, "there were no clergymen of his stature who could, by temperament or ideology, assume the leadership position he had occupied." Without the sort of prodding that Turner had provided, the independent black churches drifted ever more deeply into a kind of bourgeois respectability until the church was "no longer a primarily lower-class institution arbitrating the terms of black existence [but] . . . was becoming thoroughly middle-class and marginated."[37]

There are a number of problems with this account. The year of Bishop Turner's death was also the year Booker T. Washington died, and it might reasonably be said that it was a year in which the black church broke apart even so far as its collective level of militancy was concerned. More important, Wilmore is guilty of a double exaggeration in claiming that the black church of the 1920s fell from being "a primarily lower class institution arbitrating the terms of black existence" to being "thoroughly

middle-class and marginated." As has already been suggested, the bour-
geoisification of the black church began with its birth, not in the 1870s
nor the 1920s. Turner himself was strongly committed to a bourgeois
economic ethic and it is by no means as clear as has sometimes been
supposed that his followers were the poorest of Southern blacks.[38] It is in
any case a mistake to assume, as Wilmore seems to do, that the black
poor as a body are the bearers of a "folk religious tradition . . . [with]
radical impulses."[39] A certain kind of militantly nationalist religion has
formed a sizable and enduring constituency among the most dispossessed
members of the Afro-American population. But the black folk is made
up of a diverse range of black folks, and their religious—and political—
orientations are scarcely monolithic. So it is a considerable historical
overstatement to picture the black church of the 1920s as falling from the
paradise of an identification with the masses into the sinful embrace of
the black bourgeoisie.

It is also a considerable overstatement to claim either that the black
church ever "arbitrated the terms of black existence" or that it was
"thoroughly . . . marginated" by the 1920s. To speak, in the first instance,
of that kind of churchly domination is to dream of an ecclesiastical Eden.
It would also appear, especially from the standpoint of politics, that the
black Baptist and Methodist churches were as much at the center of the
black community in the interwar period as they had ever been. It is
arguable—I have indeed elsewhere argued it[40]—that the black Methodist
denominations lost in the twentieth century some of the cultural influence and political clout that they had enjoyed in nineteenth. But the
opposite seems to have been true among the black Baptists. The Great
Migration, which is so often seen as having undermined the mainline
black churches, in fact was the making of such powerful urban Baptist
congregations as Olivet and Pilgrim in Chicago and Abyssinian in New
York. Reflecting on the historically important role of the last named as
the base upon which Adam Clayton Powell, Jr., built his career as the
most powerful black politician of his time is a reminder of how politically
aggressive and effective the black church continued to be long after its
alleged fall in the 1920s.[41]

If the myth of modernization and the myth of the fall of the black
church are set aside, what overall picture emerges of the historical relation of the black church and politics in the United States? All I can offer
here is the merest sketch.

The main theme, as I have already suggested, is one of continuity.
Throughout our history, Afro-Americans have had continuously to deal
with "the overwhelming reality of the white presence" in America and

with the exercise of white power. To do so in the context of the political arena they have been obliged, on the one hand, to try to mobilize the full resources of the black community and, on the other, to come to terms somehow with the forces of white power. The myth of modernization suggests that the church once played a dominant role in the political mobilization of the black community but that its influence is now steadily in decline. The truth is that the church has always been and remains one base among others in the black community from which efforts to organize the community politically have been made. The myth of the fall of the black church suggests that the church at some point lost the primal militancy that allowed it to confront uncompromisingly the demonic power of whites and that it subsequently fell into a kind of political acquiescence. The truth is that the black church at every stage has had to come to some kind of bargain with the dominant political forces, however distasteful that bargain has often been. In sum, the black church throughout its history has been compelled in its political efforts to come to terms both with other forces within the black community and with the political forces of white America. That is the simple base line from which analysis must begin.

From that simple beginning, a no doubt highly complicated story can be told about the quite varied ways in which the black churches have attempted to carry out these two tasks. But to tell the tale rightly we will need to know much more than we now do about many things. On the one side, more work must be done on the precise ways in which the black church has interacted with other elements in the black community in shaping the direction of black politics. Such work needs to be highly attentive to the peculiarities of local political environments. The way the emergence of the black churches intersected with the old patterns of "Negro Election Day" was quite likely not the same in Newport, for example, as it was in New Haven; and the political environment of mid-twentieth-century New York, in which Adam Clayton Powell emerged, was not the same as the political environment of mid-twentieth-century Chicago, in which no comparable figure appeared. The peculiar political strengths and weaknesses of the different denominational structures must also be more carefully taken into account than it generally has been in the past. We need to think harder, for example, about why the nineteenth century seems to have been the Methodist age in the history of the black church and politics while the twentieth century has belonged to the Baptists.

The work that needs to be done, however, does not concern only the black church and its role within the black community but also religious and political interaction across racial lines. The encounter of black and white, as I suggested at the outset, is not a central theme only in Afro-American religious history but also in American religious history generally. Part of what needs to be done in this regard is, once again, very detailed work. We need to know more, for example, about the way the elaborate clientage networks that linked black church leaders and black politicians to white politicians did or did not parallel or intersect with networks among white church leaders. But we also need to keep our eyes more steadily on the larger ways that race, religion, and politics are intertwined in America. I have been struck, for example, by how little attention is often paid to the dependence of the political resurgence of white evangelicalism on the success of the civil rights movement. By ending segregation, the civil rights movement also ended the political segregation of the South. This not only has allowed such figures as Jerry Falwell and Pat Robertson to function as leaders in American (and not merely Southern) religion and politics; it has also made possible the reunification of the bulk of white evangelicalism—for the first time in more than a century—in a single political party. That that party is also not insignificantly building its power in the South—as its adversary did for so long—on its character as the party of white rule is simply another reminder of the disturbing persistence of racial polarity in American religion and politics.

Notes

1. Charles H. Long, "Civil Rights—Civil Religion: Visible People and Invisible Religion," in Russell E. Richey and Donald G. Jones, eds., *American Civil Religion* (New York: Harper & Row, 1974), 212, 216, 214. Long's emphasis on the interpretation of American *beginnings* is informed both by a general history-of-religions concern with the formative power of all cosmogonies and by a wide-ranging interest in the cultural and religious consequences for all humankind of modern Europe's global expansion. See Charles H. Long, *Significations: Signs, Symbols, and Images in the Interpretation of Religion* (Philadelphia: Fortress, 1986).

2. Robert N. Bellah, Richard Madsen, William M. Sullivan, Ann Swidler, and Steven M. Tipton, *Habits of the Heart: Individualism and Commitment in American Life* (Berkeley: University of California Press, 1985).

3. Vincent Harding, "Toward a Darkly Radiant Vision of America's Truth," *Cross Currents* 37, 1 (Spring 1987): 1–16.

4. A. James Reichley, *Religion in American Public Life* (Washington: The Brookings Institution, 1985).

5. Ibid., 53, 74.

6. Lipset's use of these terms in his course, Government 110, Politics and Society, Harvard University, is recorded in my class notes for April 13, 1967, but I have been unable to locate them in his voluminous publications. The basic idea is present, however, for example, in Seymour M. Lipset, "Religion and Politics in the American Past and Present," in Robert Lee and Martin E. Marty, eds., *Religion and Social Conflict* (New York: Oxford University Press, 1964), 69–126.

7. For another brief statement of this same thesis, see David W. Wills, "The Central Themes of American Religious History: Pluralism, Puritanism, and the Encounter of Black and White," *Religion and Intellectual Life* 5, 1 (Fall 1987): 30–41.

8. To speak in this way of the racial power relations that emerged "*at the beginning*" of our history is not to deny that there seems to have been more fluidity in the relations between blacks and whites in the earliest decades of Southern history than there was after the decisive shift from European to African labor occurred in the late seventeenth and early eighteenth centuries. "Beginning" here refers not simply to the very earliest years, narrowly defined, but to the broader set of initial events and processes that gradually gave enduring shape to colonial British North America.

9. The authoritative general account of the religion of the slaves is Albert J. Raboteau, *Slave Religion: The "Invisible Institution" in the Antebellum South* (New York: Oxford University Press, 1978). On the rise of black evangelicalism, see also Milton C. Sernett, *Black Religion and American Evangelicalism: White Protestantism, Plantation Missions, and the Flowering of Negro Christianity, 1783–1865* (Metuchen, NJ: Scarecrow, 1975). Two important recent works that devote considerable attention to the earlier stages of Afro-American religion as well as to the emergence of Afro-American evangelicalism are Mechal Sobel, *The World They Made Together: Black and White Values in Eighteenth Century Virginia* (Princeton: Princeton University Press, 1987); and Margaret Washington Creel, *"A Peculiar People": Slave Religion and Community Culture Among the Gullahs* (New York: New York University Press, 1988). Albert J. Raboteau, "'A Fire in the Bones': The Afro-American Chanted Sermon," an unpublished type-written essay, suggestively traces one central aspect of Afro-American religious performance styles from the slavery era to the present.

10. See Raboteau, *Slave Religion*, 289–318, for a careful and judicious discussion of "religion, rebellion and docility" among the slaves. For a provocative discussion of the relation between Afro-American culture and politics that emphasizes both the priority of the cultural and the importance of Afro-American Christianity in shaping that culture, see Cornel West, *Prophesy Deliverance: An Afro-American Revolutionary Christianity* (Philadelphia: Westminster, 1982), especially 35–36, 69–72.

11. Eugene D. Genovese, *Roll, Jordan, Roll: The World the Slaves Made* (New York: Random House, 1974), 284.

12. Long, *Significations*, 137–139, 142–143, 157–172.

13. Lorenzo J. Greene, *The Negro in Colonial New England* (New York: Columbia University Press, 1942; reprint ed., New York: Atheneum, 1969), 300–303; John Hope Franklin and Alfred A. Moss, Jr., *From Slavery to Freedom: A History of Negro Americans*, 6th ed. (New York: Knopf, 1988), 141.

14. Data from the U.S. Bureau of the Census on the black percentage of all Southern state populations in 1870, 1880, 1890, and 1900 is provided by Frederick D. Wright, "The History of Black Political Participation to 1965," in Laurence W. Moreland, Robert P. Steed, and Tod A. Baker, eds., *Blacks in Southern Politics* (New York: Praeger, 1987), 10.

15. For a recent discussion of antiblack violence during the Reconstruction era, in the North as well as in the South, see Herbert Shapiro, *White Violence and Black Response: From Reconstruction to Montgomery* (Amherst: University of Massachusetts Press, 1988), 5–29. It is Shapiro's contention (11–12) that "a key element in the race riots of this period was that usually such incidents were linked to election campaigns." See also the most important recent general survey and interpretation of Reconstruction, Eric Foner, *Reconstruction: America's Unfinished Revolution, 1863–1877* (New York: Harper & Row, 1988).

16. On Louisiana, see Wright, "History of Black Political Participation," 13–14.

17. James M. McPherson, *Ordeal By Fire: The Civil War and Reconstruction* (New York: Knopf, 1982), 501–502, 529, 542, 545, describes postwar Northern votes on black suffrage.

18. For changing percentages of blacks residing in the South, see United States Bureau of the Census, *The Social and Economic Status of the Black Population in the United States: An Historical View, 1790–1978* (Washington: Government Printing Office, [1979]); Evelyn Brooks, "In Politics To Stay: Black Women Leaders and Party Politics in the 1920s," unpublished typewritten essay; Martin Kilson, "Political Change in the Negro Ghetto, 1900–1940's," in Nathan I. Huggins, Martin Kilson, and Daniel M. Fox, eds., *Key Issues in the Afro-American Experience*, Vol. 2 (New York: Harcourt Brace Jovanovich, 1971), 167–192.

19. Wright, "History of Black Political Participation," 21–28; Margaret Edds, *Free At Last: What Really Happened When Civil Rights Came to Southern Politics* (Bethseda, MD: Adler and Adler, 1987), 6–27. See also Steven F. Lawson, *In Pursuit of Power: Southern Blacks and Electoral Politics, 1965–1982* (New York: Columbia University Press, 1985).

20. James Melvin Washington, "Jesse Jackson and the Symbolic Politics of Black Christendom," *Annals of the American Academy of Political and Social Science* 480 (July 1985): 105.

21. See Will B. Gravely, "The Dialectic of Double-Consciousness in Black American Freedom Celebrations, 1808–1863," *Journal of Negro History* 67 (Winter 1982): 302–317; William H. Wiggins, Jr., *O Freedom! Afro-American Emancipation Celebrations* (Knoxville: University of Tennessee Press, 1987).

22. Randall K. Burkett, *Garveyism as a Religious Movement: The Institutionalization of a Black Civil Religion* (Metuchen, NJ: Scarecrow, 1978), especially 2–9, 66–68, 71–99, 195–196. See also Randall K. Burkett, *Black Redemption:*

Churchmen Speak for the Garvey Movement (Philadelphia: Temple University Press, 1978).

23. This definition of power is frequently cited by the theological social ethicist James Luther Adams—for example, in his *The Prophethood of All Believers*, ed. George K. Beach (Boston: Beacon, 1986), 132. It is a central concept in his important interpretation of the relation between the voluntarism of the left wing of the Protestant Reformation and the emergence of modern democratic politics. See also James Luther Adams, *Voluntary Associations: Socio-Cultural Analyses and Theological Interpretation*, ed. J. Ronald Engel (Chicago: Exploration, 1986). Adams's views provide a standpoint from which a very illuminating study of the political role of the black churches in America could be done.

24. Emphasis added. Gravely has used this phrase in private conversation and correspondence. For a published statement of his views concerning the importance for the black church of the institutionalization of religious freedom in the early republic, see Will B. Gravely, "The Rise of African Churches in America: Re-Examining the Contexts (1786–1822)," *Journal of Religious Thought* 41 (1984): 58–73.

25. W. E. B. DuBois, ed., *The Negro Church* (Atlanta: Atlanta University Press, 1903), 10–13, 22–26, 29, discusses some of the major pieces of legislation restricting the religious activities of the slaves.

26. The most thoughtful recent overview of the emergence and early development of the black churches is Gravely, "The Rise of African Churches in America." David W. Wills and Richard Newman, eds., *Black Apostles at Home and Abroad: Afro-Americans and the Christian Mission from the Revolution to Reconstruction* (Boston: G. K. Hall, 1982), xi–xxxiii, interprets the history of black evangelicalism in the first two-thirds of the nineteenth century and offers in its notes a general survey of the literature existing at the time of its publication. Among the most important contributions to the early institutional history of the black churches that have appeared subsequently are: Albert J. Raboteau, "The Slave Church in the Era of the American Revolution," in Ira Berlin and Ronald Hoffman, eds., *Slavery and Freedom in the Age of the American Revolution* (Charlottesville: University of Virginia, 1983), 193–213; Will B. Gravely, "African Methodisms and the Rise of Black Denominationalism," in Russell E. Richey and Kenneth E. Rowe, eds., *Rethinking Methodist History: A Bicentennial Historical Consultation* (Nashville: Kingswood, 1985), 111–124; Lewis V. Baldwin, *"Invisible" Strands in African Methodism: A History of the African Union Methodist Protestant and Union American Methodist Episcopal Churches, 1805–1980* (Metuchen, NJ: Scarecrow, 1983); Clarence E. Walker, *A Rock in a Weary Land: The African Methodist Episcopal Church During the Civil War and Reconstruction* (Baton Rouge: Louisiana State University Press, 1982); and, most especially, James Melvin Washington, *Frustrated Fellowship: The Black Baptist Quest for Social Power* (Macon, GA: Mercer University Press, 1986).

27. For the post-Reconstruction history of the black churches generally, in addition to the sources cited above, see: David W. Wills, "An Enduring Distance:

Black Americans and the Establishment," in William R. Hutchison, ed., *Between the Times: The Travail of the Protestant Establishment in America, 1900-1960* (New York: Cambridge University Press, forthcoming); and Randall K. Burkett and Richard Newman, eds., *Black Apostles: Afro-American Clergy Confront the Twentieth Century* (Boston: G. K. Hall, 1978). Vinson Synan, *The Holiness-Pentecostal Movement in the United States* (Grand Rapids: Eerdmans, 1971), provides a helpful introduction to the organizational history of black Pentecostalism. The entire issue of the *U.S. Catholic Historian*, 5, 1 (1986), is devoted to the history of black Catholics in the United States. In the context of a broad interpretation of race and religion in modern America, C. Eric Lincoln *Race, Religion and the Continuing American Dilemma* (New York: Hill and Wang, 1984), 154-169, provides a succinct overview of the twentieth-century Black Muslim movement. See also the contributions of Lincoln and Lawrence H. Mamiya to Earl H. Waugh, Baha Abu-Laban, and Regula Quresh, *The Muslim Community in North America* (Edmonton: University of Alberta Press, 1983).

28. The most explicit and sophisticated application of modernization theory to black politics is to be found in the work of Martin Kilson, for example, *Political Change in Sierra Leone* (Cambridge: Harvard University Press, 1966) and "Political Change in the Negro Ghetto." Kilson emphasizes the great variability of the pattern of modernization among different nations and groups (e.g., "Political Change," 167-168) and this makes his work far less mythological and much more historically nuanced than the work criticized in the text above.

29. Adolph L. Reed, Jr., *The Jesse Jackson Phenomenon: The Crisis of Purpose in Afro-American Politics* (New Haven: Yale University Press, 1986), 43-44.

30. Reed, *Jesse Jackson,* 44, 45. An extended critique of the interpretation of Afro-American religion offered by the functionalist social scientists Reed relies on is advanced in Randall K. Burkett and David W. Wills, "Afro-American Religious History, 1919-1939: A Resource Guide and Bibliographical Essay," unpublished typewritten essay. For an exposition and analysis of Jackson's own views, which Reed much neglects, see Jesse L. Jackson, *Straight From the Heart*, ed. Roger D. Hatch and Frank E. Watkins (Philadelphia: Fortress, 1987); and Roger D. Hatch, *Beyond Opportunity: Jesse Jackson's Vision for America* (Philadelphia: Fortress, 1988). A general interpretation of black religious social thought in America is offered by Peter J. Paris, *The Social Teaching of the Black Churches* (Philadelphia: Fortress Press, 1985).

31. The literature on "Negro Election Day" includes: Greene, *Negro in Colonial New England*, 249-255; William D. Pierson, "Afro-American Culture in Eighteenth Century New England: A Comparative Examination" (Ph.D. diss., Indiana University, 1975), 211-301; William D. Pierson, *Black Yankees: The Development of an Afro-American Subculture in Eighteenth Century New England* (Amherst: University of Massachusetts, 1988), 117-140; Joseph P. Reidy, "Negro Election Day & Black Community Life in New England, 1750-1860," *Marxist Perspectives* 1, 3 (Fall 1978): 102-117; and Melvin Wade, "'Shining in

Borrowed Plumage': Affirmation of Community in Black Coronation Festivals of New England, ca. 1750–1850," in Robert Blair St. George, ed., *Material Life in America 1600–1860* (Boston: Northeastern University Press, 1988), 171–182.

32. Reidy, "Negro Election Day," 104, 105.

33. Robert A. Warner, *New Haven Negroes: A Social History* (New Haven: Yale University Press, 1940), 26; see also 8–10, 22, 28–29, 56, 78–97. Reidy, "Negro Election Day," 113, sees the conflict between Lanson and Beman as a struggle between "an older, unregenerate cultural nationalism with separatist tendencies and a local constituency" and "a newer, sophisticated reformism with assimilationist tendencies and a national constituency."

34. Mary R. Sawyer, "A Moral Minority: Religion and Congressional Black Politics," *Journal of Religious Thought* 40, 2 (Fall–Winter 1983–84): 55–66. See also Mary R. Sawyer, "Black Politics, Black Faith" (M.A. thesis, Howard University Divinity School, 1982).

35. James H. Cone, *Black Theology and Black Power* (New York: Seabury, 1969), 105, 100, 94. For discussions that emphasize—even overemphasize—the importance of the bourgeois virtues in the antebellum black churches, see Frederick Cooper, "Elevating the Race: The Social Thought of Black Leaders, 1827–1850," *American Quarterly* 24, 5 (December 1972): 604–626; and Walker, *A Rock in a Weary Land*.

36. Gayraud S. Wilmore, *Black Religion and Black Radicalism: An Interpretation of the Religious History of Afro-American People*, 2nd ed. (Maryknoll, NY: Orbis, 1983), 85–87. A recent study of the ambiguous phenomenon of black slaveholding is Larry Kroger, *Black Slaveowners: Free Black Slave Masters in South Carolina, 1790–1850* (Jefferson, NC: McFarland, 1985). See also Michael P. Johnson and James L. Roark, *Black Masters: A Free Family of Color in the Old South* (New York: W. W. Norton, 1984).

37. Wilmore, *Black Radicalism*, 135, 145.

38. I have discussed Turner's economic ethic in "Radical Justice and the Limits of American Liberalism," *Journal of Religious Ethics* 6, 2 (Fall 1978): 205–209. Even while contending that Turner's "African Dream" was more a black version of the American Dream than the expression of a genuine cultural nationalism, Edwin S. Redkey's pathbreaking *Black Exodus: Black Nationalist and Back-to-Africa Movements, 1890–1910* (New Haven: Yale University Press, 1969), insists (e.g., 5) on the "lower-class" character of Turner's following. But the book reports many instances of would-be emigrationists selling their land to go to Africa—and Southern blacks with land to sell were by no means at the bottom of the black class structure.

39. Wilmore, *Black Radicalism*, 145. Wilmore's discussion of the folk tradition, 144–145, indicates the degree to which he has been influenced, almost in spite of himself, by the highly controversial Joseph R. Washington, Jr., *Black Religion: The Negro and Christianity in the United States* (Boston: Beacon, 1964).

40. Burkett and Wills, "Afro-American Religious History" 37–38.

41. Martin Kilson, "Adam Clayton Powell, Jr.: The Militant as Politician," in John Hope Franklin and August Meier, eds., *Black Leaders of the Twentieth Century* (Urbana: University of Illinois Press, 1982), 259–275, provides a succinct analysis of Powell's career. Peter J. Paris, *Black Leaders in Conflict: Joseph H. Jackson, Martin Luther King, Jr., Malcolm X, Adam Clayton Powell, Jr.* (New York: Pilgrim, 1978), compares Powell, among others, to the pastor of the Olivet Baptist Church in Chicago, a congregation that has played an extraordinarily influential role in the National Baptist Convention, U.S.A., Inc. In an unpublished typewritten essay, "The Black Church in the Years of Crisis: J. C. Austin and Pilgrim Baptist Church, 1926–1950," Randall K. Burkett examines the career of another important National Baptist churchman and Chicago political activist.

10

Religion and Politics in Nineteenth-Century Britain: The Case Against American Exceptionalism

RICHARD CARWARDINE

I

Implicit in so much scholarly work on nineteenth-century American politics is not only an awareness that the United States, like any other country, was unique but a conviction that American political experience was truly exceptional. The United States, the "first new nation," presented Europeans from Tocqueville to Bryce with a political laboratory where they could observe a novel experiment in republicanism and democracy. Whether or not those observers regarded the experiment as foolish or brave, or both, there was a general sense that the main ligaments of the American political structure and its modus operandi constituted a departure from conventional European experience. A society that had inherited its principal, Whiggish political values from Britain set off during the second half of the eighteenth century on its own divergent path. Less and less guided by holistic maxims, and facing social changes that eroded deference and directly challenged organicist and homogeneous perceptions of the polity, men in public life found themselves operating in the early decades of the new century in a radically changing political system. By the middle of the nineteenth century that system had adjusted to the fact of universal white manhood suffrage and was organized around permanent political parties whose professional representatives competed for public favor in frequent and regular elections. For Americans in that era of emergent mass democracy the erstwhile mother country appeared as a frozen, restricted polity where class, deference, and the economic power of one group over another shaped political life, and restricted the suffrage and the political opportunities of most, and where the institutions of monarchy, lords, and commons formally embodied these unrepublican and unequal social relationships.[1]

Relations between church and state in the two countries served only to heighten this sense of the contrast between them, and indeed between the United States and European countries generally. Americans' sense of the uniqueness of their "voluntary system"—well cultivated before the removal of the last state-supported church, in Massachusetts in 1833—was implicitly and explicitly reinforced by the transatlantic stream of religious sightseers. British religious radicals and conservatives reached wholly different verdicts about the American experiment: many of the former followed Joseph Priestley's example and emigrated to the United States to escape political intolerance, while defenders of the Anglican establishment pointed to the perils of unconstrained voluntarism, including the degenerative fissiparousness of American denominational life and the enthusiastic "slaverings" of a revivalism bred by the free market in religion. But both groups were clear that the United States' religiopolitical arrangements, in shunning the traditional confessionalist state, were unique. The issues of Church disestablishment and the rights of dissenting minorities, which stood at the heart of the religious question in British politics, were largely absent from the American nineteenth-century experience.[2]

Various developments in both British and American historiography over the last quarter of a century have tended to reinforce assumptions about the divergent experiences of the two countries. Thanks to the controversial work of Lee Benson, Ronald Formisano, Paul Kleppner, and other members of the "ethnocultural school," which Robert Swierenga has described above, American historians can no longer ignore the power of religion in shaping the country's political life, and the skeptical have to address the argument that religious attachment was a major, and often the main, determinant of political loyalty amongst voters.[3] As

Daniel Howe argues elsewhere in this volume, it ill behooves any student of nineteenth-century America not to "take religion seriously."

But at the very time that American historiography has been pulled down this route, a number of trends in the writing of nineteenth-century British history have pushed in an opposite direction. Marxist and socialist historians of Britain have dramatically opened up the study of popular political culture, and not just by close focus on the laboring classes. But their writing tends to perceive religion as a peripheral element in a materialist universe, its manifestations merely epiphenomena. The persisting religious beliefs of their subjects both irritate and discomfort many of them; religion appears as an irrational, superstitious force that has impeded the advance of a rational secular socialist order. Edward Thompson's magisterial study of the formation of the English working class tells us much about this frame of mind: religious activism and revivalist enthusiasm is presented as "the chiliasm of despair," a diversion and an escape from hardheaded political activity.[4] A huge ideological chasm separates these historians from those of the "Peterhouse" or "Cowlingite" school, whose work has revolutionized and energized the study of high politics in the Victorian period. Where socialists have stressed values, ideals, and the advance of ideology, the scholarship of the high political historians over the last three decades has pushed beliefs and values to the margins of political activity and stresses instead the short-term, day-to-day considerations that determined the individual politicians' struggle for advance and survival; one of the consequences of the new "high political history" has been "to diminish our sense that ideological divisions underpinned political conflict at Westminster." Paradoxically, then, the common effect of these otherwise contending schools has been to marginalize religious belief and attachment as elements in nineteenth-century politics. And in this they have been assisted by a third group: liberal historians who, in direct lineage from an older, Whig tradition, have tended to overstress the place of rational social reformers and secular-minded radicals in the Victorian political scene; religion is marginalized in their scheme of things, too.[5]

Yet few would contend that religion was a marginal force in the culture of Victorian Britain. The revival of the historic Nonconformist churches—Old Dissent—under the stimulus of the "Arminianizing," evangelical energies of Methodism, in the last years of the eighteenth century and the early decades of the next, produced a remarkable expansion of institutional Protestantism by 1840. The religious census of 1851, taken soon after what seems to have been the proportionate highpoint of

British church membership over the past two centuries, suggested that the number attending church on census day was the equivalent of over 60 percent of the population. Since this figure was reached by counting evening attenders as additional to morning worshipers, it clearly overstated the true position. But it still suggests the powerful public place of Christianity.[6] When it is remembered that the proportion of churchgoers amongst what was a largely middle- and upper-class electorate was higher than in the population as a whole, a further point is added to the question: how, in such a Christian society, could men not carry their religious values into politics as voters, party organizers, lobbyists, MPs, and grandees?

In fact, there have been more than a few hints in the scholarship of the last quarter-century to suggest the salience of religion in Victorian politics, especially as historians have come to impose limits on the explanatory power of class and economic interest. Most recently, J. P. Parry has earnestly and persuasively argued that nineteenth-century politics in Britain "cannot be understood if it is treated merely as a secular activity."[7] Various essential elements of that Victorian conjunction of religion and politics bear comparison with integral features of American political life in the same era. In view of the current preoccupations of historians of the United States, three particular areas of the British experience seem to demand investigation: the churchgoer's sense of political duty and the degree to which churchmanship encouraged political engagement; the place of religion in shaping the discourse and practices of the political community in an era when the politics of influence were yielding to the politics of opinion; and the role of religious loyalties in creating and elaborating mutually hostile political cultures, as expressed in party conflict. In each case the evidence provides little comfort to the proponents of American exceptionalism. Rather, it indicates enough of a common transatlantic experience, particularly with regard to the electoral functions of religion, to demand a much wider contextual view of nineteenth-century American political history.

II

One of the most striking features of nineteenth-century church life in the United States, certainly up to the Civil War, was the energy with which churchmen, both laymen and their pastors, carried their religion into the public arena. The "Reformed" or "Calvinistic" perspective on political duty, driving the Christian "in a straight line from personal belief to social reform, from private experience to political activity," has always been strong in the United States. During the colonial era it was sustained in particular by the influential Congregationalist and Presbyterian traditions; it continued to exert its influence even as these Calvinist denominations were superseded by Methodism as the principal religious influence over the culture. The Civil War soured postmillennialist optimism, however, and dampened the Christian's ardor for politics and the work of reform. The withdrawal of many native "salvationist pietists" into private devotion was reinforced by the continuing immigration of Lutherans, upholders of a "two kingdoms" philosophy that kept church and politics quite separate. But even in these years of the "great reversal," the Reformed approach retained an influence and during the present century has continued to hold sway, albeit in more secular guise.[8]

Equally striking is the reflowering in nineteenth-century Britain of that same Reformed tradition in public life, by which religious Dissenters sought and achieved a position of political influence they had not known since the days of Cromwell. That they positively sought this outcome is as worthy of comment as what they achieved. For at the turn of the century many influential Nonconformists had encouraged a quietist, "no politics" approach to public affairs. These included individuals within the most vigorous Calvinist churches (the Baptist Samuel Fisher, for instance, who published *The Duty of Subjects to the Civil Magistrates* in 1794), but the most marked quietist strains were to be found amongst the Methodists and the Friends.[9]

Joseph Barker of the Methodist New Connexion later recalled how in his early days as a church member he had "thought it wrong for a Christian to meddle in political matters. . . . I thought it the duty of Christians to unite themselves together in churches, to shut themselves out from the world, to constitute themselves a little exclusive world, and to confine their labours to the government of their little kingdom." David Hempton, in a recent study, has explored the context in which such attitudes flourished. Jabez Bunting, influential high Wesleyan Tory, elaborated the idea that Christians should not challenge the existing order, because to do so would be to question God's providential goodness. When it was proposed that antislavery petition forms be sent to all Methodist circuits in 1833, Bunting objected that it would "injuriously distract the thoughts and conversation of our people, and might so divert them from the best things to subjects much mixed up, in this time of excitement, with the politics of this world, as to injure the work of God. Our duty, and our policy too, require us to be 'quiet in the land', as far and as long as we innocently can. . . . Whether we ought, *as a Missionary*

Society, to meddle with the *merely civil* or *political* part of the subject, I very much doubt." Tory-minded Wesleyans, in a manner remarkably similar to American conservative, Whiggish evangelicals of the same era, disliked political strife and party conflict. A Wesleyan electoral agent in Manchester noted: "Our ministers, as a body, meddle not with politics. The great majority belong to no party; are fearful of sweeping changes, yet friendly to sound and gradual reforms." The system of itinerancy, of course, worked against preachers exercising sustained control over electoral politics, even had they wanted to; here, too, the similarity with the experience of American Methodist itinerants is instructive.[10]

Early-nineteenth-century Quakers, too, as Elizabeth Isichei has shown, took to heart their ministers' denunciations of politics. Most appear to have remained true to the enjoinders of their Yearly Meetings not to engage in political discussions or even read newspaper reports of political events. Some, such as William Allen, Joseph Rowntree, and Joseph John Gurney, did take part in local politics, but there was strong disapproval of members who took part in electioneering. The minister Joseph Metford, a political radical, was gagged in 1834 because his "strong political bias" was inconsistent with "the peaceful quiescent spirit of a minister of the Gospel." Isichei notes, however, the paradox in the Friends' quietist rejection of politics on the one hand and their persistent and successful efforts as a centrally organized pressure group to exert influence over parliament, on the other. Petitions against slavery, church rates, or the educational clauses of the 1843 Factory Bill, for example; deputations to government ministers; using their social position to bend the ears of the great: by such means Quakers sought to shape public policy, and yet, significantly, did not regard such efforts as truly political.[11]

Gradually such attitudes shifted. Despite the "no politics" rule, Buntingite Methodists campaigned actively for Tories; Sheffield Wesleyan preachers appeared on the hustings with a Tory candidate and escaped censure; Liberal pressure groups, too, achieved more freedom within Methodism. The antislavery campaign of the early 1830s and the efforts for suffrage reform did much to change attitudes within Nonconformity towards political activity in general and voting in particular. The resort to petitioning and pressuring candidates encouraged evangelical Nonconformists, as they did Friends, "to enter the political arena with reasonably clear consciences." Like other working-class Methodists, Joseph Barker moved to a more politically oriented religious faith and practice: "I believe it my duty to . . . battle with evil wherever I see it, and to aim at the annihilation of all corrupt institutions and at the establishment of all good, and generous, and useful institutions in their places." Meanwhile

Friends, drawing ever closer to the wider Victorian society, entered local government after the repeal of the Test and Corporation Acts in 1828, stood for parliament (the first Quaker MP, Joseph Pease, was elected in 1833), and nourished an increasing respect for the activities of such radicals as Joseph Sturge (founder of the Complete Suffrage Union) and John Bright (particularly for his stand over the Crimean War).[12]

The creation of the Anti-State Church Association indicated the increasing prominence and cohesion of Nonconformists in mid-nineteenth-century politics. Sustaining this and the later political strategies of Dissenters was a "Reformed" philosophy of political duty that bore many resemblances to contemporary American Protestant ideas about active Christian citizenship. The views of George Dawson and Robert William Dale, for instance, resembled those of George Duffield, Henry Ward Beecher, and a chorus of mid-century American evangelicals, especially those of the New England tradition, in their encouragement of church-goers' participation in elections and in their denunciation of intimidation, corruption, drunkenness, and other forms of moral deficiency in politics. As D. A. Hamer has argued, "The Nonconformist was urged to regard his vote as a sacred trust conferred on him by God." Edward Miall told the Liberation Society in the 1860s: "We ought to consider that we have that power placed in our hands by the wisdom of God to bring advantage to his church." What gave particular edge to such appeals was the Nonconformists' collective memory of the discrimination and exclusion they had suffered for centuries: in the new order of things they had not only the opportunity but the duty to demonstrate their social integration and their considerable political power by using the vote constructively. Electoral abstention was frowned upon.[13]

Carrying religious energy and chapel morality into public affairs, implicit in the later term "Nonconformist conscience," did not mean that churches, as churches, were encouraged, even by their politically active members, to enter the political arena. Nor was it the case that all ministers enjoyed, or even wanted, the liberty to use the pulpit as a political soapbox. Like American ministers, they were the paid agents of their congregations and could not easily ignore reprimands along the lines of that issued to a London pastor: "We share your views, but politics are not what we come to hear from the pulpit." As David Bebbington reminds us, "The opinion formers were not so much the ministry in general, as an elite, both ministerial and lay . . . strategically concentrated in well-to-do congregations in the city centres or superior suburbs." But by the later decades of the nineteenth century these shapers of opinion within Nonconformity no longer recognized, as had their forebears a century earlier, any clear boundary between religion and politics; Silvester Horne, Congregational minister and Liberal MP, took as axiomatic that "politics may be as truly sacred a task as theology." That almost a quarter of Liberal MPs were Nonconformists by 1880 suggests both the prevalence of that outlook and the context in which such attitudes would continue to flourish.[14]

Nonconformists were equally convinced that only men of the very highest integrity should serve in public office. Cromwell and Gladstone, the latter convinced that he was a "chosen vessel of the Almighty" in his Eastern policy, provided the models. There was widespread disgust during the agitation over the Bulgarian atrocities over the remarks of the British ambassador at Constantinople, who had rebuked those "shallow politicians or persons who have allowed their feelings of revolted humanity to make them forget the capital interests involved in the question." Significantly, the term "Nonconformist conscience" was first used at the time of the moral outcry against the adulterous Irish Nationalist leader, C. S. Parnell.[15]

As well as dissolving the line between religion and politics, and scrutinizing the moral pedigree of public men, the guardians of the Nonconformist conscience also looked to a paternalistic state that would engage actively in promoting the moral well-being of its people. Bebbington sees this as the most drastic of all the changes in the chapels' outlook during the nineteenth century. Whereas in earlier years evangelical Protestants were convinced that laws could secure no more than superficial changes in personal and collective behavior, and would not secure the inner change of heart on which the creation of a truly Christian society ultimately depended, through the middle and later decades of the century attitudes changed. Increasingly the guiding power of law over public opinion, as well as behavior, came to be recognized. As in the United States, where at mid-century the argument raged between "moral suasionists" and those who looked for state action, it was particularly the urgent personal and social problems connected with the easy availability of alcohol that turned Protestant reformers more and more in the direction of legal enactment.[16]

III

The sharpened appetite of religious dissenters for politics, combined with the widening of their political opportunities through successive suffrage reform acts, inevitably affected the character of British political life in the

Victorian era. Religious sensibilities and moral imperatives were brought to bear on the discourse and practices of the political community. Whatever they might have wished, elected representatives could not avoid religious and moral issues. Politics were in no sense determined by an all-powerful "public opinion," but after 1832 the customary politics of aristocratic influence had to cohabit with pressure politics from "without" and "below." To a very considerable extent that pressure was exerted by religious groups and individuals who looked to politics as one of the routes to the inauguration of Christ's kingdom. It is worth surveying, albeit superficially, the contributions both of these energetic reformers on the outside and of the parliamentarians and other political insiders to the process by which nineteenth-century politics were "moralized." In passing we can note a number of parallels with contemporaneous American experience. The categories of insider and outsider were never mutually exclusive, and indeed with the passage of time many of the reformers were to establish what Hamer has called an integrated, or dependent, relationship with the Liberal party. But, on the whole, few men moved easily between the world of the "faddists" or "crotcheteers," with its lack of tolerance for compromise, and that of pragmatic politics.[17]

The campaigning enthusiasm of the dissenting Protestant churches against slavery in the 1830s introduced a new, evangelistic style of extraparliamentary politics, one which provided a model for further enthusiastic crusades throughout the century against a variety of secular evils that included the Corn Laws, Sabbath desecration, drunkenness, sexual license, and Romanism. In their biblicism and Manichaean worldview, as well as in the targets of their campaigns, these reforming Christians bore a close resemblance to their American counterparts (whose enthusiastic "ultraism" was equally an occasion of scorn by mainstream politicians).[18] The principal extraparliamentary reform agitations of the Victorian era—particularly the efforts of the Anti-Corn Law League for free trade, the Anti-State Church Association (later the Liberation Society) for the disestablishment of the Church of England, and the United Kingdom Alliance for temperance, for example, drew many into the orbit of politics for the first time.[19]

They brought with them an energy, determination, and suspicion of compromise and vacillation that did much to shape their electoral strategy. Between 1832 and 1867, in particular, constituencies were too large for landowners to wield their customary influence but small enough to allow a well-organized group of dedicated voters to affect the outcome of an election. In the new dispensation after the Reform Bill of 1832, reformers adopted methods that went well beyond the traditional ones of indirect pressure: petitioning, circulating tracts, holding mass meetings, and lobbying MPs. They registered like-minded voters in the face of formidable administrative complexities; elicited from them electoral pledges to vote only for dependable candidates (a favorite strategy of temperance reformers in particular); succeeded in selecting and placing sympathetic Liberal candidates; submitted lists of questions to those they did not have a hand in choosing; sometimes put up their own independent candidates; very occasionally used organized abstentions to exert what Miall's *Nonconformist* described as "restraining force"; organized a disciplined bloc vote (more easily achieved in the years of open voting before the Ballot Act of 1872, which removed an important instrument of discipline); and played the two main parties off against one another in those few circumstances where their political agents were engaged in a genuine competition for the reformers' votes.[20]

These were not uniquely British strategies: the evidence of the anti-slavery, nativist, anti-Catholic, and prohibitionist organizations, to mention only the most obvious examples, indicates that reforming American evangelicals equally sought through bloc voting, questioning candidates, electoral pledges, and independent parties to achieve a purified social order. They also debated, as did the British, the extent to which coercive electoral strategies were morally justified. The moral dilemma faced by Christian opponents of Texas annexation in 1844, for instance (when the abolitionist James Birney's candidacy offered one choice, but when a vote for the slaveowner, a duellist, and gambler Henry Clay seemed the only practicable way of preventing the election of the out-and-out annexationist James Polk), was frequently paralleled in the British context. For many Nonconformists it was axiomatic that they should not engage "in doing evil that good may (possibly) come." It was also clear to many that it was neither moral nor productive to engage in the electoral intimidation of MPs.[21]

The middle decades of the nineteenth century can be seen as the heyday of Nonconformists' political pressure. Before the 1840s their electoral power was never coordinated. But then the situation changed. Miall established his radical *Nonconformist* in 1841, with its varied diet of the religious and the secular and its shrewd, bracing commentaries. James Graham's Factory Bill, which sought to set up a network of factory schools under Anglican supervision, propelled the formation of the Anti-State Church Association in 1844. Robert Peel's decision to increase the grant to the Roman Catholic Seminary at Maynooth seemed to trumpet the need for better Nonconformist representation in parliament. The 1847 general election was the first in which Dissenters fashioned a coordinated strategy, through a Parliamentary Committee under Samuel Morley that appealed to the Christian duty of prominent Nonconformists to stand for election, and called on voters to repudiate Whig proposals to increase aid to Anglican schools. Voluntarists claimed a triumph when sixty members pledged against any endowment of religion by the state were returned.[22]

The 1850s saw Miall's election to parliament and the creation of more refined lobbying and electoral machinery, but it was in the following decade that Nonconformists, more aggressive, achieved their greatest political impact yet. Disenchanted by the failure of Whigs and Liberals to carry out their pledges to abolish church rates, Nonconformists accepted (though not without opposition) a new strategy proposed by Miall, which firmly gave the Liberation Society's interests priority over those of the Liberal party. Miall argued that Nonconformists "should act with the Liberal party in future Elections on the . . . condition, that *up to the measure of our strength on the local register the objects about which we are interested shall be advanced by the Election . . .* and, if this measure of justice be denied us, that we *resolutely withhold our co-operation*—our 'vote and influence'— *whatever may be the consequences of our abstention to the Liberal party.*" Such a strategy would create "a healthy and vigorous electoral life in the very heart of incipient electoral death." Miall's predictions seemed gloriously realized when Nonconformist abstainers claimed the credit for defeating in the Exeter by-election of 1864 a Liberal candidate opposed to the total abolition of church rates; and in the campaign of 1865 the Liberation Society's efforts again achieved a number of positive results. In the general election of 1868 Nonconformist pressure politics reached their apogee: the Liberation Society reaped the benefit of a spectacularly successful registration drive in Wales and, after the Reform Act of 1867, in the new urban constituencies where many Dissenting shopkeepers and workingmen had secured the vote; in the campaign itself it devoted all its efforts to supporting Gladstone's stand in favor of disestablishing the Irish Church. Hamer stresses "the discipline and shrewd realism" of the Liberationists in the 1860s as contrasted with the "revolt of the Nonconformists" in the 1870s, and sees a shift in the pattern of Dissenting electoral politics in the later decades of the century, as they moved away from "large-scale and heroic" strategies and became increasingly integrated within a "democratized" Liberal party. But this did not mean that Nonconformists lost their appetite for political and electoral involvement and for seeking access to party leaders and influencing public policy.[23]

If pressure on politicians from "outside" religious crusaders provided one of the shaping influences on Victorian political life, then the readiness of many politicians themselves to sustain the Protestant enthusiasm of the "faddists," and to bring religious influences to bear on the shaping of public policy, contributed another.[24] This does not mean that all those who experienced such pressure, or who benefited from Nonconformists' support, necessarily pandered to them: Gladstone was not afraid to criticize them when he thought they put their sectional interests above those of the community as a whole, and on occasions he was suspected of having engineered great national issues in order, as Guinness Rogers put it, to "shunt" the disestablishment question out of the political mainstream.[25] But at the same time he considered the voting masses likely to be as much influenced by moral as by material considerations; his admiration for Lancashire workingmen during the cotton famine of the 1860s drew him to conclude "that the masses, once relieved of the burdens which debased them, had a simple capacity for unselfish righteous judgment on great controverted questions which the 'classes' evidently had not." His Midlothian campaigns of 1879–80, landmarks in British political history, can be seen as an urgent moral crusade to bring Christian principles to bear on Ireland, Africa, and Afghanistan, and to destroy the moral incubus of government corruption, or "Beaconsfieldism." For the first time a leading statesman, consciously following American example, took his message to the people in an orchestrated series of mass rallies over several months.[26] His invitation to a Christian electorate to pass moral judgments on a range of public questions echoed the appeals of American campaigners over a long sequence of nineteenth-century elections right through to the Mugwump era of Grover Cleveland, the liberal Democrats and the Independent Republicans.[27]

Gladstone provides perhaps the most outstanding example, but he was by no means the only Victorian politician to recognize the power of religious and moral issues. Significantly, his victory in 1868 was followed in 1874 by the Conservatives' first real success for thirty-three years; in both elections arguments were employed which "capitalised on the widespread concern for the religious future." After 1832, with the enfranchisement of many well-to-do Dissenters and the advent of a new politics of persuasion, politicians faced a challenge and an opportunity. Whigs hoped to benefit, though they did not act consistently to satisfy Nonconformity (they temporized over abolishing the payment of rates for the upkeep of the state church and supported the Maynooth grant); but as Dissenters developed a greater political coherence, especially after the further extension of the suffrage in 1867, politicians were forced to harness religious energies and sensibilities and draw on the strength, political determination, language, and even organization of religious groups. Inevitably, in the early years of "mass politics" politicians had to engage the new voters' attention by addressing the issues that mattered most to them: as in the United States, where the religious enthusiasms of the Second Great Awakening were brought directly into the campaigning and public political discussions of the Jacksonian period, this meant respecting and building upon religious loyalties and preoccupations. As Parry has recently argued, this need not have meant that Victorian politicians were moved primarily by a concern for the secular consequences of extending the grip of religion (though its function as a prophylactic against social disorder and class hostility was well understood); rather, they saw religion providing men with "an inspiring and awful conception of their place in the order of things." They regarded their role as educative, teaching new voters how to promote a moral society protected by religion from the excesses of, say, French and American republicanism.[28]

Disestablishment, temperance, and education provide obvious examples of the religious and moral issues that politicians capitalized upon, but even matters whose significance might seem to have been primarily economic could be exploited as moral questions; Kitson Clark has reminded us that the anti–Corn Law campaign was "in its way a religious movement," as indeed was the cause of free trade in its wider mainfestations.[29] But, as in the United States, few issues had the explosive, fissiparous electoral force of anti-Catholicism. C. E. Brent's case study of Lewes demonstrates how both parties in the 1860s used the fear of "Popery," Tories by arguing that the end of church rates would destroy the Anglican bastion against Rome, Liberals by claiming that abolition would allow Dissenters and Anglicans at last to ally in the battle against the whore of Babylon. The Irish disestablishment issue in 1868 brought "Protestant" feeling amongst the theologically more conservative denominations to a boiling point, and Tory politicians took every opportunity to exploit a sense of the constitution in danger. Bebbington describes the frequent and enthusiastic waving of the anti-Catholic flag in the political battles of the later nineteenth century: Liberal Unionists financed the regular appearance of Irish Protestant ministers in British election campaigns from the 1880s to the 1910s, especially in areas like Lincolnshire, where Wesleyan votes might hold the balance.[30]

In certain circumstances the combined moral indignation of external pressure groups and parliamentarians could create a political explosion of extraordinary power. Such was the case in 1876 following the Turkish suppression of an attempted insurrection by Bulgarian nationalists. The news that 15,000 men, women, and children had been massacred by the Turks produced repugnance and fury against both the Islamic power and Disraeli's Eastern policy. In less than six weeks some 500 public demonstrations had provided a forum for all who felt moral revulsion at the

Turks or guilt at British policy. The agitation drew on the moral energy of those touched by the mid-century religious revivals and the Oxford Movement, including those who otherwise lacked political power, and who had learned lessons from earlier quasi-religious campaigns for anti-slavery, suffrage reform, and the repeal of the Corn Laws. Nonconformists and Anglo-Catholics, especially ministers and clergy, were prominent at every level. They included that loyal son of the Congregational manse, the crusading young Darlington editor W. T. Stead; Bishop Fraser of Manchester; Canon Liddon of St. Paul's; and Samuel Smith, Liverpool Presbyterian cotton merchant, one of those who had invited Moody and Sankey to Liverpool in the previous year, and now politically active for the first time in his career. By early September more than half the towns in England had held protest meetings. It was then that Gladstone, excited by this mass display of moral passion, lent his weight to the agitation, publishing his *Bulgarian Horrors* and addressing the great "atrocities" meeting at Blackheath on September 9. Richard Shannon characterizes that gathering as "a great revivalist rally"; certainly Stead continued to regard it as one of the most memorable scenes of his life. But there is little sign of the manipulation of public sentiment by politicians; rather, their role was reactive, one of response more than initiation. In the view of George Kitson Clark, the agitation was "by far the greatest . . . revelation of the moral susceptibility of the High Victorian public conscience."[31]

IV

Together, then, external pressure groups and politicians helped place and keep religion at the center of Victorian politics. Peter Clarke regards as emblematic the comment of a Peelite election manager that "'Maynooth' has certainly destroyed several of our friends [,] . . . 'Free Trade' hardly any," and concludes that "few would dissent from the proposition that religion entered into [electoral] politics in a fundamental way." Much of John Vincent's path-breaking work on early Liberalism sees in religious divisions "the essence" of politics, and though work on Victorian poll books and on regional complexities is much less advanced than is the analysis of American electoral behavior in that period, a variety of local studies has begun to illuminate the delicate and complex marquetry of nineteenth-century voting patterns. Those patterns were not regular. For instance, the politics of deference or landlord influence continued vigorous in the English countryside until the Reform Act of 1884, whereas in

Wales the politics of conscience were evident much earlier, and religious issues entered significantly into elections there from 1859, as Nonconformist tenants flexed their electoral muscle against Anglican landlords. Even where religious influences were clearly at work, it is not always clear how much relative importance should be attached to them, as opposed to considerations of occupation, economic location, or social subservience. David Hempton fairly summarizes the difficulty in a simple question: "did a Nonconformist employee vote with his Nonconformist employer out of economic self-interest, deference or a common religious allegiance?" There is no simple answer, but it is difficult not to approve the emphasis of Clyde Binfield, who in an evocative study of the nineteenth-century Nonconformist elite calls on William Haslam Mills, paragon of *Manchester Guardian* journalists, for his broad conclusion from the election of 1868, when the country divided "on an unmaterial issue" and when "[t]he newly enfranchised trooped to the polls in their thousands in the character of Erastians or anti-Erastians": "All the politics of the time turned indeed on creed, and when they did not turn on creed they turned on conduct."[32]

If religion was indeed fundamental to nineteenth-century politics, it remains to inquire how, broadly speaking, creed and church loyalties contributed to the competing political cultures of Victorian Britain. Thanks to the pioneering psephology of Benson and Formisano, and to Howe's brilliant study of Whig attitudes, we have a much better understanding of how religion helped shape the contrasting cultures of political parties in Jacksonian and antebellum America; Kleppner has made a similar contribution to our perspective on the Republican and Democratic parties from the 1850s to the 1890s.[33] This is not the place to review the corpus of "ethnocultural" studies, but it is worth recalling some of its fundamental perceptions: that religious creed and church affiliation (in conjunction, though not always consistently, with ethnicity) acted as positive and negative referents in social, and hence political, relationships; that reform-minded, culturally imperialist, theologically progressive, Protestant evangelicals tended to lend their support to those political agencies most likely to support social engineering, first the Whigs and later (at least until the reorientation of the 1890s) the Republican party; that, conversely, Catholics, "ritualist" Protestants, and "salvationist pietists" (their religiosity emphasizing right belief rather than social or political action) turned to the Democrats, confident of the party's opposition to state coercion in matters of private behavior. Does Victorian Britain hold any parallels?

The broad orientation of Nonconformity towards Liberalism from mid-century will already be clear. Old Dissent, in particular, looked first to the Whigs and then to the inheritors of their principles of religious liberty, the Liberals, to bring about an end to restrictive arrangements regarding the registration of births, marriage ceremonies, university education, burial services, and the payment of church rates. Politically active Dissenters were ready to challenge Whigs as much as Tories, but in the 1850s and 1860s the strategy of the Liberation Society drew them increasingly into the orbit of Liberalism. In this Nonconformists were encouraged not simply by a negative reaction against Tory Anglicans and brewers, but by a more positive sympathy for radical Liberalism, in its commitment to free trade, international brotherhood, and a class harmony developing from the prosperity and well-being of a justly ordered society. This orientation was cemented by the extraordinary relationship between them and Gladstone, for whom they came to feel a "fascination, amounting to a fetishism," despite the disquiet many felt over his Anglican high churchmanship. Bebbington argues persuasively that during the second half of the century the vast majority of the rising entrepreneurs, tradesmen, shopkeepers, and skilled workmen who made up voting Nonconformity (Methodists as well as Old Dissent) were solidly Liberal.[34] Brent's study of Lewes in the 1860s indicates that in that southern borough Dissenting ministers, and the influential townsmen and smaller self-employed electors in their congregations, were, with the exception of one chapel, overwhelmingly Liberal. Isichei confirms the clear Liberal allegiance of Quakers, at least until the Home Rule crisis. Many churches were used for party meetings, and by 1885 an Anglican bishop could complain that Congregationalism constituted a huge political organization.[35]

Nonconformity could be broadly labeled Liberal, then, and most chapelgoers could bask in Gladstone's characterization of them as "the backbone of British Liberalism." (His private reference to their "Brobdignagian estimates of their Lilliputian proceedings" would have occasioned less pleasure, but properly reminds us that by no means all Liberals were Nonconformists or "faddists," and that Liberal gentry, intellectuals, professionals, high churchmen, and secular-minded workingmen brought their own contributions to the party.)[36] Robert Kelley has argued that the Nonconformist dimension of Liberalism was one of several significant elements that made the party philosophically and politically kin to the American Democrats. The parties of Gladstone and Jackson, he argues, appealed to the "outgroups" in each society: in Britain that meant in religious terms the Dissenting Protestant opponents of the established church, the Catholics, the Celtic fringe; in America, where there was no formal church establishment or confessionalist state, the tension was between the New School Presbyterian, Congregationalist, Whiggish, re-forming, paternalist culture of New England and the "dissenting" voices of non-British immigrants, Catholics, and—particularly in the "fringes" of West and South—Baptists and Methodists, all of whom were over-whelmingly Democratic. Further, notes Kelley, Liberals and Democrats were zealously attached to the causes of honest money and free trade; they distrusted aristocracy; they accepted the need for a strong executive figure who would create the laissez-faire conditions in which minority social groups would secure equality of treatment.[37]

Nonconformists' antagonism towards the established church and aris-tocracy and their ambition to see government used to create conditions of religious and political liberty certainly shaped the political culture of Liberalism (as one Baptist minister explained, "the scruples that made him a dissenter, also made him a liberal"). Moreover, their commitment to laissez-faire led many Dissenting manufacturer-philanthropists to stand firm against factory acts and other social reform legislation.[38] But Kelley drives a useful parallel too far, and so distorts our understanding of Nonconformist-Liberal culture. Not only does he bind American evangeli-calism within a Democratic straitjacket, but he understates characteristics of British Protestant Dissenters which brought them closer to the Whig-Republican tradition than to the Democracy: their readiness in certain circumstances to countenance an interventionist state to advance a Chris-tian society, through temperance and Sabbatarian legislation, for example; and their assured, optimistic faith in new technology, economic progress, and social development, which calls to mind the postmillennialism and commercial orientation of American Whigs and, later, Republicans.[39]

At the other pole, Conservative political culture, too, was considerably shaped through the Victorian years by ecclesiastical issues, especially by its supporters' self-defense in the face of disestablishmentarians and Papists. For as long as the established church was threatened (particu-larly in the elections of 1835 and 1868),[40] raising the spectre of spoliation, a broader attack on property, and the undermining of the constitution, Anglicans of all stripes would rarely leave the Tory camp. "A Tory Dissenter," a Bristol Anglican minister asserted, "is one of the most anomolous creatures in existence, and is as rare as he is strange and unnatural."[41] The issue of disestablishment kept many Wesleyans Tory, too, in the early Victorian period. Anti-Catholicism also glued some of the most enthusiastically "Protestant"—chapelgoers as well as church-men—to the party. This was especially true when the two issues con-verged, as at the time of the disestablishment of the Irish church, which many regarded as a devilish plot hatched by Gladstone and Roman cardinals. In Salford in 1868 the Conservatives "were swept into power by a gale of hysterical Protestantism." Brent's conclusion about Tory political culture in Lewes (where the Anglicans and only the most grimly Calvinist of the Nonconformist chapels sustained Tory "Protestantism") may have a wider application: "Conservatism demanded a tightening of political and legal structures to withstand assaults from 'popery,' from 'democracy,' and from the alien in arms. Men who had . . . built up new commercial enterprises were often the most assured Liberals, while men whose upbringing, enterprises and cultural ties were interwoven with agrarian society tended to a pessimistic Toryism."[42]

The natural Toryism of the Church of England was especially evident during the Bulgarian atrocities campaign. Despite an important High Church presence amongst the leaders of the agitation, the vast majority of clergy and bishops remained hostile. Some were Liberal sympathizers like Archbishop Tait, who nonetheless believed the national Church had a duty to sustain the secular authorities, was fearful of the revived truculence of Nonconformity, and saw no proper alternative to supporting Disraeli's government. However, as Liddon told Stead, "Politically speaking, most clergymen are Conservatives. They are hard at work in their parishes, and do not know enough about European politics to entertain strong opinions: they put themselves into the hand of the Government." Only 1,000 clergy out of a total of 22,000 signed the "Clerical Declaration" against Britain's going to war on behalf of Turkey, leaving Liddon to complain: "Either men do not see the moral and religious interests at stake: or they sacrifice their Christianity to politics." Although Low Churchmen were not as homogeneously Tory as Nonconformists were Liberal, their suspicion of Anglo-Catholics meant that Shaftesbury was the only prominent Evangelical to support the agitation.[43]

Victorian politics, then, must be interpreted in "cultural" terms.[44] The judgment of Benson and his fellow ethnoculturalists, that religion was relatively the most significant determinant of voting behavior, applies as much to Victorian Britain as it does to nineteenth-century America. The abrasions between normative and comparative religious reference groups—that is, the clash of cultures and lifestyles, in an era when religion did so much to shape them—more frequently provide the key to electoral behavior than do class divisions. T. J. Nossiter's quantitative work indicates that only where Anglicanism and Dissent were strong did religion supersede other influences over voting. But, as Clarke points out, that may have meant most of the country. It certainly included Wales and most urban and industrial areas. Clarke's own study of Lancashire suggests that Tory advance in industrial areas was not based on the gathering focus of working-class consciousness, but rather on the presence of the Catholic Irish and "the essentially non-class appeal" of Tory Protestantism, in a part of the country where Anglicanism was fiercely evangelical.[45]

Issues of class, economic interest, and social welfare did, however, became more significant and explicit elements in electoral politics in the later years of the century, with the movement of the better off towards Toryism and the growing self-confidence of labor. The movement was fastest where organized religion was weak, as in London. In Lancashire by 1910, according to Clarke, political divisions were no longer based on traditional religious rivalries, and "Liberalism and Labour were working together within an essentially national framework to propagate a progressive programme with a class-based appeal." (In Wales, however, especially given the religious revival of 1904–05, there is more uncertainty over how far the essence of Liberalism had changed.) Bebbington's analysis of late-nineteenth-century Nonconformity, in part confirming Clarke's argument, suggests that there was indeed some shift of middle-class allegiance from Liberal to Tory, attributable to the growing prosperity of Nonconformists, to their unease about Liberals' toying with the concept of the redistribution of wealth, and to the relative loosening of chapel ties. But also at work was the continuing force of religion, in the form of virulent anti-Catholicism. Gladstone's support for Irish Home Rule, and its implications for the Protestant struggle against Rome, drove many Nonconformists (especially Wesleyans and the more theologically conservative denominations) into Liberal Unionism and, ultimately, the Tory party.[46] This was not the first time in the century that a party especially dependent on evangelical Protestant support had suffered eclipse for its temerity in showing sympathy to the Catholic Irish: erstwhile American Whigs, reflecting on the mid-century death of their organization, could have told Gladstone a thing or two about the destructive political force of anti-Catholicism.

This late-nineteenth-century shift in British politics from culture-based to class-oriented voting had a contemporary echo in the United States during the 1890s. There, according to Kleppner's analysis of Midwestern politics, both Democrats and Republicans consciously changed their postures. Traditionally Republicans had been seen as the party of "pietist" reformers, evangelical Protestants who looked to the state to regulate personal and social behavior. Now William Jennings Bryan appropriated these clothes for the Democrats with an appeal that combined both religious and economic elements in its talk of "moral reconstruction" and "economic equality." Republicans, just as significantly, turned to a message that was economically, not culturally, oriented, exploiting the Democrats' association with the worst economic depression of the century and addressing the general concern for recovery. By self-definition the Republicans, through William McKinley's campaign, were no longer the party of evangelical Protestants, but the party of prosperity.[47]

This, however, did not mark the beginning of the end of cultural politics in America, whereas they have been increasingly marginalized in twentieth-century Britain. The further extension of the suffrage after World War I to the least churched part of the British population ensured a reducing influence for religion and an increasing role for class and economic interest in elections. The continuing "secularization" of British society over the last hundred years has given specifically religious issues far less salience in parliamentary politics than they enjoyed in the Age of Equipoise, when at times (as in the parliamentary session before Easter 1854) half of divisons on public matters were on ecclesiastical matters.[48] For the present-day British observer of Atlantic affairs the sense of the separateness of the two countries' political cultures is underlined by the signal presence of fundamentalist evangelicals in American politics.[49] Pat Robertson and Jerry Falwell have no British counterparts—perhaps more a matter of sadness to them than to the British.

It is, however, prudent to end with two notes of warning against the view of a simple bifurcation of British and American experience since Victorian times. First, we should remember that for much of the twentieth century American politics, too, have revolved around questions of economic interest and even class, and that, broadly speaking, religion has not sustained its earlier significance. Moreover, during the middle years of the century the country enjoyed considerable political consensus; only with the return of serious ideological conflict, since the 1960s, have religious sensibilities been publicly exploited in shaping, sustaining, and validating the conservative-liberal divide. Second, we seriously misunderstand contemporary British political culture if we regard it as wholly secularized. The politics of Ulster, though not to be reduced to religious categories alone, are comprehensible only in the context of tribal divisions fed by continuing religious antagonisms; perhaps there *is* a British Pat Robertson, in the person of the Reverend Ian Paisley, MP for North Antrim. Residual tensions between Church and chapel still continue to shape some political loyalties in the 1960 and 1970s, principally in parts of the Celtic fringe.[50] In the contest for the leadership of the newly formed Social and Liberal Democratic party, guardian of historic Liberalism, it is significant that the "traditionalist" candidate, Alan Beith, an enthusiastic historian of chapel culture, made a virtue of being an elder of the United Reformed Church and a Methodist lay preacher, and reminded the party that it was part of a political tradition which "drew constant inspiration from religious belief": there is a Nonconformist conscience still.[51]

Moral questions such as the regulation of abortion and the restoration of capital punishment continue to touch consciences and religious sensibilities in politically unpredictable ways and are too dangerous to be treated as party matters. The strength of residual Sabbatarianism recently forced the government to abandon its proposals for the extension of Sunday trading. The "Thatcher revolution" in economic and fiscal affairs has generated in the churches political passions that indicate the working of more than class anger or defensive vested interests. Anglican critics of the Conservative government have made the political role of the established church a matter of public debate.[52] As part of a strategy to recapture lost electoral ground the prime minister addressed the Assembly of the Church of Scotland on May 20, 1988, offering a scriptural defense of her government's economic and social policies. The ensuing public debate drew reflections from the president of the Methodist Conference and involved politicians' self-consciously and ingloriously swapping biblical texts inside and outside parliament. During those exchanges a former Tory Cabinet minister spoke disparagingly of a "foghorn of conscience," adding: "We take a lot of our fashions from North America. . . . I do not believe that the politics of this country would be enhanced if we were to try to copy the link that has been established between some of the elements of the Republican Party and some of the elements of the revivalist movement in North America."[53] He appears not to have seen the irony that within his awful vision of the future lay elements of an honorable political past.

Notes

I am especially grateful to Drs. David Bebbington, Michael Bentley, Clyde Binfield, and John Stevenson for their suggestions and for their critical comments on this essay.

1. M. J. Heale, *The Making of American Politics* (London: Longman, 1977), takes as its theme the bifurcation of the American and British political traditions in the early decades of the new republic.

2. By way of example, see Milton B. Powell, ed., *The Voluntary Church: American Religious Life, 1740–1860, Seen Through the Eyes of European Visitors* (New York: Macmillan, 1967); Frances Trollope, *Domestic Manners of the Americans*, ed. Donald Smalley (New York: Vintage, 1960), 107–115; E. R.

Norman, *The Conscience of the State in North America* (Cambridge: Cambridge University Press, 1968).

3. Lee Benson, *The Concept of Jacksonian Democracy: New York as a Test Case* (Princeton: Princeton University Press, 1961); Ronald P. Formisano, *The Birth of Mass Political Parties: Michigan 1827–1861* (Princeton: Princeton University Press, 1971); Paul Kleppner, *The Cross of Culture: A Social Analysis of Midwestern Politics 1850–1900* (New York: Free Press, 1970); Paul Kleppner, *The Third Electoral System, 1853–1892: Parties, Voters, and Political Cultures* (Chapel Hill: University of North Carolina Press, 1979).

4. E. P. Thompson, *The Making of the English Working Class*, rev. ed. (Harmondsworth: Penguin, 1968), 385–440; Jim Obelkevitch, Lyndal Roper, Raphael Samuel, eds., *Disciplines of Faith: Studies in Religion, Politics and Patriarchy* (London: Routledge and Kegan Paul, 1987), especially 1–9.

5. J. P. Parry, *Democracy and Religion: Gladstone and the Liberal Party, 1867–1875* (Cambridge: Cambridge University Press, 1986), 1; Maurice Cowling, *1867: Disraeli, Gladstone and Revolution: the Passing of the Second Reform Bill* (Cambridge: Cambrige University Press, 1967); A. B. Cooke and J. R. Vincent, *The Governing Passion: Cabinet Government and Party Politics in Britain, 1885–86* (Brighton: Harvester 1974). It should be said that Cowling himself, unlike many "Cowlingites," supposes a serious political role for doctrine and ideas. Maurice Cowling, *Religion and Public Doctrine in Modern England*, 2 vols. (Cambridge: Cambridge University Press, 1980 and 1985).

6. A. D. Gilbert, *Religion and Society in Industrial England: Church, Chapel and Social Change 1740–1914* (London: Longman, 1976), especially 51–68; K. S. Inglis, "Patterns of Worship in 1851," *Journal of Ecclesiastical History* 11 (1960): 74–86; Richard Carwardine, *Transatlantic Revivalism: Popular Evangelicalism in Britain and America, 1790–1865* (Westport, CT: Greenwood, 1978), 59–84.

7. Parry, *Democracy and Religion*, 5.

8. Mark A. Noll, *One Nation Under God? Christian Faith and Political Action in America* (San Francisco: Harper & Row, 1988), 25 (quotation). See also George M. Marsden, *Fundamentalism and American Culture: The Shaping of Twentieth-Century Evangelicalism, 1870–1925* (New York: Oxford University Press, 1980), 85–93; David O. Moberg, *The Great Reversal: Evangelism Versus Social Concern* (Philadelphia: Lippincott, 1972).

9. Ian Sellers, *Nineteenth-Century Nonconformity* (London: Edward Arnold, 1977), 65–76; Kenneth O. Morgan, *Wales in British Politics 1868–1922* (Cardiff: University of Wales Press, 1963), 14–15. Conversely, for Dissenting political engagement at the turn of the nineteenth century, see Richard W. Davis, *Dissent in Politics 1780–1830: The Political Life of William Smith, MP* (London: Epworth, 1971).

10. David Hempton, *Methodism and Politics in British Society 1750–1850* (London: Century Hutchinson, paperback ed. 1987) 204–205, 209–210, 212–213. For Whig/evangelical antipartyism, see Formisano, *Mass Political Parties*, 56–80; M. J. Heale, *The Presidential Quest: Candidates and Images in American Politi-*

cal Culture, 1787–1852 (London: Longman, 1982), 130–132, 139–141. American Methodists' political perspectives are considered in Richard Carwardine, "Methodist Ministers and the Second Party System," in Russell E. Richey and Kenneth E. Rowe, eds., *Rethinking Methodist History* (Nashville: Kingswood Books, 1985), 134–147.

11. Elizabeth Isichei, *Victorian Quakers* (London: Oxford University Press, 1970), 16–25, 188–208.

12. Ibid., 194–197; Hempton, *Methodism and Society*, 210–213.

13. D. A. Hamer, *The Politics of Electoral Pressure: A Study in the History of Victorian Reform Agitations* (Hassocks, Sussex: Harvester, 1977), 14–15.

14. Sellers, *Nineteenth-Century Nonconformity*, 90–91; D. W. Bebbington, *The Nonconformist Conscience: Chapel and Politics, 1870–1914* (London: George Allen and Unwin, 1982), 6–7, 12; Clyde Binfield, *So Down to Prayers: Studies in English Nonconformity 1780–1920* (London: J. M. Dent 1977), 199–213. For internal criticism of Nonconformists' party political involvement, especially after the party schism of 1886, see David M. Thompson, ed., *Nonconformity in the Nineteenth Century* (London: Routledge and Kegan Paul, 1972), 209–210, 236–237, 269–272.

15. R. T. Shannon, *Gladstone and the Bulgarian Agitation 1876* (London: Thomas Nelson, 1963), 23–27; Bebbington, *The Nonconformist Conscience*, ix, 12–13.

16. Bebbington, *The Nonconformist Conscience*, 13; Ian Tyrrell, *Sobering Up: From Temperance to Prohibition in Antebellum America, 1800–1860* (Westport, CT: Greenwood 1979), 54–55, 74–75, 200–210, passim.

17. Hamer, *Politics of Electoral Pressure*, ix, 6–8. For a discussion of the survival of aristocratic control of elections after 1832, and the poverty of a "coercive" explanation of political behavior, see P. F. Clarke, "Electoral Sociology of Modern Britain," *History* 57 (February 1972): 36–40.

18. Perhaps the most celebrated study of the American "ultraist" mentality is Whitney R. Cross, *The Burned-Over District: The Social and Intellectual History of Enthusiastic Religion in Western New York, 1800–1850* (Ithaca: Cornell University Press, 1950).

19. Hamer, *Politics of Electoral Pressure*; Brian Harrison, *Drink and the Victorians: The Temperance Question in England, 1815–1872* (London: Faber and Faber, 1971); David M. Thompson, "The Liberation Society, 1844–1868," in Patricia Hollis, ed., *Pressure from Without in Early Victorian England* (London: Edward Arnold, 1974), 210–238. G. I. T. Machin's two volumes, *Politics and the Churches in Great Britain 1832 to 1868* (Oxford: Clarendon 1977) and *Politics and the Churches in Great Britain 1869 to 1921* (Oxford: Clarendon 1987), provide an essential reference point for any study of the relationship between churches and the state in the nineteenth century, and of the activities of pressure groups and parliamentarians. For Sabbatarian pressure in parliament and in the constituencies, see John Wigley, *The Rise and Fall of the Victorian Sunday* (Manchester: Manchester University Press, 1980), 90–98.

20. Hamer, *Politics of Electoral Pressure*, 9–30.

21. Ibid., 34–36.

22. Binfield, *So Down to Prayers*, 109–111; Hamer, *Politics of Electoral Pressure*, 92–94.

23. Hamer, *Politics of Electoral Pressure*, 94–121, 139–164.

24. For a highly sophisticated treatment of the way in which politicians' religious values, refracted through government and party political processes, shaped public policy, see Parry, *Democracy and Religion*, passim. This is one area in which British historians, who in the field of ethnocultural history are indebted to American scholarship, have much to teach their counterparts in the United States.

25. Hamer, *Politics of Electoral Pressure*, 6–7, 22.

26. Shannon, *Gladstone and the Bulgarian Agitation*, 11, 273; Robert Kelley, *The Transatlantic Persuasion: The Liberal Democratic Mind in the Age of Gladstone* (New York: Knopf, 1969), 209, 219–227.

27. Kelley, *The Transatlantic Persuasion*, 293–349; Heale, *Presidential Quest*, passim; Richard Carwardine, "Evangelicals, Whigs and the Election of William Henry Harrison", *Journal of American Studies* 17 (1983): 47–75.

28. William R. Brock, *Parties and Political Conscience: American Dilemmas, 1840–1850* (Millwood, NY: KTO, 1979); Richard P. McCormick, *The Presidential Game: The Origins of American Presidential Politics*, (New York: Oxford University Press, 1982); Shannon, *Gladstone and the Bulgarian Agitation*, xvi; Parry, *Democracy and Religion*, 5–6, 127–128.

29. G. S. R. Kitson Clark, "Introduction" to Shannon, *Gladstone and the Bulgarian Agitation*, xv. For the moral and cultural underpinnings of currency and banking questions in nineteenth-century America, see William G. Shade, *Banks or No Banks: The Money Issue in Western Politics 1832–1865* (Detroit: Wayne State University Press, 1972); Kelley, *The Transatlantic Persuasion*, especially 256–263, 284–286, 334–339, 415–416.

30. C. E. Brent, "The Immediate Impact of the Second Reform Act on a Southern County Town: Voting Patterns at Lewes Borough in 1865 and 1868," *Southern History* 2 (1980): 134–135; D. W. Bebbington, "Nonconformity and Electoral Sociology, 1867–1918," *Historical Journal* 27 (1984): 649. For the central place of Ireland and Romanism in the East Leeds election of 1892, see Martin Wainwright, *Ireland Not Socialism: A Leeds Election* (privately published, November 1971).

31. Shannon, *Gladstone and the Bulgarian Agitation*, v, xi, 25–30, 49–51, 84–116, and passim; Shannon argues (p. 92) that "The central function of the atrocities agitation, for Gladstone, was that it restored the moral rapport between himself and the masses which the defeat of 1874 had snapped."

32. Clarke, "Electoral Sociology of Modern Britain," 38–39, 45; J. R. Vincent, *The Formation of the British Liberal Party 1857–1868*, 2nd ed. (Hassocks, Sussex: Harvester, 1976), 106 ("There is every reason to suppose the fundamental division [in Rochdale's electorate] was denominational"); J. R. Vincent,

Pollbooks: How Victorians Voted (Cambridge: Cambridge University Press, 1967); D. G. Wright, "A Radical Borough: Parliamentary Politics in Bradford 1832–1841," *Northern History* 4 (1969): 132–166; T. A. McDonald, "Religion and Voting in an English Borough: Poole in 1859," *Southern History* 5 (1983): 221–237; R. L. Greenall, "Popular Conservatism in Salford 1868–1886," *Northern History* 9 (1974): 123–138; Brent, "Impact of the Second Reform Act"; Hempton, *Methodism and Society*, 203; Binfield, *So Down to Prayers*, 106.

33. See n. 3, above; Daniel Walker Howe, *The Political Culture of the American Whigs* (Chicago: The University of Chicago Press, 1979). See also Jean H. Baker, *Affairs of Party: The Political Culture of Northern Democrats in the Mid-Nineteenth Century* (Ithaca: Cornell University Press, 1983).

34. Machin, *Politics and the Churches, 1832–1868*, 40–41; H. J. Hanham, *Elections and Party Management: Politics in the Time of Disraeli and Gladstone* (Hassocks, Sussex: Harvester, 1978), 170–179 (for the near equivalence of Nonconformity and Liberalism in Wales); Bebbington, "Nonconformity and Electoral Sociology," 634–639. The picture that Methodism presents is confused. Hempton finds it difficult to accept E. R. Taylor's view that "the history of Methodism's relation to politics has been the story of a Liberal displacement of a strong Tory sentiment." Though much of the Wesleyan connexional leadership in the 1830s and 1840s showed a Toryism that was "a mixture of pride in Methodist achievement, and the fear that liberals, Catholics and radicals would snatch it away from them," they found it difficult to influence Methodist voters, many of whom joined other Dissenters to vote for the Whig/Liberal politicians who had enfranchised them. When and where "Papal Aggression" was a major concern, however, it contributed to fashioning a distinctive Tory populism. Hempton, *Methodism and Society*, 16, 181–216. Cf. W. R. Ward, *Religion and Society in England 1790–1850* (London: B. T. Batsford, 1972). Obelkevitch describes the growing alienation of Wesleyans in South Lindsey from the Church of England through the nineteenth century, which should have polarized them politically, but in fact most Methodists seem to have deferentially followed the lead of their landlords in this rural area. James Obelkevitch, *Religion and Rural Society: South Lindsey 1825–1875* (Oxford: Clarendon, 1976), 211–217. There are fascinating parallels between the political orientations of American and British Methodists in the nineteenth century. Neither group was as politically homogeneous as other evangelical denominations. In each case, the factors that most influenced their partisan attachments were (1) their relationship (in Britain) to the established church or (in America) to high-status denominations, the "informal establishment," especially New England Congregationalists and Yankee Presbyterians; (2) the relative strength of Romanism. When the first relationship was antagonistic, and salient, Methodists turned to Liberals or Democrats; when Catholicism threatened, they drew towards Toryism or Whiggery/Know-Nothingism/Republicanism.

35. Brent, "Impact of the Second Reform Act," 146–147, 159, 162–172; Isichei, *Victorian Quakers*, 200–201; Bebbington, *The Nonconformist Conscience*, 8.

36. Hamer, *Politics of Electoral Pressure*, 6–7, 45–46; Sellers, *Nineteenth-Century Nonconformity*, 79; Shannon, *Gladstone and the Bulgarian Agitation 1876*, 163–164; Bebbington, "Nonconformity and Electoral Sociology," 654. See Michael Bentley, *The Climax of Liberal Politics: British Liberalism in Theory and Practice 1868–1918* (London: Edward Arnold, 1987), 30–38, for the relative significance of the Nonconformist ingredients within British Liberalism.

37. Kelley, *The Transatlantic Persuasion*, 146–349.

38. Brent, "Impact of the Second Reform Act", 140–143.

39. Ibid., 172; Howe, *American Whigs*, 96–122, 181–209. Kelley sees some of the difficulties of his position, not least the sense of kinship that British Liberals felt with the moralism of American Republicans; E. L. Godkin joined that party when he arrived in America in the 1850s. Kelley, *Transatlantic Persuasion*, 269.

40. For the Conservatives' exploiting of disestablishment in 1885, see Alan Simon, "Church Disestablishment as a Factor in the General Election of 1885," *Historical Journal* 18 (1975): 791–820; Machin, *Politics and the Churches 1869–1921*, 151–159.

41. McDonald, "Religion and Voting in an English Borough," 221; McDonald's evidence for Poole suggests (232–233) that a much larger minority of Anglicans (one in four) voted solely for Liberals than the minority of Nonconformists (one in twelve) who plumped for Tory candidates. Obelkevitch, *Religion and Rural Society*, 121–122, concludes that Anglican clergy, homogeneously Tory, were the most partisan block of voters in rural Lincolnshire. Vincent, *Pollbooks*, 5, 10, also emphasizes the strength of partisanship amongst ministers, Nonconformist as well as Anglican.

42. Hempton, *Methodism and Society*, 185–186, 194, 207, 224–228; Greenall, "Popular Conservatism in Salford," 131ff; Brent, "Impact of the Second Reform Act," 172; Wainwright, *Ireland Not Socialism*, 16–17. For the deep antipopery of Protestant workingmen in Lancashire and its political consequences, see also P. J. Waller, *Democracy and Sectarianism: A Political and Social History of Liverpool, 1868–1939* (Liverpool: Liverpool University Press, 1981); J. C. Lowe, "The Tory Triumph of 1868 in Blackburn and Lancashire," *Historical Journal* 16 (1973): especially 740–743; Henry Pelling, *Popular Politics and Society in Late Victorian Britain* (London: Macmillan, 1968), 31–33. Cf. Robert Blake, *The Conservative Party from Peel to Churchill* (London: Eyre and Spottiswoode, 1970), 111–112, contrasting the Lancashire experience with that of the persisting Liberalism of 'Nonconformist' Yorkshire.

43. Shannon, *Gladstone and the Bulgarian Agitation*, 171–181.

44. For a discussion of the ethical perspectives of these two competing party political cultures, see Peter Marsh, ed., *The Conscience of the Victorian State* (Hassocks, Sussex: Harvester, 1979), especially the essays by Peter Marsh, "The Conservative Conscience," and Richard Helmstadter, "The Nonconformist Conscience," 135–172, 215–242, respectively.

45. P. F. Clarke, *Lancashire and the New Liberalism* (Cambridge: Cambridge University Press, 1971); Clarke, "Electoral Sociology of Modern Britain," 46–47.

For attempts to come to terms with the cultural, ethnic, and religious dimensions of politics in a "factory" society, and the survival of patterns of deference into the early twentieth century, see Patrick Joyce, *Work, Society and Politics* (London: Methuen, paperback ed., 1982), 240–267; Neville Kirk, *The Growth of Working Class Reformism in Mid-Victorian England* (Urbana: University of Illinois Press, 1985), especially the chapter "Class, Ethnicity and Popular Toryism." This essay, in concentrating on the respectable "Nonconformist Conscience" and the voting classes, necessarily neglects the more popular side of politics and does not consider how through the nineteenth century religion might have acted as an "integrative" force in British society, reducing class division and neutralizing the radical, potentially revolutionary, thrusts of those on the periphery of the political nation. Edward Thompson's work suggests that religion diverted working-class activism into reformist, participatory politics. It has been suggested that religious affiliation and cross-class issues like temperance might have softened class conflict and produced a "viable class society" in mid-Victorian Britain. See Harold Perkin, *The Origins of Modern British Society, 1780–1880* (London: Routledge and Kegan Paul, 1969), especially 347–364; and Brian Harrison, *Peaceable Kingdom: Stability and Change in Modern Britain* (Oxford: Clarendon, 1982), which is essential to an understanding of the social cohesion of nineteenth- and twentieth-century British society. Edward Royle, *Modern Britain: A Social History 1750–1985* (London: Edward Arnold, 1987), 325–335, offers some helpful observations on the debate.

46. Clarke, "Electoral Sociology of Modern Britain," 50–51; Bebbington, "Nonconformity and Electoral Sociology," 640–654. Michael Kinnear, *The British Voter: An Atlas and Survey Since 1885*, 2nd ed. (London: Batsford, 1981), 14, notes that as late as the election of 1923 it was possible to see a "division between West Lancashire, with its Protestant–Roman Catholic split and numerous Conservative M.P.s, and East Lancashire, with fewer Roman Catholics and fewer Conservative M.P.s." For the decline of working-class militant Protestantism in Lancashire, outside Liverpool, in the early twentieth century, and the general indifference of the working class to religion, see Alan J. Lee, "Conservatism, Traditionalism and the British Working Class," in David E. Martin and David Rubinstein, eds., *Ideology and the Labour Movement: Essays Presented to John Savile* (London: Croom Helm, 1979), 90–92.

47. Kleppner, *Cross of Culture*, 316–375.

48. Binfield, *So Down to Prayers*, 116.

49. For the greater resistance to revivalism in British culture and politics, as compared with "the dynamics of unopposed revivalism" in the United States, see George Marsden, "Fundamentalism as an American Phenomenon, a Comparison with English Evangelicalism," *Church History* 46 (1977): 215–232.

50. Bebbington, "Nonconformity and Electoral Sociology," 654; David Butler and Donald Stokes, *Political Change in Britain: Forces Shaping Electoral Choice* (London: Macmillan, 1969), 124–134; Jean Blondel, *Voters, Parties, Leaders*, rev. ed. (Harmondsworth: Penguin, 1966), 60–61; A. H. Birch, *Small-Town Poli-*

tics: A Study of Political Life in Glossop (Oxford: Oxford University Press, 1959), 111–112.

51. Alan Beith, *Leadership for Freedom* (Hebden Bridge: Hebden Royd, 1988), 15.

52. For a fuller picture of Anglicanism in modern political life, see Kenneth M. Medhurst and George H. Moyser, *Church and Politics in a Secular Age: The Case of the Church of England* (Oxford: Clarendon, 1988).

53. John Biffen, MP, quoted in *The Independent*, May 27, 1988.

11

Politics, Religion, and the Canadian Experience: A Preliminary Probe

GEORGE A. RAWLYK

In celebrating the one hundredth anniversary of the Statue of Liberty, President Ronald Reagan declared on July 3, 1986, that he had "always thought that a providential hand had something to do with the founding of this country."[1] For centuries, American leaders had been making precisely this same point about the "providential hand" and its miraculous shaping of the destiny of the "Rising American Empire."[2] Unfortunately, for Canadians at least, that providential hand has, all too often, also been pointed in a northerly direction.

The American presence has in the past, and continues in the present, to influence profoundly every aspect of Canadian development. This central reality provides the conceptual framework in which is located this preliminary probe into the often complex relationship between religion and politics in Canada. After considering some of the basic contours of Canadian nationalism and the Canadian identity, some attention is devoted to the ways in which religion may have impinged upon Canadian political life in the century or so following the end of the American Revolution. Then, in the concluding section of the paper, special emphasis is placed upon the ways in which religion or the absence of religion may be affecting contemporary Canadian political culture.

From a Canadian perspective, it seems that for many Americans, especially during the century and a half following the American Revolution, it was not enough for their new nation to be merely a republican-Christian example for the rest of the world to emulate—eventually and from a safe distance. These people were far more aggressive in their approach—advocating a determined ideological and evangelical offensive to redeem the rest of the world from its backward, sinful self. The moral, spiritual, political, and economic regeneration of the world seemed to be the special destiny of the United States. One influential American editor put it this way in 1845: "U.S. expansionism was but the fulfillment of our manifest destiny, to overspread the continent allotted by Providence for the free development"[3] of the United States. Some fifty-five years later Senator Beveridge pushed the hand of Providence far beyond the narrow confines of North America. "God has made us the master organizers of the world to establish system where chaos reigns," he intoned. The Almighty

> has marked the American people as his chosen nation to finally lead in the regeneration of the world. This is the divine mission of America and it holds for us all the profit, all the glory, all the happiness possible to man.[4]

All nations, of course, even Canada, possess a certain sense of mission. But no nation in modern history, it may be argued, especially from a vantage point north of the forty-ninth parallel, has been as preoccupied as has been the United States with the conviction that it indeed has a *unique* mission in the world and a *special* hegemonic contribution to make. The American sense of mission—its so-called Manifest Destiny—is deeply embedded in the American collective psyche. Here is to be found the conviction that an advanced form of government and a way of life was introduced in the seventeenth century to the pristinely pure New World by a people "Highly Favoured of God." The Chosen People of God—the New World People of Israel—had founded a new society in which, among other things, the individual had both freedom and liberty, where he or she was free from the entanglements of the Old World and where he or she was completely free from the heavy burdens of a bleak and prejudiced past. Here they could, with God's help, build a "Citty on a Hill." And when the eyes of the world were no longer focused on their "Citty," they could impose their "Citty" on the seemingly indifferent, the hostile, and the ignorant.[5]

Manifest Destiny, it is clear, from the time of John Winthrop to at least the late nineteenth century, explicitly expressed with respect to what is now Canada what A. K. Weinberg once referred to as "a dogma of supreme self-assurance and ambition—that America's incorporation of all adjacent lands was the virtually inevitable fulfillment of a moral mission delegated to the nation by Providence itself."[6] American "expansionism," or Manifest Destiny, with respect to what is now Canada has gone through three distinct phases and each of these has significantly affected Canadian political and cultural development. One cannot understand Canadian historical development or the evolving relationship of religion and politics without coming to grips with this central reality. The first phase of American expansion stretched from the early part of the seventeenth century to 1812–14. During this period American northern expansionism was very much shaped by economic, military, and religious forces. One thinks here of the various Acadia–Nova Scotia expeditions, the Louisbourg episode of 1745, the Chignecto campaign of 1755, the Montgomery-Arnold assault of 1775/76, and, of course, the War of 1812. Second, during much of the nineteenth century and the first decade of the twentieth, most Americans had abandoned the military approach and replaced it with a confident and assertive "ripe fruit theory."[7] They believed that through their noble republican example and because of Canadian self-interest, Canadians would jettison their British traditions and eagerly demand entry into the American Union. Then, in the post-1911 period, a profound indifference even to gobbling up "the ripe fruit" apparently affected key American decision-makers and others who were content to permit the ethos of progress to camouflage what has been referred to as "the sordid calculations of Economic Imperialism."[8] Despite some Canadian protestations to the contrary, few influential Americans during the post-1911 phase have favored sharpening the northern edge of American Manifest Destiny. Instead, they are content—very content, the Canadian nationalist would argue—to regard Canada merely as the "northern extension of the American republic." Such a point of view was cogently expressed over sixty years ago in a U.S. Department of Commerce memorandum:

> Economically and socially Canada may be considered a northern extension of the United States, and our trade with Canada is in many respects more like domestic trade than our foreign trade with other countries.[9]

In a real sense, of course, Canada in the twentieth century would be "economically and socially" very much a "northern extension of the

United States." In fact, in 1965 the brilliantly perceptive Canadian theologian-philosopher George Grant underscored what to many was this disconcerting reality in his widely acclaimed *Lament for a Nation: The Defeat of Canadian Nationalism.* Grant eloquently lamented the destruction of Canada by the insidious ethos of American liberal individualism, an ideology of material progress and consumerism that had made redundant the viable existence of any other North American independent nation-state. According to Grant, Canada had no future in the latter half of the twentieth century and beyond largely because the countervailing ideological force to the United States, Great Britain, had lost its sense of purpose and sense of ideological direction. American liberalism had undermined British conservatism—the ideology which, according to Grant, the Loyalists had introduced to North America during and after the American Revolution. "Our hope," Grant argued in describing this conservatism, "lay in the belief that on the northern half of this continent we could build a community which had a stronger sense of the common good and of public order than was possible under the individualism of the American capitalist dream."[10]

Grant's bitter and despairing lament for a conservative Canada that could no longer exist in the expanding ocean of Americanization was not, of course, accepted by all Canadians. For these men and women in the 1960s, Grant's *Lament* was, in fact, a clarion call for them to try to preserve the Canadian nation despite the odds. At the core of their neo-Canadian nationalism was a powerful critique of all things American as well as an understandable desire to exaggerate the uniqueness of the Canadian experience. Perhaps Raymond Souster best captured the intense animus of the virulent anti-Americanism that seemed to fuel the new nationalism in the 1960s:

> America
> you seem to be dying
> America
> moving across the forty-ninth parallel each
> day a stronger more death laden stench;
> wafting inshore from off the Great Lakes
> the same unmistakable stink.
>
> America
> The cracks are beginning to show
> America
> I knew you were marching to doom the night
> a young American told me: "There in Buffalo
> I saw our flag flying, when fifty yards

further on your Maple Leaf, and I
thought: thank God I'll never have to
cross that line going back again." . . .

America
your time is running out fast
America
you haven't changed at all since you
sent your New York State farm boys
across the Niagara to conquer us once
and for all, since you printed your handbills
promising French-Canadians sweet liberation
from their oppressors, since you looked the
other way as Fenians played toy soldiers
across our borders.

America
you're sitting on your own rumbling volcano . . .
America
phoney as a Hollywood cowboy main street,
laughable as Rockefeller with his ten-cent
pieces, vulgar as a Las Vegas night club . . .

America
America
there is really nothing left to do now but die with
a certain gracefulness.[11]

C. J. Newman, another Canadian poet, agreed with Souster's black
and despairing analysis of disintegrating America:

Fortress America! If only
the fortress walls were real
and high enough
to spare us having to watch
your long dark night of the soul
your reaching out for that murder
that one more murder
final murder
to purge you of murder
and of all experience
—if only . . . .

America America
the burnt seed lies by the side
of your turnpikes
auto graveyards

motel cities
military camps
the heaped-up contempt
of every dream of paradise on earth
stinking your greens
the burnt seed
shines darkly
blasting out
the sun.[12]

Not only were Canadian poets involved in shaping the new Canadian nationalism in the 1960s but there were also academics and a younger group of political activists. Perhaps the most influential group of these people became part of the Waffle Movement—a left-wing faction within the New Democratic party—Canada's democratic socialist party. (The name "Waffle" was given to the group by one of its founders, who when criticized by the NDP leadership responded that he would rather "waffle to the left than waffle to the right.") Many other nationalists, it should be pointed out, were content to work within the organizational framework of the two traditional parties, the Liberals and Conservatives. From 1969 to 1972, despite its relative weakness in numbers, the Waffle played an extremely important role in Canadian political life. Not only did it nudge the NDP further to the left in the policy realm but the Waffle also compelled the NDP to become far more anti-American than it had been. Moreover, it may be argued that the Waffle, led by Jim Laxer and Mel Watkins, because of the remarkable way in which it touched a responsive chord in the general Canadian population, pushed the Liberal party further to the nationalist left. Concerned about the threat of the NDP, the Liberals, led by Pierre Eliot Trudeau, as had the Federal Liberals in the 1940s, lurched to the left and in the process ensured their political ascendancy during the 1967–1984 period.

For the Waffle Movement in 1969, according to its widely circulated Manifesto:

The major threat to Canadian survival today is American control of the Canadian economy. The major issue of our times is not national unity but national survival, and the fundamental threat is external, not internal.

American corporate capitalism is the dominant factor shaping Canadian society. In Canada, American economic control operates through the formidable medium of the multinational corporation. . . . Canada has been reduced to a resource base and consumer market within the American empire.[13]

Then the Waffle Manifesto declared:

> The American empire is the central reality for Canadians. It is an empire characterized by militarism abroad and racism at home. Canadian resources and diplomacy have been enlisted in the support of that empire.[14]

What could then be done to rectify the situation? For the Waffle members the answer was a deceptively simple one—socialism—what they referred to as "extensive public control over investment and nationalization of the commanding heights of the economy."[15] In other words, the only viable and truly independent Canada was a Canada which was the ideological antithesis to the United States—a truly socialist Canada.

Canadian nationalists in the 1960s, as well as in the 1970s and 1980s, were not satisfied with merely criticizing all things American. Like Canadian nationalists throughout the nineteenth century they also attempted to delineate those historical and cultural attributes that seemed, to them anyway, to make Canada so different from the United States despite the movement northwards "through space" of what Allan Smith has called "American culture and the New World ethos."[16]

When attempting to define the uniqueness of the Canadian identity, Canadian nationalists have, over and over again, emphasized at least five key distinctive characteristics. First, special emphasis is placed upon the bicultural nature of Canada and the important ways in which English-French relations since the 1760s have significantly shaped the Canadian experience.[17] Second, as might have been expected from people with a powerful sense of history, the nationalists would stress that Canadians had shared quite a different historical past than had Americans, and for them this radically different historical tradition impinged on every aspect of contemporary Canadian life.[18] Third, many nationalists, especially during the past fifty years, have proudly contrasted the continuing strength and viability of democratic socialism in Canada with the fact that it remains an inconsequential, fractured, sectarian movement in the United States. It must indeed amaze most Americans that the most popular federal politician for much of the late 1980s has been Ed Broadbent, the leader of the federal New Democratic party. Moreover, if a federal election had been held in 1987, the New Democrats would have probably formed the government. Although the NDP's support declined somewhat during the campaign before the federal election of November 1988, its parliamentary candidates still polled 20 percent of the vote in that contest. It is sometimes not realized in the United States that as of early April 1988, the NDP was in power in Manitoba and in the northern territory of Yukon (though the Yukon is not yet a province). In British Columbia, Alberta, Saskatchewan, and Ontario, moreover, the NDP is the official opposition. The party has members in the legislatures of Newfoundland and Nova Scotia, but there are no New Democrats in Quebec City, Fredericton, New Brunswick, or Charlottetown, Prince Edward Island.

A fourth theme developed by Canadian nationalists is that British parliamentary democracy and the British legal system, and the conservatism associated with the Loyalists and the pre-Conquest French Canadians, have given Canada its ongoing collective obsession with "peace, order and good government" and also the suitable atmosphere to create a cultural "mosaic" rather than a "melting pot." [19]

Fifth, it has also been contended that powerful geophysical factors together with the proximity of the United States have produced in the collective Canadian psyche what Northrop Frye has called the "garrison mind" or "siege mentality" and what Margaret Atwood has argued is the Canadian preoccupation with "*Survival.*" [20] Moreover, for Herschal Hardin, because of the remarkable hold of the "siege mentality" and the concern with survival, Canada in its essentials is "a public enterprise country." The "fundamental mode of Canadian life" has always been, according to Hardin, "the un-American mechanism of redistribution as opposed to the mystic American mechanism of market rule." [21] Most Canadians, in other words, whether on the right or left in politics, expect their governments to be actively involved in the economic and social life of the nation. In a number of surveys conducted in the 1968–70 period, for example, it was discovered that 36 percent of Canadians agreed with the statement "The government should guarantee everyone at least $3,000 per year whether he works or not." The American percentage was only 14 percent. [22] Moreover, it has been recently argued, in an article suitably entitled "The Free Enterprise Dodo Is No Phoenix," that Canadian economic development has been characterized by "the pervasiveness of state intervention, regulation, and the frequent appearance of public ownership." [23] According to a 1982 study, for example,

> Of 400 top industrial firms, 25 were controlled by the federal or provincial governments. Of the top 50 industrials, all ranked by sales, 7 were either wholly owned or controlled by the federal or provincial governments. For financial institutions, 9 of the top 25 were federally or provincially owned or controlled. . . . Canadian governments at all levels exhibit little reticence about involvement in such diverse enterprises as railroads, airlines, aircraft manufacture, financial institutions, steel companies, oil companies, and selling and producing atomic reactors for energy generation. [24]

When trying to account for the five Canadian distinctives, Canadian nationalists and scholars have usually short-circuited serious discussion by simply pointing to the formative importance of the American Revolution. As far as the distinguished Canadian historian A. R. M. Lower was concerned:

> Of greater moment than the boundary settlement was the parting itself. Here surely was the profoundest depth of the Revolution. For the parting had been in bad blood. The race was broken. Neither Englishmen nor Canadians, especially Canadians, have realized to this day what Revolution really means, how wide and enduring is the gulf that it opens up between the winning and losing sides.[25]

The Revolution obviously made the republic of the United States, but it also ensured that a separate British Canada would continue to exist north of the American republic. Canada is the result of what S. M. Lipset has called a "Counterrevolution," [26] and this almost too simple fact should never be forgotten by students of any aspect of Canadian-American relations and Canadian politics.

During its formative post-Revolutionary period, the ideological and cultural shape of what is now Canada was significantly influenced by the approximately 50,000 Loyalists who pushed into the region. These people, a fairly representative sample of the strata of American society, had been compelled to leave the United States for a variety of complex reasons. It is quite obvious that all the Loyalists did not equally detest republican ideology or that they were all united in their determination to construct what was once referred to as "the foundations of the New Empire." [27] Yet some key Loyalists did indeed detest republican principles and some were eager to build a country which would be "*The Envy of the American States.*" [28] And these influential Loyalists—many of whom would indeed become members of a political and cultural elite— brought with them something more than a bitter sense of defeat and despair. They brought with them something which would shape Canadian development until the present day—a conservative ideology and frame of mind and a deep-rooted antagonism towards the United States.[29]

For the Loyalist elite, whether in present-day Ontario, Quebec, Nova Scotia, or New Brunswick, the American republican demagogues had abandoned "our priceless claim to all the rights and privileges of British subjects." [30] Instead of British stability, they perceived American republican anarchy. Instead of the British rule of law, there was the republican rule of the mob. And instead of true British liberty, which guaranteed minority rights, there was patriot-republican intimidation, which had led to sterile conformity. And, worst of all, in place of the enlightened religious and political stability produced by what Nova Scotia's first Anglican bishop called the true "Church of Christ," [31] there were the pernicious "Evils of Enthusiasm" and "Fanaticism." [32] According to Bishop Charles Inglis: "Fanatics are impatient under civil restraint & into the democratic system. They are for levelling everything sacred & civil . . . [and] are, as far as I can learn, Democrats to a man." [33]

The Loyalist elite was determined to transform the wilds of British North America into a prosperous and ordered "corner of Empire." In 1810 an influential Upper Canadian (or Ontario) Loyalist, Richard Cartwright, proudly declared: "Under an Epitome of the English Constitution we enjoy the greatest practical, political Freedom." [34] Many other Loyalist leaders located in Central Canada and elsewhere in British North America would have instinctively endorsed Cartwright's ringing declaration. They had helped to build a stratified, deferential, and British society—one which the distinguished New Brunswick Loyalist Edward Winslow once described as possessing "the most gentlemanlike government on earth." [35] The Loyalist elite considered American "Life, Liberty and the Pursuit of Happiness" to be dangerous anarchical principles that threatened to undermine their carefully constructed belief structure. Instead, the Loyalist leaders contended that proper governments—their kind—buttressed by the Church of England, should provide guiding authority, stability and, above all, order. In sharp contrast to their brand of British order, they and their successors would stress the violence and disorder that seemed to be endemic to American society.

In underscoring their "conservative principles" and their anti-Americanism, the Loyalist elite was of course reaffirming the rationale for its loyalty, but it was also attempting to facilitate their own psychological adjustment to their new and harsh environment; they were, moreover, of course attempting to consolidate their own social, religious, economic, and political power in the new land. The articulated conservative ideology was a fascinating amalgam of what has been referred to as hatred of the victor and psychological need. There was, in other words, as S. F. Wise has perceptively put it:

> The urgent necessity for a small people, in the overwhelming presence of a supremely confident neighbour, to insist not merely upon their separateness and distinctiveness, but even upon their intrinsic political and moral superiority. . . . The rigidities established by the compulsion to maintain

identity narrowed the range of political debate, channeled political thought along familiar paths, and discouraged the venturesome, the daring and the rash.[36]

What Wise has observed may help to explain, among other things, the sad, almost pathetic, state of Canadian political thought in the nineteenth and twentieth centuries. Preoccupied with the threat posed by the United States—that "providential hand"—Canadians seemed almost incapable of creative, imaginative political, social, and religious thought. They seemed to be so much better in defending or in attacking than in creating.

The worst fears of the Loyalists regarding the evils of American republicanism seemed to be confirmed by the outbreak of the War of 1812. Though apparently in a hopeless military position, the British North Americans, supported by British regulars, almost miraculously turned back the hordes of American invaders. It is not surprising that for Anglican divines from present-day Ontario to Nova Scotia, the American defeat provided convincing proof that the Almighty alone had saved Canada from almost certain destruction, and consequently the Canadians, and not the Americans, were what the Reverend John Strachan proudly called "God's Peculiar People." [37] A surprising number of Americans agreed with Strachan, contending that God was certain of the "*injustice* of" the American "cause" and "his hand" was protecting the Canadians and not the Americans.[38] "The vengeance of the Almighty," [39] it would be asserted, over and over again, had during the War of 1812 been directed at the corrupt and sinful United States and not at British Canada.

This negative American view of their involvement in the war only seemed to strengthen the growing Canadian conservative conviction, after 1814, that God had, in fact, selected Canada to do great things in the New World. The war had provided convincing proof that a Canadian "bastion of imperial power and might—a society worthy of its king and of its heroic loyalist origins . . . would not only replace, but would eclipse that which had been lost in the thirteen colonies." [40] As they sought explanations for their providential good favor, the conservative elite singled out their conservative Loyalist ideology as the most compelling reason. In the final analysis, loyalty to the king and to his church had provided them with what they would refer to as their "*Shield of Achilles.*" [41] Loyalty, as they defined it, became for Canadian conservatives in the first half of the nineteenth century and beyond *the* most important political, social, and cultural reality. Wrapping themselves in the Union Jack, they tended in periods of political crisis after 1814 to denounce their enemies as being pro-American and disloyal. And these charges were not easily sloughed off in a society which from Nova Scotia to Ontario was becoming more British and less American as the nineteenth century unfolded. Tory Anglicans, aware of their numerical weakness in pre-Confederation Ontario and the Maritimes, exaggerated their loyalty in order to consolidate political power and also to weaken the potential political strength of the non-Anglican majority. In Quebec, where the Roman Catholic Church was the dominant religious force by far, the clerical leadership from the time of the American Revolution had closely linked itself with the British governing elite. For the Roman Catholic leadership, the "political powers that be were indeed ordained of God," and they did everything in their power, despite growing opposition among younger French Canadians, to cultivate the concept of loyalty and the conservative ethos.

It is noteworthy that in all of British North America, until at least midcentury, despite the ill-fated Rebellions of 1837–38, which attempted to introduce republican forms of government into Central Canada, large numbers of so-called Nonconformists—Baptists, Methodists, Congregationalists, as well as many Presbyterians—were Reformers, opposed to what they spitefully referred to as the "Tory Family Compact." Although there were important exceptions to the rule, it may be argued that before Responsible Government was introduced into the British North American colonies in the late 1840s, the typical Nonconformist, because of his anti–Anglican-establishment view and his opposition to the preferential treatment meted out to Anglicans, would vote Reform or Liberal. The typical Anglican would vote Tory or Conservative, and after 1837 he would be joined by many Methodists and Presbyterians who had, for a variety of reasons, seen the powerful advantages of the concept of loyalty. In Quebec, it is sometimes forgotten, the Francophone majority was split, from the 1830s until the late 1890s, into two camps—an ultramontane group and an increasingly vocal anticlerical one.

It is interesting to note that from 1867, the year of Confederation, until 1896, when the Liberal Wilfrid Laurier became the first French-Canadian prime minister, the ultramontanes in Quebec successfully delivered a majority of federal seats in Quebec for the Tories. And this was despite the fact that many Anglophone Tories outside of Quebec were blatantly anti–Roman Catholic.

Something of the tremendous antagonism between Quebec ultramontanes—or the *Bleus*, as they were called—and the anticlerical element— or the *Rouges*—was captured in the infamous Guibord incident, which became a "Holy War" during the decade following Confederation. This incident clearly reveals the extent to which religion actually impinged upon Quebec political life in the 1860s and 1870s. In 1868, open warfare was declared by Bishop Bourget, the outspoken ultramontane Bishop of Montreal, against the *Institut Canadien*, the Montreal headquarters of the *Rouges*. The *Institut*'s yearbook for 1868, which contained highly controversial speeches given by Louis-Antoine Dessaules and Horace Greeley, was placed on the *Index*.[42] Moreover, from Rome, where he had gone to attend the Vatican Council, Bourget in 1869 proclaimed in a pastoral letter that it was forbidden for the faithful to belong to the *Institut*, and if they persisted in doing so they would be denied the sacrament "*même à l'àrticle de la mort.*"[43] This was an extraordinary step for Bourget to take, but he was not bluffing.

In November 1869, Joseph Guibord, a Montreal printer and prominent member of the *Institut*, died. Since he had persisted in belonging to the *Institut* despite Bourget's decree, the clergy had refused to give him the last rites of the church and would only bury him in a plot of unconsecrated land in the Roman Catholic cemetery.[44] His body found a temporary resting-place in the Protestant cemetery while several members of the *Institut* rushed to Guibord's defense and demanded that his body be buried in a Roman Catholic cemetery. They failed, however, and the Guibord case became a cause célèbre. After five years of expensive legal proceedings, the Judicial Committee of the Privy Council in London in 1874 ordered burial in the Roman Catholic cemetery.[45] In November 1875, the jubilant friends of Guibord arranged a huge funeral procession from the Protestant cemetery to the Roman Catholic one. Finding the entrance to the latter blocked by a hostile crowd, the mourners were forced to retreat. A few days later Guibord's remains were finally lowered into a plot at the Roman Catholic Côte des Neiges cemetery, and to protect the grave from possible desecration it was covered with a layer of concrete and scrap metal.[46] However, Bourget snatched victory out of the jaws of defeat by deconsecrating the patch of ground in which Guibord's remains lay.[47]

Bourget and his supporters, energized by the Guibord episode, attempted in the 1870s to consolidate their hold over the Conservative party. Among other things, they emphasized that it was essential for all French-Canadian Roman Catholics to vote only for the candidates who unreservedly supported the "Roman Catholic doctrines in religion, in politics and in social economy."[48] Moreover, they declared publicly that in any election campaign in Quebec if a choice had to be made between "a Conservative of any shade" and a Liberal, the former was to be supported. The final clause of their *Programme Catholique* clearly demonstrated to what extent the Bourget wing of the Tories actually detested the Liberals and all that they represented:

> Finally, in the event that the contest lies between a Conservative who rejects our programme and an opportunist of any brand who accepted, the position would be most delicate. To vote for the former would be to contradict the doctrine we have just expanded; to vote for the latter would be to imperil the Conservative party, which we wish to see strong. . . . In this case we shall advise Catholic electors to abstain from voting.[49]

In a February 1876 pastoral letter, Bourget explained simply and precisely how ordinary Roman Catholics were to interpret the anti-Liberal advice being provided by their priests. Any doubtful voter was instructed to seek the guidance of his priest, whose words reflected the opinions of his bishop, "the Bishop hears the Pope, and the Pope hears our Lord Jesus Christ."[50] Thus, the doctrine of papal infallibility was extended to include, in terms of Quebec politics at least, the lowliest curé. And if a simpler approach was necessary, the priest was advised to inform his parishioners that a vote for the Tories was a vote for the Almighty in the heavens, while a vote for the Liberals was a vote for the Devil and the hell he inhabited.

By 1877, however, Bourget and his supporters found themselves on the defensive as their "undue clerical influence of the worst kind"[51] was condemned by other Roman Catholic leaders in Quebec and by the courts. In addition, a pastoral letter in 1877 from the Vatican to all Roman Catholic priests in Quebec declared that they were explicitly forbidden "to teach in the pulpit or elsewhere that it is a sin to vote for such a candidate or such a political party; much more are you forbidden to announce that you will refuse the sacraments for this reason. From the pulpit you will never give your opinion."[52]

Without question, ultramontane political influence in Quebec had peaked in the mid-1870s only to decline as the nineteenth century blurred into the twentieth. In the Maritimes, however, the evidence suggests that the ultramontane influence peaked somewhat later—especially in Nova Scotia and New Brunswick—but then, too, it lost some of its political power.

Whether in Quebec or the Maritimes, however, by the last decade of the nineteenth century the ultramontanes were a largely spent force. But this, of course, did not mean that the Roman Catholic Church withdrew from the political arena. Its influence would now be largely implicit rather than explicit and for much of the post-1896 period its hierarchy would be supportive of the federal Liberals. With the death in 1891 of John A. Macdonald—the great Tory prime minister—and the election of Wilfrid Laurier as prime minister in 1896, the relationship of religion and politics in Canada underwent a significant change, a change influenced greatly by the 1885 execution of Louis Riel, the controversial Metis leader who had failed in his attempt to repulse the advancing Eastern civilization from the Canadian West. With Laurier as prime minister, the Quebec political consensus, including the support of the Roman Catholic Church, began to shift from the Conservatives to the Liberals. It may be argued that the Liberal party has retained its political hegemony in Quebec for most of the 1896–1988 period largely because it has been more sensitive to a bicultural Canada than have been the Conservatives. And in the process they have been perceived by Roman Catholics to be more open to them than the Tories with their strong tradition of anti-Catholicism. In Canada's last two federal elections a key to Conservative victory has been the much improved Conservative showing in Quebec.

It may be argued that the Liberal bias of twentieth-century Canadian federal politics has been largely the result of the fundamental shift in political alignment that took place in Quebec after 1896. As the twentieth century unfolded, the Liberal party attracted support from large sectors of the Roman Catholic and French-speaking populations outside of Quebec. With few exceptions, as was the case in 1958 and 1984, the federal Tories have had very little success in Quebec and among Roman Catholics outside Quebec as well as among Francophones. And the CCF—the Co-operative Commonwealth Federation, the forerunner of the NDP—and the NDP have failed to elect a single member from Quebec during the past fifty-five years and have had little electoral success among Francophones elsewhere in Canada and only marginally better success among non-Francophone Roman Catholics. The weakness of democratic socialism in Francophone Canada may be directly traced to a powerful antisocialist bias of the Roman Catholic hierarchy.[53] And it has only been since the late 1960s, with the secularization of Quebec, that democratic socialism, either in its Parti Québécois or New Democratic form, has become a significant force in the province.

Census data since 1911 would seem to provide great encouragement to the Liberals.[54] From 1911 to 1981, the Canadian population has increased from 7,206,643 to 24,083,495. During this same period, the percentage of Roman Catholics has grown from 39.3 percent of the population to 46.5 percent while that of the Church of England has dropped from 14.4 percent in 1911 to 10.1 percent in 1981. Even the United Church, Canada's largest Protestant church, which came into being in 1925, has declined from claiming 19.4 percent of the Canadian population in 1931 to 15.6 percent in 1981. And Canadian Baptists, who in 1911 made up 5.3 percent of the Canadian population, now only constitute 2.9 percent. In an ironic twist of Canadian religious development, the fastest-growing group in the Canadian population during the past thirty years is that which says it possesses "No Religion," up from 0.4 percent of the population in 1951 (59,679) to 7.2 percent in 1981 (1,752,380).[55] In British Columbia, it is noteworthy that, according to the 1981 census, those who have "No Religion" are members of the largest "religious denomination" in the province, with 20.5 percent of the population. Anglicans have 13.7 percent, Roman Catholics, 19.4 percent, Baptists, 3.0 percent, and the United Church, 20.2 percent. Is it merely a coincidence that the New Democratic party, at both the federal and provincial levels, has during the past two decades been supported by some 40 percent of the British Columbia population?

The possible relationship between growing socialist strength in Canada and growing secularization is one that certainly merits serious study. It is known, for example, from opinion survey data that in many areas of Canada a large percentage of activists in the NDP are people who define themselves as having "No Religion." For example, in Hamilton, Ontario, 62 percent of those very involved in the NDP in the 1970s were people who said they had "No Religion."[56] And this tendency is even more pronounced in British Columbia. If the forces of secularism continue to undermine Roman Catholicism in Quebec and both Catholicism and Protestantism in other regions of Canada, then the NDP may, in fact, be on the verge of a noteworthy political breakthrough. This development is permeated with irony, for since the 1930s the CCF and NDP have been the major political vehicles for realizing the "social gospel" in Canada. And, moreover, the NDP surge is taking place at the precise moment that Canada has been moving towards a free trade agreement with the United States. For well over two decades, the NDP has been the Canadian political party which has been most vociferous in its criticism of the United States. The Waffle Manifesto has, in the 1980s, become the rallying cry of New Democrats from Newfoundland to British Columbia. And in a remarkable reversal of political roles, the NDP, in its critique of the United States, has merely appropriated the central thrust of the nineteenth-century Tory critique of all things American and all things republican.[57]

Even as the Canadian economy is more and more integrated into the "Rising American Commercial Empire," especially with the free trade agreement ratified in December 1988, the most un-American of Canadian political parties retains a remarkable degree of popular support. The NDP, without question, has succeeded in tapping into a deep historical reservoir of Canadian-U.S. hostility stretching back to the American Revolution. It is a political party whose leadership and much of its rank and file have always been affected by an anti-American reading of the historical past. Moreover, the leadership of the party in the 1980s is also influenced to a significant degree by its social gospel heritage. Despite the powerful forces of secularism that in recent years have shaped Canadian culture in general and the New Democratic party in particular, there remains an important social gospel element in contemporary democratic socialism in Canada. T. C. Douglas, an ordained Baptist minister, the first democratic socialist premier of a Canadian province, and the first leader of the NDP, once explained his own commitment to the social gospel:

> The religion of tomorrow will be less concerned with dogmas of theology, and more concerned with the social welfare of humanity. When one sees the church spending its energies on the assertion of antiquated dogmas, but dumb as an oyster to the poverty and misery all around, we can't help recognize the need for a new interpretation of Christianity. We have come to see that the Kingdom of God is in our midst if we have the vision to build it. The rising generation will tend to build a heaven on earth rather than live in misery in the hope of gaining some uncertain reward in the distant furture.[58]

It is noteworthy that in 1935, in Alberta, another Canadian Baptist had become premier of a Canadian province. "Bible Bill" Aberhert, an "ordained apostle" of an independent fundamentalist Baptist church in Calgary, had swept into power as the leader of the Social Credit party. It has often been argued that Aberhert's political movement was a Canadian prairie variant of European Fascism, something one might expect to be coaxed into existence by a charismatic premillennialist fundamentalist. Recent scholarship, however, suggests something quite different, that Social Credit was "in fact leftist"[59] and had a great deal in common ideologically—until Aberhert's death in 1943—with the CCF. There was a growing social gospel bias in Aberhert's thought as the 1930s unfolded. The *Edmonton Bulletin* of May 24, 1943, certainly realized this fact when it declared in its obituary of Aberhert that it was

> important to remember that the social legislation [affecting health care, labor, education, oil and gas conservation, and moratoriums on foreclo-

sures] was the product of a burning sympathy for the aged and the sick and helpless. This will be his epitaph, whatever one may think of his politics, that he was the champion of the oppressed.

As leader of the federal NDP from 1961 to 1971, Tommy Douglas, another "champion of the oppressed," was disheartened to realize that his enthusiasm for building a "New Jerusalem" did not strike a more responsive chord either in his party or the Canadian electorate.[60] And it would not be until a decade after giving up the leadership of the NDP that he would see a rejuvenated social gospel, not necessarily in his party but mostly in the Roman Catholic and United churches. In fact, the Canadian Conference of Catholic Bishops has become, in recent years, one of the most outspoken critics of "the market-oriented policies of the Conservative Government."[61] Some of its critics have correctly argued that it is virtually impossible to distinguish between the CCCB statements and the democratic socialist views of the NDP. In December 1987, for example, a report entitled "A Time for Social Solidarity," largely shaped by the CCCB, demanded "a popular movement to transform the dominant socio-economic policies of this country."[62] Denouncing government policies that were encouraging the growth of "a sharply divided society of winners and losers," Canadians were urged to accept the necessity of a political program that included:

> a full employment policy, affirmative action programs, controls on investment so that capital is directed toward job creation, expansion of the public sector, pay equity, work-place democracy, improved social programs and increased taxation of the rich.[63]

Bitterly critical of the free trade agreement and closer ties with the United States, the authors of "A Time for Social Solidarity" were eager "to pull together people" who were committed not to a market economy but to "a people-oriented economy and society that puts top priority on serving people's basic needs."[64]

Here was an attempt to build a "New Jerusalem" in Canada, a kind of Christian Loyalist Elysium or "Peaceable Kingdom" but without the trappings of a pseudo-British aristocracy or an established church and free from the evils of Americanization. As might have been expected, "A Time for Social Responsibility" was endorsed by the United Church, the Canadian Labour Congress, Quebec's Confederation of National Trade Unions, and the National Farmers Union. Not surprisingly, the federal leader of the New Democratic party, Ed Broadbent, was unqualified in his support of the document.

On the surface, at least, it seems that during the past half-century or so religion has had very little impact on Canadian political life—or at least this is the general consensus reached by a myriad of scholars. Canadian voters, when compared to their American neighbors, seem strangely indifferent as to what their political leaders actually believe—in a religious sense. Since the 1930s, Canada has had as its prime ministers W. L. MacKenzie King, a Presbyterian spiritualist who was an enthusiastic advocate of the occult and a man who loved to talk to his long-dead dog and mother. There were his two Liberal successors, Louis St. Laurent, whose intense Catholicism was carefully hidden from Canadian voters, and Mike Pearson, whose lapsed Methodism was something few took seriously. Between St. Laurent and Pearson came John G. Diefenbaker, the Baptist firebrand from Saskatchewan whose Prairie Christianity seemed both pragmatic and contrived. And after Pearson, in 1967, there was Pierre Eliot Trudeau, whose lifestyle made any private or public religiosity virtually redundant. And then came Joe Clark, a Tory from Alberta whose Catholicism, when made public, surprised friend and foe alike. John Turner, who succeeded Trudeau very briefly, was a pious Roman Catholic, one of the most committed Christians to be prime minister of Canada since the time of Alexander MacKenzie, the dour Scots Baptist from Sarnia, Ontario, who served the Canadian nation from 1874 to 1878. There was some truth in John A. Macdonald's jibe that Canadians had shown in 1878 that they preferred John A. drunk to the pious Alexander MacKenzie sober. Canada's present prime minister is a Roman Catholic, but the evidence suggests that Brian Mulroney's Catholicism is not of primary importance to him. Moreover, Mulroney has made it very clear to his biographers "that his private religious principles do not carry over into politics."[65]

No Canadian prime minister in the twentieth century, to my knowledge, has publically stated that he has experienced the New Birth, and no Canadian leader of any major federal Canadian political party in recent years has attempted to appeal directly and explicitly to any religious constituency.[66] In fact, the evidence suggests that the vast majority of Canadian voters are not at all interested in the religious views of their politicians. And it is highly unlikely that this prevailing attitude will quickly change. The fact that present premier of British Columbia, Bill Van der Zalm, is what he calls a "Fundamentalist Catholic" is regarded as further proof that the Pacific province is always the peculiar exception to the Canadian norm. Van der Zalm was elected premier not because of his religious views, but despite them and because the B.C. elite desperately wanted to keep the much-feared and despised NDP out of office.

Though on the surface religion appears to have become a largely inconsequential force in late-twentieth-century Canadian political development, beneath the surface it may be of somewhat greater consequence. There may, in fact, be an important link between the increased secularization of Canada west of the Atlantic Provinces and the decline of the two major traditional parties, the Liberals and the Conservatives, in this area. The Atlantic Provinces have been recently described by Reginald Bibby as "the nation's true Bible Belt."[67] The percentage of Newfoundlanders in the "No Religion" category in 1981 was 0.9 percent; in Prince Edward Island, 2.6 percent; Nova Scotia, 4.1 percent; and in New Brunswick, 2.9 percent. These are the lowest percentages in all of Canada, and it is the Atlantic region, together with Quebec, where the Liberals and Conservatives have succeeded during the past fifty years in pushing democratic socialism to the largely inconsequential periphery of the political culture of the region.

But as more of Canada becomes more like British Columbia, especially in a profound religious sense, there is some reason to suggest that the political culture of the area west of New Brunswick will begin to reflect that of the Pacific coast rather than that of the Atlantic coast. In a sense, British Columbia may point to the future while the Atlantic region points to an increasingly irrelevant past. And this tendency could be significantly strengthened if the new social gospel thrust of the Roman Catholic Church and the United Church begins to develop into a broadly based social movement. It is of some interest that within the Roman Catholic Church, the most forceful advocate of "Social Solidarity" is a bishop from British Columbia, where socialism has, for years, been such a potent political force. And in the United Church, sometimes described by its critics as the NDP at prayer, the most committed leadership is to be found in Toronto and the West.

Even if the remarkable growth of those Canadians with "No Religion" does not in fact help to transform the federal political landscape into a genuine three-party system and even though the new social gospel may not be channeled into the NDP, Canadian politics in the 1980s is following a radically different pattern than U.S. politics. And this is taking place at the precise moment that the Canadian economy is being fully integrated into that of the United States. Because of the increasing strength of the NDP, the Liberals have been compelled to push to the left and the Progressive Conservatives have in certain respects followed suit. Politics in Canada, once again, has tilted to the left. It may be that this tilt is occurring largely to counteract the almost inexorable move to free trade. As Canada becomes a northern economic frontier of the United States, there seems to be a growing collective need in Canada to exaggerate those differences that continue to exist between the two countries. There is in this response what Freud once called "the narcissism of small differences." But there is more than this—of course.

According to Harold Innis, the influential Canadian thinker, the way in which a particular medium of communication impinges on the eye or the ear delineates the essential bias of the medium. The eye stresses space and distance and translates this sense of space and distance into a basic survival creed. Canadians, it may be argued, are a people of the eye—a people who have been overwhelmed by a sense of space and distance— and consequently they have created a survival creed or ideology that owes so much to the continuing Canadian concern with the real and imagined threat posed by the United States. They have *seen* America's "providential hand" and they have, moreover, felt its stinging impact and they realize how important it is to cultivate an ideology of community permeated by a survival creed that, in fact, may be the most coveted and cherished North American ideal. And what George Grant has called this crucially important "thrust of intention into the future" must have at its core, according to a growing number of Canadian political activists, an uncompromising Christian component.[68]

Notes

1. *The Globe and Mail*, July 4, 1986.

2. See R. Van Alstyne's often neglected volume, *The Rising American Empire* (Oxford: Oxford University Press, 1960), 1.

3. Quoted in R. B. Nye, *This Almost Chosen People* (East Lansing: Michigan State University Press, 1966), 170.

4. Quoted in ibid., 199–200.

5. This theme is developed in E. L. Tuveson, *Redeemer Nation: The Idea of America's Millenial Role* (Chicago: University of Chicago Press, 1968).

6. See A. K. Weinberg, *Manifest Destiny* (Chicago: AMS Press, 1963), 1–2.

7. This is a major theme in J. G. Snell, "'The Eagle and the Butterfly.' Some American Attitudes Towards British North America, 1864–1867" (Unpublished Ph.D. diss., Queen's University, 1970.)

8. Weinberg, *Manifest Destiny*, 7.

9. Quoted in J. Weaver, "Imperilled Dreams: Canadian Opposition to the American Empire, 1918–1930" (Unpublished Ph.D. diss., Duke University, 1973.)

10. G. Grant, *Lament for a Nation: The Defeat of Canadian Nationalism* (Toronto: Macmillan of Canada, 1971), x. There is a cogent description of the way in which Canadian nationalism in the 1900s became a kind of secular religion in R. Harris, *Democracy in Kingston: A Social Movement in Urban Politics, 1965–1970* (Montreal: McGill-Queens University Press, 1988), 12–13.

11. To be found in Al. Purdy, ed., *The New Romans* (New York: St. Martin's, 1968), 65–68.

12. Ibid., 72–73.

13. "Waffle Manifesto, 1969," in the Ontario N.D.P. Papers, Queen's University Archives, Kingston, Ontario.

14. Ibid.

15. Ibid.

16. A. Smith, "American Culture and the English-Canadian Mind at the End of the Nineteenth Century," *Journal of Popular Culture* 4 (Spring 1974): 1050.

17. This is probably the most important theme in Canadian historiography and shapes every serious discussion of virtually any aspect of Canadian historical development. See C. Berger, *The Writing of Canadian History* (Toronto: University of Toronto Press, 1977).

18. It is noteworthy that the Waffle Manifesto owed much to a small group of history Ph.D. students at Queen's University in the late 1960s, including John Smart, Jim Laxer, and Lorne Brown.

19. See S. M. Lipset, "Canada and the United States: The Cultural Dimension," in C. F. Doran and J. H. Sigler, eds., *Canada and the United States: Enduring Friendship, Persistent Stress* (Englewood Cliffs: Prentice Hall, 1985), 109–160. See also, for example, in ibid., 130, the interesting table entitled "Robbery and Murder in the United States and Canada (per 100,000 population)."

	United States		*Canada*	
	Robbery	*Murder*	*Robbery*	*Murder*
1970	172.0	7.9	54.6	2.0
1974	209.0	9.8	75.5	2.4
1977	187.0	8.8	83.6	2.9
1981	251.0	9.8	108.6	2.5

20. N. Frye, *The Bush Garden* (Toronto: University of Toronto Press, 1971); and M. Atwood, *Survival* (Toronto: University of Toronto Press, 1972).

21. H. Hardin, *A Nation Unaware: The Canadian Economic Culture* (Vancouver: J. J. Douglas, 1974), 300.

22. See Lipset, "Canada and the United States," 141.

23. A. J. T. McLeod, "The Free Enterprise Dodo Is No Phoenix," in *The Canadian Forum*, August 1976.

24. Quoted in Lipset, "Canada and the United States," 140.

25. Quoted in G. A. Rawlyk, ed., *Revolution Rejected, 1775–1776* (Scarborough: McGill-Queens University Press, 1968), 9.

26. See S. M. Lipset, *The First New Nation: The United States in Historical and Comparative Perspective* (New York: W. W. Norton, 1963).

27. Public Archives of Nova Scotia, White Collection, Vol. VIII, No. 382, William Parker and Charles Whitwith, June 8, 1784. See also Neil MacKinnon's important revisionist study, *The Unfriendly Soil: The Loyalist Experience in Nova Scotia 1783–1791* (Montreal: McGill-Queens University Press, 1985).

28. Ann Condon, *The Envy of the American States: The Loyalist Dream for New Brunswick* (Fredericton: New Ireland Press, 1984).

29. See the concluding chapter of J. C. Potter, "Is This The Liberty We Seek? Loyalist Ideology in Colonial New York and Massachusetts" (Unpublished Ph.D. diss., Queen's University, 1977), 409–434. This chapter, unfortunately, was not included in her *The Liberty We Seek: Loyalist Ideology in Colonial New York and Massachusetts* (Cambridge, MA: Harvard University Press, 1983).

30. See, for example, O. Leonard, *Massachusettensis* (Boston: Rivington, 1775), Letter V, 42.

31. See C. Inglis, *A Charge delivered to the Clergy of Nova Scotia . . . June 1791* (Halifax, 1792), reprinted in G. A. Rawlyk, ed., *New Light Letters and Songs* (Hantsport, Nova Scotia: Lancelot, 1983), 307.

32. See the Charles Inglis and Jacob Bailey letter, April 3, 1799, in Public Archives of Nova Scotia (hereinafter P.A.N.S.), MG1, Vol. 93A. See also B. Cuthbertson, *The First Bishop: A Biography of Charles Inglis* (Halifax: Waegwoltic Press, 1987).

33. Inglis to Bailey, April 3, 1799, P.A.N.S., MG1, Vol. 93a.

34. R. Cartwright, *Letters From an American Loyalist* (n.p., 1810), 2. See also G. A. Rawlyk and J. Potter, "The Honourable Richard Cartwright," *Dictionary of Canadian Biography*, Vol. 4 (Toronto: University of Toronto Press, 1983), 167–172.

35. Quoted in W. S. MacNutt, "New England's Tory Neighbours," Colonial Society of Massachusetts *Transactions*, Vol. III (Boston, 1966), 347.

36. S. F. Wise, "The Annexation Movement and Its Effect on Canadian Opinion, 1837–67," in S. F. Wise and R. C. Brown, *Canada Views the United States* (Toronto: University of Toronto Press, 1967), 96.

37. See S. F. Wise, "God's Peculiar People," in W. L. Morton, ed., *The Shield of Achilles* (Toronto: McClelland and Stewart, 1968).

38. This is an important theme in W. Gribbin, *The Churches Militant: The War of 1812 and American Religion* (New Haven: Yale University Press, 1973).

39. Quoted in ibid., 20.

40. J. Errington, *The Lion, the Eagle, and Upper Canada: A Developing Colonial Ideology* (Montreal: McGill-Queens University Press, 1987), 13.

41. See Morton, *The Shield of Achilles*.

42. O. D. Skelton, *Life and Letters of Sir Wilfrid Laurier* (Toronto: Century, 1922), I, 97.

43. Ibid.

44. See D. C. Thomson, *Alexander Mackenzie Clear Grit* (Toronto: Macmillan of Canada, 1960), 248.

45. Ibid.

46. Ibid., 255.

47. D. Creighton, *A History of Canada* (Boston: Houghton Mifflin, 1958), 326.

48. J. S. Willison, *Sir Wilfrid Laurier and the Liberal Party* (Toronto: G. N. Morang, 1903), 255.

49. Quoted in Skelton, *Life and Letters of Sir Wilfrid Laurier*, I, 128–129.

50. Quoted in ibid., I, 137.

51. C. Lindsey, *Rome in Canada* (Toronto: Williamson, 1889), 272–293.

52. Willison, *Sir Wilfrid Laurier*, I, 33.

53. G. Baum, *Catholics and Canadian Socialism: Political Thought in the Thirties and Forties* (Toronto: J. Lorimer, 1980).

54. See my discussion of twentieth-century religious patterns in Canada in my *Wrapped Up in God: Canadian Revivals and Revivalists* (Burlington: Welch, 1989).

55. See R. W. Bibby, *Fragmented Gods: The Poverty and Potential of Religion in Canada* (Toronto: Irwin, 1987), 220. By contrast, compare the percentages for religious adherence in the United States.

Religious Affiliations of Americans: 1947–84 (%)

	1947	1957	1967	1976	1984
Roman Catholic	20	26	25	27	28
Protestant	69	66	67	61	57
Baptist	—	—	21	21	20
Methodist	—	—	14	11	9
Lutheran	—	—	7	7	7
Presbyterian	—	—	6	5	2
Episcopalian	—	—	3	3	3
Other	—	—	16	14	16
Jewish	5	3	3	2	2
Other	1	1	3	4	4
None	6	3	2	6	9

Note: Because of rounding off, some percentages do not equal 100.

56. H. Jacek, J. McDonough, R. Shimizu, P. Smith, "Social Articulation and Aggregation in Political Party Organizations in a Large Canadian City," *Canadian Journal of Political Science* 8 (June 1975): 288–289.

57. For an early explanation of this development, see S. F. Wise, "The Origins of anti-Americanism in Canada," in *Fourth Seminar on Canadian-American Relations* (Windsor: The Seminar, 1962), 297–306.

58. Quoted in L. H. Thomas, ed., *The Making of a Socialist: The Recollections of T. C. Douglas* (Edmonton: University of Alberta Press, 1982), 60–61.

59. See D. R. Elliott and I. Miller, *Bible Bill: A Biography of William Aberhert* (Edmonton: Reidmore Books, 1987), 320.

60. See T. H. McLeod and I. McLeod, *Tommy Douglas: The Road to Jerusalem* (Edmonton: Hartig, 1987).

61. See *The Globe and Mail*, Dec. 10, 1987, "Church, labour form coalition to fight P.C. economic policy."

62. Ibid.

63. Ibid.

64. Ibid.

65. See R. Murphy, R. Chodus, N. Aufder Maur, *Brian Mulroney: The Boy from Baie-Comeau* (Toronto: J. Lorimer, 1984), 32.

66. This generalization is based on a careful reading of all major political statements made, during federal elections, by the Conservatives, Liberals, and New Democrats in the 1963–1983 period.

See also L. B. Pearson, *Mike: The Memoirs of the Right Honourable Lester B. Pearson*, 3 vols, ed. J. A. Munro (Toronto: University of Toronto Press, 1972, 1973, 1975); J. F. Diefenbaker, *One Canada: Memoirs of the Right Honourable John G. Diefenbaker, The Crusading Years, 1895–1956*, 3 vols. (Toronto: Macmillan of Canada, 1975, 1976, 1977); George Radwanski, *Trudeau* (Toronto: Macmillan of Canada, 1978); R. Gwyn, *The Northern Magus* (Toronto: Paper Jacks, 1981); Jack Cahill, *John Turner: The Long Run* (Toronto: McClelland and Stewart, 1984); Rae Murphy, Robert Chodus, and Nick AufderMaur, *Brian Mulroney* (Toronto: J. Lorimer, 1984). The evidence suggests that Diefenbaker's successor as leader of the Conservatives, Robert Stanfield, carefully hid his religiosity from an indifferent electorate, that David Lewis, who succeeded Douglas as NDP leader, was a secular Jew and that Ed Broadbent is a lapsed Anglican and presently someone with no religious faith. Only a few Canadian fundamentalists seem to be concerned about Broadbent's lack of Christian commitment.

67. R. Bibby, *Fragmented Gods*, 108.

68. See Grant, *Lament for a Nation*, 12: "A nation does not remain a nation only because it has roots in the past. Memory is never enough to guarantee that a nation can articulate itself in the present. There must be a thrust of intention into the future."

THE MODERN PERIOD

12

Protestant Theological Tensions and Political Styles in the Progressive Period

ROBERT T. HANDY

I

The American Protestant world at the dawn of the twentieth century was much smaller and simpler than the one we study as the century draws near its close. The nation's population, just under seventy-six million, was less than a third of what it is now. Though church statistics are notoriously unreliable, the older, historic, familiar "denominational families" of Protestantism probably then totaled somewhere around sixteen million members. The differences among the major denominational groupings, ranging in overall size from some six million to half a million— Methodist, Baptist, Presbyterian, Lutheran, Disciples, Episcopal, Congregational, Reformed—were deep-rooted in history. Some of these groups traced their origins back to the sixteenth-century Reformation separation from Roman Catholicism, others to religious movements in the centuries since. Some had existed as free churches since their beginnings, others had to learn to carry on without direct governmental assistance when the state establishments of religion disappeared, the last one in the United States voted out in 1833. They all developed somewhat

distinctive ways of governing and propogating themselves. Denominational families were internally divided along sectional, national, and
racial lines. The examples are familiar, for there were Northern and
Southern branches of Methodist, Baptist, and Presbyterian churches;
there were varieties of German and Scandinavian Lutherans; there were
Dutch and German Reformed; there were a number of denominations of
Afro-Americans, some of them sizable, for the Federal Census of Religious Bodies of 1906 reported that the black Baptists collectively were
larger than either of the two major white Baptist conventions.[1]

Not only were there these obvious divisions of Protestantism into
denominational families, large and small, but there were also sharp
tensions within most of them, sometimes because of different ethnic and
racial stocks in a given body, sometimes because of theological disputes
between parties within various denominational traditions. Because of the
intense bitterness of the fundamentalist/modernist controversies of the
1920s, especially among Baptists and Presbyterians but certainly not only
there, it has been easy to look back at the first two decades of the century
through that focus and thus to distort our interpretations of those years,
to overlook the actual spectrum of theological parties by picturing an
oversimplified dichotomy. Looking back now, after more than half a
century in which there have been various attempts to get beyond the
clashes of the 1920s between fundamentalism and modernism and perceptive efforts to probe what led up to and followed from those encoun-
ters, we can now see that the parties that waved those banners tended to
be the extremes of the larger complex movements of conservative and
liberal Protestantism.

Those movements were diverse and shifting federations of persons and
groups both within and across denominational lines, and they changed
over time. In the period of American life that historians have often
labeled the "Progressive Era," approximately the first two decades of our
century, what came to be called fundamentalism and modernism were
deepening currents in a wider theological scene.[2] Most of the denominations that bore the Protestant label defined themselves as trinitarian and
evangelical and harbored a range of theological parties across a wide
spectrum. The shape and tone of such parties related to the wider history,
polity, confessional stance, and liturgical traditions of the denomination
of which they were a part. Certainly there were tensions and debates
between them as they faced the intellectual revolutions of their time and
sought to come to terms with the rapidly changing and dynamic environ-
ing culture. There were indeed many real differences, and age-old debates
were renewed in a time of rapid social change, debates over such matters

as nature and the supernatural, sacred and secular, immanence and transcendence, revelation and reason, Calvinist and Arminian, experience and tradition, nurture and revival, postmillennial and premillennial, science and religion.

As we look back, we can see that on the organizational level it was not particularly an opportune time for such discussions as they bore on immediate decisions on how a denomination was to fulfill its task. The pace of life was steadily increasing with telegraph and telephone, railroad and motorcar; population was mounting rapidly, largely as immigrants were arriving in unprecedented numbers, the majority from other than Protestant backgrounds; and the sprawl of vast urban areas was soon to mean the shift of balance of power to the cities from rural and small-town America where Protestants had made themselves so much at home. Historically divided Protestantism was facing at once unprecedented opportunities and increasing tensions in the progressive period.

There was, nevertheless, a strong sense of unity in the major Protestant churches of that period, especially among those that were steeped in the British Protestant tradition and/or were grounded in the Calvinist tradition. They had much in common that held in considerable check the centrifugal forces that had divided them and that still persisted as a continual threat. They were well aware of sectarian tendencies that, for example, had led to departures into Holiness and Pentecostal movements. The major sources of what gave a certain sense of unity and identifiability to the Protestantism they professed are important to note for a full understanding of religion in the progressive era. In the following analysis, particular attention is given to matters that may have relevance for understanding political leanings.

- These Protestants shared a common devotion to the Bible, very evident in their patterns of preaching, worship, and Sunday school education. Familiar biblical phrases and cadences informed the way they spoke and wrote. They could, and often did, disagree over ways of interpreting "the word of God," yet it continued to operate as the central written point of reference for Christian life in church and world.

- Their piety and theology was prevailingly Christocentric in orientation, for they believed that God was in Christ, that God was revealed in the person and work of Jesus Christ as Lord and Savior. When they articulated their Christocentrism in sermonic and theological discourse, differences of interpretation emerged among the various parties. Those attached to historic confessionalism or revivalistic pietism tended to express this in more traditional terms, while the Christocentric liberals, in affirming belief in the unique divinity of Jesus Christ, often endeavored to ground that divinity in the ontological being of God and were troubled when some of their number tended to move toward more naturalistic or humanistic positions, though that rarely became significant in the progressive period. As Hutchison explained, "Few, if any, Protestant liberals—modernistic or otherwise— denied normative status to Christ and to the Christian tradition."[3]

• They looked forward to the coming Kingdom of God, freely citing relevant biblical passages as they expounded this theme. While some dwelt on the eschatological aspects of the Kingdom's coming, others spoke more freely of the "building of the Kingdom" on earth, seeking a fuller following of God's will in human affairs. Szasz has noted that the "vagueness of the Kingdom ideal . . . allowed for varying interpretations."[4] But it was effective in encouraging leaders of congregations and denominations to work together as they appealed to their people in a time when, as Washington Gladden put it, the Kingdom was prominent among the ruling ideas of that age.[5]

• Protestantism in the progressive period was wholeheartedly behind the foreign missionary movement, then immensely popular and a principal cause for which the churches, with the help of various voluntary agencies, maintained extensive home bases, raised vast sums, and sent hundreds of missionaries abroad. Noting that by 1910 the Americans had surpassed the hitherto dominant British in the numbers sent out and in the financing of missions, in his recent *Errand to the World* Hutchison observed that Protestant leaders "spoke with remarkable unanimity across the theological spectrum. . . . Opposing forces could collaborate because the principal common enterprise, converting the world to Christ, seemed more compelling than any differences; but also because they shared a vision of the essential rightness of Western civilization and the near-inevitability of its triumph."[6]

• The progressive period was one in which concern for reform was widespread, though the scope and purpose of reforming measures were quite differently understood among those who advocated them. Within Protestantism, concern for social problems had increased noticeably in the last decade of the nineteenth century, in part because of the effects of the depression of 1893 and the impact of the populist movement, one of the predecessors of progressivism. In the progressive era, many Protestants across the religious spectrum spoke and acted on behalf of social reform. It is surprising to some of us to find that *in those years* persons we now remember as prominent fundamentalists contributed to reform efforts, such persons as Mark A. Matthews, William Bell Riley, and John Roach Straton.[7] The term "social gospel" has sometimes been expanded to include all those active in reform movements; it is more clarifying and reflective of the situation then, I believe, to use that term primarily for those reform-minded Protestants who were challenging the individualistic social ethic so dominant at the time and seeking to stress both social and individual salvation, though that balance was not easy to keep. It is also surprising for some to find that many persons now remembered as prominent theological liberals were *not* significantly involved in reform movements or in challenging the dominance of individualistic ethics.[8] They did not align themselves with the social Christian movement, even as broadly defined, while some of the conservative evangelicals at work in the slums did "produce extensive social programs and close identification with the needy," as Norris Magnuson's *Salvation in the Slums* makes very clear.[9] Though the tension between the social gospel, which in most cases was rooted in theological liberalism, and the other types of Christian reformers was real, the wider concern for social evils did serve to keep the discussion open and, in some cases, encourage cooperation.

• A major reforming thrust of the progressive years was even more clearly unitive, for most evangelical Protestants of various backgrounds and leanings supported the drive for prohibition. Again, we tend to look back at the prewar crusade for a constitutional amendment through our understandings of the 1920s, when prohibition had become a matter of law and order, and hence forget that it had been part of the larger temperance movement for social and humanitarian reform, had been a favorite cause of many leaders of the social gospel, and with one exception had enlisted the official support of all the denominations that had been permeated by the social gospel.[10] Thousands of congregations participated in the activities of the Anti-Saloon League, which claimed to be the political arm of the churches, "the church in action," though it operated as an independent single-issue group that was instrumental in securing the adoption of the Eighteenth Amendment in 1919. Prohibition was popular among Protestants in the South, and was one of the major links between Northern and Southern evangelicals.[11] In the 1920s the more negative, even repressive, side of the movement became more conspicuous, though its continuity in holding the loyalty of much of Protestantism was illustrated in that it was one of the factors at work in the defeat of Alfred E. Smith for president in 1928.

• A less dramatic but even more common force for unity among most Protestants was the support for public schools. Protestant backing for the public schools had developed out of the common school movement of the previous century. Few churches found either the will, the need, or the resources to develop their own network of primary and elementary schools; and as Protestantism entered the new century as a dominant cultural force in American life, its leaders believed they could safely entrust the educational task to the public schools. More than that: they believed that such institutions could contribute significantly to the molding of a more homogeneous people, socializing and Americanizing those from many immigrant backgrounds and providing them with a set of moral values. Early in the new century, as Robert W. Lynn has noted, came "the development of a new theme which up until now had been largely implicit in Protestant writings: the school is symbolic of both our national unity and God's handiwork in history. As such it was a sacred cause, worthy of religious devotion." [12] What Protestants were largely unable to see was that what for them was a "common" value system was to other eyes, especially those of Catholics, a specific one rooted in Protestant perspectives. Criticism of public education only heightened the devotion of Protestants of that period to it and strengthened its unitive force among them.

• In view of later developments within and against cooperative Christianity, it is not easy now to remember how far it reached across the Protestant spectrum when what became the Foreign Missions Conference of North America was founded in 1893, followed by the Interdenominational Conference of Woman's Boards of Foreign Missions three years later, and, in 1908, the Home Missions Council, the Council of Women for Home Missions, and, climactically, the Federal Council of Churches. The cooperative mission agencies represented many denominational boards, but the Federal Council was officially sponsored initially by thirty-three denominations. Among its members were many of the larger evangelical denominations, including those from both the North and the South, a major Lutheran synod, and two black Methodist communions. The movement thus reached across racial lines at a time the trend toward increased segregation was strong, and provided one of the few effective links between white and black evangelicals. As the Episcopal Address of 1904 of the African Methodist Episcopal Church put it, "The pronounced tendency to unity of spirit and cooperation in Christian work, and, indeed, to organic union, is hailed with delight." [13] The Federal Council had no authority over its members, but encouraged and provided channels for cooperation in evangelism, missions, education, and social service—the influence of social Christianity and of the social gospel was evident from the start. But so was its concern for missions as it allied itself with the cooperative mission agencies, and in the progressive period it succeeded in holding the loyalty of denominations whose memberships included vast groups—probably majorities in many cases—of those whose religious sympathies leaned toward the conservative side. In 1919 William Jennings Bryan, now remembered as a champion of fundamentalism, called the Federal Council "the greatest religious organization in our nation" and served on its commission on temperance. [14]

• The evangelical world was further linked by a spirit of patriotism. Though the churches were divided in their attitude toward what to do about Cuba after the sinking of the battleship *Maine* early in 1898, majority opinion settled in favor of intervention about the time that the Spanish-American War was declared. That struggle was short and precipitated an intense discussion about imperialism, but even most of those opposed to retaining the Philippines and other islands that were the fruits of victory accepted a distinction between imperialism and expansionism and were willing to support missionary work wherever it was possible. The new century opened with the spirit of patriotism at a high point, as illustrated, for example, when the General Conference of the Methodist Episcopal Church voted in 1900 permanently to display the American flag on its platform in order that "with our loyalty to the King eternal may be advanced our love of country and its institutions." [15] American entry into World War I on Good Friday, 1917, quickly brought a surge of patriotism to the fore again. Though much of the literature about the war has tended to overemphasize the jingoistic statements in which some Protestant voices indulged, John Piper's recent book on the churches and World War I make clear that there were other, more moderate statements. The most comprehensive Protestant agency to guide church war work was under the aegis of the Federal Council of Churches, which sought a middle ground between pacifists and militants. A statement prepared by the most representative group yet gathered by the Council pledged its support and allegiance to the nation "in unstinted measure," but insisted that "we owe it to our country to maintain intact and to transmit unimpaired to our descendants our heritage of freedom and democracy" and pledged "to be vigilant against every attempt to arouse the spirit of vengeance and unjust suspicion toward those of foreign birth or sympathies." [16] Though not all of the nearly eighteen million persons related to the Federal Council through their churches' membership—two-thirds of the total number of Protestants— abided by that pledge, it was an important leaven. The patriotism expressed did serve as a unifying force toward the end of the progressive period and even led to a limited degree of practical cooperation between Catholic and Protestant leaders.

• The latter was a somewhat new development because anti-Catholicism had long been one of the defining characteristics of Protestantism, evident across its divisions and tensions. The contentions between Catholics and Protestants went back to the bitter struggles of the Reformation of the sixteenth century and the religious wars and persecutions that followed. Many events across several centuries intensified the anti-Catholicism of English life. Catholics were a small and persecuted minority in the colonial period, and deep into American history were generally considered to be an alien element in an essentially Protestant nation. As their numbers dramatically increased during the course of the nineteenth century—the Roman Catholic had become the single largest church in America by mid-century—fear of the "Romanist peril" had important political consequences, as in the nativist Know-Nothing movement of the 1850s. As the patterns of European immigration brought in increasing numbers of Catholics—an estimated three million between 1870 and 1900, and two million more in the first decade of the new century—Protestant reactions intensified. For example, the American Protective Association (APA) was founded in 1887 and the more moderate National League for the Protection of American

Institutions (NLPAI), two years later.[17] The Catholic perception that the public schools reflected what to them was a "sectarian" Protestant ethos led to the determination in 1884 to extend the parochial school network to every parish where that was possible. This infuriated many Protestants and others who were committed to public education; the result was the blockage of public funds for private educational institutions.[18] Catholics were frequently labeled un-American, and it was said they opposed the tradition of religious freedom. Such statements as that of the titular head of American Catholicism, James Cardinal Gibbons, that "American Catholics rejoice in our separation of Church and State; and I can conceive of no combination of circumstances likely to arise which would make a union desirable either to Church or State," were dismissed as mere rhetoric.[19] Even a man of ecumenical spirit, Howard B. Grose, called by Martin E. Marty "the least anti-foreign and anti-Catholic among Protestant experts" in the church extension field, could argue for the conversion of Catholics because "the foundation principles of Protestant Americanism and Roman Catholicism are irreconcilable."[20] The awareness of what was conceived as a common enemy served as a unifying force among Protestants of many types.

The preceding analysis has endeavored to illustrate the point that to many Protestants leaders and followers the centripetal forces at work seemed to be winning out over the centrifugal ones. It is not intended to minimize the latter but to see them in perspective. Despite certain unitive trends within denominational families and a marked increase in federative movements, boundaries between denominational traditions remained quite clearly marked and various theological tensions remained unresolved.

For the reasons summarized above, however, the Protestant sense of a larger unity despite diversities does allow us to speak of Protestantism in the singular, if we do it with care. The view that in recognizable ways this many-sided movement did have distinguishable common characteristics helped it to enter the twentieth century in a mood of self-confidence, assurance, and glowing optimism. As noted evangelical layman William E. Dodge declared as he helped to prepare for the famous Ecumenical Conference in New York in 1900, "We are going into a century more full of hope, and promise, and opportunity than any period in the world's history."[21] Those present at that gathering could feel they were close to the centers of power as they were addressed by a past, present, and future president of the United States—Benjamin Harrison, William McKinley, and Theodore Roosevelt. Protestants shared in and in many ways contributed to the optimistic spirit that was widespread among the nation's opinion-makers. In 1901 another future president, then Professor Woodrow Wilson, wrote that "we have become confirmed in energy, in resourcefulness, in practical proficiency, in self-confidence."[22] One who lived through it all was later to write:

> The first fifteen years of the twentieth century may sometimes be remembered in America as the Age of Crusades. There were a superabundance of zeal, a sufficiency of good causes, unusual moral idealism, excessive confidence in mass movements and leaders with rare gifts of popular appeal. The people were ready to cry "God wills it" and set out for world peace, prohibition, the Progressive Party, the "New Freedom" or "the World for Christ in this Generation." The air was full of banners, and the trumpets called from every camp.[23]

The Protestantism of the progressive period not only reflected the crusading spirit of the wider culture, but was also a generator and intensifier of it.

II

Political progressivism is difficult to define, but it set the tone for both major parties in the early twentieth century, which was, as Henry F. May has aptly stated, "a time of sureness and unity, at least on the surface of American life."[24] Its roots were diverse as it drew on various reform movements, such as the populism of the 1890s, social scientism, and social Christianity. Those who have attempted to picture it often refer to the many strands it attempted to weave together. Walter Dean Burnham observed that "this movement is a remarkable mixture of contradictory elements: a striving for mass democracy on the one hand and corporatist-technocratic elitism on the other."[25] Dewey Grantham discussed "the paradoxical nature of progressivism: its vitality but its lack of focus; its materialistic emphases but its humanistic achievements; its romanticism but its realism; its particularistic purposes but its nationalistic values."[26]

As a political movement, progressivism was reformist rather than radically reconstructionist. On the one hand, it was a movement that attracted the idealists, the humanitarians, the municipal reformers, and the social Christians—Szasz reported that a 1906 survey discovered that only 15 percent of a large number of social crusaders were not somehow connected with the evangelical Protestantism of that time, and Robert Crunden has observed that though Catholics, Jews, and people of no religious affiliation found progressive goals attractive, "Protestantism provided the chief thrust and defined the perimeters of discourse."[27] In a study of the progressive intellectuals who were the conspicuous articulators of the movement's ideals, Jean Quandt observed that they used their skills in communication not only as agents of scientific reform and social harmony, but also as "the redemptive agents of the kingdom of God in America."[28] Many of those on that side of the progressivist spectrum, including a number of prominent social gospel leaders, wanted to use the powers of the democratic state for the public good, with particular attention to the underprivileged. On the other hand, moving away from interpretations of progressivism that stem primarily from the rhetoric of leaders of the movement and those who followed their lead, some historians of the last three decades who have focused on the actual practices of economic, political, and social groups have gathered a lot of evidence to emphasize another side of progressivism. In studying in considerable detail the realities of urban reform—one of the jewels in the progressive crown—Samuel P. Hayes, for example, found that "the leading business groups in each city and the professional men closely allied with them initiated and dominated municipal movements."[29] In a more sweeping interpretation, Gabriel Kolko declared:

> Because of their positive theory of the state, key business elements managed to define the basic form and content of the major federal legislation that was enacted. They provided direction to existing opinion for regulation, but in a number of crucial cases they were the first to initiate that sentiment. They were able to define such sentiment because, in the last analysis, the major political leaders of the Progressive Era—Roosevelt, Taft, and Wilson—were sufficiently conservative to respond to their initiatives.[30]

That progressivism was indeed a web of many strands can be deduced in that among its interpreters through the years some have emphasized its upper-class orientation, others its middle-class nature, and still others its appeal to the lower classes. Yet its accomplishments were considerable as, for example, it secured amendments for a federal income tax, the direct election of senators, prohibition, and woman suffrage; passed antitrust legislation and provided regulatory commissions in the areas of transportation and manufacturing; advanced the cause of conservation; and in many states instituted the direct primary, the initiative, and the referendum.

Clearly, there was conspicuous support for various progressive measures across the Protestant spectrum: one has only to mention the reforming role of certain social gospel leaders, the Social Creed of the Churches as adopted by the Federal Council of Churches, and the social

Christian stance of such a political figure as William Jennings Bryan. But adequate generalizations as to the way elements in the Protestant population actually functioned at the polls are not as readily framed as can be done for some earlier periods. Paul Kleppner, a prolific author in the field of voting behavior, has noted how difficult it is to do that whether one approaches the question from the side of politics or religion. He has said that "No political party has ever wholly conformed to retrospective descriptions of it. . . . Party activities and behaviors have always been sufficiently varied to elude simple descriptive generalizations."[31] He has also emphasized that analysis of voting must deal with the spectrum of ethnocultural values relating to famiy, religion, education, and community, which implies that it may be difficult to be precise about any one factor, such as religion, in the chain.

It is possible to make more satisfying generalizations about religion and political parties for the period before the political realignments of the 1890s, as we have seen in earlier chapters. In the later nineteenth century, the situation was such that the relation of religious allegiance to voting was somewhat clearer than it later became. In his probing book *The Winning of the Midwest: Social and Political Conflict, 1888–1896*, Richard J. Jensen went so far as to delcare that then "religion shaped the issues and the rhetoric of politics, and played the critical role in determining the party alignments of the voters." He identified two polar theological positions, the pietistic and the liturgical, which "expressed themselves through the Republican and Democratic parties, respectively."[32] He found these two positions in conflict in every denomination, though he had some trouble fitting both Presbyterians and Lutherans into his schema because of their divisions. The liturgically minded German Lutherans, for example, largely identified themselves with the Democrats, where they were political partners with their religious enemies, the Catholics, while the pietistically oriented ones often gravitated to the Republicans. Despite nuances, however, the evidence points to a fairly clear religiopolitical picture. Jensen's book deals with the Midwest, but in a more recent study of the national scene, Kleppner came to a similar conclusion for the late nineteenth century, observing that "as party behaviors began to evoke common meanings for activists, officeholders, and voters, *Democrat* came to represent the outlooks of antipietists, and *Republican* came to resonate emotionally with the dispositions of evangelical pietists." He quoted contemporaries who observed that "'Catholics . . . think one is not a Catholic if he is a Republican'; or, alternatively, when they pointed to the inconsistency involved in going 'to the Lord's table on Sunday and vot[ing] for Cleveland on Tuesday.'"[33]

The twentieth-century situation was quite different, however, for certain dramatic alterations in that familiar pattern came about in the 1890s. There were many reasons for the change; a major one was clearly economic. A Democratic administration under Grover Cleveland had the misfortune to be inducted in 1893 as a financial panic, followed by mounting unemployment and hard times, was developing. A careful, well-documented book on the political shift that climaxed in 1896 is appropriately titled *The Politics of Depression*. But religious factors were also involved in the political realignment that followed. They contributed not only to the Republican victory of 1896 but to a strengthened party that dominated the political scene for the first three decades of our century, except for the period when a party split allowed the Democrats to place Wilson in the White House for two terms. The story is complex, but a summary of several aspects of it is relevant here.

As some among the rapidly increasing numbers of Catholics were attracted to the Republicans, the party learned to accommodate to that reality. It was reported, for example, that there were some 70,000 Republican Catholics in New York State by 1894. Nationally, the eloquent Archbishop John Ireland of St. Paul was an ardent Republican who developed considerable influence in party affairs and was among those who absolved the party of anti-Catholic tendencies and deplored Catholic identification with the Democrats.[34] He accepted the concern for temperance that was strong in his chosen party, was a central figure in the Catholic Total Abstinence Union, and even helped to found the Anti-Saloon League.[35] Meanwhile, the party had been broadening its scope by resisting the more extreme, ultraist Prohibitionist interpretations of temperance in favor of more moderate stands. Jensen's case study of Iowa in the early 1890s suggested that the GOP there had to draw the line between "responsible temperance and control of the saloon on the one hand, and irresponsible, millenarian prohibition, with its secret dives and bootleggers on the other"; and, having moved toward the softer position, regained control of the state in 1893, thereby laying the groundwork for a critical plurality for McKinley three years later. Similar trends were taking place elsewhere in the Midwest and the North generally; the middle road proved to be politically viable. Ironically, Republican moderation came in part because pragmatic professional politicians were taking a larger role in party affairs, just as the American Anti-Saloon League was founded in 1895. The League eventually attained its goal of prohibition largely because it also relied on the professionals.[36] In the middle 1890s, Republicans were finding that they could repudiate connections with anti-Catholic organizations such as the American Protective Association without significantly losing the support of traditionally anti-Catholic Protestants—that is, they could advantageously take the middle road. A sign of the new stance was that they chose a rabbi to open their national convention in 1896, so as to avoid offending either their traditional Protestant supporters or their growing Catholic constituency.[37]

According to those who have studied the 1896 returns in depth, the Republicans under McKinley won decisively in what came to be called the urban-industrial heartland of the Northeast and Midwest, where they gained support among Catholics and confessional German Lutherans. The Democrats under Bryan retained strength in the South and West, gathered votes from some who had supported the Populist and Prohibition parties and some who had long espoused the moral integration of society. But he did not go over well among many old-line party regulars, who did not favor strong central government. As Kleppner put it, "Bryan's advocacy of an active and interventionist government, a posture articulated in evangelically toned rhetoric, repelled many of the party's normal ethnic and religious support groups." So, though Bryan did hold the support of many urban native-stock Protestant voters, there was little enthusiasm for him among many Catholics and German Lutherans. Thus, Kleppner can conclude, "As a consequence, at its social base, Bryan's Democratic party was more agrarian and evangelical than that party had been at any earlier point in the second half of the nineteenth century."[38] An important but very unfortunate result of the election was further steps in the disenfranchisement of Southern blacks to insure that the section remain solidly Democratic, thereby in effect nullifying the Fifteenth Amendment and civil rights legislation. Kleppner has concluded that "the demobilization that occurred in the post-1900 South was the largest, most extensive, and most enduring that this country has ever witnessed."[39] After the realignment, the basic political realities continued to go against the Democrats nationally as they lost the presidential prize in the next three elections, in two of which (1900, 1908) Bryan was again the nominee. The progressive movement became a powerful political force during the administration of a victorious party that was striving to be open religiously without offending its traditional Protestant supporters, which makes simple generalizations about its religious components somewhat suspect.

The problem of assessing Protestant political leanings in the progressive period is compounded by the way the separation of church and state has often been understood. Progressivism as an effective force in politics was over long before the flood of Supreme Court cases focused great attention on the religion clauses of the First Amendment, but in 1878 the Court had quoted Jefferson's 1802 interpretation of the establishment clause as "building a wall of separation between church and State."[40] Then, as now, many seemed to assume that this also inhibited political expression by churches and clergy, or at least it often made them hesitate to speak out on partisan matters, though less so on causes understood to be moral—in some cases very much less so. Some well-known preachers were reluctant to bring political matters to the pulpit, as was the famous Boston pastor of Trinity Church, Phillips Brooks, who remained an influential model long after his death. Though remembered as the leading prophet of the social gospel, Walter Rauschenbusch, in the book that made him famous in 1907, was stating prevailing opinion when he declared that the church appropriately cooperates with the state in implanting religious impulses toward righteousness and training moral convictions, "but if it should enter into politics and get funds from the public treasury or police support for its doctrine and ritual, it would inject a divisive and corrosive force into political life," so "the machinery of Church and State must be kept separate."[41] Though this was a time when the missionary crusade was high on the list of denominational agenda, and when missionaries often had visions of a new international order, James Reed has observed that both at home and abroad, with a few exceptions, they "generally cultivated indifference to the daily realities of power" and "tended to avoid explicitly political questions."[42] They seemed to mirror faithfully the predominant opinion of those who commissioned and sent them.

In part because of the defense of slavery that had explicitly or implicitly been accepted by many Southern white Christians, the patterns of excluding political matters from the pulpit in the South had become widespread, and only slowly was there a shift to such nonpartisan matters as supporting prohibition, upholding Sabbath laws, and opposing gambling. Szasz provides some illustrations of his generalization that "virtually every urban black minister of any standing took positions on such issues as prohibition, black teachers in public schools, and equal rights."[43] There were, of course, Protestant leaders who did engage directly in partisan politics; for example, Bishop Charles Fowler actively campaigned for fellow Methodist layman William McKinley as president in 1900, and the Reverend Alexander J. McKelway, a fiery editor who actively supported fellow Southern Presbyterian Woodrow Wilson for president in 1912, was able to get twenty out of twenty-three suggestions incorporated into the Democratic platform in 1916.[44] Such directly partisan activities by clergy seem to have been the exceptions rather than the rule.

As the progressive movement emerged with growing strength in the twentieth century and pressed for reform to deal with social problems resulting from the unregulated expansion of cities and their new industries, it became a political force that made its way through local and state levels to the national scene. When the ambitious Theodore Roosevelt moved into the presidency after the assassination of McKinley, he shrewdly held the support of business and financial interests while encouraging many progressive measures. At first under attack from Roman Catholics for some of his Philippine policies, he was concerned to listen to their opinions and deal fairly with them in appointments to various offices in the islands, working with the civil governor, William Howard Taft. Roosevelt did earn the respect of many Catholics, and then found the razor's edge a little uncomfortable as he was assailed by some Protestants as being too pro-Catholic. But in his victory at the polls in 1904, as Frank T. Reuter's researches disclosed, he won in places where there were "large concentrations of Catholic voters, areas that had supported Bryan in 1896 and 1900."[45] Now president in his own right by a sizable plurality, Roosevelt took it as a mandate for progressivism as he interpreted it, so that some historians date the "era" as beginning in 1905. From then until 1920, leading candidates on both sides waved a progressive banner. It was Taft versus Bryan in 1908, but as Taft backed away from Roosevelt's policies, the latter bolted the Republicans to form the Progressive party, a split that opened the door for Democrat Woodrow Wilson to carry his progressive banner to success in 1912. Christians oriented by differing approaches to social reform could therefore find reasons for supporting as progressive their major party of choice throughout the period. The mood of the country was indeed "progressive," and it was in that atmosphere that social Christianity flourished. One could be drawn either to its more conservative or liberal social gospel, or even to the more radical and reconstructionist socialist camps, and be in tune with the times; one could opt for working directly through a political party, through a denominational or interdenominational agency, or through a voluntary crusade for a given political objective and be relevant to the needs of the age as defined in a progressive era.

It was at the height of progressive enthusiasm and in his most programmatic book that Rauschenbusch made the controversial and oft-criticized claim that political life in America, along with the family, church, and education, had been Christianized, that is, had passed through constitutional changes that made it to some degree part of the organism through which the spirit of Christ can do its work in humanity. "To Americans this may seem a staggering assertion," he wrote in 1912, for of all corrupt things surely our politics is the corruptest. I confess to some misgivings in moving that this brother be received among the regenerate, but I plead on his behalf that he is a newly saved sinner. Politics has been on the thorny path of sanctification only about a century and a half, and the tattered clothes and questionable smells of the far country still cling to the prodigal.

His purpose was to emphasize that it was the fifth social institution of society that needed regeneration: business, "the seat and source of our present troubles." He sought to use the channels of government to help correct economic abuses, a familiar progressivist strategy. At the end of his long book, evidently sensing that it might seem to many to pay too little attention to religion and thus sag to the level of mere economic discussion, he insisted that the work's "sole concern is for the kingdom of God and the salvation of men. But the kingdom of God includes the economic life; for it means the progressive transformation of all human affairs by the thought and spirit of Christ."[46]

There were, however, those touched by the enthusiasm of the social gospel with its prevailingly liberal theological base who did focus much of their attention on social and economic matters; some took up careers in social work, labor organization, or politics, and some drifted away from the church. Reflecting on the previous three decades, a church historian in 1933 spoke of a type of theological modernism that "results from a shift of interest from all these things [rigorous thought, proved scientific facts, philosophical doctrines] as well as from the authorities and the conclusions of the older orthodoxy. Temperamental liberals find in the contemporary social situation both an opportunity and an incentive for a type of liberalism which represents a great deal of human sympathy but very little careful thinking."[47] Some others were drawn outside of the moderate reformism of the social gospel into the social reconstructionism of Christian socialism.[48] In his last book, conscious that the emphasis on social salvation had weaned some away from an emphasis on the personal, Rauschenbusch wrote a chapter entitled "The Social Gospel and Personal Salvation," in which he insisted that "the salvation of the individual is, of course, an essential part of salvation. Every new being is a new problem of salvation. . . . The burden of the individual is as heavy now as ever."[49] Though that was consistent with the tenor of his life and writings, there were representatives of the social gospel who let the critique of an individualist ethic so evident then in much church life, liberal and conservative, minimize their attention to the individual in their concern for the social.

By the time Rauschenbusch wrote his last book the cleavage within evangelical Protestantism, with its range of parties on both sides of the divide, was widening noticeably. Many conservatives who had been active in the wider movement of social Christianity were already pulling away from their concern with reformist thought and action, as George Marsden has indicated in his thorough *Fundamentalism and American Culture*. Among the proto-fundamentalists in the era before World War I, he explained, "progressive political sentiments were still common, even though conservatism prevailed," but he noted "the rather dramatic disappearance of this interest—or at least its severe curtailment—by the 1920s."[50] Reaction to the social gospel, its liberal premises, and its attachment to an American culture that was very optimistic and self-confident was among the reasons conservatism pulled back, so that eventually the centripetal forces at work in Protestantism were weakened because of developments on both sides of the widening cleavage.

At first, American entry into World War I seemed to reinforce some of the motifs of the progressive period. The crusading spirit was renewed as a "Great Crusade" in support of "the war to make the world safe for democracy" was launched. A new surge of patriotism swept across the land, at times with a backlash that left some bitter tastes later. Some progressive hopes came to fulfillment in transportation, child labor, and conservation, and the prohibition and woman suffrage amendments were passed. Both Catholic and Protestant churches worked in voluntary cooperation with governmental agencies as they carried out religious and social ministries for soldiers and certain groups of civilians. But progressivism was a web of many strands, and in an article that summarized the evidence, Arthur S. Link concluded that under the impact of the stresses of the war, "the Wilsonian coalition gradually disintegrated from 1917 to 1920 and disappeared entirely during the campaign of 1920."[51] But though the movement evaporated as moods of disillusionment dampened earlier idealistic hopes, much that progressivism had accomplished was not swept away, such as the beginnings of zoning, planning, and social insurance movements; the maturing of factory legislation; and the laying of foundations for the development of hydroelectric power. Some of the weaknesses of the movement lived on after it: immigration restriction was motivated in part by racism, nativism, and anti-Semitism. But certain of its ideas and ideals were carried into the new political era of the 1930s, to contribute to another period of reform.

The last stage of the progressive period, 1917–20, however, was marked by a hardening of the theological tensions that had been growing in Protestant life. Probing the "logic of modernism" during and just after the war, Hutchison concludes that one result among some of its thoughtful representatives "was an increasing sense that the progressivist component of modernism, its reverently hopeful interpretation of the immanence of God in culture, had become deeply problematic." But that shift did not seem to extend to the characteristic liberal postmillennialism, while during the war period, fear of the demise of Christian civilization itself led many conservatives to accentuate their premillennialist views emphatically as a key to understanding God's will for the nation.[52] The progressive period had been one in which the centripetal forces in Protestantism seemed to be winning over divisive centrifugal pressures, but as the era ended in the aftermath of war the latter were becoming resurgent. The social Christian movements had largely opted for a liberal political cast, while various groups that were just gathering around the then new term "fundamentalist," though politics were not high on their agendas, were drawn more and more to conservative positions. The changing alignments that can be discerned as the progressive period drew to its close continued to be of significance in the political turmoil of the 1920s and 1930s.

Notes

1. Estimates based on the work by Edwin Scott Gaustad, *Historical Atlas of Religion in America*, rev. ed. (New York: Harper & Row, 1976), Part II, and on summaries of the Federal Census of Religious Bodies in C. Luther Fry, *The U. S. Looks at its Churches* (New York: Institute of Social and Religious Research, 1930), appendix, esp. 141.

2. Indispensable works for understanding these movements are: Kenneth Cauthen, *The Impact of American Religious Liberalism*, 2nd ed. (Washington: University Press of America, 1983); William R. Hutchison, *The Modernist Impulse in American Protestantism* (Cambridge: Harvard University Press, 1976); George M. Marsden, *Fundamentalism and American Culture: The Shaping of Twentieth-Century Evangelicalism, 1870–1925* (New York: Oxford University Press, 1980); C. Allyn Russell, *Voices of American Fundamentalism* (Philadelphia: Westminster 1976); Ferenc M. Szasz, *The Divided Mind of Protestant America, 1880–1930* (University, AL: University of Alabama Press, 1982).

3. Hutchison, *Modernist Impulse*, 8. See also H. Shelton Smith's chapter, "The Christocentric Liberal Tradition," in Smith, Robert Handy, and Lefferts Loetscher, *American Christianity: An Historical Interpretation with Representative Documents* (New York: Scribner's, 1963), II, 255–308.

4. Szasz, *Divided Mind*, 44.

5. Washington Gladden, *Ruling Ideas of the Present Age* (Boston: Houghton, Mifflin, 1895).

6. William R. Hutchison, *Errand to the World: American Protestant Thought and Foreign Missions* (Chicago: University of Chicago Press, 1987), 95.

7. Russell has chapters on Straton and Riley in *Voices,* and an article entitled "Mark Allison Matthews: Seattle Fundamentalist and Civic Reformer," *Journal of Presbyterian History* 57 (1979): 446–466.

8. Hutchison, *Modernist Impulse,* 165. Though his work does not deal with the progressive period, Henry F. May's treatment of American social Christian movements in the late nineteenth century under the headings of conservative, progressive (social gospel), and radical social Christianity is relevant also to the twentieth: *Protestant Churches and Industrial America* (New York: Harper & Bros., 1949), esp. Part IV.

9. Norris Magnuson, *Salvation in the Slums: Evangelical Social Work, 1865–1920* (Metuchen, NJ: Scarecrow, 1977).

10. This point has been strongly made by Paul A. Carter, *The Decline and Revival of the Social Gospel: Social and Political Liberalism in American Protestant Churches, 1920–1940* (Ithaca: Cornell University Press, 1956), 2nd ed. (Hamden, CT: Archon, 1971), ch. III. The exception was the Episcopal church. See also K. Austin Kerr, *Organized for Prohibition: A New History of the Anti-Saloon League* (New Haven: Yale University Press, 1985).

11. John Lee Eighmy, "Religious Liberalism in the South During the Progressive Era," *Church History* 38 (1969): 363–365.

12. Robert W. Lynn, *Protestant Strategies in Education* (New York: Association Press, 1964), 30.

13. *Journal of the Twenty-second Quadrennial Session of the African Methodist Episcopal Church* (1904): 186–187.

14. Szasz, *Divided Mind,* 113, referring to Bryan's *Commoner* 19 (May 1919).

15. Journal of the General Conference of the Methodist Episcopal Church (1900): 186–187.

16. As quoted by John F. Piper, Jr., *The American Churches in World War I* (Athens, OH: Ohio University Press, 1985), 15–16.

17. Donald L. Kinzer, *An Episode in Anti-Catholicism: The American Protective Association* (Seattle: University of Washington Press, 1964), discussed the NLPAI in the course of his treatment of the APA.

18. The literature is vast; for an overall survey, see Lloyd P. Jorgenson, *The State and the Non-Public School, 1825–1925* (Columbia: University of Missouri Press, 1987).

19. Gibbons made this statement in an article in the *North American Review* in 1909, quoted by John Tracy Ellis, *Perspectives on American Catholicism* (Baltimore: Helicon, 1963), 5.

20. Martin E. Marty, *Modern American Religion,* Vol. I: *The Irony of It All, 1893–1919* (Chicago: University of Chicago Press, 1986), 155. The Grose quotation is from his *The Incoming Millions* (New York: Fleming H. Revell, 1906), 99.

21. *Ecumenical Missionary Conference in New York, 1900,* 2 vols. (New York: American Tract Society, 1900), I, 11.

22. "Democracy and Efficiency," as reprinted in part by Richard M. Abrams, ed., *The Issues of the Populist and Progressive Eras, 1892–1912* (New York: Harper & Row, 1969), 275.

23. Gaius Glenn Atkins, *Religion in Our Times* (New York: Round Table, 1932), 156.

24. Henry F. May, *The End of American Innocence: A Study of the First Years of our Own Time, 1912–1917* (New York: Knopf, 1963), 18.

25. Walter Dean Burnham, "The System of 1896," in Paul Kleppner et al., *The Evolution of American Electoral Systems* (Westport, CT: Greenwood, 1981), 166.

26. "The Progressive Era and the Reform Traditions," reprinted in part by David M. Kennedy, ed., *Progressivism: The Critical Issues* (Boston: Little, Brown, 1971), 118.

27. Szasz, *Divided Mind*, 43; Robert M. Crunden, *Ministers of Reform: The Progressives' Achievement in American Civilization, 1889–1920* (New York: Basic Books, 1982), ix–x.

28. Jean Quandt, *From the Small Town to the Great Community: The Social Thought of Progressive Intellectuals* (New Brunswick: Rutgers University Press, 1970), 75.

29. Samuel P. Hayes, "The Politics of Reform in Municipal Government in the Progressive Era," in Kennedy, *Progressivism*, 91.

30. Gabriel Kolko, *The Triumph of Conservatism* (Glencoe, IL: Free Press, 1963), 134.

31. Paul Kleppner, *Who Voted? The Dynamics of Electoral Turnouts, 1870–1980* (New York: Praeger, 1982), 76.

32. Richard J. Jensen, *The Winning of the Midwest: Social and Political Conflict, 1888–1896* (Chicago: University of Chicago Press, 1971), esp. chs. 3 and 7; the quotations are on 58; on the Lutherans see 67, 83.

33. Kleppner, *Who Voted?*, 45, 46.

34. Samuel T. McSeveney, *The Politics of Depression: Political Behavior in the Northeast, 1893–1896* (New York: Oxford University Press, 1972), 76, 105–106.

35. Robert D. Cross, *The Emergence of Liberal Catholicism* (Cambridge: Harvard University Press, 1958), 110, 128–129.

36. Jensen, *Winning of the Midwest*, 195–208, quoted words on 202.

37. McSeveney, *Politics of Depression*, 37–38, 85.

38. Kleppner, *Who Voted?*, 75. See also John L. Hammond, *The Politics of Benevolence: Revival Religion and American Voting Behavior* (Norwood, NJ: Ablex, 1979), 152–160.

39. Paul Kleppner, *Continuity and Change in Electoral Politics, 1893–1928* (New York: Greenwood, 1987), 165; see also his *Who Voted?*, 56, 65–66.

40. The letter is reprinted in John F. Wilson and Donald L. Drakeford, eds., *Church and State in American History: The Burden of Religious Pluralism*, 2nd ed. (Boston: Beacon, 1987), 78–80; the citation by the Supreme Court is from *Reynolds* v. *U.S.*, 98 U.S. 145 (1879).

41. Walter Rauschenbusch, *Christianity and the Social Crisis* (New York: Macmillan, 1907), 380.

42. James Reed, *The Missionary Mind and American East Asia Policy, 1911–1915* (Cambridge: Harvard University Press, 1983), 96.

43. Szasz, *Divided Mind.* 49.

44. Fowler's role is mentioned by Frederick A. Norwood, *The Story of American Methodism* (Nashville: Abingdon, 1974), 347; on McKelway, see Hugh C. Bailey, *Liberalism in the New South: Southern Social Reformers and the Progressive Movement* (Coral Gables: University of Miami Press, 1969), esp. ch. 10, "National Politics."

45. Frank T. Reuter, *Catholic Influence on American Colonial Policies, 1898–1904* (Austin: University of Texas Press, 1967), 135.

46. Walter Rauschenbusch, *Christianizing the Social Order* (New York: Macmillan, 1912), 148–149, 156, 458.

47. Winfred E. Garrison, *The March of Faith: The Story of Religion in America Since 1865* (New York: Harper & Bros., 1933), 267.

48. See my article, "Christianity and Socialism in America, 1900–1920," *Church History* 21, (1952): 39–54.

49. Walter Rauschenbusch, *A Theology for the Social Gospel* (New York: Macmillan, 1917), 944.

50. Marsden, *Fundamentalism and American Culture*, esp. chs. 10, 16, and 23; quotations on 207, 85. Also relevant is ch. 5 in Timothy P. Weber, *Living in the Shadow of the Second Coming: American Premillennialism, 1875–1925* (New York: Oxford University Press, 1979).

51. Arthur S. Link, "What Happened to the Progressive Movement in the 1920's?" *American Historical Review* 54 (1959): 839; also reprinted in Kennedy, *Progressivism*, 153.

52. Hutchison, *Modernist Impulse*, 226–256, quotation on 256; see also Marsden, *Fundamentalism and American Culture*, 141–153.

13

Roman Catholics and American Politics, 1900–1960: Altered Circumstances, Continuing Patterns

JAMES HENNESEY, S. J.

The chronological limits set for this essay take all the fun out of it. Well, not all, but a great deal. The "Americanism" controversy is over before we begin and, at the other end, John F. Kennedy has been elected but not inaugurated, while the Second Vatican Council is in a preparatory stage little similar to the actual event. Rehearsing the six decades that lie in between is not easy. And while I am committed to the proposition that examining those sixty years will provide some leverage on present concerns, I am not totally sanguine about the outcome of the exercise. The change in world, and even more in the church, has been so great since 1960 as to give even the most committed historian pause in the enterprise of illuminating the present by reference to the past. That is, nevertheless, the task.

"Politics." What do we mean? In his recent *Caesar's Coin: Religion and Politics in America*, Richard McBrien writes that "politics has to do with the public forum and with the process of decision making that occurs there."[1] I take that as my ballpark. Roman Catholics in the first sixty years of the twentieth century ran for public office and served in appointive posts at all levels of government. They were involved as commentators upon and occasionally as movers and shakers in some of the major public issues of the time.

Officeholding and public involvement came in two ways, corporate and individual. For Roman Catholics of the period, corporate involvement meant the Holy See—the pope and/or officials of his central administration—or it meant the involvement of American bishops. "The Church" in the latter case might be represented by an individual bishop or, from the 1920s on, in the peculiar style of collegial voice harbored in the National Catholic Welfare Conference. Individual priests, sisters, and brothers were likewise often perceived as "the Church." The extent to which they might fairly be said to represent the Catholic community was subject to interpretation. The same was true of lay Catholics. The first six decades of the century saw an enormous proliferation in the number of Roman Catholic officeholders on all levels of government. Sheer numbers had a certain sociological importance. The extent to which Roman Catholics running for or holding public office or commenting in a significant way on public affairs reflected well-informed Catholic theological, political, or social thought was something else again.

The century began for the country's approximately twelve million Roman Catholics amid the shambles of the intramural quarrel which Pope Leo XIII had brought to an end with a sentence in an 1899 encyclical letter: "We cannot approve the opinions which some comprise under the head of Americanism."[2] The pope immediately took pains in the letter *Testem Benevolentiae* to distinguish the religious Americanism he was proscribing from its political cousin, but at the very least his terminology was embarrassing to his American co-religionists, many of whom had already read enough of the widespread newspaper coverage of disagreements among their bishops.[3] At issue was the inclination of some American Catholic bishops, as William Halsey summarized it, to espouse "the activist individualism, self-confident mystique and optimistic idealism" prevalent in American society at the end of the century.[4] William Clebsch thought they were trying to "fit Catholicism into the live-and-let-live pluralism of the American denominations" and singing "the current songs of the middle-class denominations: progress, social reform and shared religious traditions."[5] But the "Americanists" were hardly liberal Protestants, as closer inspection of any of them—Ireland of St. Paul, Gibbons of Baltimore, Keane of the Catholic University, O'Connell of the

American College in Rome, and the rest—reveals. Thirty or more years ago, Robert Cross fixed it in our minds that the Americanists represented a liberal kind of Catholicism.[6] Others preferred the term "progressive." But easy categorization falls apart when confronted by the dynamic progressivism of a "conservative and reactionary" McQuaid of Rochester or the near-nativist obscurantism of "liberal" John Ireland's treatment of eastern-rite Catholics.

Be all that as it may, American Roman Catholics as the new century began faced on the East Coast the "banner immigrational decade" between the years 1900–10, in which nearly one-half of the total net immigration were people religiously Roman Catholic, the great majority of them southern Italians, Hungarians, or Slavs from the Austrian and Russian empires.[7] Across the Pacific and in the Caribbean, tens of thousands of fellow Catholics had come under the American flag, even if President McKinley did seem to think that some of his new empire had yet to hear the gospel.[8] The Americanist episode and its Roman condemnation was followed in Catholicism by a largely European "modernist" crisis that was put down far more severely than had been Americanism. Historical and speculative thought in Roman Catholic theological circles went into a half-century eclipse, particularly in the United States. American Roman Catholics had both the need and the opportunity to devote their energies to the social and political problems of the new century.

Writing in the 1840s of the church that he consigned to the *purgatorio* of "non-evangelical denominations," Robert Baird listed "three things that have occurred to arouse the American people in relation to Rome and her movements":

> 1. The simultaneous efforts which have been made of late by her hierarchy in many of the States to obtain a portion of the funds destined to the support of public schools, and employ them for the support of their own sectarian schools, in which neither the Sacred Scriptures, nor any portion of them, are read, but avowedly sectarian instruction is given. . . .
> 2. The efforts made by the hierarchy to bring all the property of the Roman Catholic Church . . . into the possession of the bishops.
> 3. The disposition, long well known, of some of the leaders of the great political parties, to court the Romanists for their vote at the elections, and the willingness of the hierarchy to be regarded as a "great power in the State," and as, in fact, holding the "balance of power."[9]

Schools, property titles, and politics had been constants in nineteenth-century squabbles, both within the Catholic body in the United States and in Catholics' relationships with the larger society and with the state.

Schools and politics remained factors in the twentieth century. In the mainstream American Catholic church, battles between bishops and civil trustees of church property were rare, but flare-ups among newer ethnic groups entering the country helped keep alive Catholicism's authoritarian image.

Conflict between Roman Catholics and other Americans over the kind of primary schools the nation should have goes back to the early nineteenth century, when Roman Catholics sought a share in the public funds being allocated, first, to openly denominational schools and, later, as the reform movement associated with the name of Horace Mann took hold, to schools that Catholics and others saw as Protestant Christian, but most Protestants saw as properly "nonsectarian."

The first school money disbursed in Chicago went in 1834 to schools located in Presbyterian and Baptist churches; only in 1910 were religious influences finally eliminated under pressure from an alliance at various times attracting support from Catholics, Jews, Unitarians, Universalists, and liberal Protestants, as well as atheists and agnostics.[10] In New York City, Bishop John Hughes in 1841 declared open war on the Public School Society. In cooperation with Whig boss Thurlow Weed, the bishop ran a competing slate in a legislative election that cost the Democrats seats in the New York Assembly. It is the only such example of direct political action by a Catholic bishop in our history. The Democrats felt the sting of the bishop's power, but he got no funds for his schools.[11] Disputes in Philadelphia during the spring and summer of 1844 over religious observances and exclusive classroom use of the King James version in the common schools led to rioting, church-burning and confrontations between armed Protestant and Catholic militia units.[12]

The phenomenon was not limited to the East and Midwest. In the newly minted state of California, a law passed in 1853 to allow funding of church-controlled schools was repealed in 1855 after Catholic Archbishop Alemany of San Francisco tried to take advantage of it.[13] On the opposite side, thanks to the efforts of Santa Fe Archbishop Lamy, most teachers in the public as well as in the parochial schools in the New Mexico Territory were in the mid-1870s Roman Catholic sisters, brothers, or priests, and almost all textbooks used in both private and public schools were printed by the Jesuits' Rio Grande Press. The Catholic monopoly was a factor delaying New Mexican statehood. The situation was not helped when Jesuit Donato Gasparri ("the carpetbagger from Naples," Territorial Secretary W. G. Ritch called him) sat on the Speaker's bench during legislative debate on a public education bill he had denounced as a "Cancer which corrodes and consumes the societies of the United States."[14]

The nineteenth-century Catholic house was not a monolith on the school question. The "progressionists" or "anti-absolutists," a band of liberal New York priests, had long opposed parochial schools and other church-sponsored institutions paralleling those of the state.[15] The intramural "schools controversy" of the early 1890s revolved around efforts somehow to integrate Catholic and public education.[16] But as the new century began, the Catholic church in the United States was officially committed to a policy of separate schools. Where government aid was available, as it was on Indian reservations after a United States Supreme Court decision in 1908, Catholic missionaries took it; but there was a general policy of suspicion that government control would follow financial aid.

In 1925 the Supreme Court struck down an Oregon law that would have created an educational monopoly for state schools for all children aged eight to sixteen. Religiously affiliated schools were among those that had their status secured. Public debate on another issue was already under way: the question of federal aid to education and the creation of a federal department of education. Cardinal Gibbons of Baltimore, the unofficial but acknowledged leader of the American hierarchy, was not disinclined to deal with "a few intelligent men in Washington" rather than with "so many petty, narrow officials of each state," but the bishops voted in 1919 to oppose any such scheme.[17] A 1922 release explained their opposition to the postwar growth of the federal bureaucracy, which they called "foreign to everything American . . . unconstitutional and undemocratic." "It means officialism," they declared, "red tape and prodigal waste of public money. It spells hordes of so-called experts and self-perpetuating cliques of politicians to regulate every detail of life. It would eventually sovietize our government."[18]

A bishop with a different vision was John Glennon, from 1903 to 1946 archbishop of St. Louis. He had taken a hard line, both with fellow bishops and in his diocese, in the matter of parochial primary and secondary schools, but tight money in the immediate postwar period made him cast about for new sources of funding. Arguing that education must provide moral training, "which must have a religious basis, background and sustenance," he called for tax assistance to Catholic schools such that it would "establish a reasonable equity between the sources and the disposal of taxes."[19] Glennon tried to raise national discussion of state aid to private schools, but it was an issue still two decades away.

The 1950s found America's Catholics embroiled on three interrelated fronts in the schools conflict. Cardinal O'Hara of Philadelphia, a former president of the University of Notre Dame and a bishop who placed great emphasis on diocesan schools, held firmly to the 1920s position of no government aid. Partly he based his opposition on "the waste of public funds that goes on in public school construction and operation," but his major fear was the control that would inevitably follow government financing.[20] O'Hara was, however, now a minority voice among the bishops. In June 1949, their official representative announced as a new major premise, in testimony before a congressional committee, that "every school to which parents may send their children in compliance with the compulsory education laws of the State is entitled to a fair share of the tax funds."[21] The Glennon view had prevailed.

Bitter controversy soon engulfed the issue. Rep. Graham Barden of North Carolina had filed a bill for federal aid that would be based on the total school population in a given state, but restricted in distribution to public schools. Cardinal Spellman of New York, declaring himself in favor of such aid "for needy States and needy children," vehemently protested exclusion of parochial school children from its benefit. Spellman's vitriolic rhetoric, strewn with references to "bigots" and "unhooded Klansmen," provoked an uproar that attracted attacks from other churches and involved him in an unseemly episode with Mrs. Eleanor Roosevelt, for which he had to apologize.[22] The waters were badly muddied just as the Supreme Court began to hand down the first in a series (at this writing forty years old and still running) of decisions interpreting and applying below the federal level the free-exercise and nonestablishment clauses of the First Amendment to the Federal Constitution.

Beginning with the Supreme Court's judgment in *Everson* v. *Board of Education* (1947), jurisprudence in this area has been a complex maze, and I shall not enter that maze. Nonetheless, what I wrote nearly a decade ago still seems to be true, that Roman Catholics generally read the Constitution

> as allowing some accommodation between church and state. Advocates of this view appeal to the historical origin of the nonestablishment clause of the First Amendment (designed to prevent a single national state church), to the same amendment's free exercise clause, and to the Fourteenth Amendment's equal protection clause. This approach adopts the philosophical principle of distributive justice. . . . Historically it accepts the thesis that in America church-state separation was conceived in cooperation and not, as in Europe in the aftermath of the French Revolution, in hostility.[23]

This is a position that, to sum it up in metaphor, does not accept that there is in the Constitution a necessary "wall" of separation between church and state, as that Jeffersonian phrase has been used after its reintroduction in *Everson*.

Catholic schools and their claims on the state were one perduring "Baird" issue. Direct involvement in partisan politics on the part of the hierarchy was another, but there the evidence has been much less clear.

John Carroll, later the first Catholic bishop in the United States, accompanied the new nation's first diplomatic mission, sent by the Continental Congress in the spring of 1776 to Quebec. He did so for patriotic reasons, but with some reluctance because "I have observed that when the ministers of Religion leave the duties of their profession to take a busy part in political matters, they generally fall into contempt; & sometimes even bring discredit to the cause, in whose service they are engaged."[24] The theme is one repeated over and over and over again with other bishops. With few exceptions they react with near horror to the suggestion that they be involved in "politics." Open partisanship is what they mean.

It is easy in John Carroll's writings to trace his development from enlightened, historically conscious thinker to more cautious Burkean conservative. He also introduced a long tradition of what might be called "a word in your ear" political involvement. When in 1784 he learned that Roman authorities, without consulting the American clergy, were trying to negotiate church affairs with Congress through the agency of U.S. Commissioner in Paris Benjamin Franklin, he expressed satisfaction at Congress's rejection of the proposal, but added:

> Had I received timely information before Congress sent their answer, I flatter myself it would have been more satisfactory to us, than the one which was sent, tho' a good one. My Brother's triennium in Congress has just expired; and Mr. Fitzsimmons, the only Catholic member beside, had just resigned: these were unfortunate circumstances.[25]

His cousin, Charles Carroll of Carrollton, was president of the Maryland State Convention when John Carroll wrote him about a state law that forbade Roman Catholics to be guardians of Protestant children: "I make no doubt but you will be able to obtain a general repeal of this and all other laws and clauses of laws enacting any partial regards to one denomination to the prejudice of others."[26] On another occasion he announced opposition to a plan under which the state legislature would impose a compulsory church tax, to be paid to the denomination of one's choice. His opposition was not to the principle, but because

> from certain clauses in [the proposed law], and other circumstances, we, as well as the Presbyterians, Methodists, Quakers and Anabaptists are in-

duced to believe, that it is calculated to create a predominant and irresistible influence in favour of the Protestant Episcopal Church.[27]

The coming of the nineteenth-century immigrants brought a different tone. "Irishmen fresh from the bogs of Ireland," a Boston Yankee politician complained, "are led up to vote like dumb brutes."[28] The Irish learned to play machine politics and did it with considerable skill. Occasional bishops like John Hughes indulged openly. But the basic tradition remained that of a quiet word to the political leader when it seemed needed.

There were exceptions. On November 25, 1894, Bishop Bernard McQuaid of Rochester mounted the pulpit of his cathedral. He first announced his own position on bishops in politics. For twenty-seven years he had not even voted in public elections, "out of anxiety not to put it in any man's power to say that I had voted for one party or the other." "It has been traditional in the Church of the United States," he continued, "for Bishops to hold aloof from politics." But the burden of his pronouncement that day was to pillory Archbishop John Ireland of St. Paul for violating that taboo. Ireland, an unabashed Republican party activist, had openly campaigned in New York State against McQuaid's candidacy for legislative election to the Board of Regents of the University of the State of New York. McQuaid noted the uniqueness of Ireland's activity and declared his unequivocal opposition:

> I want it understood that it is the policy of the Catholic Church in this country that her bishops and priests should take no active part in political campaigns and contests; that what bishops can do with impunity in political matters priests can also do; that neither have any right to become tools or agents of any political party; that, when they do so, they descend from their high dignity, lay themselves open to censure and bitter remarks from those whom they oppose, remarks which recoil on the sacred office which they hold and expose themselves and [their] office to the vituperation so common in electioneering times.[29]

No doubt, the distinction of what was "political" and what was not was at times more in the mind of the cleric than it was in the logic of the facts, but careful students have noted the generally ambivalent relationships that existed between prominent Catholic prelates and predominantly Catholic city machines. R. Laurence Moore has confidently declared that "What bothered Ireland about his New York colleagues . . . was their comfortable acquiescence in the marriage of many Irish Catholics with the very American institution of Tammany Hall." The archbishop's misgivings, Moore thinks, "reflected his staunch ties to the Republican Party."[30] Perhaps, but more detailed study is needed on when and why Archbishop's House on Madison Avenue became known in New York political circles as "The Powerhouse"—and on when and why it lost that sobriquet.

Case studies abound. In San Francisco, Peter Yorke was a priest and the crusading editor of the diocesan newspaper *The Monitor*. His initial focus was on the influence in local politics of the openly anti-Catholic American Protective Association (APA). In 1896 he helped end the senatorial aspirations of John D. Spreckels on the score of the latter's association with the APA. By 1898 Yorke's field of fire was broader as he attacked Catholic political figures on issues unrelated to religion. One of them was San Francisco Mayor James D. Phelan, who at his death would bequeath ten million dollars to Catholic institutions. But through it all, Archbishop Patrick Riordan serenely proclaimed that, while the clergy were free to make their political views known, "the Catholic Church never dictated a political policy to its clergy and laity." Yorke himself, Riordan biographer James Gaffey states, "genuinely believed that he had never violated the sane tradition that Catholic priests must not interfere in politics." "He belonged," Gaffey explains, "to no political party, viewing Democrats and Republicans, Socialists and Populists, with what was termed 'benevolent neutrality.'"[31] Would-be senator Spreckels and senator-to-be Phelan might have entertained other views.

Many currents that disturbed the West Coast scene flowed also in the East. John Webb Pratt's analysis of the New York State constitutional convention of 1894 is instructive, showing as it does how Archbishop Corrigan of New York, working through lay representatives, accepted a "sectarian amendment" to the state constitution prohibiting public aid to church-related charitable institutions.[32]

The Boston scene had its own dynamics. Cardinal William O'Connell, archbishop from 1907 to 1944, preferred the company of Yankee politicians to that of Irish Catholics, from whom he kept "a studied distance." Asked once for support by James Michael Curley, his reply was negative, because "our religion has nothing to do with it."[33]

Massachusetts had its own battle over a "sectarian amendment" to its constitution in 1917. A difference was that the amendment was supported by two prominent Roman Catholics, the later Speaker of the U.S. House of Representatives, John W. McCormack, and Boston political boss Martin Lomasney, known as "the Mahatma of the West End." Their constitutional amendment struck not only at schools, but at nonpublic institutions of any type. O'Connell declared the proposal a "gratuitous insult" to Catholics; Lomasney's reply was: "Tell His Eminence to mind his own business."[34]

O'Connell lost the 1917 fight. He was not fazed and soon took on bigger fish. Montana Democratic Senator Thomas J. Walsh sponsored in 1924 a child labor amendment to the Constitution. Monsignor John A. Ryan of the Catholic University of America had assisted in drafting the document. For Cardinal O'Connell it was but another example of "overblown government" interference, this time with parental rights. It was, besides, "nefarious and bolshevik."[35] Thirty years later similar arguments served Cardinal O'Hara of Philadelphia arguing against federal aid to education.

Catholic Governor David I. Walsh brought woman suffrage to a vote in Massachusetts in 1915, and there was a vigorous women's Catholic movement there in its favor. O'Connell and the clergy stayed out of the argument, but opponents of adoption on the state level included Katherine Conway, editor of the archdiocesan newspaper *The Pilot* and antisocialist crusader Martha Moore Avery, who feared votes for women to be another manifestation of the "red menace" threatening America. The woman suffrage amendment to the Federal Constitution was ratified in 1920. It had drawn opposition from such different Catholics as Cardinal Gibbons of Baltimore and radical labor agitator "Mother" Mary Harris Jones, each playing on some variation of the theme that woman's place was in the home.[36]

Mary Jo Weaver has identified Lucy Burns as "the only Catholic woman in the radical wing of the suffragist campaign," bringing "a fierceness and resolution to the American woman suffrage movement that was rarely equalled." She "organized parades, took trainloads of women to campaign against Wilson in western states, gave speeches, lobbied, educated other women, and published a newspaper."[37] Weaver neglects to mention the many women in Massachusetts' "Margaret Brent League" and the suffragist record of Archbishop Austin Dowling of St. Paul. Most of his peers opposed or were doubtful about suffrage for women, but there is no evidence for Weaver's statement that "The official Catholic position toward suffrage was negative." There was no "official" position.

Friendly persuasion of public officials to carry out Catholic purposes continued into the 1920s. A *New York Times* headline proclaimed in 1921: "Birth Control Raid Made by Police on Archbishop's Orders." The target was the first American Birth Control Conference; the archbishop at whose instances the New York Police Department shut it down was Patrick J. Hayes, who voiced the extraordinary judgment that, while taking human life "after its inception is a horrible crime, to prevent human life that the Creator is about to bring into being, is satanic."[38] More politic, but as determined to work his will in the public forum, was George W. Mundelein, who arrived from Brooklyn to be archbishop of Chicago in 1915, and stayed until his death in 1939. He passed orders in 1917 to the Speaker of the Illinois House of Representatives to "bury" bills unfavorable to Catholic orphanages, and when ultimately that tactic failed, he took the matter up with Chicago's mayor and the governor of the state. Discovering Roman Catholics to be underrepresented on the Chicago Board of Education (they held five of twenty-one seats), he sent Mayor William Hale Thompson the names of two Catholics for appointment, noting that he had selected them "with a great deal of care."[39] That was in 1917, soon after Mundelein's arrival. His political influence grew with the years and was even symbolized by the license plate on his car: it read "Illinois 1."

The approach in Pennsylvania was more sophisticated. In a move that foreshadowed the lobbyists, who in modern days represent Catholic church concerns in state capitals across the country, Philadelphia Archbishop Dennis Dougherty in late 1918 agreed with Bishop McDevitt of Harrisburg that it was time for the Pennsylvania dioceses to hire a lawyer to watch over their interests in the state legislature. For over thirty years Dougherty dominated the Pennsylvania scene. A biographer summed up his public involvement this way:

> He would move quickly but astutely into the political arena when the welfare of the Church was concerned, and personally followed all legislation involving the welfare of the Church or its institutions. In the best sense he knew how to work behind the scenes, avoiding publicity unless it was necessary as a final measure to procure his goal or alert his subjects.[40]

Finally, there was Cardinal Richard Cushing, archbishop of Boston. He succeeded O'Connell in 1944 and retired in 1970. Cushing reveled in the company of politicians and entered into their world. He gave and demanded favors. When in 1962 the Kennedys' effort to ransom prisoners taken in Cuba in the Bay of Pigs fiasco was foundering, it was the archbishop who raised, by borrowing, the needed million dollars. And when the bishops' national education department sought his help during another round in the never-ending battle over aid to church-related schools, he wrote: "'Holler' if I can do anything more. These men [Congressman Thomas P. O'Neill, Jr., and Senator John F. Kennedy] should be standing by ready to serve me. . . . I have done enough for both of them."[41] In Cushing's world, church and state were co-operators.

He disclaimed any right to tell people for whom to vote, but "religious people must be interested in the application of moral and ethical principles to public policy."[42]

In theory this was hardly different from the thought of William O'Connell. What was different was the close relations between Cushing and political leaders and the unabashed way he organized the Catholic forces for political combat. The 1948 campaign against liberalization of Massachusetts' laws on contraception was an example, complete with voter-registration drive, reminders of the citizen's moral obligation to vote, use of an advertising agency to orchestrate radio and newspaper coverage, billboards, flyers and pamphlets, distribution to parish priests of sample sermons, and organization of cadres of responsible adults in each parish to hand out "Vote No" literature near the polling places. The campaign was successful; a new style of active political involvement was born.[43]

Cushing's approach is startlingly like approaches growing out of post–Vatican II "political theology," with its collapse of the dualities that separated and stratified church and world, secular and sacred, clergy and laity. But, in fact, his style owed much to his native environment as a child of "Southie," South Boston, where politics is as natural as air. The substance of his approach was heavily influenced by longtime aide John J. Wright, himself later a cardinal in Rome. Wright's doctoral dissertation was entitled "National Patriotism in Papal Teaching." His ideas reflected those popular in the time of Pius XI, pope from 1922 to 1939, when identification of the Kingdom of God with the Roman Catholic Church was very close. Wright urged on Catholics the obligation to establish the Kingdom in their homelands ("fatherlands," he called them). Direct and open involvement of the clergy in the political process was not taboo. In Cushing's Boston it was very real.[44]

World War I was a great turning point in the relationship between American Roman Catholics and their compatriots. The 1920s would be a decade of sharp contrasts. On the domestic front anti-Catholicism flared in the activities of the Ku Klux Klan and in many of the less savory attacks on the candidacy of New York Governor Alfred E. Smith, first for the vice-presidency and then for the presidency of the United States. There were also the thoughtful probings of people like Episcopalian attorney Charles G. Marshall, who wondered in print how a conscientious Roman Catholic could reconcile American understanding of church-state relations with the view of Pope Leo XIII in his 1885 encyclical letter, *Immortale Dei*. Al Smith's spontaneous and plaintive "Will somebody please tell me what in hell an encyclical is?" spoke volumes.[45] Historians of religion point to the truism that a religious tradition is passed on through many channels. There is the channel of the theologians, with their precisions and philosophizing; that of the community's public worship, with its delicately nuanced multiple ways of conveying meaning; that of official documents and canonical niceties; and there is the channel of the *sensus fidelium*, in this case the instinctive sense of people in the Catholic tradition of who they are and why they are that way. The channels are generally parallel, but they are complementary, not wholly identical. A learned man like Charles Marshall knew about Leo XIII's medieval views on the relationship of church and state. American Catholics in the main did not, although they had been repeated by John A. Ryan and Moorhouse Millar in a 1922 book. Their impact on the thinking of American Catholics was slight, as Smith's reaction suggested, but Marshall and others could hardly be expected to sense that, especially when they put it together with more pedestrian examples of church-state "unionist" thought.

An aspect of 1920s' Catholicism highlighted in William Halsey's *The Survival of American Innocence* was its rather confident return from the exile into which conflict with the nineteenth-century world of science, progress, prosperity, and the liberal faith had plunged it. Catholics in the United States found "a new sense of identity, an enthusiasm for ideals, and a rather disconcerting confidence in their beliefs."[46] The approach contrasted with the depression that settled in among heretofore dominant religious groups. It found support in the powerful style of Pius XI, pope from 1922 to 1939. Disdainful of the League of Nations and of the Versailles Treaty, he sought "the peace of Christ in the kingdom of Christ." His world was the church; he was Christ's vicar. Theologically the church was seen as the kingdom; under his successors other metaphors would take pride of place: the Body of Christ, later the People of God.

Pius XI thought in terms of spiritual conquest. He planned to win Russia from both Bolsheviks and Orthodoxy; he established a mission to convert Islam. He shunned ecumenical cooperation, since to participate would admit the presumption that the Church of Christ was not already existent and identical with the Roman Catholic Church. Some thought him in the pocket of the Western totalitarians. He was no doubt an autocrat, but Owen Chadwick is also right to see in him "one of the world leaders in the fight against Nazism and Fascism."[47] Important for his impact on American Catholics was the sense he communicated of their church as a proud isolationist world of its own, outside of and superior to other worlds.

The new Catholic spirit found expression philosophically and in literature, in an American version of what German theologian Karl Rahner called the "Pian Monolith."[48] It corresponded with the growing "arrival" of lay Catholics in business and government circles, a development accelerated during the presidencies of Franklin D. Roosevelt. Catholic social doctrine enunciated in Leo XIII's 1891 letter, *Rerum Novarum*, and in Pius XI's 1931 reprise, *Quadragesimo Anno*, found American expression in the 1919 Bishops' Program of Social Reconstruction and in the activities of its author, the "Right Reverend New Dealer," John A. Ryan, and others like him.

How influential Ryan was on the New Deal thinkers, or on the president, is debatable, but the labor movement produced a number of national figures knowledgeable in papal social teachings, while in many cities Catholic labor schools combatted communist influence as well as union corruption. FDR courted bishops. He would have liked a favorite, Bernard J. Sheil of Chicago, as archbishop in Washington, and he found Cardinal Mundelein of Chicago sympathetic. But the most public of the bishops was Francis J. Spellman, archbishop of New York from 1939 until his death in 1967. His position as the Catholic church's supervisor of military chaplains and his closeness to Pius XII, pope from 1939 to 1958, founded his influence. He personified the old clerical culture that was dying even as he lived out his final years.[49]

Radicalism growing out of the immigrant segment of American Catholicism was not unknown before the 1960s, but the vast mass of American Catholics has been socially and politically conservative. Until recent years that did not translate into membership in the Republican party, although Catholic Republicans were not unknown. John Ireland was perhaps the most prominent. Francis C. Kelley, a priest and founder of the Catholic Church Extension Society, was another. A sometimes violent opponent of Woodrow Wilson's Mexican policy, he provoked Secretary of State William Jennings Bryan to the outburst: "When our side of the Mexican story is told, there are some Catholic Republicans who are going to feel very uncomfortable."[50] Political reasons operated: Rhode Island Franco-American Catholics voted Republican because they could not get a look-in with the Irish-controlled Democrats. Sometimes the motivation was economic. My own immigrant grandfather, who had done well as a cotton trader, told his children he voted for the Republicans because he "didn't want the cheap foreign goods following him in." On my mother's side, we were Democrats, in the style of Mayor Frank Hague's Jersey City, surely one of the more conservative baronies in the Roosevelt coalition.

Social historians can probe the American (and European peasant) roots of American Catholic conservatism. It was mightily encouraged by the authoritarian cast that developed in Roman Catholicism during the nineteenth century and the first half of the twentieth. To be sure, not until 1950, and then only in the single matter of the Assumption of Mary, did a pope exercise the infallibility defined in 1870 by the First Vatican Council. An aura of authority nonetheless settled over officeholders in the church. Scholarship was discounted. Donna Merwick summed up much of it when she described Archbishop William O'Connell of Boston as "authority's answer to intellectual curiosity." Michael Gannon has documented the "intellectual isolation of the American priest" early in the present century.[51] The situation was ready-made for simplistic single-issue demagoguery. Nineteenth-century Catholicism had known it in immensely influential editors like Louis Veuillot of *L'Univers* and, in the United States, James A. McMaster of the New York *Freeman's Journal*. In France and in America, no journals had greater circulation among Catholic clergy.

Twentieth-century counterparts were "Radio Priest" Charles E. Coughlin and, two decades later, Senator Joseph R. McCarthy. Neither can be dismissed as aberrations in the Catholic community. They spoke to deep-seated fears, prejudices, and insecurities and provided simplistic answers. Coughlin preached voodoo economics long before George Bush coined the term, supported an abortive third-party movement in the presidential campaign of 1936, degenerated into anti-Semitism, and was finally forced from the air by a combination of church and federal government pressure. During the long night of the Cold War, McCarthy's anticommunist rampage attracted widespread support from Catholics. Both he and Coughlin remain folk heroes in certain circles. An eleven-cassette set of Coughlin's talks is on sale, offering "Fr. Coughlin's predictions of the days to come."

The final decade before the Second Vatican Council opened in October 1962 saw American Catholic political reliability once again under fire. Paul Blanshard's 1949 *American Freedom and Catholic Power* covered, as Barbara Welter remarks, much the same territory as had Maria Monk's *Awful Disclosures* a century earlier. Catholic Americans were pilloried for their un-American servility to the "absolute rule of the clergy," and the parochial school system was denounced as divisive and undemocratic. "Protestants and Other Americans for Separation of Church and State" kept an eagle eye cocked for Catholic miscreancies.[52] President Harry S. Truman did not help matters with his nomination in 1951 of General Mark Clark as ambassador to the Holy See. The last

United States diplomat regularly accredited to the Holy See had left Rome in 1867; the time was not ripe for resuming diplomatic relations. Nor, beyond a small number of bishops, had the idea ever particularly appealed to American Catholics. Proposed in the early 1950s, it stirred a hornets' nest.[53]

Simultaneously, within the American Catholic community a debate was in progress, unnoticed save by scholars. Joseph Clifford Fenton, professor at the Catholic University in Washington, was vigorously engaged in defending then-standard Catholic positions on relationships between church and state, and on religious liberty, against the challenge of the Jesuit John Courtney Murray, professor at nearby Woodstock College in Maryland. Fenton argued that the ideal arrangement was one in which the state supported the church. Derogation from that ideal and equality of free exercise of religion might be tolerated in given circumstances, but only as the lesser of two evils. Murray argued that in the modern world the state's "care of religion" consisted in assuring the church's ability to operate. He grounded his assertion of the compatibility of Catholicism and American democracy in a natural-law analysis of individual human dignity and its consequences. His defense of the acceptability of separation of church and of religious liberty as a natural right led the way to the Second Vatican Council's declaration on religious liberty in 1965.[54]

Towards the end of the 1950s, in October 1958, Angelo Giuseppe Roncalli became pope. He took the name John XXIII. Under his leadership and that of his successor, Paul VI (1963–78), a radical shift took place in Roman Catholic thinking that materially affected the approach to the political world both of the official church and of Catholic people. A static and conceptual approach to reality yielded to one more biblically and historically conscious. Secular and sacred, church and world, clergy and laity became less contrasted, less stratified. The Council singled out as its primary metaphor for the church that of the People of God. The sense grew throughout the community that "we"—all of us—are the church. Canon lawyer Rose McDermott spelled out some consequences: a sense that "all the faithful enjoy a radical equality prior to any functional diversity . . . [and] share in the teaching, sanctifying and governing mission of the Church."[55]

The Council's constitution on the church in the modern world charted a new turning to direct concern by church members for the actual needs of the world and the people in it. Moving away from possessive attitudes like that of Pius XI, the document explicitly accepted "the autonomy of many areas of life" and urged Catholics to express their religious belief precisely in and through and by secular activity, penetrating the secular world with a Christian spirit. Involvement in culture, personal and family values, economics, trades, and professions were all seen as ways of participating in the church's mission and apostolate.

Marking in 1981 the eightieth anniversary of Pope Leo XIII's land- mark social encyclical letter, *Rerum Novarum*, Paul VI, in *Octogesima Adveniens*, departed from the deductive approach of his predecessor. He accepted the possibility of a plurality of solutions to problems, given the diversity of human situations and the reality of historical pluralism. The pope had grown up in an Italy where until World War I Catholics were forbidden by papal fiat to participate in the political life of their nation. "Ne eletti ne elettori" was the motto. They were not to stand for office or to vote. In *Octogesima* he wrote that politics represent a demanding way, although not the only way, of living a Christian commitment to others.

The sequel has been interesting. Presidential candidates and Supreme Court nominees are no longer questioned on their Catholic beliefs in the way that a Smith or Kennedy was questioned. But neither can they any longer fob off inquirers with inadequate simplicities on the plea of theological ignorance. Throughout most of our history, at least since Charles Carroll of Carrollton retired from active political life, few Catholic politicians have represented a well-informed Catholic point of view, however personally devout they may or may not have been. That is changing, and politicians have emerged who are not only conversant with contemporary philosophical and theological trends and with Catholic thought, but are unafraid to speak out of that background. The change has not been total. While some bishops produce thoughtful documents on contemporary problems, others remain lineal descendants of those depicted in these pages, and the same is true for lay men and women and sisters and priests. The actors have changed, and so have many of the lines; large bits of the play remain the same.

Notes

1. Richard P. McBrien, *Caesar's Coin: Religion and Politics in America* (New York: Macmillan, 1987), 20.

2. John Tracy Ellis, ed., *Documents of American Catholic History*, 3 vols. (Wilmington, DE: Michael Glazier, 1987), 2, 546.

3. James Hennesey, S.J., *American Catholics: A History of the Roman Catholic Community in the United States* (New York/Oxford: Oxford University Press, 1981), 196–203.

4. William Halsey, *The Survival of American Innocence: Catholicism in an*

Era of Disillusionment 1920–1940 (Notre Dame/London: Notre Dame University Press, 1980), 4.

5. William A. Clebsch, *American Religious Thought: A History* (Chicago: University of Chicago Press, 1973), 114.

6. Robert Cross, *The Emergence of Liberal Catholicism in America* (Cambridge: Harvard University Press, 1958).

7. Gerald Shaughnessy, S.M., *Has the Immigrant Kept the Faith?* (New York: Macmillan, 1925), 172.

8. Hennesey, *American Catholics*, 205.

9. Robert Baird, *Religion in America*, ed. Henry Warner Bowden (New York: Harper & Row, 1970), 261–262.

10. James W. Sanders, *The Education of an Urban Minority: Catholics in Chicago 1833–1965* (New York/Oxford: Oxford University Press, 1977), 20, 25.

11. Diane Ravitch, *The Great School Wars: New York City 1805–1973* (New York: Basic Books, 1974), 27–76.

12. Hugh J. Nolan, "Francis Patrick Kenrick, First Coadjutor Bishop," in James F. Connelly, ed., *The History of the Archdiocese of Philadelphia* (Philadelphia: The Archdiocese, 1976), 167–186; Michael Feldberg, *The Philadelphia Riots of 1844: A Study of Ethnic Conflict* (Westport, CT: Greenwood, 1975).

13. Louis B. Wright, *Culture on the Moving Frontier* (New York: Harper & Row, 1961), 141.

14. Howard Roberts Lamar, *The Far Southwest 1846–1912: A Territorial History* (New York: W. W. Norton, 1970), 167–169.

15. Robert Emmett Curran, S.J., "Prelude to 'Americanism': The New York Academia and Clerical Radicalism in the Late Nineteenth Century," *Church History* 47 (1978): 48–65.

16. Daniel F. Reilly, O.P., *The School Controversy 1891–1893* (Washington: Catholic University Press, 1943).

17. John Tracy Ellis, *The Life of James Cardinal Gibbons, Archbishop of Baltimore, 1834–1921*, 2 vols. (Milwaukee: Bruce, 1952), 2, 545.

18. John B. Sheerin, C.S.P., *Never Look Back: The Career and Concerns of John J. Burke* (New York: Paulist, 1975), 66.

19. Nicholas Schneider, *The Life of John Cardinal Glennon, Archbishop of St. Louis* (Liguori: Liguori, 1971), 62–63.

20. Thomas J. McAvoy, C.S.C., *Father O'Hara of Notre Dame, the Cardinal-Archbishop of Philadelphia* (Notre Dame/London: Notre Dame University Press, 1967), 401.

21. Hennesey, *American Catholics*, 297.

22. For a pro-Spellman view, see Robert I. Gannon, S.J., *The Cardinal Spellman Story* (Garden City: Doubleday, 1962), 312–322. See also John Tracy Ellis, *Catholic Bishops: A Memoir* (Wilmington: Michael Glazier, 1983), 93.

23. Hennesey, *American Catholics*, 298–299.

24. Thomas O'Brien Hanley, S.J., ed., *The John Carrol Papers*, 3 vols. (Notre Dame/London: Notre Dame University Press, 1976), 1, 46.

25. Ibid., 1, 152.

26. Ibid., 1, 82.

27. Ibid., 1, 168.

28. Carleton Beals, *Brass-Knuckle Crusade: The Great Know-Nothing Conspiracy 1820–1860* (New York: Hastings House, 1960), 99.

29. Frederick J. Zwierlein, *The Life and Letters of Bishop McQuaid*, 3 vols. (Rochester: Art Printing Shop, 1925–1927), 3, 207–210.

30. R. Laurence Moore, *Religious Outsiders and the Making of Americans* (New York/Oxford: Oxford University Press, 1986), 62. Essays in Robert E. Sullivan and James M. O'Toole, eds., *Catholic Boston: Studies in Religion and Community 1870–1970* (Boston: The Archdiocese, 1985), are helpful in assessing the relationship of Catholics and church officials to big-city Irish politics. See, particularly, James M. O'Toole, "Prelates and Politics: Catholics and Politics in Massachusetts 1900–1970," 15–65. Also illuminating are Susan S. Walton, "To Preserve the Faith: Catholic Charities in Boston 1870–1930," 67–119; and James W. Sanders, "Catholics and the School Question in Boston: The Cardinal O'Connell Years," 121–169.

31. James P. Gaffey, *Citizen of No Mean City: Archbishop Patrick Riordan of San Francisco (1841–1914)* (Wilmington: Consortium, 1976), 150–155, 162–175.

32. John Webb Pratt, *Religion, Politics, and Diversity: The Church-State Theme in New York History* (Ithaca, NY: Cornell University Press, 1967), 225–256.

33. O'Toole, "Prelates and Politics," 20.

34. Ibid., 25–27; 21.

35. Ibid., 27–31.

36. Hennesey, *American Catholics*, 232–233.

37. Mary Jo Weaver, *New Catholic Women: A Contemporary Challenge to Traditional Religious Authority* (San Francisco: Harper & Row, 1985), 18–20.

38. Hennesey, *American Catholics*, 327.

39. Sanders, *Education of an Urban Minority*, 128–130.

40. Hugh J. Nolan, "Native Son," in Connelly, *Archdiocese in Philadelphia*, 358.

41. O'Toole, "Prelates and Politics," 59–60.

42. Ibid., 46.

43. Ibid., 49–57.

44. Ibid., 48.

45. Hennesey, *American Catholics*, 246–247, 252–258.

46. Halsey, *Survival of American Innocence*, 8.

47. Anthony Rhodes, *The Vatican in the Age of the Dictators 1922–1945* (New York: Holt, Rinehart & Winston, 1973); Owen Chadwick, *Britain and the Vatican during the Second World War* (Cambridge: Cambridge University Press, 1986), 19.

48. Fergus Kerr, O.P., "Rahner Retrospective: Rupturing Der Pianische Monolithismus," *New Blackfriars*, 61 (1980): 226.

49. Gannon's biography, *The Cardinal Spellman Story*, is still the best available.

50. James P. Gaffey, *Francis Clement Kelley and the American Catholic Dream*, 2 vols. (Bensenville: The Heritage Foundation, 1980), 2, 20.

51. Donna Merwick, *Boston's Priests 1848–1910: A Study of Social and Intellectual Change* (Cambridge: Harvard University Press, 1973); Michael V. Gannon, "Before and after Modernism: The Intellectual Image of the American Priest," in John Tracy Ellis, ed., *The Catholic Priest in the United States: Historical Investigations* (Collegeville, MN: St. John's University, 1971), 293–383.

52. Barbara Welter, "From Maria Monk to Paul Blanchard: A Century of Protestant Anti-Catholicism," in Robert N. Bellah and Frederick E. Greenspan, eds., *Uncivil Religion: Interreligious Hostility in America* (New York: Crossroad, 1987), 43–71.

53. James Hennesey, S.J., "Papal Diplomacy and the Contemporary Church," *Thought* 46 (1971): 55–71; James A. Coriden, "Diplomatic Relations Between the United States and the Holy See," *Journal of International Law* 19 (1987): 361–373.

54. Donald E. Pelotte, S.S.S., *John Courtney Murray: Theologian in Conflict* (New York: Paulist, 1976); and, in a scholarly critique, Charles E. Curran, *American Catholic Social Ethics: Twentieth-Century Approaches* (Notre Dame/London: Notre Dame University Press, 1982), 171–232.

55. Rose McDermott, S.S.J., "Women in the New Code," *The Way Supplement* 50 (1984): 27–28.

14

The Twentieth Century:
Protestants and Others

MARTIN E. MARTY

Politics: What It Is in a Republic

What one has to say about religion and politics depends greatly on what one conceives politics to be. One hears about "political theology" in totalitarian, authoritarian, monarchic, and theocratic states, but the relation of religion to politics differs greatly in all such cases from the situation in a republic. Even the way one conceives a republic has much to do with how politics looks in relation to religion. The Federalists and Anti-Federalists, advocates of democracy and republicanism, and other partisans in American history had different definitions of the political order. Here it is necessary, then, to defend one ordering of politics as being an appropriate conception of the American Founders' intentions and the worked-out experience over two centuries.

Aristotle, in his *Politics*, set the context for a discussion of religion and American politics, politics within a constitutional republic. He accused Plato of trying to reduce everything in the *polis*, the human city, the political entity, to a unity. Aristotle refers to and then argues against Socrates:

The object which Socrates assumes as his premiss is . . . "that the greatest possible unity of the whole *polis* is the supreme good." Yet it is obvious that a *polis* which goes on and on, and becomes more and more of a unity, will eventually cease to be a *polis* at all. A *polis* by its nature is some sort of aggregation. If it becomes more of a unit, it will first become a household instead of a *polis*, and then an individual instead of a household. . . . It follows that, even if we could, we ought not to achieve this object: it would be the destruction of the *polis*.[1]

The American republic, whose motto is *E pluribus unum*, by analogy to the *plures* which were the colonies that became states, was and is made up also of other kinds of aggregates. Many familiar models come to mind. Johannes Althusius spoke of a *communitas communitatum*, made up of *symbiotes*, components of subcommunities that lived off each other, that lived together.[2] Edmund Burke used a hierarchical model which can be translated to an egalitarian one when he spoke of the "little platoons" that make up a society.[3] Constitution drafter James Madison, in *The Federalist*, No. 10, spoke of "factions" and "interests" and "sects" that make up "the scheme of representation" in a republic.[4] Justice Felix Frankfurter, even as he called for "the binding tie of cohesive sentiment" in a free society, spoke of "all those agencies of mind and spirit" that make it up.[5]

These aggregates, symbiotes, platoons, factions, or agencies that make up the American "scheme of representation" and do not permit the American *polis* to "go on and on" include Madison's "variety of sects dispersed over the entire face" of the Confederacy, the "multiplicity of sects" (*The Federalist*, No. 51) that help assure the security of civil rights. They possess, as he knew, actual political rights and potential political power that may or may not be "adverse to the rights of other citizens, or to the permanent and aggregate interests of the community."

A modern gloss on how these aggregates interact and influence society comes from British political scientist Bernard Crick. In *In Defence of Politics*, Crick shows that he knows that politics is not the only way to solve the problem of order in society, that a constitutional and representative republic is not the only way to address politics. But in the republican context, very much in the Aristotelian spirit, Crick adds to the picture of the situation in which religious denominations and movements or interests act in America in the twentieth century (and before it):

> Politics, then, can be simply defined as the activity by which differing interests within a given unit of rule are conciliated by giving them a share in power in proportion to their importance to the welfare and the survival of the whole community.[6]

Needless to say, no one "gives" the interests their share in power; they have to win it through "publicity" and "activity."[7]

Politics: "Everybody in Religion Does It"

Protestant churches from 1607 or 1787 to the present have, by their majority, their diversity, their access to publicity, and their propensity, been the major active religious interests in American politics. We are to observe twentieth-century "Protestants and Others." "Others" here can mean "everyone else," or selected or presumed elements among "everyone else" (as in the early name of an organization, "Protestants and Other Americans United for Separation of Church and State"), or Protestants "over against Others."

It would be impossible to make a contribution by trying to speak of all the "Others," the hundreds of non-Protestant groups that find a place in *The Encyclopedia of American Religion.*[8] It would be possible and may be valuable to conceive this assignment as being fulfilled by posing the development of what today is often called "mainstream" Protestantism, the older hegemonic cluster, in the face of the other agents that make up what today is always called a "pluralist" society. The increasing sharing of space, the progressive yielding of place, and the gradually increasing recognition on the part of this Protestantism that other religious groups have a "share in power" make up much of the main plot of twentieth-century American "religion and politics."

Even in this context one must select; but selection is not difficult, for certain groups quite obviously show their importance, their potential "in proportion to their importance to the welfare and the survival of the whole community." An assessment of how religious groups appear in the 1988 United States presidential campaign (or any of the seven that preceded it) brings these obvious candidates to the fore. As important as they may be in the economy of American politics, Eastern Orthodox, Eastern, Occult, "New," New Age, and similar religious groups have not been major actors; Mormons are a special case, though politically they generally match "conservative Protestants."

A General Social Survey (GSS) collation of eleven surveys of "noninstitutionalized English-speaking persons living in the continental United States" (using 17,052 individual cases) is a guide to the groups that are candidates to "share in power," to use Crick's model. Thus the 25 percent who "prefer" Catholicism—a figure that might grow slightly if one included "non-English-speaking" people like many Hispanics—is obviously the major other aggregate of interests. Black Protestants (9.1 percent) are another. "Conservative Protestants" (15.8 percent) (Southern Baptists, Churches of Christ, Nazarenes, Pentecostals/Holiness, Evangelicals/Fundamentalists, Assemblies of God, Churches of God, and Adventists,

among others) make up a third set of *symbiotes*. "No religious preference" (6.9 percent) would include the studied secularists who appear
regularly on the Protestant screen, as do Jews (2.3 percent).

This leaves "Unitarians-Universalists" (0.2 percent) among the "Others," and they tend politically to cluster with the "Moderate Protestants"
(24.2 percent) and "Liberal Protestants" (8.7 percent) who together survive as an approximate one-third of the whole sample and who make up
the main plot of what we are here calling simply, if with an imperial
definition, "Protestants." They are the ones who once held, or felt that
they had had, hegemony which they have been yielding to these "Others."
And these "Others" are all visible in contemporary presidential, to say
nothing of state and local, politics.[9]

Very few people in any of these groups joined them or grew up and
remained with them because they represented this or that political stance
or in order to express politics through such a group or movement. People
are religious for all the reasons that they are religious: inheritance,
tradition, habit, ethnic or racial context, geography and demography,
choice, conversion, and the like. Politics does not save souls; Crick
reminds that "it does not claim to settle every problem or to make every
sad heart glad." It happens that for whatever reason people are in a
religious group, they may on occasion or even constantly find that group
expressing, contradicting, or representing some element of their political
interests or beliefs.

The book title by H. M. Kuitert, *Everything Is Politics but Politics Is
Not Everything*, suggests the borders within which the political postures
of "Protestant and Others" appear.[10] On one extreme, there may be
Protestants and Others who would make "politics everything." To visit
Crick penultimately, "the attempt to politicize everything is the destruction of politics," and, one might say in retrospect about some Protestant
factions, of religion. At the other extreme, there is no escape, in a
political society, from political context and activity. Crick, finally, having
reminded that "politics is not religion, ethics, law, science, history, or
economics. . . . Politics is politics," then describes its reach. "The person
who wishes not to be troubled by politics and to be left alone finds
himself the unwitting ally of those to whom politics is a troublesome
obstacle to their well-meant intentions to leave nothing alone."[11]

Willy-nilly, then, all religious groups in America are actors in the
political drama, even if mainstream Protestants and Catholics were often
seen as the only two movements that were overt about their political
choices. Some, in what I once called a "private," as opposed to an overtly
"public" Protestant party, late in the nineteenth century organized them-

selves with the intention not to be political and gave some appearances until late in the twentieth century that they were consistently following that intention.[12] But in a more basic and profound sense, they could never be nonpolitical.

Putatively nonpolitical, passive, or "private" Protestantism is a set of agents on the political scene in the American republic just as religious dissenters, who claim that their interests are transcendent only, are components in what passes for politics in totalitarian societies. Indeed, the American would-be nonpolitical types are necessarily political for a reason that connects with life in a republic. As the (Leo) Straussian neoconservative political scientist Walter Berns accurately points out: a constitutional republic necessarily solves its "religious problem" through "the subordination of religion."[13]

Subordination is not necessarily subservience. It has to do with polity, with ordering, with ordaining, with assigning a legal and political "place" to religion and religious groups. It would be impossible to have a republic that separates church and state (Jefferson) or draws a "line of distinction" between religion and the civil authorities (Madison), as America does and as the overwhelming majority of its citizens say they want it to, without such subordination.[14]

Obviously, religious groups do not subordinate the political order. The state does not ask the church to be relieved of participation in its stewardship drive as the church gets a charter, incorporates, and requests tax exemption from the state. Religious groups may in the spirit of prophetic transcendence act in the name of a Higher Law, but they may suffer civil penalties for doing so. Otherwise, they are subordinated; they must live by a "law" of conscientious objection, and must live within the politically set context of tax-exemption, zoning, police, fire, and any number of other laws.

Being "subordinate," religious groups have to be political to assert their rights and protect their interests. One can create an instantaneous and effective ecumenical movement of "Protestants and Others," including those who "wish not to be troubled by politics and to be left alone," or who want to create the impression that they so wish. All that is necessary is to provide a platform for these "subordinates" to react against what, in one conference, was called "government intervention in religious affairs." Such reaction was "publicity" and "action" of a political sort.

The book of proceedings of this conference (Dean Kelley, ed., *Government Intervention in Religious Affairs*) is necessarily political from front to back. Chapter titles include: "Frontier Issues of Tax Exemption for Religious Organizations," "The IRS Cracks Down on Coalitions," "Concordia College Challenges the IRS," "A Baptist Seminary Resists the Equal Employment Opportunity Commission," "The Potential in Recent Statutes for Government Surveillance of Religious Organizations," "Current Issues in Government Regulation of Religious Solicitation," "Obtaining Information from Religious Bodies by Compulsory Process," "Government Restraint on Political Activities of Religious Bodies," "The Use of Legal Process for De-Conversion." These, among others, bring together the traditionalist wings of the Southern Baptist Convention, the Lutheran Church—Missouri Synod, "cults," Jehovah's Witnesses, Bible churches, fundamentalists, and others who often described themselves as nonpolitical. They are political even if only to assure their "share in power in proportion to their importance to the welfare and the survival of the whole community." So alert, concerted, and aggressive are they that William Lee Miller found it in place to respond with a chapter titled "Responsible Government, Not Religion, Is the Endangered Species."[15]

Beyond this minimal if aggressive participation in politics, virtually every group has some zone of beliefs it would protect, some ideology on whose basis it would be politically belligerent, some temperature at which it reaches a boiling point. The best illustration is the controversy over abortion of fetuses. Various traditionalist, Catholic, Missouri Synod Lutheran, Southern Baptist, and fundamentalist groups, who say that they disdain politics and who criticize their own fellow believers and "Others" who mix religion and politics—even on so drastic a "life" issue as nuclear disarmament or the protection of the environment—will work actively for a constitutional amendment outlawing abortions. To them, this issue is qualitatively different from all others; to all others looking on, it may be quantitatively more controversial and demanding or urgent, but it belongs on the continuum with other political issues.

In short, "everyone does it," if doing it means to realize that religious groups are all components who share a political society, aggregates and interests that express themselves politically in some set of circumstances or other. Exceptions among Amish or Hutterites (who usually are acted for politically by the American Civil Liberties Union or others) are statistically insignificant, though often morally vivid. And if "everyone does it," then it falls to us to see when and how "Others" are politically activated and what their agency during the twentieth century has done and does to the Protestantism, which once was more or less hegemonous in the American republic. Needless to say, there have been changes during this century, and these changes change Protestantism and Others and the republic at once.

Politics: Power Shifts in the Twentieth Century

1901-1932: Mainstream Hegemony

While, in respect to the religious engagement with politics, "everyone does it," the mainstream (moderate plus liberal) Protestants held hegemony during the first third of the century. The Catholics increasingly moved to challenge this privileged position; the Bishops' Program of 1919 represented a formal effort toward political involvement. However, Catholicism was still an insecure minority, impelled to prove that it belonged in America and uncertain about the moves it should make. In a famed passage in a 1927 book, French visitor André Siegfried could still say with plausibility that Protestantism was America's "only national religion."[16]

Protestant, yes, but of what kind? Black Protestants aspired to find political expression through their most important institutions, the black churches. But they were in no position to set the terms for anyone outside those highly segregated institutions, and were often overlooked. Jews were interested in self-defense and developed organizations to promote this, and their liberals often coalesced with Protestant and other liberals; but the Zionist cause was still a specialty of Jewish minorities and did not represent a major intrusion into the conventional zones of American politics. Much of secularized America was "post-Protestant," which is a way of saying that if it paid heed to religion in politics, it knew chiefly the mainstream sort. As for conservative Protestantism, out of which Pentecostalism, fundamentalism, and what was later called evangelicalism were developing, most of its leaders steadfastly insisted that churches should shun political involvement. They engaged in more "social activism" than they used to receive credit or blame for, but most of them criticized moderates and liberals for mixing religion with politics.

As for these mainstream groups, which means roughly those that formed the Federal Council of Churches in 1908, political action meant both continuity with nineteenth-century expression plus some innovation. I have always seen their turn-of-the-century and subsequent endeavors as attempts to diagnose, address, and transcend "the modern situation" of churches and religious organizations. "Modern," in such a context, meant chiefly "differentiation," the "chopping up" of life into specialties, and choice. This differentiation had included the separation of ethnicity from religion (for modern Jews), the separation of church and state (a trauma for modern Catholics), the division into competitive denominations, and the sundering of the "sacred" from the "secular" (for Protestants and others in the free worlds). In the path of these separations, people were impelled to choose their religious commitments.[17]

In this understanding, leaders in the "old-time" religion, once called New Light, New School, New Side, or advocates of New Measures, first understood modernity. They settled for specialized religion (of a "private," soul-saving, spiritual sort, for the most part), and, through their evangelists, asked people to decide for their brand of conversion.

In the course of a century of adjustment, the mainstream Protestant party undertook acts of what we might call dedifferentiation and aspired to restore integrity or wholeness. Josiah Strong gave classic statement to this goal, which included politics, when he described two parties, the second of which was usually seen as liberal-modernist. He wrote that there were "two types of Christianity, the old and the older. The one is traditional, familiar, and dominant. The other, though as old as the Gospel of Christ, is so rare that it is suspected of being new, or is overlooked altogether."[18] This "new" type was overtly a political agent through the first three decades of the century.

This Christomonistic liberalism sought to advance the "Kingdom of God" through political and social action. On occasion it could link with other Protestant elements, for example, to produce prohibition. Normally, it attempted to speak for religion, whether to the government during World War I or to the whole society through the 1920s. A symbolic date, 1932, signals the beginning of a change in eras with the publication of Reinhold Niebuhr's self-critical and "neoorthodox" *Moral Man and Immoral Society* and the election of Franklin Delano Roosevelt.[19]

1933–1951: Internal Schism and External Challenge

During the Depression and pre–World War II years the mainstream Protestants did not retreat from politics; they found it necessary to engage it ever more strenuously, whether through moves to Right or Left, as Robert Moats Miller convincingly documented in *American Protestantism and Social Issues, 1919–1939*. The "Protestantism" of his book title characteristically meant moderate-to-liberal groups; blacks receive a few pages of mention, for what white churches did or did not do to or for them; fundamentalism makes an appearance in its antievolutionist crusade, a harbinger of future political involvement. The hardly mentioned conservative Protestants were organizing an American Council of Christian Churches and a National Association of Evangelicals in the early 1940s. These could not help but have political implications and consequences, but they organized with explicit attacks on Federal Council of Churches-type mixture of religion and politics. It was still the mainstream hegemonic Protestants who held center stage.[20]

Through the period, however, they increasingly felt threatened by the rise of political Catholicism. While the two movements might make common cause—for example, in support of various New Deal measures—suspicion grew that ascendant Catholicism might grow to the point where, because of its size, its presumed internal unity, its hierarchical structure and authoritarian system, and its international practices, it would "win" America. Protestants and Other Americans United for Separation of Church and State, which took shape late in the 1940s, included some conservative Baptists but was still largely the expression of now insecure mainstream Protestantism of moderate and liberal sorts.

This period closes with the end of the Roosevelt-Truman era, Protestant disaffection with President Truman's attempt to send General Mark W. Clark to the Vatican as an ambassador in 1951, and, symbolically, with a *Christian Century* editorial in 1951, "Pluralism: A National Menace."[21] Meanwhile, a new element was also becoming politically expressive: organized religious Judaism. The Holocaust in Europe and the birth of Israel in 1948 meant the effective end of anti-Zionism within Judaism—only eccentric Jewish minorities held out against Israel—and the permanent institutionalization of a political movement with religious bases and auspices. While many premillennial fundamentalists sided with Zionists because of dispensational views of the place of a restored Israel in the plot of Jesus' Second Coming, this sympathy went generally overlooked. Meanwhile, many moderates and liberals, the *Christian Century* among them, feared that Zionism had meant a particularization of religious nationalism that threatened the American fabric. It was also part of the pluralism that was "a national menace."

Internal criticism and a tendency toward schism, meanwhile, weakened the mainstream Protestants. Most notable was the controversy between the pacifists and near-pacifists, who opposed preparation for American participation in World War II, and the Niebuhrian Christian Realists, who strenuously worked for such preparation and involvement. It was hard to hold the hegemonous position when on this and other profound issues, including the rise of Israel, there was such patent division within this Protestant house.

1951–1968: Four-Faith Pluralism and Civil Religion

During the next two decades it was clear that the old hegemony was going, and eventually it was gone. Jewish sociologist-theologian Will Herberg's *Protestant-Catholic-Jew* in 1955[22] and Jesuit Father John Courtney Murray's *We Hold these Truths*[23] in 1960 described the new terms of trifaith or, in Murray's case, a "four-conspiracy" approach to American polity. Murray added the "secularist" option in his vision of American religious pluralism. The kind of Protestantism represented by the *Christian Century* progressively came to terms with the fact of Israel and supported Israel. With the coming of Pope John XXIII in 1958 and the Second Vatican Council in 1962, it turned from its ancient anti-Catholicism to support for inclusion of Catholicism in ecumenical designs. In both cases, political alliances also developed, with Protestant anti-Catholicism effectually ending with the election of Catholic President John F. Kennedy in 1960.

Meanwhile, the civil rights movement brought about a kind of integration of white and black Protestantisms with "Other" Americans on a religiously based moral and political cause through the 1960s. At last the profoundly rooted (in local communities, and beyond) churchly character of black politics was exposed to view as Reverends King, Abernathy, Shuttlesworth, Fauntroy, Young, Jackson, Bevel, and scores more, drew upon and mobilized the hitherto hidden-from-view (of whites) political bases in their churches. The old white Protestant establishment often took signals from Catholics, Jews, and black Protestants, forming shifting alliances with them.

In turn, "Others" knew that moderate and liberal Protestants were the prime agents on the political-religious scene. When James Forman, representing Christian "Black Power," posted a Black Manifesto seeking reparations from white America, this symbolic act did not take place at the huge and powerful Fundamentalist First Baptist Church in Dallas. Forman knew that he could get his best hearing by presenting it at the old flagship church of liberal Protestantism, Riverside Church in New York.[24] The Federal Council of Churches, not the American Council of Christian Churches or the National Association of Evangelicals, developed an agency for dealing with issues of race and civil rights. The cast of politically engaged churches was considered complete by 1968; it excluded the fundamentalist, Pentecostal, or evangelical churches. Most of these still saw themselves as nonpolitical, antipolitical, or apolitical.

The new religious if nonchurchly agent on the scene was what Sidney E. Mead called "The Religion of the Republic" and Robert Bellah termed "Civil Religion." This ideology and ethos, informally institutionalized, of course was political, for it had no clarified structure in the churches and synagogues; its home was in the *polis*, where, whether in right-wing populist forms or in moderate-to-left academic expressions, it was another aggregate, subcommunity, platoon, or agency of mind and spirit.

1968-1988: The Public Engagement of Conservatives

After the upheavals symbolized by radical politics, protest against racism and the Vietnam War, theological and social radicalism ("New Morality," "hippies," and the like), Americans in the 1970s reacted against the patterns of the 1960s. The mainstream Protestantism experienced losses in statistics and status as it yielded to its new partners where once it had held hegemony. But during these two decades, the old "private" Protestant parties "went public." By the 1976 campaign of evangelical Jimmy Carter their presence was coming to be felt nationally, and the elections of Ronald Reagan in 1980 and 1984 found them the most visible, most controversial, and most political actors on the scene. A New Christian Right represented many (but by no means all) elements in fundamentalism, evangelicalism, Pentecostalism, Southern Baptist, and other conservative churches.

As they made their move, passing from action based on constantly expressed *ressentiment*, bone-deep resentment for the neglect they faced or the contempt they felt, to the will-to-power that comes with groups being in range of power, their leaders made no secret of the fact that their language in the 1980s represented a 180-degree turn from that which they had used in the 1960s. Then, said Jerry Falwell, one of the most prominent leaders, "we" had said it was a sin for churches to enter politics. Now, he said, it was a sin for the churches not to do so.

This is not the place to revisit the familiar story of conservative Protestantism's intrusion into the most visible space in churchly politics. Some was occasioned by the felt need to give political voice to support of Israel, as part of premillennial schemes. More came in support of anti-abortion and pro-"school prayer" legislation, or to advance other causes tabbed "social issues." Technology made much of the mobilization possible; television, computers, and rapid mail procedures were some of the techniques used. Mass media had also inspired some of the reaction, for they brought signals that eroded or corroded the boundaries and defenses of once-insulated fundamentalism, evangelicalism, and Pentecostalism.

The move into politics during the 1980s did not attract all conservatives, many of whom insisted that they were apolitical or made clear that the charismatic leaders and organized movements did not speak for them. But now the political celebrities in religion came from this New Christian Right flank; it was they who had access to the White House, who lobbied strenuously, and who were motivated to try to see the courts take a new turn. Whatever the future power of this cluster, it had demonstrated two things: no one religious movement held hegemony in the midst of pluralism; all major components were now actors on the scene, and on similar terms.

Of course, techniques varied from group to group. Catholics combined "pastoral letters" of bishops with every form of organization by movements. Jews concentrated on support of Israel as their domestic liberal coalitions divided and became diffuse and some leaders became political "neoconservatives." Blacks stayed on the scene, their church organization often being the main agent in seeing to the election of black mayors in major cities and in supporting Jesse Jackson, the first plausible black presidential candidate. Mainstream Protestants engaged in some retreat, partly because of reaction against a bureaucratized approach to political action that, it was argued, did not often represent actual constituencies and therefore lost political potency. But on local levels and on some issues, they remained as engaged as ever. They simply were surrounded by the "Others" of my title, and this changed their posture and possibility considerably.

Tomorrow: The Terms of Political Engagement

What is clear from this brief accounting of episodes and shifts in nine American decades is that nothing lasts in American religious politics. Hegemonic powers divide and have to yield their power. Overlooked groups like black churches become ever more visible to others. Jews come to prominence in support of an international issue, defense of Israel, but can change domestic alliances. Once antipolitical groups can become most political. In the immediate future, it looks as if none of them will prevail. They all represent sorts of caucuses with which politicians must deal. They all include elements of internal criticism and conflict that lead them to be cautious about the extent and nature of their political involvements.

Along the way, the plot of political participation has made denominational boundaries almost irrelevant. The divisions and alliances cross denominational lines. On most substantial issues—for example, abortion or nuclear armament—one kind of Catholic faction will be allied with a similar kind of Jewish or mainstream, black, or conservative Protestant, against another kind of Catholic, Jew, or Protestant in the three movements just mentioned. On another issue, the coalitions will shift. Radical secular feminists make common cause with fundamentalists in opposing pornography while premillennialists, who have nothing in common with most Jews' domestic programs, are their most staunch allies in support of Israel.

The overall trend through the century has been one which has seen religious group after group grow discontented with and restless about what we might call the informal "modern pact." This was the tacit agreement that churches could hold sway in respect to individuals' private, leisure, residential, "sacred" life—so long as they left social, public, productive, working-place, and "profane" life to secular powers. It was the apparent invasion of the private and sacred zone by forces which religionists considered alien, subversive, or disruptive that occasioned their reactions. Meanwhile, having yielded so much to secular forces, element after element on the religious scene found reasons and ways to aspire to recover some vision of the whole, some means to address all of life.

Inevitably, there are and will remain clashes between these visions and means. The difference that separates the beginning from the end of the century lies most patently in the fact that no important element consistently and permanently abstains from political involvement. Protestants, the pioneers, and "Others" share the scene, and will continue to do so, risking some of their constituents' support at times, pleasing them at others, winning some and losing some—for "that's politics"—and making some compromises and adaptations to advance their purposes—for "that's politics," too. They seem to be dynamic, proof of Charles Peguy's old observation, "Everything begins in mysticism and ends in politics."

It is hard to resist a postscript that reports on a countertendency or would insert a kind of theological reservation. Kuitert's book title also belongs to the expression of those who know that temporal politics as an "end" can also mean a limit of the spiritual, the eternal, the transcendent. There are, and are reasons for, counterforces that, in Kuitert's terms, insist that it is only in the temporal realm that "everything is politics" even as they remind that "politics is not everything."

Notes

1. Quoted by Bernard Crick, *In Defence of Politics* (Baltimore: Penguin, 1964), 171.

2. Frederick S. Carney, ed., *The Politics of Johannes Althusius* (abridged from *Politica Methodice Digesta atque Exemplis Sacris et Profanis Illustrata*, 3rd ed.) (Boston: Beacon, 1964), 12.

3. Edmund Burke, *Reflections on the Revolution in France* (Garden City, NY: Doubleday, n.d.), 59.

4. Alexander Hamilton, John Jay, and James Madison, *The Federalist Papers* (Washington: Robert B. Luce, 1976), 339–340.

5. *Minersville School District* v. *Gobitis* 310 U.S. 586 On Writ of Certiorari to the United States Circuit Court of Appeals for the Third Circuit (1940).

6. Crick, *In Defence of Politics*, 21.

7. Ibid., 20, 25.

8. See, for example, J. Gordon Melton, *The Encyclopedia of American Religions*, 2 vols. (Wilmington, NC: McGrath, 1978).

9. Wade Clark Roof and William McKinney, *American Mainline Religion: Its Changing Shape and Future* (New Brunswick, NJ: Rutgers University Press, 1987), 82, 253–256.

10. H. M. Kuitert, *Everything Is Politics but Politics Is Not Everything* (Grand Rapids, MI: Eerdmans, 1986).

11. Crick, *In Defence of Politics*, 16.

12. Martin E. Marty, *Righteous Empire: The Protestant Experience in America* (New York: Dial, 1971), 179.

13. Walter Berns, *The First Amendment and the Future of American Democracy* (New York: Basic Books, 1976), 26.

14. See Sidney E. Mead, *The Nation with the Soul of a Church* (New York: Harper & Row, 1975), 78–94, for an elaboration of this Madisonian distinction.

15. Dean M. Kelley, ed., *Government Intervention in Religious Affairs* (New York: Pilgrim, 1982), includes essays on these subjects. See especially pp. 51–56.

16. André Siegfried, *America Comes of Age* (New York: Harcourt, 1927), 33.

17. Martin E. Marty, *Modern American Religion*, Vol. I, *1893–1919: The Irony of It All* (Chicago: University of Chicago Press, 1986), 251–316, develops the concept.

18. Josiah Strong, *The Next Great Awakening*, 10th ed. (New York: 1913), iii, as quoted in Marty, *Righteous Empire*, 177.

19. Reinhold Niebuhr, *Moral Man and Immoral Society* (New York: Scribner's, 1932).

20. Robert Moats Miller, *American Protestantism and Social Issues, 1919–1939* (Chapel Hill: University of North Carolina Press, 1958), 63–130.

21. "Pluralism: A National Menace," *The Christian Century*, June 13, 1951, cover.

22. Will Herberg, *Protestant, Catholic, Jew* (Garden City, NY: Doubleday, 1955).

23. John Courtney Murray, S.J., *We Hold These Truths: Catholic Reflections on the American Proposition* (New York: Sheed and Ward, 1960).

24. For comment on the Black Manifesto, see C. Eric Lincoln, ed., *The Black Experience in Religion* (Garden City, NY: Doubleday, 1974), 180, 183.

15

Quid Obscurum:
The Changing Terrain
of Church-State Relations

ROBERT WUTHNOW

In his hauntingly memorable description of the Battle of Waterloo, Victor Hugo makes a startling observation. The opening lines of his narrative are these:

> If it had not rained on the night of June 17, 1815, the future of Europe would have been different. A few drops more or less tipped the balance against Napoleon. For Waterloo to be the end of Austerlitz, Providence needed only a little rain, and an unseasonable cloud crossing the sky was enough for the collapse of a world.[1]

What is startling, though, is not the idea that the future of Europe, or even the outcome of the battle, hinged on something as seemingly trivial as an unexpected rainstorm. Such explanations fill the annals of military history. Had not the British expeditionary force been able to evacuate from Dunkirk under cover of heavy fog during the week of May 26, 1940, the German army might well have gone on to win the war. Those who tread the battlefields near Gettysburg, Pennsylvania, view the heights along Culp's Hill and Cemetary Ridge and wonder what the outcome would have been had Lee's troops occupied those favored positions instead of Meade's. The great turning points of history, it appears, sometimes hinge less on what people do than the conditions under which they have to do it. The flukes of nature—or, as some would maintain, the hand of God—intervene willfully at portentous moments.

And yet, we in contemporary society, schooled as we have been in the complexities of history, know how tenuous these arguments often prove to be. Battles may be won or lost on the basis of a sudden turn of the weather, but wars are not and neither is the course of history. What if, by some chance, Lee's troops had occupied the heights at Gettysburg? Would Meade's then have run the bloody gauntlet that became immortalized as "Pickett's charge"? Or would the Federal army have faded away to fight on more opportune terms? Lee, we learn from modern analysts of the battle, was forced to fight, despite the unfavorable terrain, because he desperately needed to win. Supplies were running low and Confederate agents needed to be able to demonstrate to their European creditors that they could win. And the reason supplies were running low lay deep in the South's agrarian economy, compared with the North's industrial economy, and even deeper in the triangular trade that had developed between the South, Great Britain, and West Africa. Lee was forced to fight; Meade could have slipped away.

What startles us as we proceed with Victor Hugo's account is that he succeeds so well in defending his thesis. A soggy battlefield was indeed a decisive factor. But as so often is the case in Hugo's narratives, it was the larger terrain—and the uncertainties inherent in this terrain—that constituted the framework in which the decisions of the two commanders had to be made. An unexpected rainstorm made it impossible for Napoleon to deploy the full force of his artillery. This was a factor that could not have been anticipated, an element of the battle that in essence remained obscure.

The *quid obscurum* in Hugo's account, though, is at once more simple and straightforward than this and more elusive as well. There was, running through the battlefield, interposed directly between the two armies, a ditch. It extended across the entire line that Napoleon's cavalry would have to charge. It was a deep chasm, made by human hands, the result of a road that had been cut as if by a knife through the natural terrain. It was hidden from view. The cavalry charged, and then faced the terror. Hugo recounts:

> There was the ravine, unexpected, gaping right at the horses' feet, twelve feet deep between its banks. The second rank pushed in the first, the third pushed in the second; the horses reared, lurched backward, fell onto their

rumps, and struggled writhing with their feet in the air, piling up and throwing their riders; no means to retreat; the whole column was nothing but a projectile. The momentum to crush the English crushed the French. The inexorable ravine could not yield until it was filled; riders and horses rolled in together helter-skelter, grinding against each other, making common flesh in this dreadful gulf, and when this grave was full of living men, the rest marched over them and went on. Almost a third of Dubois's brigade sank into the abyss.[2]

The *quid obscurum*, quite literally, was a hidden fracture with enormous consequences.

The second, and deeper, meaning of Hugo's reference to the *quid obscurum* is that of the broader uncertainties evoked by the clash of two armies. Only in the heat of battle do the unforeseen contingencies become evident; only then do the plans of the commanding generals prove to have missed important features of the broader terrain. In the struggling line of soldiers engaged in hand-to-hand combat, one begins to realize that the expenditures are greater than expected. The consequences of seemingly unimportant conditions turn out to be incalculable. It is left to the historian to calculate, with the advantage of hindsight, what the role of these previously obscured realities was.

My purpose in drawing attention to Hugo's discussion is also twofold. At the more literal level, there is a great fracture, like the ravine cutting across the plateau of Mont-Saint-Jean, running through the cultural terrain on which the battles of religion and politics are now being fought. It is a fracture that deserves our attention, for it is of recent creation, a human construction, unlike the timeless swells of culture through which it has been cut. And it has become a mire of bitter contention, consuming the energies of religious communities and grinding their ideals into the grime of unforeseen animosities. At a broader level, this fracture also symbolizes the unplanned developments in the larger terrain that did not become evident until the battles themselves began to erupt. With the advantage of hindsight, we can now discover the importance of these developments. We can see how the present controversies in American religion were affected by broader changes in the society—the consequences of which remained obscure at the time but have now become painfully transparent.

The ravine running through the culturescape of American religion is as real as the one made by the road between the two villages on the Belgian border. It differs in one important respect, though. It is not simply a fissure in the physical environment, a ditch that creates the downfall of one of the protagonists. It is to a much greater extent the product of battle itself. The chasm dividing American religion into separate communities has emerged largely from the struggle between these two communities. It may have occurred, as we shall suggest shortly, along a fault line already present in the cultural terrain. But it has been dug deeper and wider by the skirmishes that have been launched across it.

Depending on whose lens we use to view it through, any number of ways of describing it can be found. Television evangelist Jimmy Swaggart has described it as a gulf between those who believe in the Judeo-Christian principles on which our country was founded and those who believe in the "vain philosophies of men." On one side are the "old-fashioned" believers in "the word of almighty God," who are often maligned as "poor simpletons"; on the other side are the "so-called intelligentsia," those who believe they are great because they "are more intelligent than anyone else," "socialists," believers in "syphilitic Lenin," and the burdened masses who have nothing better to get excited about than football games and baseball.[3] In contrast, a writer for the *New York Times* depicted it as a battle between "churches and church-allied groups" who favor freedom, democracy, and the rights of minorities, on the one hand, and a right-wing fringe interested in setting up a theocracy governed by a "dictatorship of religious values," on the other hand.[4]

Apart from the colors in which the two sides are portrayed, though, one finds general agreement on the following points: (a) the reality of the division between two opposing camps; (b) the predominance of "fundamentalists," "evangelicals," and "religious conservatives" in one and the predominance of "religious liberals," "humanists," and "secularists" in the other; and (c) the presence of deep hostility and misgiving between the two. An official of the National Council of Churches summarized the two positions, and the views of each toward the other, this way:

> Liberals abhor the smugness, the self-righteousness, the absolute certainty, the judgmentalism, the lovelessness of a narrow, dogmatic faith. [Conservatives] scorn the fuzziness, the marshmallow convictions, the inclusiveness that makes membership meaningless—the "anything goes" attitude that views even Scripture as relative. Both often caricature the worst in one another and fail to perceive the best.[5]

To suggest that American religion is divided neatly into two communities with sharply differentiated views is, of course, to ride roughshod over the countless landmarks, signposts, hills, and gullies that actually constitute the religious landscape. Not only do fundamentalists distinguish themselves from evangelicals, but each brand of religious conservatism is divided into dozens of denominational product lines. Similar distinctions can be made on the Religious Left. In the popular mind, though, there does seem to be some reality to the cruder, binary way of thinking.

A national survey, conducted several years ago (even before some of the more acrimonious debates over the role of religion in politics had arisen), found both a high level of awareness of the basic divisions between religious liberals and conservatives and a great deal of actual hostility between the two. When asked to classify themselves, 43 percent of those surveyed identified themselves as religious liberals and 41 percent said they were religious conservatives. The public is thus divided almost equally between the two categories, and only one person in six was unable or unwilling to use these labels.[6] Judging from the ways in which self-styled liberals and conservatives answered other questions, the two categories also seem to have had some validity. As one would expect, conservatives were much more likely than liberals to identify themselves as evangelicals, to believe in a literal interpretation of the Bible, to say they had had a "born-again" conversion experience, to indicate that they had tried to convert others to their faith, and to hold conservative views on such issues as abortion and prayer in public schools. Liberals were less likely than conservatives to attend church or synagogue regularly, but a majority affirmed the importance of religion in their lives, tended to regard the Bible as divinely inspired (if not to be taken literally), and held liberal views on a variety of political and moral issues. Some denominations tended to consist of more conservatives than liberals, or vice versa. But, generally, the major denominational families and faith traditions—Methodists, Lutherans, Presbyterians, Catholics, Jews—were all divided about equally between religious conservatives and religious liberals. In other words, the cleavage between conservatives and liberals tends not, for the most part, to fall along denominational lines. It is a cleavage that divides people within the same denominations—as recent struggles within the Southern Baptist Convention, the Episcopal church, the Presbyterian Church U.S.A., and the Roman Catholic Church all bear witness to.

The study also demonstrated the extent to which the relations between religious liberals and religious conservatives have become ridden with conflict. A majority of the public surveyed said the conflict between religious liberals and conservatives is an area of "serious tension." A substantial majority of both groups said they had had unpleasant, or at best, "mixed," relations with the other group. And these relations were said to have taken place in fairly intimate settings: in one's church, among friends and relatives, even within the same Bible study or fellowship groups. Moreover, each side held a number of negative images of the other. Liberals saw conservatives as rigid, intolerant, and fanatical. Conservatives described liberals as shallow, morally loose, unloving, and unsaved. The study also demonstrated that, unlike other kinds of prejudice and hostility, the ill feelings separating religious liberals and religious conservatives *did not mitigate* as the two groups came into greater contact with one another. The more each side came into contact with the other, and the more knowledge it gained about the other, the less it liked the other.

Viewed normatively, it is of course disturbing to find such levels of animosity and tension between religious liberals and conservatives. We might expect nothing better from communists and capitalists or Democrats and Republicans. But deep within the Hebrew and Christian traditions lies an ethic of love and forgiveness. In congregation after congregation prayers are routinely offered for unity among the faithful. Creeds are recited stating belief in the one, holy, catholic church. And homilies are delivered on Jesus' injunction to love one's neighbor as oneself.

If these findings are disturbing, they are not, however, surprising. They accord with the way in which American religion is portrayed in the media and in pulpits, and with the way in which American religion seems to function. The major newspapers and television networks routinely publicize the bizarre activities of fundamentalists and evangelicals: the conservative governor who prays with his pastor and hears God tell him to run for the presidency, the television preacher who prays (successfully, it turns out) that an impending hurricane will be averted from the Virginia coast, the fundamentalists in Indiana who deny their children proper schooling and medical care, the evangelical counselor in California who is sued by the family of a patient who committed suicide, the deranged member of a fundamentalist church in Maine who mows down his fellow parishioners with a shotgun. Conservative television preachers and conservative religious publications make equally vitriolic comments about their liberal foes: how an Episcopal bishop is condoning sexual permissiveness within his diocese, how Methodist liberals are encouraging homosexuality among the denomination's pastors, how zealous clergy in the nuclear disarmament movement are selling the country out to the Russians, how religious conservatives are being discriminated against in colleges and universities. It is little wonder that the labels begin to stick. Sooner or later it does in fact begin to appear as if the world of faith is divided into two belligerent superpowers.

But this picture of the religious world is not simply a creation of the sensationalist media. At the grass roots, one can readily find denunciations of liberalism from conservative pulpits and diatribes against fundamentalism from liberal pulpits. One can readily observe the split between liberals and conservatives in church meetings and discussion groups. Liberals freely express doubts about the historical authenticity of the Bible. Conservatives appeal for greater faith in the supernatural, the miraculous, and argue for more emphasis on sin and personal salvation. Beneath the innocent statements of each are deeper feelings about right and wrong, truth and error. Beyond these simple exchanges, the two also isolate themselves in different communities of support and action: liberals in the nurturing environment of local groups promoting peace, the forum on AIDS, the movement to lobby for equitable and affordable housing; conservatives, in the womb of Bible study groups and prayer fellowships. One can also readily observe the polarizing tendencies of national issues on the religious environment. Pick up the latest issue of *Christian Century* or *Christianity Today*. Observe the number of articles that deal with politics. Note the paucity of material on theology or even personal spirituality. Or open the mail. Count the letters from Moral Majority, Christian Voice, People for the American Way, the American Civil Liberties Union. The issues are now national, rather than local or regional. They concern an appointment to the Supreme Court, a constitutional amendment on abortion, a preacher running for president. They are supported by one faction of the religious community and opposed by another. They induce polarization.

But to say that there are many reasons why the chasm between religious liberals and conservatives exists is still only to describe it—to parade the colors of the troops engaged in the great battle of which it consists. It is a chasm deepened and widened by political debate. It is a chasm around which religious communities' participation in public affairs divides. It has become a predictable feature of the contemporary debate over church-state relations. To understand it, though, we must look at broader developments in the social terrain. We must try to discover why this particular fracture line existed in the cultural geography in the first place.

In one sense it is, of course, a fracture line that can be found in the soil of American religion as far back as the years immediately after the Civil War. Even in the eighteenth century and during the first half of the nineteenth, one can identify the beginnings of a division between religious conservatives and religious liberals insofar as one considers the effects of the Enlightenment on elite culture. Skepticism, atheism, anticlericalism, and of course deism constitute identifiable alternatives to the popular piety of Methodists and Baptists and the conservative orthodoxy of Roman Catholics, Jews, Presbyterians, and others during this period. But to an important degree the potential division between conservatism and liberalism before the Civil War is overshadowed by the deeper tensions to which the society is subject. Nationalism and regionalism, differences between the culture of the Eastern seaboard and the expanding Western territories, and increasingly the tensions between North and South provide the major divisions affecting the organization of American religion. Not until the termination of these hostilities and the resumption of material progress after the Civil War does it become possible for the gap between religious conservatives and liberals to gain importance. Gradually in these years the discoveries of science, the new ideas of Charles Darwin, and by the end of century the beginnings of a national system of higher education provide the groundwork for a liberal challenge to religious conservatism. The culmination of these changes, of course, comes at the turn of the century in the modernist movement and its increasingly vocal opponent, the fundamentalists. In the long view, the present division between religious liberals and religious conservatives can be pictured simply as a continuation or outgrowth of this earlier conflict. The inevitable forces of modernization produced a secular freedom in matters of the spirit and voiced skepticism toward a faith based in divine revelation, and this tendency evoked a reactionary movement in which religious conservatism was preserved.

That, as I say, is the impression gained from taking a long view of American history. If one takes a more limited perspective, though, a rather different impression emerges. One is able to focus more directly on the immediate contours of the religious environment and to see how these contours are in the short term shaped by specific events. This, I suppose, is the advantage of taking the perspective of the sociologist—which seldom extends much before World War II.

At the close of that war, the condition of American religion was quite different than it is now. It contained seeds that were to germinate and grow, like weeds in the concrete, widening the cracks that have now become so visible. But the basic divisions ran along other lines. Tensions between Protestants and Catholics had reached new heights as immigration and natural increase contributed to the growth of the Catholic population. Tensions between Christians and Jews also ran deep, even though they were often less visible than the conflicts dividing Protestants and Catholics. There was, as Will Herberg was to describe it a few years later, a "tripartite division" in American religion: to be American was to be Protestant, Catholic, or Jewish.[7] In addition, denominational boundaries also played an important role in giving structure to the Protestant branch of this tripartite arrangement. Ecumenical services were beginning to erode some of these boundaries (often for the explicit purpose of displaying Protestant unity against the threat of papal expansion). But ethnic, national, and geographic divisions—as well as theological and liturgical divisions—continued to reinforce denominational separatism.

In all of this, there was little evidence of any basic split between liberals and conservatives. To be sure, fundamentalism was alive and well; but its very success proved in a deeper sense to be its limitation. By the mid-1930s, fundamentalist spokesmen had largely conceded their defeat in the major Protestant denominations and had withdrawn to form their own organizations. As the Great Depression, and then the rationing imposed by the war, made travel more difficult, these organizations also grew farther apart from one another. By the end of the war, they consisted largely of small, isolated splinter groups on the fringes of the mainline denominations. Most of the population that continued to believe in such doctrinal tenets as biblical inerrancy, the divinity of Jesus, and the necessity of personal salvation remained within these larger denominations. And even the official policies of these denominations reflected what would now be considered a strong conservative emphasis. Evangelism, door-to-door canvassing of communities, revivalistic meetings, biblical preaching, missions—all received prominent support. Also of significance was the fact that many of the more outspoken conservative religious leaders were quietly beginning to build their own organizations. As yet, though, these leaders were able to build quietly and were content largely to maintain ties with the major denominations, rather than break away like their fundamentalist counterparts. Certainly there were differences of opinion about such matters as the literal inspiration of the Bible or the role of churches in political affairs. But these were as yet not the subject of mass movements or of widely recognized cultural divisions. Only the terms "fundamentalist" and "liberal" suggest continuity between this period and our own; a more careful examination of issues, personalities, and organizations indicates discontinuity.

In the years immediately following World War II we do find evidence, though, of the conditions that were to predispose American religion to undergo a major restructuring in the decades that followed. Three such predisposing conditions stand out in particular. In the first place American religion was on the whole extraordinarily strong. The largest churches now counted members in the thousands. Overall, the number of local churches and synagogues ranged in the hundreds of thousands. Some denominations sported budgets in the tens of millions. And collectively, religious organizations took in approximately $800 million annually—a figure, the historian Harold Laski observed, that exceeded the budget of the entire British government.[8] In comparison with Europe, the American churches were especially strong. They had not been subjected to the same limitations on government spending that the churches in England, France, and Germany had faced, nor had they faced the mass withdrawal of the working classes that these churches had experienced; and, of course, they had not been subject to the extensive destruction resulting from the war. They had been weakened by the Depression and by shortages of building materials during the war. But, curiously perhaps, this very weakness turned out to be a strength as well. It prompted major building programs after the war, allowed the churches to relocate in growing neighborhoods, and generally encouraged what was to become known as the religious revival of the 1950s. The critical feature of the churches' massive institutional strength for the coming decades, though, was the fact that religion was able to adjust to a changing environment. Rather than simply wither away—or maintain itself in quiet contemplative seclusion—it adapted to the major social developments of the post-war period. In this sense, we owe much of the present controversy in American religion to the simple fact that it had remained a strong institutional force right up to the second half of the twentieth century.

The second predisposing condition was the strong "this-worldly" orientation of American religion. Not only was it able to adapt to changing circumstances; it also engaged itself actively in the social environment by its own initiative. When the war ended, religious leaders looked to the future with great expectancy. They recognized the opportunities that lay ahead. They were also mindful of the recurrent dangers they faced. Indeed, a prominent theme in their motivational appeals focused on the combination of promise and peril. A resolution passed by the Federal Council of Churches in 1945, for instance, declared: "We are living in a uniquely dangerous and promising time."[9] It was a dangerous time because of the recurrent likelihood of war, the widely anticipated return to a depressed economy after the war-induced boom had ended, and of course the invention of nuclear weapons. It was a promising time because of new opportunities for missionary work and evangelism. The stakes were high, so persistent activism was the desired response. In the words of a Methodist minister, who reminded his audience of the perilous opportunities facing them: "That requires . . . a great godly company of men and women with no axe to grind, desiring only to save, serve, help and heal."[10] The result was that religious organizations deliberately exposed their flanks to the influences of their environment. Programs were initiated, education was encouraged, preaching confronted issues of the day—all of which, like the rain on Napoleon's troops, would reveal the churches' dependence on the conditions of their terrain.

The third predisposing factor was reflected in the relation understood to prevail between religion and the public sphere. This is especially important to understand, because it provides a vivid contrast with the ways in which we now conceive of religion's influence in the political arena. In the 1940s and 1950s there appears to have been a fairly widespread view among religious leaders, theologians, and even social scientists that values and behavior were closely related. Find out what a person's basic values were and you could pretty well predict that person's behavior. If persons valued democracy, they could be counted on to uphold it in their behavior. If a person worked hard and struggled to get ahead, you could be pretty sure that person valued success and achievement. More broadly, writers also extended this connection to the society. A nation's culture essentially consisted of values, and these values were arranged in a hierarchy of priority. The society was held together by this hierarchy of values. It generated consensus and caused people to behave in similar ways.

For religious leaders, this was a very convenient way of conceiving things. It meant that the way to shape people's lives was by shaping their values. And this was what the churches did best: they preached and they taught. They influenced the individual's system of values. They shaped the individual's conscience. Their conduit to the public arena was thus through the individual's conscience. Shape a church person's values and you could rest assured that your influence would be carried into the public sphere. That person would vote according to his or her conscience, would manifest high values in his or her work, would behave charitably, ethically, honestly. All the churches needed to do was preach and teach.

This was a view that also gained support from the public arena itself. Public officials spoke frequently and fervently about their commitment to high moral principles. They lauded the work of religious leaders in reinforcing these principles. Truman, Eisenhower, Dulles, and others spoke of their own religious faith and commended this faith as a source of societal cohesion and strength. It was easy for religious leaders to believe their efforts really were having an impact.

Already, though, there were signs that this worldview was coming apart. The problem was not that political leaders were suspected of hypocrisy, although this may have been a problem. Nor was the problem, as some have suggested, that this was basically a Protestant view and thus was being undermined by the growing pluralism of the society. Catholic and Jewish leaders in the 1950s articulated it too. The idea was not that religious faith channeled behavior in specifically Protestant or Catholic or Jewish directions. The idea—at least the one expressed in public contexts—was that a deep religious faith gave the individual moral strength, conviction, the will to do what was right. But the premises on which this worldview itself was based were beginning to be questioned. Doubts were beginning to be expressed about the basic connection between values and behavior. What if one's basic values did not translate into actual behavior? What if one's behavior did not stem from one's convictions but was influenced by other factors? As yet, these questions were only raised occasionally. But the very fact that they could be raised suggested the presence of a cultural fissure, a fault line along which a more serious fracture could open up. Values constituted one category, behavior another. The two categories were connected—had to be connected closely for arguments about the impact of conscience on public affairs to be credible. But this connection itself was becoming tenuous.

How, then, did these predisposing conditions in the 1950s become transformed to produce the chasm between religious liberals and conservatives that we experience at the present? How did Herberg's tripartite system, in which the basic religious and *religio-political* divisions occurred between Protestants and Catholics and between Christians and Jews, come to be replaced by what some have called a "two-party system"? The answer, of course, is enormously complex because it involves not only the relations among all the major religious groupings, but also the relations between religion and the forces shaping the broader society. It is, however, enormously important, for it brings together all the decisive factors that have shaped American religion in the period since World War II. We can, of course, touch only the basic contours.

In picturing the transformation as a tripartite division being replaced by a two-party system, we should not think that the latter simply superimposed itself on the former or that the one led directy into the other. It helps to divide the process in two and seek answers for each of its phases separately. The first phase (not temporally but analytically) amounted to an erosion of the basic divisions comprising the tripartite system. The second phase amounted to developments reinforcing a new, different cleavage between liberals and conservatives. These processes combined to create what many have sensed is a new dynamic in the relations between church and state, or between religion and politics more generally. But they are also analytically separable. It also helps to identify an interim phase between the two. Three categories of religious organization did not simply melt into two. Thinking of it that way causes us to miss the violence associated with any social change as basic as this. Natural communities were torn asunder, their parts flung into the air and scattered in strange configurations, before the subterranean forces at work in the society finally rearranged them in the patterns we see today. We have to recognize the upheaval and displacement associated with this process if we are to tap the wellsprings from which much of the present political fury arises.

The erosion of the divisions separating Protestants and Catholics, Jews and Christians, and members of different denominations came about gradually. It was legitimated from within by norms of love and humility that promoted interfaith cooperation. It was reinforced from without by changes in the larger society. Rising education levels, memories of the Holocaust, and the civil rights movement all contributed to an increasing emphasis on tolerance. Regional migration brought Catholics and Protestants, and Christians and Jews, into closer physical proximity with one another. Denominational ghettos, forged by immigration and ethnic ties, were gradually replaced by religiously and ethnically plural communities. Rates of interreligious marriage went up. And it became increasingly common for members of all religious groups to have grown up in other groups, to have friends from other groups, and to have attended other groups. The denominational hierarchies, seminaries, pension plans, and so forth, still played a significant role in the organization of American religion. But the ground was in a sense cleared of old demarcations, thereby making it easier for new alliances and cleavages to emerge.

For those who had spent their entire lives within particular denominational ghettos, these changes in themselves represented major disruptions, of course, especially when it was their pastor who began welcoming outsiders, their denomination that lost its identity by merging with another, or their child who married outside the faith. Most of the upheaval, though, came during the 1960s and was closely associated with the upheaval that pervaded the society in general. Young people were particularly subject to this upheaval. Many were the first ever in their families to attend college. For many attending college meant leaving the ethnoreligious ghetto for the first time. The campuses themselves were growing so rapidly that alienation and social isolation were common experiences. And, of course, the civil rights movement and antiwar protests added to the turmoil. Among the many ways in which this upheaval affected religion, two are especially important.

First, the tensions of the 1960s significantly widened the gap between values and behavior that was mentioned earlier. The two major social movements of this period were the civil rights movement and the antiwar movement, and significantly, both dramatized the disjuncture between values and behavior. The civil rights movement brought into sharp relief what Gunnar Myrdal had called the "American dilemma"—the dilemma of subscribing to egalitarian values in principle, but engaging in racial discrimination in practice.[11] Here was a clear example of values and behavior being out of joint. The antiwar movement pointed up a similar disjuncture. On the one hand, Americans supposedly believed deeply in such values as democracy and the right of people to determine their own destiny. On the other hand, the country was engaged in a war in Southeast Asia that to many seemed to deny these principles. Military force was being used, at best, in an effort to determine another people's destiny for them or, at worst, to prop up an ineffective nondemocratic regime. Both movements drove home, often implicitly, the more general point that people of high values and good consciences could not always be counted on to manifest those virtues in their day-to-day behavior.

The wedge that these movements drove into the earlier connection between values and behavior was to prove increasingly important in separating religious liberals from religious conservatives. Although this picture was to be modified somewhat by the 1980s, in the late 1960s it essentially consisted of conservatives grasping the value side of the equation and liberals seizing the behavioral side. That is, conservatives continued to emphasize preaching and teaching, the shaping of high personal moral standards, and above all the personally redemptive experience of salvation. Whether behavior would result that could alleviate racial discrimination or the war in Southeast Asia was not the issue; the issue was what one believed in one's heart and the motives from which one acted. Liberals, in contrast, increasingly attached importance to behavior. Believe what one will, it does not matter, they said, unless one puts one's faith on the line, takes action, helps bring about change. And changing social institutions was especially important, because institutions provided the reason why values and behavior did not correspond. People with good intentions were caught up in evil systems that needed to be overthrown. For the time being at least, liberals argued for religious organizations' taking direct action in politics, while conservatives remained aloof from politics entirely, preferring instead to concentrate on matters of personal belief. Indeed, the two often gave lip service to the higher principles held by the other, but expressed disagreement over the tactics being used. Thus, conservatives often expressed sympathy with the ideal of racial equality, but argued against the direct-action techniques in which liberal clergy were becoming involved. Liberals often continued to express sympathy with the ideal of personal salvation, but argued that personal salvation alone was not enough of a witness if church people did not become actively involved in working for social justice as well.

The second consequence of the turmoil of the 1960s that stands out is the increasing role of higher education in differentiating styles of religious commitment. In the 1950s, perhaps surprisingly so in retrospect, those who had been to college and those who had not were remarkably similar on most items of religious belief and practice. By the early 1970s, a considerable education gap had emerged between the two. The college educated were much less likely, even than the college educated of the previous decade, to attend religious services regularly. Their belief in a literal interpretation of the Bible had eroded dramatically. They were more tolerant of other religions. And they were more interested in experimenting with the so-called new religions, such as Zen, Transcendental Meditation, Hare Krishna, and the human potential movement. Those who had not been to college remained more committed to traditional views of the Bible, were more strongly interested in religion in general, continued to attend religious services regularly, and expressed doubt about other faiths, including the new religions. In short, educational differences were becoming more significant for religion, just as they were being emphasized more generally in the society. Higher education was becoming a more significant basis for creating social and cultural distinctions. And for religion, it was beginning to reinforce the cleavage between religious liberals and religious conservatives.

For a time, perhaps even as recently as 1976, it appeared that the gap between religious liberals and conservatives might be bridged by a significant segment of the evangelical community. Many of its leaders had participated in the educational expansion of the previous decade. They were exposed to the current thinking in higher education, had been influenced by their own participation in the civil rights and antiwar movements, and had come to hold liberal views on many political issues, and yet retained a strong commitment to the biblical tradition, including an emphasis on personal faith. Their voice, however, was soon drowned out by the more strident voices of the Religious Right. Television hookups and direct-mail solicitations replaced the evangelical periodical, seminary, and scholarly conference as a more effective means of forging a large following and extracting revenue from that following. Issues such as abortion and feminism provided platforms on which the Religious Right could organize. Educational differences continued to separate the more conservative from the more liberal. But other issues began to reinforce these differences. Issues arose that also reflected the success of women in gaining higher education and becoming employed in professional careers, or the exposure one gained in college to the social sciences and humanities as opposed to more narrowly technical educations in engineering or business. The Religious Right also borrowed the more activist style of political confrontation that had been used by the Left during the 1960s. It began to renew the connection between values and behavior. Its commitment to personal morality remained strong, but it now urged believers to take political action, to organize themselves, to infuse their morality into the basic institutions of government. Each side developed special-purpose groups to gain its objectives, either within more narrow denominational contexts or in the national arena.

There are, then, deeper features of the social and cultural terrain that underlie the present fracture between religious liberals and religious conservatives. Had it simply been, say, the Supreme Court's 1973 decision on abortion that elicited different responses from liberals and conservatives, we might well have seen a temporary flurry of activity followed by a gradual progression of interest to other matters. Instead, the religious environment is characterized by two clearly identified communities. Each has developed through events spanning more than a quarter of a century, if not longer. The two are located differently with respect to the basic social division that has been produced by the growth of higher education. Other bases of differentiation, such as regionalism, ethnicity, and denominationalism, that might have mitigated this basic division have subsided in importance. And each side has mobilized its resources around special-purpose groups. It is, therefore, highly likely that specific issues concerning the relations between church and state, cases in the federal courts involving religion, and religious issues in electoral campaigns will continue to evoke strong—and opposing—responses from these two communities.

At the same time, we should not conclude without mentioning several forces that may work to contain or reduce this polarization of religion in the public arena. One is the fact that neither community is actually organized as a single party. Each side is still divided into dozens of denominations, is represented by dozens of different national leaders, has mobilized its political efforts through dozens of special-purpose groups, and at the grass roots consists of thousands of separate congregations. For either side to operate effectively as a political bloc, it must forge coalitions among these various organizations. And, despite the fact that both sides have been able to transcend old divisions, matters of theology, liturgical tradition, and even region still present formidable barriers to be overcome.

Another mitigating factor is that both sides continue to register, at least at the grass roots, a healthy suspicion of government. It sometimes appears that each side is anxious to use government to achieve its goals. But grass-roots mobilization of church people, whether liberals or conservatives, has been more effective in opposing government than in cooperating with government. During the civil rights movement, churchgoers who became most active in politics at the grass roots were those who opposed the actions being taken by the government. During the Vietnam War, it was again those who opposed the government's actions. And in recent years it has been those who opposed the government's role on abortion and welfare spending. In each of these periods, moreover, churchgoers who felt government was becoming too powerful were more likely to become politically active than churchgoers who did not feel this way. The reason, I suspect, lies in the fact that there is a long history of concern, expressed specifically in the First Amendment to the Constitution, over the threat that government poses to religious freedom. In any case, this suspicion of government seems likely to dampen enthusiasm for any strong theocratic orientation of the kind that has sometimes been projected.

Finally, it must be remembered that the involvement of either religious faction in political life cannot succeed without active support from leaders in the political arena itself. Under the Reagan administration, at least an impression of such support was often taken for granted. At the same time, officials of both political parties have often expressed consternation over the activities of religious groups. Lack of political experience, extremist rhetoric, disinterest in routine party activities, and single-issue orientations have been cited as reasons for this consternation. Moreover, religious liberals and religious conservatives have often been courted by factions within the political community for entirely secular purposes: because they supported stronger defense initiatives, or because they favored a freeze on nuclear weapons, or because they wanted a tougher policy against communism in Latin America. Changes in the larger international arena, either militarily or economically, can radically alter the nature of these issues and, therefore, the likelihood of religious factions being courted.

We return, then, to the point at which we began. The relations between faith and politics are contingent on the broader terrain on which they occur. Like the Battle of Waterloo, the battle between religious conservatives and religious liberals is subject to its environment. A deep cultural ravine appears to separate the two communities. Whether this ravine can be bridged depends on raising it from obscurity, bringing it into consciousness, and recognizing the surrounding contours on which these efforts must rest.

Notes

1. Victor Hugo, *Les Misérables* (New York: New American Library, 1987 [1862]), 309.

2. Ibid., 328–329.

3. From a broadcast in February 1987 titled "What Is the Foundation for Our Philosophy of Christianity?" I wish to thank Victoria Chapman for the transcription of this sermon.

4. E. J. Dionne, Jr., "Religion and Politics," *New York Times*, September 15, 1987.

5. Peggy L. Shriver, "The Paradox of Inclusiveness-that-Divides," *Christian Century*, January 21, 1984, p. 194.

6. At the extremes, the public was also about equally divided: 19 percent said they were very liberal; 18 percent, very conservative. These figures are from a survey conducted in June 1984 by the Gallup Organization under a grant from the Robert Schuller Ministries. Some of the study's findings were reported in the May and June 1986 issues of *Emerging Trends*, a publication edited by George Gallup, Jr. The results of additional analyses of these data appear in my book *The Restructuring of American Religion: Society and Faith Since World War II* (Princeton: Princeton University Press, 1988).

7. Will Herberg, *Protestant-Catholic-Jew* (Garden City, NY: Anchor, 1955).

8. Harold Laski, *The American Democracy* (New York: Viking, 1948), 283.

9. "The Churches and World Order," reprinted in *Christian Century*, February 7, 1945, pp. 174–177.

10. C. Stanley Lowell, "The Conversion of America," *Christian Century*, September 29, 1949, p. 1134.

11. Gunnar Myrdal, *An American Dilemma* (New York: Harper & Brothers, 1944).

16

Religion, Voting for President, and Party Identification, 1948–1984

LYMAN A. KELLSTEDT AND MARK A. NOLL

For the sake of the self-respect of modern academics, it would be encouraging to report that we knew as much about the connection between religion and politics in America for the mid-twentieth century as for the nineteenth. Unfortunately, we do not. For reasons outlined in the historiographical introduction to Robert Swierenga's chapter, social scientists studying twentieth-century politics have assumed, until quite recently, that religion in America is a private affair of little public influence. From this assumption, the conclusion followed that it was not worth studying religion with the same care that sociologists and political scientists devoted to race, income, education, and other important social variables. Scholarship on nineteenth-century America should have shaken these assumptions, but it took the recent surge of the Religious Right to alert academics to the continuing salience of religion in political life.[1] Over the last quarter-century a much fuller range of data has in fact been gathered on religious convictions and practices that can be linked with political behavior. Nonetheless, social scientists have often betrayed a reluctance to study the configuration of religion as carefully as the configuration of other social realities, and efforts to interpret systematically the growing mass of potentially useful data remain in their early stages. The result is that we still know more about the religious factor in almost any presidential election from 1832 to 1896 than we do about any presidential election since 1932, with the possible exception of John Kennedy's narrow victory over Richard Nixon in 1960.[2]

Another reason that analysis of modern connections between religion and politics has lagged behind the ethnoreligious research of the nineteenth century is the increasing gap between ethnicity and religion. Explanatory models built upon the mutually reinforcing political effects of religious affiliation and ethnic identification become less helpful when, as in recent decades, the religious-ethnic tie itself becomes less salient. To be sure, ethnicity still reinforces religion (and vice versa) for a great number of American Jews, a significant proportion of American Catholics, and a surprisingly diverse range of Protestants. In addition, the most prominent division in the political landscape remains an ethnic one—the divide between black and white. Yet a number of circumstances, all intensifying since World War II, have worked against the ties that once bound ethnic and religious identification so closely to each other.[3] The rapid expansion of higher education, the movement of large numbers of the middle classes from cities to suburbs, the great growth of the national economy and the attendant mobility of managers, professionals, and laborers—all have weakened ethnoreligious ties. For many Americans, ethnicity has become one thing and religion another.

Again, existing models for charting religious-political connections are undermined by important shifts in the contours of American religion. Denominations with once predictable ethnic or social-economic characteristics have changed (Pentecostals and Roman Catholics, for example, now include a much higher number of Hispanics than in 1940). Some of the older denominations have simply failed to keep up with general population growth. And new denominations with indistinct ethnic ties have emerged as important players on the American religious stage. The *Yearbook of American and Canadian Churches* provides comparative information over time for a number of denominations that have maintained especially good records. These include nine denominations that showed a membership of at least 1 million in 1940. By 1986, that number had grown to eleven. The numerical fate of these large denominations over the intervening forty-six years suggests the extent of the recent changes. Roman Catholic affiliation increased from slightly more than 21 million (roughly 16 percent of the total population) to about 53 million (or 22 percent of all Americans); the older Protestant denominations showed only a very slight gain (Methodists, Presbyterians, Episcopalians, United Church of Christ [formerly Congregationalists], and the Christian Church [Disciples of Christ] taken together grew from about 16 million members to 17.5); the three major Lutheran denominations increased from slightly more than 4 million to nearly 8 million; the Southern Baptist Convention nearly tripled in membership, from less than 5 million to nearly 15 million; and two previously marginal "sects" showed, among these large denominations, the most spectacular gains: Mormons up over fivefold, from 725,000 to 3,860,000, and the pentecostal Assemblies of God up over tenfold, from 199,000 to 2,135,000.[4]

A complex story lies behind these bare figures for each of the denominations. But some messages for social scientists are clear. Catholics—all internal divisions and shifts in ethnic proportion notwithstanding—loom *very* large in contemporary American society.[5] For national purposes, "Protestant" now should be taken to mean much more "Baptist" than "Episcopalian-Presbyterian-Congregationalist-Methodist."[6] Efforts to maintain a generic "Protestant" category mean less and less. Above all, the stereotypical divisions within American religion that helped summarize developments for the nineteenth century are badly in need of renovation today.

Given recent changes in both religion and society, social scientists need sharper, not blunter, instruments to measure religious adherence and the possible connections between religion and politics. Denominational identifiers remain a convenient way of classifying religious Americans, but groupings that transcend or divide denominations are often just as important (for example, "charismatics" and "evangelicals" among Protestants or "traditionalists" and "progressives" among Roman Catholics). New models for describing religious people together, reaching out broadly as the "pietist" and "liturgical" categories did for the nineteenth century, are also necessary. Perhaps they will come from measures of belief, of actual religious practice, or of attitudes toward the nature of morality.[7] It is also necessary to make a more careful discrimination between "communal" and "associational" types of religious allegiance. These terms, from a 1961 study of religion in Detroit by Gerhard Lenski, represent an effort to tease apart the loyalties folded together in ethnoreligious politics.[8] As Lenski used the phrases, "communal" values speak of inherited bonds with family, neighborhood, and ethnic traditions, including religious identification. "Associational" values, on the other hand, relate more to one's own actively chosen groups or associations, including churches. Thus, for instance, individuals who identify themselves as "Baptists" or "Catholics," but who rarely attend church and belong to no other religious organizations, exhibit a "communal" loyalty to their denomination. Those who alongside the denominational identity also go to church regularly and take an active part in religious organizations show an "associational" loyalty. Distinctions of this sort, which turn out to have a remarkable effect on political relationships, make for a clearer picture of religion and politics for Americans as a whole.

Social-scientific surveys have begun to adjust to the new realities of American religion. As a consequence, their data have become increasingly useful for tracing connections between religion and politics. Nonetheless, sophisticated religious measures are still fairly recent, and they are still in need of refinement. Despite noteworthy progress, the surveys that have done the best job of discriminating varieties of religion are weak in tracing political relationships, while those which excel in recording political variables have been weak on religion.[9]

The data available from the Center for Political Studies (CPS) at the University of Michigan, which are made available through the Inter-University Consortium for Political and Social Research, are a case in point. The CPS data, gathered every presidential election year since 1952 (and every off-year congressional election since 1958) by means of extensive interviews with a wide cross-section of Americans (the number of respondents in a given year is usually 1,500 or more), add up to an immensely useful record. Unless otherwise noted, this is the information put to use in this chapter for an analysis of recent trends in religion and politics. CPS questions range widely to cover age, region, income, sex, education, and occupation of respondents. They also have a few questions about religion. But the sophistication of the religious questions has only gradually begun to match the sophistication present from the beginning for other areas. Until 1960, CPS questionnaires inquired only if respondents were Protestants, Catholics, or Jews, and if they went to church regularly. Beginning in 1960, the survey began to ask Protestants for a somewhat more specific designation of denomination, but it was not until 1972 that CPS data distinguished members of the Southern Baptist Convention from other Baptists. And, with rare exceptions, it was not until 1980 that the survey began to ask questions about the importance of religion in a respondent's life and whether the respondent had been born again or considered the Bible to be God's inerrant word. The result is that, while earlier surveys reveal a great deal about religious-political connections, only in later years do we have responses that begin to account for some of the most critical divisions in modern American religion.

Much of what data like the CPS surveys reveal about religion and politics in America is commonplace, but some conjunctions hidden in the data sets are as unexpected as they are important for America's political life. In what follows, we hope to show how levels of political activity, political partisanship (i.e., identifying oneself as a Republican or a Democrat), and voting for president are related to religion. Available data make it possible to generalize on such matters for several groups, including Catholics, Jews, blacks, "evangelical Protestants" (defined below), and other Protestants. Such generalizations are informative for general purposes, but especially for addressing the role of religion in the possible political realignment of recent decades. Political scientists have documented the tendency of American voters to loosen ties to the Democratic party in recent decades and have attributed the change to younger whites and white Southerners. But the potential effects of religious commitment have been mostly neglected.

A table comparing the vote for president between the population at large and the religious groups denominated in the CPS data provides a quick introduction to relationships between religious allegiance and political behavior (see Table 16-1, next page).

Several conclusions fairly leap out from this table:

- Roman Catholics since World War II have voted consistently Democratic, but in steadily decreasing proportions. Through 1960, regular church attendance among Catholics was associated with a stronger Democratic vote. Since 1960 church attendance has made little difference.
- Jews have voted overwhelmingly Democratic, as have blacks who regularly attend church.
- White Protestants have voted consistently Republican, and white Protestants who attend church regularly have voted even more consistently Republican. The size of Republican pluralities varies from denomination to denomination and year to year, but not the fact of the support.
- The year 1964 was a crucial year for political-religious connections among churchgoing blacks. Since that time these votes have gone almost entirely to the Democratic candidates.
- The presidential elections of 1960 and 1976 were the most interesting recent elections from a religious point of view. The election of 1960 marked the high point of Roman Catholic support for the Democratic party and the low point for regularly attending Protestants. In 1976, evangelicals (especially Baptists and Pentecostals) gave their fellow evangelical, Jimmy Carter, a larger than normal proportion of their vote.

More detailed interpretation of these and related data for questions of political activity and partisanship becomes possible when the major religious groups are examined separately.

Table 16-1. Religious Groups and Presidential Vote, 1948-1984:
Comparison with National Pecentages for Democratic Candidates

	1948[a]	1952	1956	1960	1964	1968	1972	1976	1980	1984
Democratic %	49.5	44.4	42.0	49.7	61.0	42.7	37.5	50.1	41.0	40.6
White Protestants	-1	-11	-8	-16	-3	-18	-14	-9	-7	-12
Roman Catholics	+21	+7	+3	+33	+17	+12	0	+6	+3	+4
Jews	+36	+40	+35	+39	+28	+47	+32	+21	+15	+29
W-RA Protestants	-3	-15	-10	-25	-8	-22	-19	-14	-9	-17
RA Roman Catholics	+25	+10	+5	+37	+17	+14	+1	0	-4	+4
RA Blacks	+30	+25	+28	0	+39	+54	+47	+48	+53	+48
W-RA Baptists[b]		-1[c]	-25	0	-28	-31	-11	-26	-29
W-RA Southern Baptists			(data not available)				-17	-8	-4	-18
W-RA Methodists			-5	-19	-4	-25	-13	-18	-8	-5
W-RA Lutherans			-24	-25	-4	-21	-13	-20	-15	-14
W-RA Presbyterians			-18	-28	-16	-24	-21	-25	-18	-23
W-RA Pentecostals [d]			-42	-50	-61	-23	-38	+12	+9	-28
W-RA Episcopalians [d]			-29	-38	-34	-21	-16	-50	-1	-10
W-RA Northern [e] Evangelicals [f]			-25	-36	-10	-21	-28	-11	-8	-29
W-RA Southern [e] Evangelicals [f]			-20	-19	+5	-18	-23	-4	-7	-11

+ = Percentage points more Democratic; - = Percentage points more Republican
W = White
RA = Regular church attenders (weekly or more)

[a] Figures for 1948 were obtained by questions in 1952 about the 1948 election.
[b] Before 1972, Baptists include members of the Southern Baptist Convention.
[c] Figures for 1956 were obtained by questions in 1960 about the 1956 election.
[d] Total numbers are quite small and so more susceptible to sampling error.
[e] Southern means residence in Alabama, Arkansas, Florida, Georgia, Kentucky, Louisiana, Mississippi,
   North Carolina, Oklahoma, South Carolina, Tennessee, Texas, and Virginia.
[f] "Evangelical" is defined below.

Roman Catholics

The social-demographic profile for Roman Catholics has changed considerably since World War II. One of the clearest indications of that
change has to do with levels of education. CPS data from the 1950s show
that only 13 percent of interviewed Catholics had any college experience.
This compared with 19 percent of white Protestants and 24 percent of
Jews. The percentage of Catholics attending college climbed steadily
thereafter, surpassing in the 1960s the proportion of evangelical Protes-

tants who had gone to college, and coming close in the 1980s to the percentage of college-educated among the other Protestants. By the mid-1980s, 43 percent of the Catholics had college experience compared with 32 percent of the evangelicals, 45 percent of nonevangelical Protestants, and 71 percent of Jews. These figures indicate the general transformation of American Catholicism from a population of lower-middle-class, poorly educated people to a group almost as well educated as the mainline Protestants, the traditional elite group in American society. In addition, the Catholic population had become even younger relative to the other religious groups than was the case in the 1950s. Since younger age groups are more likely to have experienced college than their older counterparts, we could expect a higher proportion of college-educated Catholics than college-educated mainline Protestants by the year 2000.

These social-demographic changes are no doubt related to recent changes in religious and political practice as well. Church attendance, for example, has witnessed a dramatic change over the past forty years. In the 1950s, two-thirds of Catholics attended church at least weekly, while for Protestants the corresponding figure was only one-third (45 percent in the South). By the 1980s, weekly or more than weekly church attendance among Catholics had dropped to slightly below 44 percent and was almost identical to that of white evangelicals.[10]

These educational and ecclesiastical developments among Catholics have occurred during a period when the church itself underwent great changes, with the reforms of the Second Vatican Council and the move of many Catholics from cities to suburbs being only the most obvious. Exact accounts of cause and effect may be blurred, but no doubt exists that American Catholics entered a new era in their history after the war.[11]

As could be expected, these changes in American Catholicism have been related to political shifts. Growing middle-class status, as reflected by college education, would lead us to expect a growing Catholic identification as Republicans, the party of the middle class. In fact, however, this has proved to be a relatively late trend. In the 1950s approximately 65 percent of Catholics identified themselves as Democrats, compared to 27 percent as Republicans. Even as education and income improved, however, this partisan gap widened in the 1960s, perhaps reflecting the impact of John Kennedy's election in 1960, which, as Table 16-1 shows, was supported by an overwhelming majority of Catholics. In the 1970s, only 27 percent of Catholics identified themselves as Republicans, but by the mid-1980s this figure had grown to 35 percent, while the Democratic percentage had fallen to 53.[12]

Actual voting by Catholics has tended to become more Republican in recent presidential elections (see Table 16-1), but the fact remains that Catholics have remained attached to the Democratic party. Recent Republican gains seem to be as closely related to short-term factors, like candidates and issues, as they do to long-term gains in socioeconomic status. Yet, despite these gains, Catholics have voted for Democratic presidential candidates at higher rates than Protestants in every presidential election since 1948, and they retain their Democratic partisanship (although with decreasing strength) despite achieving educational levels as high as mainline Protestants, who began and ended the period with consistently high identification as Republicans.

Why have Roman Catholics retained their identification as Democrats? The answer probably has something to do with ethnoreligious factors as well as with the 1960 election. For Catholics, communal ties (i.e., identification with the group) seem to have remained strong while associational ties (in this case, church attendance) have weakened. These communal ties—to put it generally, the "ethno" of ethnoreligious—are strong enough to overcome the otherwise natural affinities of middle-class socioeconomic status, suburbanization, and the Republican party. In addition, the long-term impact of the 1960 election, when John Kennedy became the United States' first Catholic president, should not be underestimated. Catholic vote totals for president had been drawing closer to the national totals in the first three elections after World War II. But in 1960 Catholics gave an overwhelming plurality (82.5 percent) to Kennedy. This surge for the Democratic candidate seems to have carried over throughout the 1960s. Almost certainly it played a part in checking what might well have been a more rapid drift toward the GOP.[13] The following graph illustrates why it is reasonable to suppose that the 1960 election checked the Catholic move toward the Republican party.

For Catholics it is as important to note internal differences as it is for other groups. Regular attendance at mass (an "associational" loyalty) seems to be connected with a stronger vote for the Democratic presidential candidate from 1948 through 1960 (see Table 16-1). From 1964 through 1972, regular attendance does not seem to affect the presidential vote. For 1976 and 1980, the Catholic pattern began to resemble the Protestant pattern, where regular church attendance is associated with a higher Republican vote, while in 1984 church attendance made no difference.

Recent interpretations of Catholic political behavior connected with a major study of Catholic parishioners reveal even further discriminations

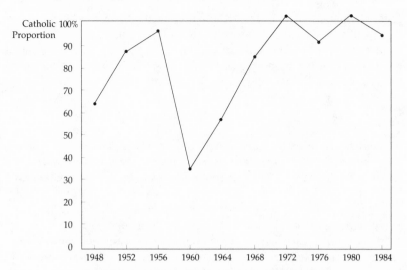

(The Catholic proportion is figured as the percentage of Republican support among Catholics divided by the nation-wide percentage for Republicans. Thus, a proportion above 100%, as in 1972 and 1980, means that the Republican percentage among Catholics was greater than the Republican percentage nation-wide.)

FIGURE 16–1. Ratio of Catholic Percentage of Republican Vote to National Percentage of Republican Vote, 1948–1984

among Catholics. The "Notre Dame Study of Catholic Parish Life" shows that Catholic political preferences reflect common national patterns, like those related to age or region of residence. But it also suggests that among active Catholic parishioners more education does not lead to a shifting of partisan identification to Republicans, while a rise in income does tend in that direction. Furthermore, Catholics who describe their own religious identities in terms of involvement in parish life are more predictably Democratic than those who describe their religious identities in terms of beliefs. In addition, it seems to make considerable difference if religious beliefs focus on individual values or on communal values, with the former more closely associated with "conservative" political positions and the latter with "liberal."[14] From even this bare summary of only a few of the important findings of the Notre Dame study, it is clear that a number of factors come to bear on the political activity of American Catholics today. One very important conclusion of the study follows naturally. As the Notre Dame researchers put it, "It is decreasingly probable that a single theory will offer an encompassing explanation for the mosaic of issues that informs the political consciousness of active Catholics and provokes political action."[15] In other words, every bit of the nuance that has been applied to ethnoreligious aspects of nineteenth-century American politics is warranted for the present as well.

Jews

The number of Jews in the national samples for any one survey is small, but when totals from the various years are combined, it is possible to speak with greater confidence about political orientations. Compared with Christian groups, Jews show far higher levels of education. They are also much less likely to attend their places of worship regularly. Compared with all major groups of Christians, Jews tend to be more active politically, more Democratic in partisan identification, and more Democratic in voting choice. Jewish identification with the Democratic party has ranged from four or five to one over the past generation. Jewish support for Democratic presidential candidates has declined somewhat in the 1970s and 1980s, but still remains very high (see Table 16-1).

Jews present a picture of a group with weak associational ties (i.e., synagogue attendance), but very strong communal ties. It may safely be assumed that these communal ties play a crucial role in political behavior. Jewish voters are notably distinct in one area, for they contradict the usual American association between high income and high education with Republican partisanship. For the period after World War II, strong traditions of political liberalism, a definite sense of standing over against the dominant WASP culture, and support for the state of Israel seem to have been the dominant motivation factors for Jewish voters, not socioeconomic position.[16]

Blacks

CPS data suggest that blacks rank high in church attendance compared to the population at large. Historical studies, like those cited by David Wills, above, would lead us to expect the high importance of religion for blacks, and this is in fact what contemporary social-scientific data show. Blacks in general rank a close second to conservative white Protestants in their religious involvement (church attendance, commitment to denominations, membership in church-related groups), and ahead of Catholics, Jews, and moderate and liberal Protestants. Not surprisingly, CPS surveys show that in the aggregate blacks are younger and less well educated than white groups, although levels of higher education have risen rapidly since the 1950s.[17]

Politically, there have been important changes for blacks since World War II. All measures of politicization (interest in politics, voter turnout, campaign activity) show dramatic gains in the past four decades. Due to increased black political mobilization, civil rights legislation, and a decline in overt discrimination, black voter registration more than doubled between 1952 and 1984, and percentages of blacks voting for president have begun to approach national averages, particularly in the North. As is also true for white groups, blacks who regularly attend church show consistently higher percentages of involvement in all areas of political activity.

Throughout the postwar period blacks have identified as Democrats and supported Democratic candidates. But that identification and support increased throughout the 1960s, no doubt because Democratic figures took the lead in sponsoring civil rights legislation.

An untold and most interesting religious-political story among blacks since World War II concerns the relation of evangelical beliefs and practices to political partisanship. A higher proportion of black churchgoers than white churchgoers may be identified as evangelicals (either through the patterns of belief explained below or through association with theologically conservative denominations). Furthermore, these black evangelicals hold social views very similar to those of white evangelicals. In 1984, for example, 232 whites and 71 blacks in the CPS survey responded that religion was very important in their lives, that they had been born again, and that they believed the Bible was literally true. Among these black and white "evangelicals" very similar percentages opposed abortion on demand and favored prayer in the public schools. (White and black Protestants who were not "evangelical" by these criteria favored abortion on demand and opposed prayer in the public schools by 15–30 more percentage points.) But on questions of party identification and presidential vote, white and black evangelicals were poles apart. Among white evangelicals, 54 percent identified themselves as Republicans and 75 percent voted for Ronald Reagan, while only 14 percent of black evangelicals said they were Republicans and only 8 percent voted for Reagan. To say the least, the evangelical-Republican affinity is monochromatic.[18]

Could it have been different? Might the strong Republican gains of recent years among white evangelicals have been matched by a corresponding growth of black evangelicals in the GOP? The number of black respondents in the CPS surveys is not sufficient to allow us to speak with complete confidence, but it does seem as if an important "realignment that never happened" lurks in fairly recent history. CPS measures before 1980 do not allow for the identification of evangelicals on the basis of beliefs, but they do record church attendance. And given the preponderance of evangelical Protestants among blacks generally, it is a fair conclusion that most blacks who regularly attended church had evangelical convictions. What CPS data show is an increasing Republican vote among regularly attending blacks from 1948 through 1960. In three out of four of those elections, regularly attending (and therefore probably more evangelical) blacks voted much more for the Republican than blacks who did not attend church regularly (regular attenders voted more Republican by 17 percentage points in 1948, more Republican by 23 percentage points in 1952, more Democratic by 10 percentage points in 1956, and more Republican by 37 percentage points in 1960). In 1960, the vote among CPS respondents for Richard Nixon over the Catholic John Kennedy reached 50 percent. Even assuming sizable sampling error, this finding is surprising, to say the least. Evidently, black evangelicals shared in the suspicions of the Catholic candidate that pushed all white Protestant vote totals to record Republican proportions for that year. In 1960, the trend among black evangelicals seemed to be moving toward the Republicans, and there was probably a residual stigma attached to the Democrats for running a Catholic candidate.

It seems as if the Republican hour had arrived among black evangelicals. But if there ever was such an hour, it quickly ran its course. For whatever reason—moves made by the Kennedy administration toward blacks, the national outpouring of grief at Kennedy's assassination, Lyndon Johnson's sponsorship of the 1964 Civil Rights Act, Barry Goldwater's opposition to civil rights legislation—black evangelicals turned resolutely away from the Republicans. All 114 church-attending blacks polled in the 1964 survey voted for Johnson. And since 1964 black voting for Democratic presidential candidates has never fallen below 85 percent, with no measurable difference between blacks who regularly attend church and those who do not. (In 1984, where measures of belief could be used, 8 percent of black evangelicals voted for Reagan compared to 10 percent of blacks who were not evangelicals.) The graph that follows, which duplicates the format of the previous figure for Roman Catholics, shows how decisive the election of 1964 was.

Ethnicity may have become less of a factor for other parts of the American electorate. For blacks, religion is associated with increased political activity, but it is race that explains partisanship and voting.

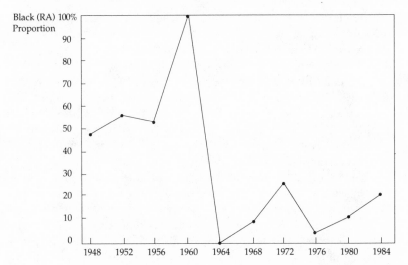

RA = Regular church attenders
(The black proportion is figured as the percentage of Republican support among blacks divided by the nation-wide Republican percentage. Thus, 1960 is the only year reported here when the percentage of the Republican vote among blacks who regularly attended church equalled the nation-wide percentage for the Republicans.)

FIGURE 16-2. Ratio of Black (Regular Church Attenders) Percentage of Republican Vote to National Percentage of Republican Vote, 1948-1984

"Evangelical" Protestants and Other Protestants

Designations among Protestants are as tricky in the mid-twentieth century as they were in the mid-nineteenth. For general purposes, a three- or fourfold categorization is probably necessary. Roof and McKinney's *American Mainline Religion*, one of the best recent studies of Protestantism, identifies clusters of "liberal," "moderate," and "conservative" Protestants.[19] Further distinctions may also be warranted, perhaps among Roof and McKinney's "conservatives," between "independents," whose churches shun associations with other congregations, and "connectionals," who are part of larger, self-conscious movements. For political purposes, however, a simpler distinction seems to aid interpretation, or at least the kind of interpretation allowed by the nature of the data collected in national surveys. This distinction is between "evangelical" Protestants and other Protestants. Word choice is precarious here, because some of those we group as "evangelicals" do not use the name for themselves, but rather prefer designations like "Bible believing," "fundamentalist," or "Spirit-filled." On the other hand, some we group with the other Protestants are clearly in an "evangelical" tradition. Lutherans, for example, will figure as "other Protestants" here, although they are the American counterpart to Germany's *evangelische* churches.[20]

The distinction between "evangelical" and "other" Protestants depends upon an analysis of beliefs and behaviors.[21] Survey data show that individuals who respond as attending church regularly, as finding religion important in their lives, as being born again, and as believing that the Bible is the Word of God (or that it is inerrant) are more likely to be identified with some denominations than others. In turn, denominations that stress certain doctrinal beliefs—the urgent necessity of spreading the Christian message, the divinity of Christ, Christ as the only way to salvation, and an inerrant Bible—regularly show up in social-scientific surveys with high numbers who have been born again, for whom religion is very important, and (obviously) who believe in an inerrant Bible. This clustering of beliefs and denominational affiliations constitutes a reasonably coherent "evangelical" category, set off from Catholics by distinctly Protestant emphases, from "European evangelicals" like the Lutherans by attitudes drawn from American experience, and from older American denominations by the evangelical embrace of the revivalist tradition. Presbyterians, Lutherans, and Methodists, for example, count here as "other Protestants" because their members responding to surveys rank considerably lower on orthodox beliefs than those in the "evangelical" denominations listed below. In the 1984 CPS data, members of these three groups who regularly attended church were less likely to have been born again, by 31 to 55 percentage points, than members of the evangelical bodies who regularly attended church, and their members were less likely to believe in biblical inerrancy by 21 to 51 percentage points.

Like any classification scheme, this one has ambiguities and unavoidable errors. Nonetheless, it is possible to group together denominations in a way that combines attention to the nature of religious groups and accessibility to the data collected by social-scientific surveys. For the CPS data, therefore, we count as "evangelical" denominations the Southern Baptist Convention, all other Baptists (Primitive, Free Will, Missionary, Fundamentalist, Gospel), the Evangelical and Reformed, Christian Reformed, Disciples of Christ, Christian Church, Mennonite, Church of the Brethren, Church of God, Nazarene, Free Methodist, Church of God in Christ, Plymouth Brethren, Pentecostal, Assembly of God, Church of Christ, Salvation Army, Seventh Day Adventist, and Quaker. It should be noted in passing that regular churchgoers who claim these denominational affiliations are much more likely to hold the evangelical beliefs specified above than those with only nominal attachment to these denominations. Most surveys do not have sufficient respondents from any one of these groups for reliable conclusions. Taken together, they provide a sufficient quantity for examining connections between religion and politics.

Other Protestants

America's "old guard" churches—Episcopalians, Congregationalists, Presbyterians, and Methodists—along with major Old World groups like the Lutherans, turn out to have a standard profile socially, politically, and religiously. Throughout the past forty years, this group of denominations has consistently outranked other white Christians (evangelical Protestants and Catholics) in their proportion of older citizens as well as in their levels of higher education. In addition, a small and diminishing proportion of this group resides in the South (from 26 percent in the 1960s to 17 percent in the mid-1980s). They are also less likely to attend church regularly than either evangelicals or Catholics.

Politically, this group has several distinctives. Throughout the past three decades, these "mainline" denominations have shown greater interest in politics than evangelicals or Catholics, have turned out to vote at much higher rates than evangelicals (and somewhat higher rates than Catholics), and have engaged in more campaign activities than members of the other two groups. In other words, the white, Anglo-Saxon Protestants continue to play a large political role in American society, just as they always have. Among these denominations, it is the Episcopalians who are the most politicized, followed closely by the Presbyterians.

Denominational preferences provided by members of the U.S. Congress testify to the continuing political salience of these denominations. Only about 5 percent of Americans now identify themselves as Presbyterians, Episcopalians, or members of the United Church of Christ (Congregationalists). Yet almost a quarter of the members in the 100th Congress that gathered in January 1987 were members of these three denominations (60 Episcopalians, 57 Presbyterians, and 16 from the United Church of Christ).[22]

As our mass sample data show, members of the old Protestant denominations have been a mainstay of the Republican party. During the 1960s, 43 percent identified as Democrats and 54 percent as Republicans, with similar but somewhat greater support for the Republicans during the next two decades (1970s: 37 percent Democrats, 50 percent Republicans;

1980s: 38 percent Democrats, 56 percent Republicans). Among Episcopalians and Presbyterians, the proportions identifying with the GOP are even higher, with usually more than two Republicans for each Democrat.

This group of Protestants gave a plurality for every Republican candidate for president since 1948, with the exception of 1964, when 53 percent of their number supported Lyndon Johnson over Barry Goldwater. Even in 1964, however, Episcopalians and Presbyterians lent a majority of their support to the Republican candidate. Among the individuals from these denominations who regularly attend church, the Republican vote, expressed as a percentage of the national Republican vote, has gone as high as 200 percent (Episcopalians in 1976). Rarely has it been as low as the 108 percent from Methodists in 1984. In terms of vote choice, the percentage of Republican ballots from regularly attending Episcopalians, Presbyterians, Lutherans, and Methodists has usually been one-third to two-thirds higher than the national Republican percentage.

As for all white Protestants, regular church attendance has been associated with higher Republican pluralities. Among the four largest families differentiated by CPS data, church attendance seems to make the most political difference among Lutherans, least among Methodists. Since 1960, with but four exceptions, regular churchgoing Presbyterians, Lutherans, Episcopalians, and Methodists have voted more Republican than their fellows who do not attend church regularly.[23] Churchgoing seems especially important among Lutherans, where Republican presidential candidates have received from 13 to 23 more percentage points from regular attenders than from the irregular. These figures suggest that, as the most ethnic of these Protestant bodies, Lutheran "associational" values have a greater political weight than "communal" values.

The most important conclusion about the politics of this cluster of Protestants, however, concerns its size. These descendants of the "Protestant establishment" of previous generations no doubt retain considerable clout in public life. But as their numbers have declined relative to the total population, so has their political importance.

Evangelical Protestants

The group of Protestants we have distinguished as "evangelicals" shows distinct demographic characteristics. They are far more likely to come from the South than the other religious groups. In addition, they are less likely to have attended college. These findings fit common stereotypes. But to focus on the stereotypes ignores some important changes taking place within the evangelical community. Since the 1960s, the number of college-educated evangelicals has doubled to where in the mid-1980s almost one-third of the group had some higher education. Among Northern, regular church-attending evangelicals, close to one-half have had college experience.[24]

The CPS data also reveal important age trends among evangelicals. In the 1960s about one-quarter of the group was under 35, while one-third was over 55. By the mid-1980s, the proportion of evangelicals in the younger age group had grown to 37 percent while the percentage in the older group remained the same. Hence, we have an evangelical population in the 1980s that is younger and better educated in comparison with the preceding generation. These trends hold out the prospect that evangelicals will experience a liberalization of social attitudes similar to that taking place in other groups with younger and better-educated members. One example of such liberalization is attitudes toward Roman Catholics. Figures from the 1960 election make it clear that anti-Catholic sentiment was strong in the evangelical community and was directed against the candidacy of John Kennedy. By the 1980s, such sentiment was much less common.[25]

The white evangelical community seems also to be growing when compared with other Protestants. During the 1960s, the CPS surveys placed 43 percent of Protestants in the evangelical denominations, a figure that had risen to 47 percent by the mid-1980s. Evangelicals are also more likely to be influenced by their religion because their associational ties are so strong. Roof and McKinney rank "conservative Protestants" (roughly equivalent to the "evangelicals" of this chapter) as the American grouping most thoroughly involved in their churches and in religious activities.[26] During the 1960s, according to CPS data, evangelicals attended church about as frequently as the other Protestants and about half as regularly as Catholics. But by the mid-1980s, the consistency of evangelical church attendance had caught up with Catholics and far surpassed the other Protestants.

Politically, evangelicals in the 1960s were less likely to be interested in politics, less likely to vote in presidential elections, and less likely to be involved in campaign activities than other religious groups. Despite the rise of the Religious Right, these trends continued into the mid-1980s. Such findings partly reflect the Southern regional bias of evangelicals. Because of the one-party tradition, levels of political involvement for all groups tend to be lower in the South. Educational levels among evangelicals may also explain low levels of political involvement, since the two are related for all groups. Yet even among Northern, regular church-attending evangelicals (the subgroup most like other Protestants demographically) politicization is lower than for other Protestants.

Church attendance, however, does make a difference. Taking all evangelical respondents from 1960 through 1984, and dividing them by region of residence and frequency of church attendance, Northern, regularly attending evangelicals showed the greatest interest in politics, turned out to vote most frequently, and engaged in the most campaign activity. Southern, regular-attending evangelicals ranked next. Northern evangelicals who attended church only irregularly came next, and Southern irregular attenders showed the least political involvement.

One factor affecting conclusions about evangelical political activity is the low level of interest by Pentecostals. In the 1960s not one Pentecostal interviewed in the CPS surveys engaged in campaign activity. The same results appeared in 1984. CPS data point to similar conclusions for the independent, fundamentalist denominations. Even if the 1988 campaign of Pat Robertson for the Republican presidential nomination increased levels of political activity among Pentecostals and fundamentalists, it is still the case that general levels of evangelical political activity are low. Baptists, including Southern Baptists, for example, have ranked below Episcopalians, Presbyterians, Lutherans, and Methodists in measures of political activity throughout the past three decades.

On the question of party identification, evangelicals show a marked change since World War II. In the 1960s, the Democratic edge over the Republicans was almost two to one, 59 percent to 31 percent. (Projecting data from 1960 back into the 1950s, it seems safe to conclude that evangelicals were at least two to one Democratic in that period.) In the 1970s the gap had narrowed to 49 percent for the Democrats to 36 percent for the Republicans. By the mid-1980s Democrats were in the minority, 41 percent to 47 percent. This is a remarkable transformation that has been missed by scholars, and shows a very different pattern from the other groups examined in this chapter. Before attempting to explain

Table 16-2. Partisan Identifications of Evangelical Sub-Groups, 1960s -1980s

Evangelical Groups	1960s		1970s		1980s		GOP gains 1960s-80s
	Dem	Rep	Dem	Rep	Dem	Rep	
Northern, RA	34.9%	57.4%	38.7%	47.5%	21.7%	71.7%	14.3
Northern, LT-RA	50.4	41.5	43.3	37.4	43.8	43.8	2.3
Southern, RA	69.3	21.4	57.0	31.6	51.0	39.0	17.6
Southern, LT-RA	70.1	19.0	53.9	28.9	45.0	37.9	18.9

RA = Regular church attenders
LT-RA = Less than regular church attendance

this dramatic shift in partisan identification, a comparison of the same four evangelical subgroups discussed above is relevant (see Table 16-2). The subgroup differences are substantial. Republican gains in partisanship are greatest among the Northern regular attenders and among Southerners. The former group has been Republican throughout the past three decades and has become even more so, resembling the other Protestants in its partisan identities. These data show also that church attendance has a much greater impact on partisanship in the North than in the South. This may be due to the fact that in the North regular church attendance makes a person stand out more from the surrounding culture and makes a religious influence more likely. Finally, the importance of this partisan shift is heightened by the fact that it is strongest among younger voters, and so portends a great deal for the future.

A comparison of party preference between 1980 and 1984 illustrates the dimensions of recent changes. When evangelicals are divided according to their denominations, frequency of church attendance, age, and region, most categories show modest gains for the Republicans (2 percent more of all Southerners, for example, called themselves Republicans in 1984 compared to 1980, as did 9 more percent of Northerners under 35 from other Protestant denominations). Republican gains, however, were nothing short of spectacular for evangelicals under 35 who regularly attended church; they vastly exceeded Republican gains in all other possible categories: 26 more percent for Southerners, 31 more percent for Northerners.[27]

Evangelical partisan realignment appears also when examining specific denominations and denominational groups. The following figures in Table 16-3 show changes in party identification in the last two decades among regularly attending evangelicals.

In this breakdown, the other Baptists and Pentecostals are predominately from the North, so the movement toward the Republicans is not

Table 16-3. Partisan Identification of Selected
Evangelical Denominations, 1970s and 1980s

Evangelical Denominations	1970s		1980s		GOP gain 1970s-80s
	Dem	Rep	Dem	Rep	
Other Baptists	44.7%	43.2%	16.7%	75.0%	31.8
Southern Baptists	59.8	32.1	42.1	50.9	18.8
Pentecostals	49.4	31.0	43.8	43.8	12.8

simply a Southern phenomenon. But when consideration is given to the size of the Southern Baptist Convention, the largest Protestant denomination in the United States, these results increase in significance.[28]

Among the factors that have led to these partisan changes in the past three decades are the improving socioeconomic status of evangelicals, the anti-Catholic/anti-Kennedy vote of 1960, early opposition to the civil rights movement throughout the 1960s, the emergence of the social issue agenda in the 1970s, the embrace of this agenda by the Republican party in the 1980s, and the mobilization efforts of the Christian Right in the late 1970s and early 1980s. The evangelical move away from the Democratic party seems to have been stimulated negatively by Democratic candidates like George McGovern and positively by Republicans like Ronald Reagan.

While evangelical voting for president offers several points to ponder, the most immediately obvious result from CPS data is that evangelicals in the 1960s and 1970s were voting for Republicans even while maintaining Democratic identity (see Table 16-1). Only for Lyndon Johnson in 1964 did more evangelicals vote for the Democrat than for the Republican. No doubt the "habit" of voting Republican in presidential elections made the transformation of party loyalties to the GOP an easier process.

Among evangelicals, regular attendance at church makes even more difference than for other Protestants. The comparisons for elections since 1960, broken down again by region and frequency of attendance, are shown in Table 16-4.

Table 16-4. Evangelical Vote by Region and
Regularity of Church Attendance, 1960-1984

	North RA	North LT-RA	South RA	South LT-RA
Democratic % 1960	14.0%	44.4%	30.6%	57.3%
Democratic % 1964	51.1	68.9	65.5	67.2
Democratic % 1968	21.4	25.6	24.4	19.4
George Wallace % 1968	2.4	14.1	34.1	41.7
Democratic % 1972	9.9	25.8	14.5	25.0
Democratic % 1976	39.4	48.9	46.5	53.7
Democratic % 1980	33.3	42.1	34.0	38.9
Democratic % 1984	11.4	35.5	29.2	36.1

RA = Regular church attenders
LT-RA = Less than regular church attendance

Regional differences are not unimportant here, for the traditional bent of the white South to the Democratic party certainly stands in the way of a thorough evangelical-Republican alliance. At the same time, differences between regular and less regular attenders are more striking than differences between regions. In 1960, the differences are the greatest—most regular-church-attending evangelicals were unwilling to support Kennedy. Anti-Catholic sentiment among these regular churchgoers almost certainly accounted for the voting. In each of the remaining elections, regular attenders were somewhat more supportive of Republican candidates than those who attended less frequently. And George Wallace's candidacy in 1968 won significantly less approval from evangelicals who regularly attended church than from those who did not, although the Wallace vote among Southern regular attenders was very high.

Figures for individual denominations support these conclusions. In 1960, regularly attending Baptists, including Southern Baptists, gave Kennedy 25 percent of their votes as compared with 51 percent of Baptists who did not attend church regularly. By contrast, in the next election the gap was much smaller. Anti-Catholic sentiment in 1960 seems, in other words, to have accounted for much of the Nixon vote among regularly attending Baptists.

No doubt Watergate retarded the swing of evangelicals toward the Republican party. But CPS data indicate that the candidacy of a born-again Southern Baptist, Jimmy Carter, in 1976 and 1980 also slowed the evangelical move to the Republicans. In 1976, regularly attending Northern evangelicals gave Carter a higher proportion of their votes (relative to nationwide percentages) than to any other Democratic candidate measured by the CPS surveys. Also in 1976, Southern Baptists and other Baptists voted more heavily for Carter than they had for any Democrat since Lyndon Johnson. In 1976 and 1980, Pentecostals, who regularly vote overwhelmingly Republican, gave Carter a plurality of their votes. By contrast, percentages for Carter in both 1976 and 1980 among regularly attending Methodists, Lutherans, Presbyterians, and Episcopalians were no more than, and sometimes less than, the percentages these groups normally gave to the Democratic candidate. Although Carter did less well among evangelicals in 1980 than in 1976, his candidacies seem to have checked the evangelical move toward the GOP. In this regard, Jimmy Carter may have exerted an effect on Protestant evangelicals that resembled the effect of John Kennedy's candidacy on Catholics.

In summary, political shifts among evangelicals have been substantial in the past generation. Social-demographic changes have brought evangelicals into the cultural mainstream, although they remain more Southern and less educated than other religious groups in the 1980s. Somewhat less involved in politics than other groups, evangelicals have moved dramatically toward the Republican party in terms of identification while strongly supporting Republican candidates in presidential elections throughout the last generation. By the mid-1980s, it can be said that evangelicals had realigned and had become members of the Republican party coalition.[29]

The Question of Causation

Figures that link religion and politics do not by themselves answer questions of causal relationship. No doubt more Catholics, proportionately, voted Republican in 1984 than in 1948, for example, because levels of Catholic income and education now come closer to matching levels of income and education of those who regularly vote Republican. To take another example, members of the Southern Baptist Convention now may identify themselves more often as Republicans because Southerners as a whole are doing so. The question remains, as Lenski put it in 1961, whether religion is "cause or correlate of party preference."[30]

Social scientists, however, have several techniques by which to determine the relative importance in a large population of several factors that might come to bear on vote choice or political attitudes. One of these, multiple classification analysis, has been used in studies of possible links between religion and social attitudes. Its purpose is to compare the influence of religious affiliation and practice with other social variables (like region of residence, income, levels of education). The application of this technique turns out to support roughly the same conclusions as analagous techniques discovered for the nineteenth century. Although many other things come into play, religion is an important factor—for some groups, the most important factor—in shaping political attitudes and behavior. Roof and McKinney, for example, demonstrate by this technique that religious affiliation bears a very strong connection with moral attitudes.[31] A recent study of social issue positions among evangelicals has a similar result. Factors like region and age certainly have an influence, but the more important religion is for a group and the more important evangelical convictions are, the more religion is associated with a conservative social agenda, especially for residents of the North.[32]

Much more work is required to speak confidently about connections between religion and politics in the middle and late twentieth century. Changes that separate modern society from the society of antebellum

America are as obvious as they are important. Yet continuities may be stronger than conventional assumptions allow. Of these continuities, one of the most significant arises from the simple observation—however it may be interpreted—that religious affiliation and religious practice have remained, at least for very many Americans, a vitally important part of political life since World War II.

Notes

1. Among the best studies of this phenomenon are Robert C. Liebman and Robert Wuthnow, eds., *The New Christian Right* (Hawthorne, NY: Aldine, 1983); Tod A. Baker, Robert P. Steed, and Laurence W. Moreland, eds., *Religion and Politics in the South* (New York: Praeger, 1983); David G. Bromley and Anson D. Shupe, eds., *New Christian Politics* (Macon, GA: Mercer University Press, 1984); and Stephen D. Johnson and Joseph B. Tamney, eds., *The Political Role of Religion in the United States* (Boulder, CO: Westview, 1986).

2. For a particularly helpful analysis of the religious dimensions of that election, see Philip Converse, *Elections and the Political Order* (New York: Wiley, 1966), chs. 5 and 6.

3. Two superb recent studies on the religious impact of those changes are Robert Wuthnow, *The Restructuring of American Religion: Society and Faith Since World War II* (Princeton: Princeton University Press, 1988); and Wade Clark Roof and William McKinney, *American Mainline Religion: Its Changing Shape and Future* (New Brunswick, NJ: Rutgers University Press, 1987). A solid general study, which also puts to use the materials of the Center for Political Studies that we use in this chapter, is Paul Lopatto, *Religion and the Presidential Election* (New York: Praeger, 1985).

4. Constant H. Jacquet, Jr., ed., *Yearbook of American and Canadian Churches: 1988* (Nashville: Abingdon, 1988), 20–61.

5. For social-political and theological-political analyses of this fact, see, respectively, Andrew M. Greeley, *The American Catholic: A Social Portrait* (New York: Basic Books, 1977), and Richard J. Neuhaus, *The Catholic Moment* (San Francisco: Harper & Row, 1987).

6. It is well to remember that there are at least as many Baptists not part of the Southern Baptist Convention as who belong to the SBC. For figures, see *Yearbook of American and Canadian Churches*, 246–256.

7. Wuthnow, *Restructuring of American Religion*, 61–64, 148–149, as well as in his chapter above, shows how changing attitudes toward the relationship between convictions and behavior, leading to a sharp divide between moral absolutists and moral relativists, constitute a new basis for religious classification.

8. Gerhard Lenski, *The Religious Factor: A Sociological Study of Religion's Impact on Politics, Economics, and Family Life* (Garden City, NY: Doubleday, 1961), 157–160, 164–168.

9. A prime example of the former is the 1978 Gallup survey conducted for *Christianity Today* magazine. The election studies from the University of Michigan, cited below, and the National Opinion Research Center at the University of Chicago are examples of the latter.

10. For similar data on the decline of religious practice among American Catholics, see Roof and McKinney, *American Mainline Religion*, 56. Roof and McKinney draw their data from the General Social Surveys of the National Opinion Research Center.

11. Good accounts of that recent history are found in James J. Hennesey, S.J., *American Catholics: A History of the Roman Catholic Community in the United States* (New York: Oxford University Press, 1981), 307–331; and Jay P. Dolan, *The American Catholic Experience* (Garden City, NY: Doubleday, 1985), 421–454.

12. Our references to the 1970s include materials from the 1972, 1976 and 1980 surveys in order to balance the figures reported for the three election years of the 1960s.

13. This is also the opinion of Lopatto, *Religion and the Presidential Election*, 80–93.

14. As the Notre Dame researchers note, the same sort of connections between individual-conservative and communal-liberal have shown up in a study of members of Congress. See Peter L. Benson and Dorothy L. Williams, *Religion on Capitol Hill: Myths and Realities* (New York: Harper & Row, 1982).

15. David C. Leege and Michael R. Welch, "The Roots of Political Orientations: Examining the Relationship Between Religion and Politics among American Catholics," *Journal of Politics*, forthcoming.

16. For a fuller picture of Jewish demographic trends and their relation to American religion, see Roof and McKinney, *American Mainline Religion*, 16, 96–97, 183–184.

17. Ibid., 101, on black religious practice, 112–113 on black socioeconomic status.

18. See Lyman A. Kellstedt, "The Meaning and Measurement of Evangelicalism: Problems and Prospects," in Ted G. Jelen, ed., *Religion and American Political Behavior* (New York: Praeger, forthcoming), Table 2.

19. For the denominations making up these three categories, see Roof and McKinney, *American Mainline Religion*, 253–256.

20. On the complicated historical question of defining "evangelicals," see Cullen Murphy, "Protestantism and the Evangelicals," *The Wilson Quarterly* 5 (Autumn 1981): 105–116; George M. Marsden, "Introduction: The Evangelical Denomination," in Marsden, ed., *Evangelicalism in Modern America* (Grand Rapids: Eerdmans, 1984), viii–xvi; Timothy L. Smith, "The Evangelical Kaleidoscope and the Call to Christian Unity," *Christian Scholar's Review* 15 (1986): 125–140; and Mark A. Noll, *Between Faith and Criticism: Evangelicals, Scholarship, and the Bible in America* (San Francisco: Harper & Row, 1986), 1–5.

21. An extended rationale for the distinctions used here is found in Kellstedt,

"Meaning and Measurement of Evangelicalism." It is also developed in James Guth, Ted Jelen, Lyman Kellstedt, Corwin Smidt, and Kenneth Wald, "The Politics of Religion in America," *American Politics Quarterly* 16 (1988): 357–397.

22. A full list of these religious preferences was printed in the *Washington Post*, Jan. 10, 1987, p. G8. Among the Representatives and Senators were also 144 Roman Catholics, 74 United Methodists, 55 Baptists, 37 Jews, 23 Lutherans, 22 "Protestants," 11 Mormons, and 10 Unitarian-Universalists, to cite the other groups with at least ten members.

23. The exceptions were Presbyterians in 1964, Methodists in 1984, and Episcopalians in 1960 and 1980. Episcopalian results may be suspect because of the small number of Episcopalians interviewed in each survey.

24. On the effects of college training on evangelicals, see especially James Davison Hunter, *Evangelicalism: The Coming Generation* (Chicago: University of Chicago Press, 1987).

25. These conclusions are reached from CPS data not presented here. Levels of anti-Semitism among evangelicals and fundamentalists are also no higher than among the population at large, if adjustments are made for the social-demographic characteristics of these groups, according to Gregory Martire and Ruth Clark, *Anti-Semitism in the United States: A Study of Prejudice in the 1980s* (New York: Praeger, 1982), 68–76.

26. Roof and McKinney, *American Mainline Religion*, 101.

27. For further discussion, see Lyman A. Kellstedt, "Religion and Partisan Realignment: The Impact of the Evangelicals," in Jelen, *Religion and American Political Behavior*.

28. For a similar movement of clergy in the Southern Baptist Convention toward the Republican party, see James L. Guth, "Political Converts: Partisan Realignment Among Southern Baptist Ministers," *Election Politics* 3 (1985): 2–6.

29. Other important dimensions of evangelical political behavior in the 1980s are mapped by Corwin Smidt, "Born-Again Politics: The Political Behavior of Evangelical Christians in the South and Non-South," in Baker et al., *Religion and Politics in the South*, 27–56; and Smidt, "Evangelicals and the 1984 Election: Continuity or Change?" *American Politics Quarterly* 15 (October 1987): 419–444.

30. Lenski, *The Religious Factor*, 126.

31. Roof and McKinney, *American Mainline Religion*, 186–228. Leege and Welch put to use a similar technique, multiple regression analysis, in the Notre Dame Parish study as a basis for some of their judgments about which religious factors relate positively to partisan political attitudes.

32. See Kellstedt, "Evangelical Religion and Support for Social Issue Policies: An Examination of Regional Variation," in Robert P. Steed, Laurence W. Moreland, and Tod A. Baker, eds., *The Disappearing South? Studies in Regional Change and Continuity* (University, AL: University of Alabama Press, 1989).

17

Afterword: Religion, Politics, and the Search for an American Consensus

GEORGE M. MARSDEN

Attempting an overview on so complex a subject as American religion and politics is a hazardous enterprise. Still, it may be worth the effort to make an informal attempt to identify some persistent themes and to relate them to some twentieth-century developments, if only to stimulate others to do the same.

Religion, especially when combined with ethnicity, has been the best predictor of political behavior throughout most of the history of the United States. From the early colonial settlements through at least the election of 1896, significant correlations existed between religious and political sentiments. This did not mean that religion was always or usually the primary determinant of political behavior, since many other variables came into play, including all those involved with ethnicity. Nonetheless, it is undeniable that, historically, religion has been a major component in American political life. Moreover, it was for centuries a divisive element, or at least a feature of the political scene fitting in with disruption more than harmony.

For our present purposes it is necessary only to mention the formidable role that religion played during the American colonial era. Throughout the period a central theme was the extended cold war between Protestants and Catholics. This deep rivalry dominated American thought on international politics in a way not unlike the way the Cold War overshadowed everything after World War II. Anti-Catholicism, of course, was far from the only political consideration for the overwhelmingly Protestant colonies, but for many influential people it was a major concern, one that could elicit their strongest loyalties.

Related was the theme of anti-Anglicanism. For Puritan New England this was originally the primary religious-political issue, one for which their coreligionists in England went to war and for which the English Puritans experienced bitter suffering after the Restoration of the monarchy in 1660. Although eighteenth-century New Englanders accepted the Anglican political establishment for a time, they never reconciled themselves to it.

In the middle colonies and the inland Southern settlements of the eighteenth century, anti-Anglicanism was likewise often a dominating passion for the militant Scotch-Irish Presbyterian settlers. They too had a religious-political score to settle. Their anti-English and anti-Anglican sentiments were important ingredients in making the Revolution possible.[1]

Dissenting Protestants in eighteenth-century England also articulated resentments against the Anglican establishments in a respectable enlightened republican form. Such motifs were conspicuous in the Real Whig political writings that shaped much of American Revolutionary thought. In the American Southern colonies this tradition was often attractive to those who were by birth Anglicans, but who, because of their provincial location, were outsiders to the British and Anglican political-religious establishment. Such leaders, of whom Jefferson is the prototype, were themselves secularizing, thus giving them an additional reason to oppose the Anglican religious establishment in America.

The American republic was thus shaped by a dissenting Protestant and Enlightenment coalition against Anglican political power in the colonies. Of course, the issue was neither so simple nor so explicit, but religion was still a major feature of the conflict. The animus of many colonials, just before the Revolution, against the possibility of the appointment of an American Anglican bishop was one manifestation of the widespread perception that Anglican ecclesiastical establishment and political power went hand in hand.

Formally, the new nation was defined in secular terms. The reason for that, as John Wilson suggests in his significant observations on the Constitution, was not because religion was unimportant to the colonists, but rather because it was too important. Clearly many of the revolutionaries were not in principle opposed to all church establishments, since several states retained them. Rather the primary explanation is that which Wilson presents. Only by staying away from the disruptive question of religion could a successful political coalition be forged among these contentious religious-ethnic groups.

Hence one basis for political consensus in the United States is the recognition that the nation is divided tribally into ethnoreligious groups, which means that it is best to stay away from religion in public life. This tradition emphasizes the acceptance of diversity as a moral duty. It presumes that other ethical principles necessary for the survival of civilization will emerge from nongovernment sources.

Many within the dominant classes in the new nation, however, shared another heritage that demanded a more integral relationship between Christianity and public life. They were not satisfied with tribal diversity, but were intent on uniting the nation under divinely sanctioned right principles. The revolutionary tradition going back to the Puritan commonwealth included this motif. The mythology that was part of eighteenth-century American Revolutionary republicanism contained a version of this theme also. According to this outlook, based in part on the Real Whig republican political thought of eighteenth-century English dissenting Protestants, religious authoritarianism and political authoritarianism were related historically and ideologically. On one side of the ledger were Catholicism, Anglicanism, centralized monarchical power, corruption, and tyranny; on the other side were Protestantism, Puritanism, representative government, virtue, and freedom. The American way thus had strong religious and ethical dimensions.

Particularly important in the early nineteenth century was an evangelical version of this outlook with a strong New England component and Puritan heritage. The Great Awakening of the eighteenth century had provided a bridge between Puritanism and democratic revolution. The Second Great Awakening, continuing throughout the first half of the century and longer, expanded the cultural influence of revivalist or evangelical Protestantism. Especially in the North, this heritage furnished the religious rationale for the cultural outlook that became one of the long-standing components in the basic patterns of American political life.

Those who adopted this outlook were usually English and religiously evangelical (or Unitarian). Culturally aggressive New England Yankees provided the leadership for this party. Reflecting the Puritan heritage, they sought the conversion of individuals and also strongly favored applying Christian principles to the transformation of society. This transformation would be accomplished by converted individuals who cultivated virtues of industry, thrift, and personal purity, but also by voluntary societies of such individuals who would band together for religious, educational, and political causes.

One of the early political expressions of this impulse was a phenomenon that, outside of this context, would appear as a total anomaly in American political history, the Anti-Mason party. The secret order of the Masons appeared to these evangelicals as an ominous false religion, one that appealed especially to freethinkers. In 1828 Anti-Masons were numerous enough to deliver nearly half of New York's electoral votes to John Quincy Adams. They soon merged with the new Whig party and became the base for that party's important "conscience" wing, including such strong proponents of antislavery as Thaddeus Stevens and William H. Seward. Evangelist Charles Finney was an ardent anti-Mason. (After the Civil War, when the antislavery issue was settled, Finney returned to the unfinished business of anti-Masonry, allying himself with Jonathan Blanchard, president of Wheaton College in Illinois.)

While the Whig party of the 1830s and 1840s included a substantial New England element, which promoted the effort to regulate society according to evangelical principles,[2] the drive took on a new shape with the demise of the Whig party.

The new factor in the equation was the rise of Catholic political power. Before the mid-nineteenth century the American rivalries had been intra-Protestant. The Scotch-Irish, for instance, were pivotal in American politics through the nation's first half-century. Disliking the New Englanders and New England schemes for moral regulation, they allied themselves with the South, which dominated the politics of the early era. In the 1850s, however, the Catholic threat changed the picture. Catholics who also did not like Yankee ideals of a monolithic Protestant moral commonwealth swelled the ranks of the Democrats. The Scotch-Irish despised the Catholics even more than they disliked the New Englanders and so left the Democratic fold. So did some Baptists and Methodists. As Robert Kelley observes, whereas previously the party of culturally aggressive Protestantism had been *English*, now it was a *British* lineup against the detested Irish Catholics.[3]

Explicit anti-Catholicism emerged as the major political issue of the early 1850s. In 1856 the anti-Catholic, nativist Know-Nothing party won 21 percent of the popular vote for its presidential candidate, Millard Fillmore. Then it merged with the antislavery and purely regional Republican party.

The result was that the Republican party had a strong Puritan-evangelical component, bent on regulating the society according to Christian principles. Antislavery was the great achievement of this outlook; but antialcohol and anti-Catholicism were just as much its trademarks.

One thing this party was doing was establishing an insider-versus-outsider mentality toward America and Americanism. Ethnically it was predominantly British; economically it was thoroughly allied with the dominant business community. Both these features reinforced its insider view of itself. The Puritan-Methodist ethic of self-help, moral discipline, and social responsibility dominated much of American education and defined its version of Americanism.

In the meantime, the Democratic party after the 1840s was becoming increasingly the party of outsiders. Its two strongest components were Catholics and Southerners, two groups who had almost nothing in common except their common disdain of Republicanism, with its self-righteous evangelical penchant to impose its version of Christian morality on the whole nation. Northern evangelicals, such as Methodists, most Baptists, Congregationalists, and New School Presbyterians, usually voted Republican. High Church, liturgical,and confessional Protestants, including some German Lutherans, all groups who had reservations about the evangelical-Puritan version of a Christian America, on the other hand, were more likely to vote Democratic. So were an important group of evangelical Protestants who, in the tradition of Roger Williams, were sufficiently sectarian to question the possibility of ever establishing a Christian political order.[4]

Though the Republican party was a pragmatic coalition and not simply an evangelical voluntary society writ large, a clue to its image of itself as building a Protestant Christian moral consensus is found in the notorious remark by James G. Blaine during the presidential campaign of 1884. The Democrats, he said, were the party of "Rum, Romanism, and Rebellion." On the one hand, it is revealing of the party's Protestant nativist and moral reform heritage that a shrewd politician such as Blaine would make such a remark. On the other hand, since the quip was thought to have cost Blaine the election, it may be taken as signaling the end of the era, begun with the anti-Mason campaigns, when evangelical Protestantism would be an explicitly partisan factor in American political life. Although the symbolic evangelical issue of prohibition remained prominent for another half-century, neither party could afford to be as overtly sectarian as before. The parties were closely enough matched that Republicans had to cultivate some Catholic support and Democrats, some evangelical. This situation was a major change from a period when religion had largely worked against national consensus.

The real turning point to the reorientation of American politics came in 1896, when the Democrats ran the evangelical William Jennings Bryan for president. By the time Bryan had run twice more, in 1900 and 1908, the Democratic party included an interventionist reformist element, much like the Republican party, including even strong sentiments for the archevangelical cause of prohibition.[5] Democrats ended the progressive era by electing Woodrow Wilson. Though a Southerner, the Presbyterian Wilson was as Puritan as any New Englander who ever held the office.

Just as revealing, however, was what was happening to the Republicans in the meantime. The party of McKinley and Mark Hanna had toned down its evangelical image and attracted some Catholic constituency. Nonetheless, as Robert Handy shows, they were still an overwhelmingly Protestant party with strong assimilationist goals. They represented centripetal forces in America attempting to counter centrifugal tendencies accentuated by immigration. Public education became sacrosanct as one means for teaching immigrants the American way and American virtues. The social gospel was a program for Christianizing America, but without the offense of the old exclusivist gospel of revivalism. In other words, Republicans were still building a Christian consensus, but were suppressing the exclusivist evangelical Protestant elements so as to be able to absorb the new immigrants within their domain.

In effect, the liberal Protestantism and slightly secularized social reform of the progressive era allowed the heirs to accomplish once again what their more explicitly evangelical fathers and mothers had achieved in the 1860s, Northern Protestant dominance. As Robert Kelley puts it, the party patterns set in the progressive era, from 1894 to 1930, coincided with "the years of Northern WASP ascendency in all things, including government, literature, scholarship, the arts, and the economy."[6]

So we see an instance of what Martin Marty long ago pointed out as an American pattern of secularization. Secularization in America took place not by a developing hostility between religion and the dominant culture, but by a blending of their goals. So Republican-Protestant hegemony no longer had to be explicitly Protestant. It just represented, as Handy makes clear, a certain concept of civilization. Civilization was equivalent in most minds to Christian civilization. It could be advanced by reforming progressive moral principles that people from all traditions might share. Many Democrats of the era, represented by Bryan and Wilson, adopted this slightly secularized Protestant vision as much as did Republicans. The immense American missionary enthusiasm of this era, sweeping through its colleges, reflected this same impulse to help the world by advancing Christian civilization. Wilson's secularized postmillennial vision of the American mission—to make the world safe for democracy—reflected a similar outlook. Religion, in short, had begun to work toward consensus.

Nonetheless, despite this softening of the Protestant hegemony into a melting-pot ideal of citizenship, democracy, and values taught to all in the public schools, the realignment of 1896 did not entirely disrupt the older party patterns.[7] At least through the election of 1960 the strongest bases for the Democratic party were the solid South and Catholic communities. Old-line Protestants still tended to be disproportionately Republican. With the coming of the Depression and the New Deal, however, economic issues dominated party politics. Except when the Democrats ran Catholics in 1928 and 1960, explicit religion was relegated to a ceremonial role.

As James Hennesey's essay shows, although there were a number of politicians who were Catholics during this era, there were almost no Catholic politicians in the substantive sense of elected leaders applying Catholic principles to politics. Rather, Catholic politicians were Americanizing. And the price of being an American politician if you were a Catholic was to leave your substantive Catholicism at the church door. Al Smith's remark, "What in hell is an encyclical?" perfectly summarizes the stance. Catholics had learned to play the twentieth-century game of appealing to the nation's religious heritage, but in a purely ceremonial way. So John F. Kennedy's public use of religious symbolism qualified him to become Robert Bellah's exhibit number one in his famous characterization of American civil religion.

After the progressive era, almost the only place where religion worked against the political consensus was in the civil rights movement. Blacks, whose political style had been set by mid-nineteenth-century Republican models and for whom the clergy were traditional community spokespersons in the pattern of Puritan New England, could still challenge the collective conscience of the nation. During the Lyndon Johnson era, they too were finally incorporated into the consensus, although largely in formal and superficial ways.

The wider pattern was a growing ideal of secularized consensus extending from 1896 to about 1968. Despite the persistent ethnoreligious patterns, some differing economic policies, and differing degrees of cold warriorism, the two parties were now much alike. With some significant exceptions, it was difficult to find any principal difference between them.

Rather, the genius of American politics seemed to be that the two parties did not stand for much of anything. George Wallace's campaign slogan of 1968 that there was not "a dime's worth of difference" between the two parties seemed accurate. Supporters of Eugene McCarthy could agree.

Martin Marty has referred to a "four-faith" pluralism that emerged in consensus America of the 1950s. As Will Herberg showed in 1955, although American Protestants, Catholics, and Jews had differing formal religions, they had much in common in the operative religion of faith in the American way of life.[8] Marty adds the fourth faith of secularism, acceptable as a private option and still fitting within the consensus.[9]

From our retrospective vantage point, one of the striking things about this accurate portrayal of American public life in the consensus era is the lack of any role for explicitly evangelical Protestantism.

What had happened was that, as mainline Protestants blended into a secularized consensus, fundamentalists, conservative Protestants, or explicit "evangelicals" were forced out. After the 1920s they lapsed into political inactivity, or rested quietly on the fringes of American political life, often on the far Right, as quietly conservative Republicans in the North or as birthright Democrats in the South. But in this separation, it is important to note, evangelicals were beginning to nurture dissent that would one day threaten the consensus. They dissented first of all against the liberal theology that made the consensus possible, but also against some of the progressive social policies that grew out of the social gospel.

One of the remarkable things that has happened since 1968 is the emergence of this group as an active political force. By 1968 the liberal New Deal consensus had broken down. The Vietnam War, the rioting of the blacks, and the counterculture brought down the illusion of a liberal-Protestant-Catholic-Jewish-secular–good citizenship–consensus America. While progressives tried to rebuild a more thoroughly secular and more inclusivistic and pluralistic consensus, conservatives sharply disagreed. Capitalizing at first on what seemed a largely secular backlash, as suggested by Vice President Spiro Agnew's popularity in claiming a "silent majority," they mobilized around anticommunism and love-it-or-leave-it Americanism. Then, after the Vietnam War and the presidency of Richard Nixon, a new, more religious coalition began to coalesce around ethical issues such as anti-abortion, anti-pornography, anti-ERA, and symbolic religious issues such as school prayer.

After 1976 it became clear that a substantial evangelical, fundamentalist, and Pentecostal-charismatic constituency could be mobilized around these issues. Only a portion of theologically conservative evangelicals, however, adopted this stance on the political Right. The evangelical movement itself was a divided coalition that at best maintained a tenuous anti-liberal theological unity among a myriad of subgroups and denominations. Although a solid contingent of evangelicals could be organized, as in the Moral Majority or in the Pat Robertson campaign, evangelicalism was far from unified as a political force.

What those who did mobilize helped to do, however, was very significant for the patterns of American political life. They helped supply a rhetoric to bring one wing of the Republican party back toward its nineteenth-century heritage. A striking element that was gone, however, was the anti-Catholicism. Evangelicals and conservative Catholics (as well as Mormons and members of the Unification Church) now made common cause on anti-communist and family issues. Such remarkable alliances suggested that, despite the explicitly evangelical stance of the leadership of the Religious Right, it also was forming a political consensus in which the exclusiveness of evangelicalism would be toned down. At the same time the New Religious Right drew in the natural Protestant evangelical constituency of the South, which adopted the renewed Christian American ideal with particular fervor. Though not overtly racist, the new coalition had forsaken its nineteenth-century heritage of advocating the black cause.

As was true for nineteenth-century evangelical Republicans in the era of Ulysses S. Grant, what conservatives actually got in the White House with the victory of Ronald Reagan fell far short of the Christian America of their rhetoric. The mixture that combined high moral aspirations for Christian civilization with a foreign policy built around militant anti-communism and the pragmatic acquisitive individualism of business interests always compromised the ideal.

Despite these anomalies, which demonstrated that the conscience wing of Republicanism had not yet taken over, an important component of the American political heritage had been revived. Nineteenth-century anti-Masonry and the contemporary war on secular humanism are generically related, even if the center of gravity has moved south. In the face of growing pluralism and moral inclusivism, which became increasingly the trademarks of the Democratic party, one significant wing of Republicanism recovered the ideals of building a coalition around a militant, broadly Christian, anti-secularist, and anti-communist heritage. As the end of the twentieth century approaches, this view of the essence of what it means to be an American conflicts sharply with a more inclusivist moral vision. Once again, as a result, religion seems to be working against political consensus, rather than for it.

Robert Wuthnow points out that political conservatives are not the only ones to have a religious-moral vision for the nation. Rather, he observes, America has two civil religions:

> The conservative vision offers divine sanction to America, legitimates its form of government and economy, explains its privileged place in the world and justifies a uniquely American standard of luxury and morality. The liberal vision raises questions about the American way of life, scrutinizes its political and economic policies in the light of transcendent concerns and challenges Americans to act on behalf of all humanity rather than their own interests alone.[10]

Just as Americans generally are divided concerning these competing moral visions, so are evangelicals divided. Disproportionate numbers of white evangelicals have adopted the conservative exclusivist vision; but the vision more critical of nation and self-interest is an equally venerable part of a heritage that goes back at least to Roger Williams. Likewise strong is a view with roots in the Revolutionary era, which recognizes that America is divided tribally into religious-ethnic groups and that therefore a high moral principle in public life is to keep explicit religion out of politics. Jimmy Carter, who held something like this view, was the only evangelical to be president during the 1980s, a simple fact to take into account when considering why most evangelicals did not vote for Pat Robertson. Robertson, Jerry Falwell, and other leaders of the Christian Right do represent the revival of an American political heritage, one that has a long tradition of attempting to set evangelical moral standards for the nation; but even for evangelicals, it is only one of America's religious heritages.

Notes

1. Robert Kelley, *The Cultural Pattern of American Politics* (New York: Knopf, 1979), 71–72.
2. Daniel Walker Howe, *The Political Culture of the American Whigs* (Chicago: University of Chicago Press, 1979), provides an excellent discussion of these themes.
3. Kelley, *Cultural Pattern*, 278–279.
4. Howe, *Political Culture*, 17–18, 159–167. A very detailed and sophisticated analysis of these typologies for a later period is offered by Philip R. VanderMeer, *The Hoosier Politician: Officeholding and Political Culture in Indiana: 1896–1920* (Urbana: University of Illinois Press, 1985), 96–120.

5. Paul Kleppner, *Who Voted: The Dynamics of Electoral Turnout, 1870–1980* (New York: Praeger, 1982), 77–78. Cf. Kleppner, "From Ethnoreligious Conflict to 'Social Harmony': Coalitional and Party Transformations in the 1890s," in Seymour Martin Lipset, ed., *Emerging Coalitions in American Politics* (San Francisco: Institute for Contemporary Studies, 1978), 41–59.

6. Kelley, *Cultural Pattern*, 285.

7. VanderMeer, *Hoosier Politician*, shows that in general the old patterns held in Indiana during the progressive era.

8. Will Herberg, *Protestant-Catholic-Jew* (Garden City, NY: Doubleday, 1955).

9. In *The New Shape of American Religion* (New York: Harper & Row, 1958), 76–80, Marty was already talking about America's fourth faith as "secular humanism" (following John Courtney Murray in the usage). He also remarked that "it has an 'established church' in the field of public education." Presumably, discussions such as Murray's and Marty's were behind Justice Hugo Black's famous reference to "secular humanism" as a religion in a 1961 Supreme Court decision. Such sober roots for the term run against claims (as by Sean Wilentz, "God and Man at Lynchburg," *The New Republic*, April 25, 1988, p. 36) of "the invention of secular humanism as a mass religion" by fundamentalists.

10. Robert Wuthnow, "Divided We Fall: America's Two Civil Religions," *Christian Century*, April 20, 1988, p. 398. Wuthnow's *The Restructuring of American Religion* (Princeton: Princeton University Press, 1988) contains the outstanding discussion of political and religious realignments.

Index